The Emerald Brooch

The Celtic Brooch Series, Book 4

Katherine Lowry Logan

Copyright © 2015 by Katherine Lowry Logan
Print Edition

This is a work of fiction. Names, characters, places, and incidents are the product of the author's imagination, or are used fictitiously, and any resemblance to actual persons living or dead, business establishments, events, or locales is entirely coincidental.

All rights reserved. No part of this book may be used or reproduced in any manner whatsoever without written permission of the author, except in the case of brief quotations embodied in critical articles or reviews.

Story Consultant and Editor: Faith Freewoman
Cover Art by Damonza
Interior Design by BB eBooks

Website: www.katherinellogan.com

DEDICATED TO

~

The Boys of Pointe du Hoc and the Mighty Eighth Air Force

And

McKenzie Anne Hicks

David McBain can do the impossible with one hand tied behind his back, but miracles take him a wee bit longer…

Two deployments in Afghanistan couldn't prepare Major David McBain and Captain Kenzie Wallis-Manning for the week leading up to D-Day – June 6, 1944.

From the bombed-out streets of London to the huts at Bletchley Park and an interview with Alan Turing to the 2nd Battalion Army Rangers and the beaches of Normandy, this high-stakes, time-travel World War II romantic adventure will keep you enthralled, awake into the wee hours, and racing toward the end, only to wish it had never arrived.

West Point graduate Kenzie Wallis-Manning planned to make the Army her career, but after being severely wounded during her second deployment, and suffering from PTSD, she retires from the military and enrolls in law school.

While studying in England, she receives a package containing an emerald brooch with a Gaelic inscription. As soon as she sounds out the words engraved on the stone, she is whisked back in time to May 28, 1944.

When Elliott Fraser learns his friend's half-sister, Kenzie, has disappeared, he sends David McBain and Jack Mallory to the past to find her, and bring her and her soul mate back to the future.

Will David discover the mission pits him against the best interests of Britain? Will Jack's penchant for getting in trouble put his life at risk again? Will Kenzie find her soul mate, or will she lose more on the battlefield of this war than she did in Afghanistan?

The Celtic Brooch Series

THE RUBY BROOCH (Book 1): Time Travel Romance – Oregon Trail 1852 – Kit MacKlenna and Cullen Montgomery's love story. Introduces: Elliott Fraser and Braham McCabe.

THE LAST MACKLENNA (Book 2): Contemporary Romance – Meredith Montgomery and Elliott Fraser's love story. Introduces: David McBain and Kevin Allen.

THE SAPPHIRE BROOCH (Book 3): Time Travel Romance – Civil War, 1864-1865 – Charlotte Mallory and Braham McCabe's love story. Introduces: Jack Mallory and includes Elliott, Meredith, David, Kevin, Braham, Kit, and Cullen

THE EMERALD BROOCH (Book 4): Time Travel Romance – World War II, London, June 1944. Introduces Kenzie Wallis-Manning. Includes: David, Jack, Elliott, Meredith, Kevin, Charlotte, Braham, and the children.

THE DIAMOND BROOCH (Book 5): Time Travel Romance, coming in 2016

1

Wolverhampton, England, Present Day

KENZIE WALLIS-MANNING SLOSHED through the shoe-sucking mud of The Tough Guy Full Brutal Marathon, feeling like a herd of buffalo was bearing down on her. After miles of swinging Tarzan ropes, belly-flopping under razor wire, and frequent trips in and out of sub-zero water obstacles, she had been torture-tested to the limit of her endurance, often unable to breathe or even see where to plant her next step. But now she raced toward the finish line, only seconds from a personal record and a possible podium finish.

You got this, Kenz.

She dashed across the finish line with her muddy arms raised. According to the clock, she had PR'd. Not only had she run her best time, but she should be one of the top three finishers in her age group.

She didn't stop for congratulations, but ran straight to the security-guarded barn for her backpack, then off to the hot showers, where she stood in line shivering. "It's so cold I'll chip my teeth on the soup in the food tent."

The woman standing in front of her laughed. "You got that right."

"It's so cold Starbucks is serving coffee on a stick."

"Keep going, girl. Every time I laugh I warm up a degree," another woman said.

"Here's one more," Kenzie said, her teeth chattering. "It was so cold we had to chop up the piano for firewood, but only got two chords."

By now the entire line was laughing. When she finally entered the shower stall, the water was tepid at best. "Damn. The water's not hot, and I haven't taken a cold shower since I was a sexually frustrated lieutenant in Afghanistan."

"You were in the service? No wonder you handled those cargo nets so well," a woman in the adjoining stall said.

"I've climbed my share, that's for sure." Kenzie scrubbed the mud from her body's nooks and crannies, taking special care around the scars that crisscrossed her hip and upper thigh.

"Hey, soldier," the next woman in line yelled. "Did you ever have hot sex after finishing a mission? I heard lots of soldiers hook up after tense engagements."

Kenzie turned off the water and wrapped her hair in one towel and her body in another. "Only once, and it was *hot*, but it wasn't with another soldier." She stepped out of the shower, freeing it up for the woman who had asked the question.

"Not a soldier, huh? Must have been one of those independent contractors."

"Yep. I'd known him a couple of months. My adrenaline was redlined because an insurgent group set off an IED in front of our convoy. He crossed my path as soon as we got back to camp, asked how I was doing. I said I'd feel much better if he could spare me five minutes. We slipped off to a supply tent. I think it only took three."

A chorus of laughter rippled through the shower tent.

She would never forget that night. A week later, a suicide bomber waltzed into camp. Her best friend, Trey Kelly, sensed something was wrong and yelled for her to take cover a second before he tackled her. The bomber blew himself up. Her hook-up was killed instantly, but that split second, and the protection of Trey's body, saved her life. Trey survived a few hours before succumbing to his injuries. Images of those moments were permanently embedded in her brain, and still exploded into consciousness now and then, replaying in slow motion when she was stressed, or for no reason at all.

"The awards ceremony starts in ten minutes," someone shouted from the tent's entrance.

The woman stepped out of the stall and made room for the next muddy racer. "You better hurry, soldier. With your time, I bet you finished in the top three."

Kenzie did. She took second place in the twenty-six to thirty age group. In three months, she'd bump up to a new age division, and a bigger field to compete with. She accepted her medal, saluted Trey in her heart, and caught the next train back to London.

When she opened the front door to her apartment complex on Regent Square, after a ten-minute walk from King's Cross station, she ran smack into Postman Joe.

"Afternoon, Miss Wallis-Manning. You're just in time to save me a trip up the stairs." He held out a shoebox-shaped package wrapped in brown paper and tied with twine.

She held up her hands and stepped back. "You know I don't accept packages like that. You never know what's inside."

He fixed her with his gray eyes. "All my packages go through a scanner. When I saw it was for you, I ran it through again. There's no bomb inside."

"Maybe not a bomb, but it could still explode."

"Our bomb-sniffing dog passed on it, too. It's safe, and look…" He pointed to the return address. "It's from a solicitor in Scotland. If he was going to blow someone up—"

Kenzie cringed and drew back another step.

"—he wouldn't have put his name on it, now would he?"

"You have a point," she said. "But I don't know anyone in Scotland…" Her voice faded as she glanced at the return address. Her mother had been from Inverness, but her family disowned her when she married Kenzie's father. Kenzie had never met any of the Wallises, even though she carried their name. "If I blow up, you'll tell the authorities about this, won't you?"

"I will if you'll tell me a postman joke."

Kenzie tapped her cheek with her index finger. "Okay, here goes. Why do postmen laugh three times when they hear a joke?"

Joe's eyes narrowed. "Hmm. Don't know."

"Once when it's told, once when it's explained, and once when they finally get it."

He threw back his head, laughing. "*When they finally get it.* That's a good one. I'll tell the lads in the mailroom. They ask every day if I have a new Kenzie joke. You're famous."

She faked a smile. "Or infamous, if you ask my dad." She began climbing the steps to her third floor flat, enjoying the sound of Postman Joe's laughter filtering up the stairwell. She might have started out telling jokes in high school as a way to gain acceptance at new schools when her father moved every other year, but she told them now because she loved to hear people laugh.

"Have a good day, Joe, and remember to tell the police…"

Joe was one of several reasons she enjoyed living here. Making the daily, slightly-under-one-hour commute to Cambridge had gotten old within the first six weeks, but living in London, where she could walk to the best museums and libraries, made the added expense and inconvenience worthwhile. She lived frugally to make up the difference.

When she reached the second floor, she put the package to her ear and then scolded herself for being so suspicious. But how could she not be? Even if the package didn't contain an explosive device, it could still hurt her. It came from Scotland, for God's sake, and the only thing good to ever come from there had been her mother. If the Wallises were sending her a package now, it was twenty years too late. She unzipped the top of her backpack and shoved the parcel in as far as it would go.

Her neighbor, a well-sculpted, handsome man in his mid-forties, stepped out of his apartment just as she reached the third floor. "Hey, Kenzie. How was the race?"

"I PR'd and came in second in my age group." He raised his hand and she slapped it. "It was fun, but brutal. Glad it's over."

"Congratulations, girl. I knew you'd do it." He leaned away and framed her with his hands, nodding appreciatively. "I like the Lulu look you got going on. That's their new running jacket, right? I saw it in the store." He pinched the edge of her sleeve, rubbing the fabric between his fingers. "Nice. Busted your budget again, didn't you?"

"Yep."

"You look fabulous in it. The cut shows off your curves and muscular arms."

"Only you would notice, Howard."

"I'm gay, but I'm not blind." He removed the clip from her hair, letting it fall to her shoulders. "Those golden red locks are movie-star glam. You might be a little small at the top, but the rest of you is a body to die for."

"Scars and all," she said.

He glanced down her leg, tsking. "I've seen those scars. Your memory of how you got them is worse than the marks on your body. They're hardly noticeable."

"Well, thanks. You're good for my self-esteem."

"My last appointment is at five o'clock. If you want a massage, stop by the salon at six. I'll work you in. I bet your legs are really tight."

"My arms are worse. I'll be there."

"Oh, I slid a newspaper article I read this morning under your door. It's about Churchill and Bletchley Park. I thought you might be interested, since we just watched that Alan Turing movie."

"You're a godsend, Howard. You take care of my body, my mind, and my wardrobe."

"And you, my lovely," he kissed her forehead, "make me laugh. Tell me a food joke and I'll be on my way."

"Food? You love to randomly pick topics, don't you? Hmm. What do you call a honeymoon sandwich?"

His brows knitted, then he tsked again. "Don't know."

"Lettuce alone."

"Let us?" Behind his big blue eyes was a vivid imagination. It took a second before they widened. "*Lettuce*? Oh, that's *awful*." Then he laughed. "I'll see you later and expect to hear a better one when you arrive. The salon staff loves your jokes, too."

"I'll work on it." She turned in the direction of her corner apartment, but Howard tugged on the top of the package, stopping her.

"*What's this?* Were you trying to hide a new purchase?" His mouth curved into a knowing grin. "You bought new running shoes. Didn't you?"

"I wish. It's from a solicitor in Scotland, and Postman Joe promised it wasn't a bomb."

"Ooh," Howard's smile slipped. "That doesn't sound good. Do you think it's from your mum's family?"

She hugged herself. "Probably."

His mouth set in a hard line, and he moved behind her and put his magic fingers on her shoulders and kneaded them. "I'm sorry I asked."

"As long as you don't stop, you can ask again. That feels wonderful."

His hands moved up her neck, digging into her muscles, and she blissfully closed her eyes. "Listen to me," he said. "First, make sure no one sent you shoes, and then throw the damn box into the trash."

"I can always count on you for the best advice."

"What good's a neighbor if he doesn't dole it out unsolicited? See you at six."

She groaned when he stopped the mini-massage. "After that teaser, I wouldn't miss it for the world."

Kenzie opened the door to her apartment and tossed the box into the trash.

Her cell phone rang. She rummaged through her backpack, digging through sweaty clothes and leftover snacks until she found her phone. The display flashed a picture of her father. *Oh, Dad, don't ruin my day, please.* She squeezed the phone in her hand, debating whether to take the call or let it go to voicemail. If the colonel got her voicemail, he'd call right back.

Ever since she retired from the Army, he had become progressively worse, both in his tone and in the way he treated her. His abuse had never been physical, but verbal abuse left bruises, too. On the fourth ring, she answered. "Hi, Dad. I just got home. Can I call you later?"

"You're five hours ahead of me. Your *later* will be the middle of *my* night, and I'll be asleep."

"I'll call you in an hour, then. I just got home from a race…" She sucked air between her teeth, cringing. She hadn't meant to tell him. "I need to take a shower," she added quickly. She wanted a long, lingering one using her special soap.

"You had time to race…"

She tensed, bracing herself for a verbal assault. She had learned to control her emotions to a certain extent, so at least her face wouldn't show the stabs of hurt his words caused. Sometimes it worked. Sometimes it didn't. Today she didn't even have to look in the mirror to know it wasn't working. Hot tears burned the backs of her eyes.

"But you don't have time to talk. You never should have left the Army—"

Here it comes.

"I told you not to, but you wouldn't listen. I also told you a law degree from Harvard was all you needed. You didn't listen to me about that, either. Now you're spending too much money living abroad."

"It's. My. Money."

"I don't give a damn. Investing in risky commodities will deplete your retirement fund. I'm not leaving you an estate to lose with futures trading."

"I don't want your money."

"Good, because you're not getting any. I'll give it to charity."

Damn him. She said nothing, thinking hard, swallowing, and blinking harder, but that didn't stop the tears. She dropped into the chair, shoulders slumping. He had opened her mail instead of collecting it to send, a month's worth at a time. She had opted for convenience and not changed her mailing address. He had read her monthly investment statement, and she could only blame herself for the invasion of her privacy.

She glanced at the package in the trash. The combination of her father's irritation and the package from Scotland was more brutal than the race. What would he say if she told him about the package? He didn't have any use for the country or its people, any more than she did.

In a tight voice that hurt her throat, she said, "You wouldn't know what I'm investing in unless you opened my mail. I asked you not to do that." She tightened not only her voice but her resolve not to cave in to him. "Did you get drunk…or bored?"

"Soldier, watch your tongue."

"I'm not a soldier. I'm your daughter."

"My daughter?" He slammed a glass with clinking ice against a hard surface. "My daughter would never have embarrassed me by quitting the Army."

She had not discussed her final decision to retire with him, and he would never forgive her. She changed the subject. "I came in second in my age group in the race today."

"You should have stayed home and studied so you can be first in your class. But no, you wanted to waste money on entry fees. How much did the race cost?"

"It's my money, Dad." How many times had she said that to him? He never listened to her, and if he did, he only picked up on more things to complain about. She leaned forward, elbows on her knees, phone in one hand, and palm to her forehead with the other. It was time to change the mailing address on all of her accounts.

"The way you're investing it, you won't have any funds left in six months. When you're broke, don't ask me for a goddamn entry fee."

A tight knot clenched her stomach. "Here's a joke for you, Dad. How do crazy runners go through the forest?"

He gave a mirthless laugh before slurring his words. "I don't give a damn about the punch line."

"I'm going to tell you anyway. They take the psycho path." From the other end of the phone came steaming silence. "I've got to go,

Dad. I've got work to do."

"If you have so much goddamn work to do, then why the hell were you racing today?"

The colonel had clearly consumed more than his usual three martinis, because he was slurring his words. She tried once more to lighten the mood. "The trouble with jogging is that by the time you realize you're not in shape for it, it's too far to walk back."

The sound of liquid sloshing into a glass came from his end of the phone. "Damn it, Kenzie…"

"You're drunk. I'll call you tomorrow. Good-bye, Dad."

She disconnected the call. Several times in her life she had actually made him laugh. She never quit trying to make it happen again.

A pressure cooker couldn't be more rattled and on the verge of explosion than she was at the moment. She took several deep breaths to calm her churning emotions. The dim remembrance of her mother's soft voice and gentle hands holding her tightly flickered in the corner of her mind. The colonel could so easily ruin her day if she let him. He was a son of a bitch, and he drank too much, but he was the only family she had.

She pushed empty cartons of Chinese food aside, dumped her backpack on the table, unloaded muddy running gear, and tossed a T-shirt and shorts onto the dirty clothes pile on the floor. Then she stripped out of her running jacket and pants and added them to the pile. She sniffed, scrunching her nose. The flat was beginning to smell like the inside of a locker room. But it was her own stink, and that made it tolerable.

Life as an Army brat, four years at West Point, and five years in the Army, had turned her into a neat freak. So when it mattered, she could be neat. Right now it didn't. Not when she was sore, hungry, and cold, colder than she had been before the call.

She used a half a bottle of shampoo to clean her hair, and a bar of luxury soap to wash away the mud the first shower had missed. She splurged during a recent shopping trip to Penhaligon's, hoping she'd have a date while in London, but it didn't seem likely at this point. The research for her thesis on *Settlement of International Disputes*, with a particular emphasis on Winston Churchill, had turned into a part-time job. It didn't help that she had developed a severe fangirl crush on the late Prime Minister.

A car backfired outside the window. In a split second she was once again a ten-year-old being told her mother died in a crash. Panting hard, Kenzie pressed her hand against her chest, trying to push her heart back into its regular rhythm. But it wouldn't go. Then a bomb blast rattled her teeth. People screamed, and a heavy weight fell on top of her. Blood. So much blood. She slid down the wall and collapsed into the bathtub, where she pulled her knees to her chest. Lukewarm water poured down on top of her head and mingled with hot tears streaming from her eyes.

2

London, England, Present Day

KENZIE DIDN'T KNOW how long she'd been sitting in the shower. Cold water beat down on her, and she was chilled to the marrow. It could have been seconds or minutes…maybe even hours.

The flashbacks didn't happen often, and weren't as severe as they had been a couple of years earlier, thank God. The memories were like obstacle-course cargo nets, connected yet full of gaps and holes, and so slippery she wasn't sure how accurate they were anymore.

The flashbacks followed the same pattern. A sound, a smell, or her father's anger would trigger memories of her mother's tragic death or the bombing in Afghanistan, and she would have a meltdown. She'd been through therapy, taken medication, and her therapist was pleased with her recovery. She wasn't healed yet, but she was managing.

She couldn't even remember what had set her off.

Shaking, she turned off the water, gripped the towel bar, and climbed out of the tub.

The bathroom was warm and toasty and smelled like a garden of green clover, lavender, and geranium. Safe, calming scents that cleansed her mind of bad memories and switched her focus to the here and now, and not on what had been. She inhaled for a count of six, then exhaled for a count of six, several times. After a minute or two, she held out her hands. They were now steady enough to fire a weapon and hit the center of the target.

While drying off, Kenzie noticed the bruises on her arms and legs from the cargo nets, and the scratches on her shoulders from the barbed wire obstacle. She had crawled underneath it, fast and careless. She knew better.

In other words, the race had beaten the crap out of her.

A few squirts of Neosporin and a couple of ibuprofen and she'd be back to normal in, what? Twelve to twenty-four hours? The only difference between torture and a marathon mud race was the torture didn't end after a few hours, or so she'd been told.

After steeping a cup of tea, she rummaged through her small clothes closet. Small, but big enough for everything she needed to store, even when all her clothes were clean. She traveled light wherever she went, a habit honed after years of listening to her father complain about moving boxes of her crap.

She pulled out a new navy peplum dress and paired it with neutral pumps. Despite what her father believed, she did quite well managing her portfolio and could afford new clothes as long as she didn't go shopping every day. A white and blue checked scarf and a white sweater completed her ensemble. As good as she looked, and as nice as she smelled, maybe—just maybe—she'd meet someone interesting.

Her West Point class ring and the diamond-stud earrings her father gave her for graduation were the only jewelry she ever wore.

She shoved her laptop into her computer bag. One of these days she would have to empty the bag of old receipts, gum wrappers, half-eaten candy bars, the dog-eared map of London, her comb, brush, and makeup case, or there wouldn't be any room for her notebook and laptop.

She shouldered her bag and happened to glance into the trashcan. *What the heck.* She dug her fingers into a fold of the paper wrapping and ripped it open. What she found gave her that surprise *wham*, and she was bowled over.

In her shaking hands was an antique puzzle box, approximately six by four by two inches in size. The box was inlaid with dogwood and cherrywood to create elaborate geometric patterns, and it gleamed from years of polish that enhanced the beauty of the wood grain.

She pushed the pause button on her excitement and studied the name on the wrapping paper again. Who was Mr. Digby? And why had he sent her the box? Did he know she had an obsession for solving puzzle boxes, riddles, and mathematical problems? Her friends knew. They teased her relentlessly with gifts of Rubik's Cubes shaped in spheres and triangles, conspiring to find a unique one she couldn't solve. They had yet to stump her.

If she looked in the mirror right now, she knew she would see an inquisitive frown. She consciously relaxed her forehead, a self-taught method to open her mind to possibilities. What was the obvious that needed to be ignored? *My mother and the connection to Scotland.* Perfect. Now, focus solely on the puzzle. The reason for the gift might eventually prove more important than the gift, but for now it was a distraction.

The rumbling of faint hunger reminded her that, while her post-race meal had restocked her glycogen supply, she needed to have lunch soon. A big, juicy steak from the restaurant down the street—instead of a pasta dish from the Italian restaurant—was calling her name. Afterward, she would give the puzzle her full attention.

The backpack had enough room for the puzzle box in one of the side mesh pockets. She carefully squeezed it in, then slung the backpack over one shoulder and hurried out of the apartment.

3

London, England, Present Day

Hours later—with a full stomach and several articles to read on Churchill's war years she had downloaded while using the free Wi-Fi at Starbucks—Kenzie collapsed on the sofa in her apartment, ready to solve the puzzle box.

She had found nothing on solicitor Digby, other than the address of his law office. No specialties. No partners. No awards for making exquisite puzzle boxes. A shadow lawyer. But a shadow for whom?

Although she hadn't been fiddling with the puzzle box, the patterns in the wood had been chugging away in the back of her mind like a slot machine trying to line up three reels with identical pictures. But the same pictures never lined up on the pay line. She envisioned a mysterious old lawyer, looking like the Wizard of Oz, superimposing his face on one of the reels, frustrating her. If she didn't get the answers she wanted when she opened the box, she'd be forced to travel to Edinburgh. *Yuk*. The thought didn't sit well at all.

She put her feet up on the coffee table and started moving sliders on the top, sides, and bottom of the box, trying to determine the solution's algorithms. It took her about fifteen minutes to get the box to pop open.

She high-fived the air above her head.

But what she found inside wiped the grin of accomplishment off her face and replaced it with open-mouthed shock. *"My God."*

Her hand shook as she carefully lifted an antique emerald brooch with a Celtic design out of the velvet-lined box. The brooch was old, exquisite, and expensive-looking, but the sender was probably a member of her mother's family, and Kenzie wanted nothing to do with people who abandoned her mother and even refused to come to her funeral.

She would return the jewelry to solicitor Digby. Maybe next weekend she would take the train to Edinburgh and tell him thanks but no thanks.

Then she noticed a distinct pattern in the silver tracery, and she followed the interconnecting lines with her fingernail. The emerald warmed against her finger, and she jerked it back. The tip of her finger had turned red from the heat. *Weird.*

Whoever made the jewelry was a master craftsman. Kenzie had never seen such extraordinary workmanship outside a museum. Now she was even more curious about the identity of the sender.

If she hadn't been studying the intricate design so closely, she wouldn't have noticed the clasp hidden in the tracery. She pressed it with her fingertip and the stone popped up, revealing words she recognized as Gaelic engraved on the stone. She rubbed her finger over the words, sounding them out: *"Chan ann le tìm no àite a bhios sinn a' tomhais a' gaol ach 's ann le neart anama."*

A peat-scented fog rose up around her, engulfing her, choking the breath from her lungs. She jumped to her feet and tried to escape from the fog, but when she moved, the cloud moved with her, and then took over. It jerked her left, then right, then back to the left again, tossing her about on a demon of a rollercoaster without a seatbelt or guardrail. She wanted off. Now. Her queasy stomach forced its contents up to the back of her throat. If she didn't get loose quickly, she'd have to clean her lunch off the floor.

After a terrifying few moments, the whiplash ride stopped and the pressure eased. Instead of the scent of peat, she was assaulted by the rank smells of smoldering ash and gunpowder. Her heart jackknifed to her throat. She patted her sides, searching for weapons, but she had nothing.

She swatted at the fog. "Go away. Get off of me."

As suddenly as the cloud had materialized, it evaporated, and she could see again. And what lay before her terrified her more than her own worst fears.

A siren wailed and a bomb blast rent the air.

4

Fraser House, the Highlands, Scotland, Present Day

DAVID MCBAIN'S FINGER hovered over the Send button while he mentally reviewed his editor's comments. He had responded to each one with deep edits to the heroine's rescue and the trial of the Lincoln assassination conspirators. Satisfied, he clicked Send, and his latest manuscript soared into cyberspace.

He pushed back in his chair, crossed his arms and allowed a smile to surface. The story he'd just returned to his publisher was based on his adventures back in time to 1865 to rescue his friend Jack Mallory from a hangman's noose. Jack was writing a mystery about his misadventure, while David's story was more a fantasy, or a romantic adventure, which in some ways hadn't turned out particularly well for him, though he did get a second godson out of the deal. Wee Lincoln McCabe and laddie James Cullen Fraser were the stars around which David's life revolved.

His phone beeped, announcing another text message. He'd ignored the last two, but ignoring the outside world came with limitations…or consequences. He had too many responsibilities to go unaccounted for longer than a few hours, enough time for a satisfying escapade between the sheets, or to meet a deadline, but nothing more. Whoever was looking for him now would assume the former, not the latter, except for his mother, who would continue to harass him until he answered.

He rustled through the papers in his lap to find his mobile

phone buried in the midst of chapter twenty-five, which was titled *The Trip to Washington*. He shook his head briefly to dispel a wee memory of Charlotte, one that often caught him unaware and reminded him of how deeply he had loved her. Time and necessity had masked those feelings, until now they were the color of steely, locked-down gray.

The messages were from Alice, his mum, and read: *Come to the house, please*. The third message didn't include the word *please*.

He responded, tapping the keys easily with his large, dexterous fingers: *Coming*.

Alice had been the housekeeper at Fraser House for more than forty years. Since Elliott Fraser split his time away from Scotland jet-setting between MacKlenna Farm in Kentucky and Montgomery Winery in Napa, Alice had most of the responsibility for the upkeep of the estate. She managed two full-time grounds keepers, but depended on local maintenance workers to tend to daily repairs. When David was in residence, he did what he could, but he generally traveled with Elliott and Meredith, managing most of the Thoroughbred breeding operation, and also spending time at the Mallory and McCabe plantations in Richmond, Virginia.

Besides his mum, David had sisters scattered throughout Scotland, in London, and a few in America. They weren't actually his sisters, but women who would change plans at a moment's notice to spend an evening with him. No commitments. No expectations. No drama.

The term had been coined during his teenage years to keep the relationship with his first sweetheart a secret from his mum. "We're like brother and sister," he had told her. The description had stuck, and although Alice knew he didn't have brother/sister relationships with the women he spent time with, calling them sisters somehow kept life less complicated.

He pushed his work aside and stood to stretch. He was still achy from the workout the day before with his trainer. She had pushed him hard as payback for not getting to the gym for almost a week. David had wanted a no-sympathy hardass to keep him in shape. The sweet, wee, busty blonde he paid to torture him did it with aplomb.

He stuffed his saxophone into a cupboard and snagged his leather jacket off the back of a chair. The sax was his private indulgence. Ever since his drunken father tripped over it and laid into him for leaving it out, David kept the instrument and his musical talent hidden from everyone, including his mum, though it had happened more than twenty years ago.

He shrugged into the jacket and left the cottage, tucking his hands into the pockets.

The centuries-old path, along a broad stone terrace with a carved railing led from the original grounds keeper's restored cottage where David lived to the rear of the house that locals referred to as a castle. As a lad he had counted the stones one by one as a delaying tactic when Auld Fraser summoned him to the room on the second floor he used as a private study. It was where the man meted out punishment to those who broke the rules. Every time David broke some godforsaken rule, he received an arse-whipping for it. But he never complained.

The whistle of the wind blew across an expansive, pie-shaped wedge of the moor, bringing a nip in the air, crisp and cool, and the earthy scent of heather cloaked in a colorful palette of dazzling lavender, copper, and magenta. There was no place he would rather be in the spring than the Highlands. Although central Kentucky during the spring meeting at Keeneland was quite beautiful, nothing compared to home, not even MacKlenna Farm, situated smack in the middle of Bluegrass Country.

David moved at a brisk jogger's pace, his leather boots grating on the gravel. Before entering the kitchen, he scraped mud from the bottoms of his shoes rather than risk his mum's ire.

Inside the four hundred-year-old house, two pots steamed and bubbled on the gas stove. He sniffed. *Vegetable soup with barley and split peas.* One of his mum's many specialties.

He had supervised the renovation of the kitchen following his return from Afghanistan, back when he wasn't sure what he wanted to do with himself. He installed industrial-sized appliances and repurposed the old vintage cupboards. The biggest change, though, was the replacement of the multi-paned windows to let in as much natural light as possible. The new panes also put a stop to the stern rattle of the wind through the cracks and crevices that had surrounded the ancient glass. Now the room was warm and cozy, and his mum sang while she cooked. She only did that when she was in a rare good mood.

The door to the wine cellar stood open. "Who's downstairs?" he asked.

"Mrs. Fraser spotted bats in the cave last week and asked Ned to get rid of them."

"What the hell was Meredith doing down there? She never should have been back that far. It's more dangerous than a minefield." He rocked back on his heels and shifted his gaze to his mum. "Ye' shouldna' have let her go down there by herself."

"Ye'd gone to Inverness, and hisself was looking at a sick horse. And I never go farther than the door to the steps to the cellar."

"If Ned's down there now, he needs to get out. Even a handyman could get in trouble with the loose rocks and weak beams."

David's own mouth went dry when he went anywhere near the back part of the wine cellar. From the stories he had heard as a child, the first cave-in occurred in the early seventeen hundreds, but left a narrow path from the wine cellar to a secret entrance hidden among the ancient Caledonian pines a half mile from the house. The second cave-in happened in the 1960s, and had sealed the cave, at least to people.

He strode to the top of the stairs and yelled, "*Ned.*" There was no answer. "Damn it." David clomped down the new enclosed wood stairs. "*Ned.*" Still no answer. Sound carried in the cellar. If Ned didn't hear him, he was either too far into the cave, or something had happened to him. Either way, David needed to get him out of there.

He eased his way down the long aisle through rows of oak racks stacked floor to ceiling on each side. Hundreds of bottles of wine filled the racks, some dating back two hundred years. The high humidity and cool temperature provided the perfect environment for the collection, which had been valued at several million dollars. The bottles weren't as dusty as they had been before Meredith took an interest in their preservation, but then she was the vintner in the family. Before she married Elliott and they had James Cullen, her Napa Valley Winery had been her life.

The aisle narrowed, the musty scent thickened, and the temperature dropped at least ten degrees when he left the front portion of the cellar and traveled closer to the cave. His pace slackened. His heart rate increased. He hated the cellar and despised the cave. As a child, he had stumbled upon the cave's entrance in the pine trees and crawled in to explore. When his lantern burned out, he'd been left in the dark. He managed to find his way and crawled out hours later, hungry and terrified, and had never entered it again.

"*Ned*," David yelled.

"I'm back here," Ned said, calm as you please.

The four-inch-thick wood door separating the cellar from the cave stood open. David's feet refused to step over the threshold. He gripped the old wood beams that formed the door frame. The sides were likely not sturdy enough to withstand an invasion, but sturdy enough to keep out a few men. He hung from the overhead beam to test its strength. The beam was as solid as the day it had been placed there.

"Ned, let's get out of here."

"Mrs. Fraser wants me to get rid of the bats."

"Leave them. I want this door bolted. The cave can be a permanent home for the wee buggers for all I care."

"Ye'll have to deal with the missus, then. She's determined to expand the wine collection. She's been down here for hours mapping portions of the cave and tracking the temperature."

"I'll make some calls and get a mining engineer in here to do a feasibility study. Until then, this door will be bolted, and Meredith is not to have the key."

Ned came through the door and closed it, sliding the bolt into the socket and locking it in place. He handed David a large ring of keys. "Ye' take these and keep them away from Mrs. Fraser. If I don't have them, I can't let her in."

David slipped the ring into his jacket pocket. "Let's get out of here. Alice has hot coffee on the stove."

A few minutes later, the local handyman stood near the large open hearth in the kitchen sipping steamy brew from a mug and warming his backside. "David has the keys now, Alice. If herself wants back into the cave, she'll have to talk to yer son."

Alice stomped toward David, clicking her sensible shoes on the stone floor. He was at the kitchen sink scrubbing dust and dirt from his hands. "Ye' need to remember, lad, she's Elliott's wife, not yers. She's happy down there."

"I'm not locking her out of the cellar," David said, drying his hands, "only the cave."

He easily spotted nuances in a person's tone, and his mother's had changed. She was worried, and trying hard to disguise her concern. If he and his mum had been alone in the room he would press her for an explanation. For now, he would let it pass. She probably wouldn't tell her secrets anyway. Once her mind was set, she could be like a plow mule walking in a furrow, too stubborn to turn.

"She might as well be mine," he said more gently. "Who do ye' think she comes to when she wants a project done without argument, or needs Elliott persuaded to her point of view?" Elliott was David's mentor and friend and the closest thing he had to a father. He respected Elliott, loved him, and would take a bullet for him. But when Elliott and Meredith had problems, David always took her side. The sun came out the day she entered Elliott's life, and she kept him grounded. Without her, Elliott wouldn't survive.

"Certainly not ye'. Nothing gentle or persuasive about yer manner."

"Aye, if that's true, ye've only yerself to blame."

Something in that comment evidently amused her, because she smiled and then laughed. His mother's deep chuckle followed him through the house and into the study, which was set off of the main hall by a short corridor. He kicked the door closed behind him. Regardless of what his mum said, David could be gentle when situations demanded, such as when dealing with wee lads, or skittish horses, or first-time lovers.

Elliott had a serviceable desk that had been made for the laird long before the Jacobite Rebellion of 1745, but it wasn't mammoth like the one at MacKlenna Farm. Oriental carpets covered the stone floor, and tapestries dating back three hundred years hung on the walls. A set of windows overlooking the front entry had been added a few years before World War I.

The history of Fraser House was well documented, except for the cave-in. There was no recorded date or cause. It might have happened when the castle burned during the Rebellion, but no one knew for sure, not even Auld Fraser, Elliott's grandfather.

A table lamp squatted to the right of the desk, its oval shade angled perfectly to cast light where he needed it most. He flipped through the Rolodex for the name of the qualified mining engineer he had worked with previously. If the expert couldn't do the excavation of the partial cave-in, he would know who could.

His cell phone rang to the beat of a Disney song. David glared at the device as if it had dropped from Mars—splat in the middle of the desk.

James Cullen MacKlenna Fraser.

David had dozed off while reading to Elliott and Meredith's lad a couple of nights earlier. The wee toerag must have changed ring tones on the phone then. Kit MacKlenna Montgomery, Elliott's goddaughter, used to do that to Elliott to annoy the hell out of him. David wasn't annoyed. The tyke could drop the mobile in the toilet and David wouldn't get angry with him.

The caller ID on David's phone identified the caller as Jim Manning, Elliott's attorney and longtime friend. David answered with one word, "McBain."

"It's Jim. I need help."

David eased into Elliott's desk chair and grabbed a pen. "Whatever ye' need, just ask."

"I was hoping you'd say that," Jim said. "My half-sister—"

"Didn't know ye' had one."

"It's a long story. I'll tell you later." The brusque tone of voice David rarely heard from Elliott's consigliere told David the story was not only a long one, but complicated as well.

"Kenzie, my sister," Jim continued, "is in a joint degree program to earn a J.D. from Harvard and an LL.M. from Cambridge. She's had a flat in London since August. Sometime in the last four days she's gone missing. The police are investigating. They have her cell phone and are calling her contacts, but so far they have nothing. She was supposed to return her father's call Monday. She didn't."

Jim paused and took a heavy breath. "I hate to ask you to do this, but you have experience finding people who don't want to be found. Will you look into it? She's probably shacked up and doesn't want to talk to him. I don't blame her, but we'll put my feelings aside for the moment. Her father is convinced something has happened to her."

"I'll fly to London this afternoon. Do you have an address?" David jotted down the information. "What's her full name?"

"Kenzie Wallis-Manning. It's a hyphenated last name."

David wrote down the name and circled the word *Wallis*. An impression formed in his mind of a tall, nondescript, brown-haired lass. Jim, a former basketball player at the University of Kentucky, was a nice-enough-looking man, but without his height, he would go unnoticed in a crowd.

"Wallis is a Scots name," David said. "Where's her family from?"

Jim cleared his throat, and the sound of rustling papers came from his end of the phone. "Her mother grew up close to the Frasers, but I never met her."

"Never?"

"She died in a car accident when Kenzie was ten." He paused and drew another long, heavy breath. If David had been standing next to Jim instead of listening over the phone, he imagined the man's taut face would express his true emotions, because the roughness in his voice indicated there was deep emotional pain associated with Kenzie Wallis-Manning.

"Look, I've never met my sister. I only found out she existed a few years ago, and as far as I know, she still doesn't know about me."

Quoting James Cullen, David said under his breath, "And Bingo was her name."

David and Jim had been through a lot together over the last decade. They had a solid working relationship, and of course David would do everything he could to relieve his friend's distress.

"Check into it, will you?" Jim asked. "See what you can find out. If you reach the same conclusion as the police, let it go. I want as little to do with *our* father as possible. Call me after you visit her apartment."

"If you dislike him so much, why are ye' helping him out?"

"Judy insisted," Jim said. "She's pushing for reconciliation, but I'm not interested."

David knew Jim's wife, and it was rare she didn't get her way. "Where's the key to Kenzie's flat?"

"Don't have one. The building superintendent might be able to help you."

The last person David intended to ask was a nosy super. Besides, he didn't need a key. He had learned to pick locks, hotwire cars, and open safes—not as a form of criminal activity, but out of necessity. Elliott threw keys away as fast as he had once thrown back shots of whiskey. Although Elliott no longer drank, he still couldn't hold on to a key.

"I was going to talk to Elliott about this during our conference call an hour ago," Jim said, "but he sounded so distracted. When I asked him what was on his mind, he blew me off. That's not like him. Did he say anything to you?"

In the thirty years David had known Elliott, he had never discussed Elliott with anyone except Meredith. If Elliott didn't want to share information with his closest confidante, it wasn't David's place to do it. "If there's anything Elliott wants the inner circle to know, he'll tell us."

"By the way, you were supposed to be on that call to discuss the Syndication Agreement with the Sheik. Where were you?"

"Sorry I missed it. I was sending off my manuscript. I'll catch up later. The Sheik probably still wants too much for his stallion's breeding rights. Elliott will work it out." Although Elliott had an impeccable international reputation when it came to Thoroughbred breeding and racing, he wasn't focused on horses at the moment. David wasn't sure what had his attention, but he intended to find out.

"I'll call ye' later." David disconnected the call, scrolled through his contacts, and called the MacKlenna Farm pilot, who was staying at Louise's B&B in Edinburgh. After a short conversation, David hung up. Five minutes later, the pilot called him back with an itinerary. David would meet the plane at the Inverness Airport in ninety minutes, followed by a ninety-minute flight to London. He'd be in the city by noon.

His next call was to Jack Mallory, who answered on the second ring. "If you're calling me, you must have sent off your manuscript."

"I did. I'll be in London at noon. Meet me for lunch?"

"Sure. Come to the Ritz. We'll eat downstairs."

"There's something I have to check out first, and I need yer take on a situation that's just developed. Meet me out front. We'll eat afterwards."

"I'll be at the side entrance at noon. Don't be late. I hate waiting."

David was about to disconnect the call when he glanced at the notepad where he had jotted down the names of the two universities Jim mentioned: Cambridge and Harvard. "Hold up a minute. What do ye' know about the joint degree program to earn a J.D. from Harvard and an LL.M. from Cambridge?"

"Only that the program exists. Why?"

"Check it out, will ye'? How hard is it to get into?"

Jack laughed. "You're talking about Cambridge, not Podunk University."

"Just check it out." David hung up and sat in front of Elliott's computer, which was tucked into the corner behind the desk. He logged into the network, Googled Kenzie Wallis-Manning, and found her on Facebook. Several pictures had been posted Sunday after a mud race in Wolverhampton. She hadn't posted them. Instead, she had been tagged by friends. He wasn't even sure from the layer of mud what color hair she had, but she did have large, hazel eyes and full, expressive lips.

He had crawled through mud in the Army and had no desire to do it for fun. "What makes it fun for you, Wallis-Manning?" David said to the picture. "What does it say about your character that will help me find you?"

Her profile picture was a pair of muddy running shoes, and the cover photo, a lush green spot standing in stark contrast to a surrounding desert, looked hauntingly familiar. Had to be Afghanistan.

David also found her on Pinterest. She had several boards labeled: ENDURANCE RACES, FIREARMS, ENGLAND, RESTAURANTS, and VACATION SPOTS. But the board that caused his shoulders to square as though standing at attention was labeled WEST POINT.

Following a link on the board, he clicked on a YouTube video of Kenzie running the Indoor Obstacle Course Test at the U.S. Military Academy. A note at the bottom of the video said she held the record for the fastest time. David was rarely impressed, but he was now.

He clicked back to her Facebook page and noted there were large gaps of time between the public postings. She probably didn't use Facebook often while deployed; some soldiers were active on social media, others not so much. As soon as he found her email address, he would hack into her account. He had no qualms about invading her privacy if it helped him find her. He'd work on it during the flight to London.

He squinted at the picture of a woman, her face in shadow, sitting in the front row of cadets, dressed in white gloves and skirt, gray jacket with maroon sash, sword at her side. The look of a competent woman. A woman of strong character and mind. It was Kenzie, and from her stoic body language, she wasn't the type of woman who would shuck responsibility and disappear.

He knew in his gut that Kenzie Wallis-Manning hadn't left of her own volition.

If he hadn't seen a muddy post-race picture of her laughing, he'd consider looking in the local hospital for her, thinking she might have broken a bone or worse. But he was sure the police had already reviewed hospital admissions.

David checked the time. He had thirty minutes before he was scheduled to meet the plane, and he had yet to pack an overnight bag and text Elliott to let him know he was taking the plane to London. Unless Elliott needed him, David would stay the weekend. One of his sisters might have a free evening.

5

London, England, May 28, 1944

KENZIE STOOD AMID the rubble of a burned-out building. The stench of death and burning debris saturated the cool, crisp air, and her low-heeled shoes sank deep into thick dust that irritated the inside of her nose. The nasty smell of damp plaster and dirty coal triggered a sudden sneeze. Her heart pounded so hard against her ribs she thought they would crack. Even a simple sneeze could give away her position, and the Afghan insurgents would be on her in a heartbeat.

Where the hell was she? And where was the rest of her unit?

A blackout had siphoned all light and color from the street, but there was some light from above, from the stars and the full moon—a bomber's moon.

The shrill sound of an air raid siren blasted through the night. Doors opened and slammed shut, and voices yelled, "Hurry. They're coming."

English voices. That made no sense. She had to move. Find her unit.

She studied the aircraft moving through the searchlight beams. The planes were Ju 88s, medium bombers used by the German Luftwaffe. "Impossible." The Afghans didn't have World War II German bombers.

She had to find cover. But where? A viselike grip of terror held her rooted to the spot while the roar of engines soared overhead.

Deafening explosions sundered the air and rocked the ground, windows rattled and shattered, and a shower of glass spiked the sidewalk and street, crunching and grinding. More explosions followed.

Move, soldier.

She jumped at the command and darted away just as a brick wall collapsed onto the spot where she'd been standing. Sweat ran between her breasts as she made a mad dash across the street, arms pumping, to take cover behind a water tank. She patted down the pockets of her dress. Where was her weapon? She didn't have one, unless she decided to use the miniature Rubik's Cube keychain with her apartment key attached or the brooch's pin to gouge out someone's eye. She fumbled and stuck herself once, but finally managed to pin the brooch to the inside of her pocket to keep company with the cube.

Nearby came the sound of machine gun fire. *Bratatat, bratatat, bratatat.* Opposing forces were firing at the planes. Was her unit the one firing the machine guns, or the one dropping the bombs? American forces never flew German bombers. That meant her guys were on the ground. She would find them and get her orders. She didn't know where they were or how she had become separated from them.

She trained her ears on the droning planes. They were turning, flying away. The engines grew faint, then fainter still…until they disappeared entirely. *Thank God.*

Her problems were almost over.

She raised her head. Her eyes had adjusted to the darkness, and from her position she could see a row of brick townhomes directly in front of her. Afghanistan didn't have houses like that. The buildings on her left had been destroyed by bombs, the innards scooped out, leaving only brick walls standing as sentries to guard the remains. The buildings to the right had minimal damage, a sure sign of indiscriminate bombing.

The only vehicles on the street were black taxis passing by at random intervals. They belonged in London. Not Afghanistan.

Farther down the street, silhouetted against the blackness, a single church steeple rose from debris like a wicked scepter pointing a finger. "Don't point at me. I didn't do this."

Do what? Destroy a city in the United Kingdom or Afghanistan? Neither. She was having a flashback or a nightmare. This couldn't be real. *Wasn't* real. Her dream was mixing up her current life with her former. She licked her dry lips. The front of her dress was soaked now with perspiration. It was time to wake up.

She glanced up. No planes were caught in the searchlight, but something else was. Standing tall in the middle of the lights was Big Ben—London's iconic landmark.

It might seem like a nightmare, but the sulfur stink of bombs and fires made the scene much too real.

The sirens blasted again, and she jumped, startled by the sharp sound. Were the planes returning? This time the signal was a single, continuous note. Not an air raid warning, but the all clear. When it ceased, the quiet was as disturbing as the wailing siren had been.

It was time to find her unit. She walked toward the light of the fires.

Halfway down the next block she was met by a stream of old men and women climbing up out of a bomb shelter, speaking with English accents. This was definitely not Afghanistan.

She passed buildings with boarded-up windows and acres of bombed sites with piles of bricks neatly stacked nearby. A haze of black dust covered sidewalks and storefronts. Shelter signs with big white letter S's were clamped to lampposts like street signs. Beneath the S was the word SHELTER, with a white arrow pointing toward particular buildings. Water tanks were tucked in between stores and residences, and firefighting equipment was scattered helter-skelter.

Across the street, women with string bags hanging from their arms stood in a queue outside a market which was reopening now the all clear had sounded. Amid the gloom, there were dim blue lights saying PUB or RESTAURANT. A group of GIs stood outside an open door, smoking. The sight of her unit stopped her in the dust. She walked toward them, warmed with relief.

They whistled. One of the GIs stepped forward and jerked off his cap. "If you're going inside the pub, can I have a dance?"

Another GI shoved him aside. "He don't know his left foot from his right. Dance with me."

"I'm...I'm not dancing with anyone. Excuse me." She pushed her way through the gathered men and hastened her pace with no destination in mind. *Jerks. What was wrong with them?*

"You're American," another GI exclaimed.

"Who'd you expect? The Queen?" Her head was splitting, pounding in confusion.

Waking up was her only option, because she had no identification, money, or connections. But she did have her West Point ring. All she had to do was tap it against a hard surface—an unobtrusive signal to all Pointers present. She spun the black onyx and gold class ring with her thumb. She had earned it with her blood and sweat. The ring was a symbol of the perpetual bond of the Long Gray Line.

They would help her.

She continued her walk with the words *don your rings* playing in her mind. That was the moment she had begun to feel invincible. The bomb blast in Afghanistan that almost killed her had shattered that belief. Now she struggled to regain what West Point had bolstered and the war had smashed to pieces.

At Piccadilly Circus a labyrinth of blackout curtains had been pushed aside, and a mixture of light and noise and uniforms spilled from open doorways. Another group of GIs stood laughing and smoking on the corner of Shaftesbury Avenue in front of the Rainbow Corner Club.

She had run across several references to the American Red Cross club in her World War II research. It was a slice of Americana in the midst of London.

This was the craziest flashback she'd ever had. Or was she dreaming?

Three women approached the Rainbow Corner Club from the opposite side of the street, drawing the attention of every soldier standing outside the club. Kenzie used the distraction to sneak into the building without anyone noticing.

A Bing Crosby sound-alike was singing on a small stage, blending in with the clinking of bottles. Not beer bottles. Coca-Cola. A haze of smoke formed a canopy inside the club from the bountiful supply of American cigarettes that had turned a generation of men into smokers. She tried to wave away the dense clouds of smoke, then gave up. Not even a chainsaw could do the job.

Where was the ladies' room? She wanted to wash her hands. A sign to the facilities hung above the checkroom with an arrow pointing to the left. Before she could make the turn, a soldier grabbed her hand and whisked her onto the crowded dance floor.

"Dance with me."

Before she could object, she was triple-stepping to the beat of Glenn Miller's "Jukebox Saturday Night." Her much taller, smiling partner had an easy rhythm about him, and they moved across the dance floor as easily as partners who had danced together for years. He was that good a dancer, and she forgot about tired racing legs and bombs and flashbacks. She was lost in the heart and soul of music that reflected the pain of the country, yet it remained upbeat and positive. It was music that defined a generation; music she loved.

When she finally took time to study her partner, she lost the beat and stumbled, but he caught her and twirled her around like a pro. His face had perfect symmetry. Had an artist drawn half of his face and held a mirror to the drawing? Oh, wait. His nose wasn't completely straight. A small bump on the bridge indicated a previous break, but it didn't take away from the clean lines of his jaw and cheekbones. Nice hair, dark blond hair, parted on the side and cut in careless layers that angled down to brush his shirt collar.

And he smelled of leather and courage.

Both corners of his mouth turned up, revealing even rows of teeth. And then she gazed into his eyes, intense and beautifully blue, and her heart skipped several beats. If she didn't know for certain that John F. Kennedy served in the Navy in the South Pacific, she would have thought she was dancing with a blond-haired version of the late President. Dressed in the Army's olive drab wool trousers and four-button tunic with leather belt, by God, he was gorgeous, for a lanky kind of guy with pilot's wings pinned to his jacket.

Mr. Blue Eyes had light feet and strong hands. Whatever type of plane he flew, with those hands it had to be a gentle ride.

The dream was changing from dangerous to erotic, and that wasn't so bad.

When the band started playing Irving Berlin's "With My Head in The Clouds," she asked, "What do you think about when you're up in the sky?"

Without missing a beat he said, in a strong Boston accent, "Next time, I'll be thinking of you."

She didn't flirt with soldiers. Never had. Never had one for a lover, either. But Mr. Boston Blue Eyes was making a case for reconsideration. Dream sex. That's all she'd had since…since before she'd been hurt. She shook the thought out of her mind. Any man would be turned off by her scars, and she never wanted to see rejection in another man's eyes. Her father had given her The Look of rejection and disappointment too many times.

"You ready for a backflip?" Blue Eyes asked.

"An inverted flight?" Sure, she was game. With his large hands, she would land lightly on her feet. "Let's do it."

"Put your hands on my shoulders." He wrapped his right hand behind her lower back and his left behind her knee. "Ready? Jump into the lift," he coached. She braced her hands on him and jumped, landing softly.

Other dancers had stopped to watch and were now applauding. She took a quick bow. "You've done that before."

"Nah, but I've always wanted to try."

The first dance led to another one and another. She couldn't remember the last time she had danced and laughed so much. Was it the music or the company? Could be either. Could be both.

Bobbing her head to the beat, she leaned in close to his ear. "Great music."

Her partner grinned. It must be the adrenaline, because she was ready to grab his hand and go find a room.

"Music is the food of love," he said.

He must be having the same thoughts. "That sounds like Shakespeare."

He nodded, his eyes wide, obviously pleased she recognized the reference. *Twelfth Night*.

"Then 'play on. Give me excess of that.'"

A low, delighted laugh rumbled from him. "A Shakespeare devotee."

She waggled her hands, iffy-like. "Suffered through a high school English class with a teacher who was a huge devotee."

Two Army officers tapped Blue Eyes' shoulder to cut in, but he shook them off. When the band switched to Johnny Desmond's "Speak Low," they danced cheek to cheek to a song about speaking low when you speak love. Sensations Kenzie hadn't had in months, if not a few years, tickled her, toe to nose and back again.

He was hot and sexy, a great dream sex partner, and if she was reading body language correctly—when they danced cheek to cheek—he wanted her as much as she wanted him.

"Would you like a Coca-Cola?" he asked.

She lifted her hair to cool her neck. "*Yes*, please."

His glance followed the curve of her neck, and when his eyes met hers, he smiled, not with the smile of a starving man, but with the smile of a hungry man who knew the art of savoring the feast set out before him.

This pilot had style, and she liked that about him.

He laced his fingers with hers and led the way toward the bar, brushing off soldiers who tried to pull Kenzie back to the dance floor. "Take a number," Blue Eyes said. He leaned close and said, "You're a hit, sweetheart."

"You made me look good," she said.

He winked. "No ma'am. You don't need me."

He bought drinks, and they moved to two empty stools at the quieter end of the bar. He took a long pull on the bottle and then another, and she watched with fascination as he drank the entire bottle, swallowing only twice. Funny the things she noticed about men, about him in particular. He set the bottle on the bar and nodded to the bartender for another round.

"I haven't seen you here before."

What could she say? This was just a dream and she was liking it now. "It's a new experience for me."

His brow lifted with either surprise or delight. She couldn't tell. "You're American. What are you doing in London?"

"Dancing with you." She took a long drink, stalling, while taking a moment to deal with the niggling sensation peppering her arms. She set down the bottle, saying "Will you excuse me? I need to go to the ladies'."

He stood, put his hands on her shoulders, and turned her in the direction she should go. "Straight ahead. If anyone bothers you, send them to me. I'll save your seat."

"I'll be back."

The band returned, and she snapped her fingers and boogied her way down the hall. A small table was jammed against the wall holding copies of the *Stars and Stripes,* the military newspaper packed with reports from the battle zone, sports features, and news from the States. She'd read several old copies on microfilm in the last few weeks.

She scanned the masthead for the date—May 28, 1944.

The date was a slap to her face. A bucket of cold water over her head. A wake-up call. An alarm. The music dimmed and crept into the background noise. Cold sweat broke out all over her. The hall closed in on her, and she leaned her hand against the wall for support.

Sweet Jesus. This might be real.

Walking her fingers along the wall to make sure she didn't fall over, she made her way to the ladies'. Inside the two-stall bathroom, she collapsed in a straight-backed chair and dropped her head down between her legs, sending the blood back to her heart and brain.

The door burst open, and Kenzie jerked at the sudden intrusion. The brisk click of high heels against the tile floor stopped at her chair. "Are you sick, my dear?" The woman's voice, definitely English, was slightly deep, in a smooth, alluring way, not husky like Kenzie's.

Kenzie groaned. "Worse, I'm out of time." Humor had the habit of finding its way into the most dreadful of situations.

"Like Cinderella at midnight?" the woman asked cheerfully. "I don't see any glass slippers on your feet."

"They have cracks in them. They didn't make the trip."

"That's for the best. German bombs are breaking all the glass around here."

Kenzie chuckled at the absurdity of the situation.

"You also have smart shoes. What you need is a cold compress. You'll be spiffing again in no time." The woman turned on the water facet and a slow stream of water trickled into the basin. After a bit of sloshing, she gently raised Kenzie's chin and placed a towel on her forehead. "I can find smelling salts if you need them."

"Commonly called a *lady reviver*." Kenzie's groans turned to moans. "I think I've been sucked into a bad Victorian novel."

"You're funny. Are you better now?"

"How can I *ever* feel better? I have a nose that runs and feet that smell."

While the woman laughed, Kenzie raised her head and encountered the warm brown eyes of a gorgeous blonde with a Veronica Lake hairstyle. Even the woman's red angora sweater, which showed a nice bit of cleavage, was nauseatingly sophisticated. Kenzie buried her face in the damp towel again and prayed the sickening turmoil stirring in her stomach would settle before she threw up all over Miz-Too-Perfect.

Kenzie knew fear and pain and war well enough to know she wasn't dreaming. How had her life come to this? Had she unfriended someone on Facebook who wreaked revenge by sticking a pin in a voodoo doll?

"You're the lady Cav was dancing with."

Her insanity-inducing situation didn't appear to be improving, and was likely to get worse. "Cav?"

"The handsome American pilot who had his arms around you. Most of the women in the club are green with envy."

"Oh, right."

"Lieutenant Joseph Cavanaugh. Every girl's dream."

The way the woman said *every girl's dream*, though, was more matter-of-fact than dreamily, as if she was repeating gossip, not wishful thinking. "He's come in here a few times, but never danced. The girls assumed he couldn't, and they all wanted to give him lessons. Guess he was waiting for the right partner to walk through the door."

Kenzie sat up straight and tossed the towel in the basket next to the sink, taking a closer look at the woman's angora sweater with a black belted waist. The pilling on the arms showed its wear, but Kenzie picked up the faint scent of laundry detergent. Clean but worn. Said a lot about the woman. Said a lot about the times. A straight black line had been drawn with ink up the backs of her bare legs to resemble stocking seams. Women made do during the war, but never gave up the attempt to be fashionable.

The woman extended her hand. "I'm Molly Bradford." Her clasp conveyed both strength and warmth, and Kenzie shook her hand, liking Molly's confidence.

"I'm Kenzie Wallis-Manning. Thanks for your help."

Molly whipped out a black and white checkered neckerchief from her purse and tied it around her collar. The scarf was cute, too. Then she painted her lips with a bright red lipstick and combed her thick waves.

Glamorous, high cheekbones, and great hair. And if Kenzie wanted to make herself really jealous, she'd also acknowledge Molly's too-cute figure with soft, feminine curves, not hard and muscular like Kenzie's. Her mother had been like Molly, all stylish and soft and sweet-natured.

Kenzie worked up a smile. "He's the best dance partner I've ever had. He wore me out." It had been a long day for her. Sunrise had come with a starting gun for the marathon.

Molly primped in front of the mirror, fluffing the bottom of her perfect hair again. "I can tell you're feeling better. Your face is more pink than white now. If you're ready, I'll walk out with you in case you get faint again. That fly-boy should have come with a warning sign."

"What's the difference between a fighter pilot and God?" Kenzie asked.

"I don't know," Molly said, cocking her head curiously.

"God doesn't think He's a fighter pilot."

Molly laughed, held her side, and laughed some more until tears streamed down her cheeks. "I'll have to remember that one. It's spot on."

"You go," Kenzie said, feeling a bit better. "I need to use the toilet. Would you tell the lieutenant I'll be a couple more minutes?"

"You mean God?" Molly asked, wiping her face. "Sure thing, honey."

Molly flitted out of the restroom, laughing, and Kenzie hunkered down in one of the stalls, perched on the edge of a toilet, and leaned heavily against the wall, trying her best to figure out how—and why—she had suddenly appeared in London on May 28, 1944.

6

London, England, May 28, 1944

KENZIE WAS SITTING on the edge of the toilet in the ladies' room at the Rainbow Corner Club trying to figure out what in the world had happened to her. She gripped her head between her hands and gave it a gentle shake; like that was really going to stir the answers loose. It didn't work, of course, and the jarring impact only intensified her headache.

When she had flashbacks, or episodes, as she called them, she often lost track of time—an hour, two hours—and she never regained her memory for those periods of time. What was the last thing she remembered? Think. If she could recall everything that happened, then she had a serious situation on her hands.

She remembered sitting in her flat. Doing what? Reading her mail. No, not reading. Opening a package from Scotland. From a man named Digby. So far, her memory wasn't faulty.

Inside the package was a box, and inside the box was a brooch with a huge emerald. Okay. All good so far. Then what happened?

She had found a small latch and the emerald popped open. *And I read Gaelic words.*

Exactly. Then what? A fog appeared. It was peat-scented, and it carried her away. To where? To here. To now. To London in 1944.

Impossible.

It might seem impossible but it's what happened. No memory loss. No unaccountable hours. No unexplainable bumps or bruises.

I was minding my own business and look where I ended up.

Had solicitor Digby been hired by someone who wanted to wreak havoc with her life? Off to the past you go. *Poof.*

She didn't want to be in London in 1944. There was a frigging war going on. Studying World War II was one thing; living it was at the bottom of her list of things she wanted to do.

In less than forty-five minutes, she experienced a London air raid, danced with a sexy pilot, chatted with Molly, gotten a sense of London in Churchill's day, and was now hiding in a stall in a ladies' room at the famous Rainbow Corner Club.

For an adventure, this time travel jaunt deserved a five-star review. No. Only three stars. The air raid was a bit overdone.

If she said the words again, would the fog take her home? Only one way to find out. Try it and see.

She was all thumbs trying to unpin the brooch from her pocket and stuck her finger. "Ouch." The stone didn't warm in her hand as it had done the first time. A small detail, but an important one. She felt calm and cool that this would resolve itself perfectly. No. That was a damn lie. She felt cold, icy cold.

What do you call a time-traveling emerald brooch? It took two seconds to conjure a punch line. *Jewelry with a mission.* The stupid joke didn't make her laugh. Not even a chuckle. That was a bad sign, too.

She pressed the clasp, and the stone opened. She took a moment to be sure she was ready to go home. She could stay a few days and do some real research.

Impossible. She and war zones didn't see eye-to-eye. "There's no place like home." She clicked her heels and spoke the Gaelic words, sounding each one out just as she had done in her flat.

Nothing happened. No dizzying fog. No loud roar. No scent of peat. Nothing. Zip. Zero.

She tamped down the escalating fear and repeated the words, enunciating carefully: *"Chan ann le tìm no àite a bhios sinn a' tomhais a' gaol ach 's ann le neart anama."*

Again, nothing.

Faster: *"Chan ann le tìm no àite a bhios sinn a' tomhais a' gaol ach 's ann le neart anama."*

Nothing.

Slower: *"Chan ann le tìm no àite a bhios sinn a' tomhais a' gaol ach 's ann le neart anama."*

It's not working.

Obviously…

Her finely honed self-preservation instincts seemed to vanish like animals on the endangered species list. The realization that she was stuck in 1944 would have taken her legs right out from under her if she'd been standing.

Clowns to the left of me…jokers to the right…here I am, stuck in the middle…And I'm wondering what it is I should do.

She had no money, no clothes, no identification, and no friends to call for help. Did they even have telephones in 1944? Of course they did. She'd seen that old movie about a switchboard operator—*Ladies Should Listen* with Cary Grant.

Get a grip. Think. Had there ever been a puzzle she couldn't solve when she put her mind to it? No. Well, then, first things first.

Food. She needed to eat.

She re-pinned the brooch to the inside of her pocket, but her hand shook so hard it took several tries to snap the bar pin clasp. Was there a warranty for the damn thing? She should return it to the store and demand a refund, claiming the stone didn't meet her expectations. You'd think that if you were given a brooch with time traveling propensities, the stone would come with a round trip ticket. But hey, she wasn't the purchaser. The stone was a gift. Maybe the sender was Scrooge, and he kept the other half of the ticket for his next dream sequence.

Thanks a lot.

If she sold the jewelry, she'd have money for food and a place to sleep. While a sale would solve one problem, the transaction might create another one. What if the brooch was only temporarily out of order?

That's a lovely thought.

How was she supposed to fix it? Take it to a jeweler and tell him it wouldn't transport her back to the future. Yeah, right. Or maybe he could use his soldering iron and solder the magic back into the stone.

Get a grip, soldier.

A chorus of inner voices chanted, *Hold on to the emerald brooch. Although it doesn't work now, it might work later.*

Her best option was to cling to the possibility that the brooch was on holiday. After she jumped through whatever hoops it had in mind, maybe she could return home. If she intended to cling to that scenario, she would pray for the courage to endure whatever lay ahead.

If she was stuck in 1944, she needed to get out of London before the next air raid. If she could find somewhere in the countryside, away from bombs and the shadow of death lingering on every corner, she'd be okay, and the flashbacks would stop—maybe.

She was a smart person. Although she didn't have any money, she had a brain. At least she didn't have to go to Oz to figure that one out. And she had a heart, too. Courage? Well, that was debatable.

Kenzie's resume boasted perfect scores on her SAT and GRE. She wasn't cute like Molly, but she was a pretty decent stand-up comedienne. Her biggest asset, at least in 1944, was her knowledge of the future. Surely she could use information for her benefit. How? She shrugged. The answer wasn't clear yet, but she would figure it out. In the meantime…

"Hey," she said, pinching her earlobes. She wasn't without resources after all. The first weight on a scale toward balance was a delightful piece of news. There was a diamond in each earlobe, and on any jeweler's scale, they would weigh a carat each. Her father had paid a small fortune for the graduation present, but she wouldn't have to sell both of them unless…

A shiver raced down her spine and settled in her gut.

Unless…she couldn't find a way home.

First things first. Get through tonight. Tomorrow she would sell a diamond and travel out of London. To where?

How about Scotland? Since the brooch was an antique, and the words were Gaelic, what better place to look for her ticket home? The history of the brooch might be buried in old parish records in the Highlands, or the National Archives in Edinburgh. As much as she hated the thought, her mother's home country would have to be her starting point. The answer was there. It had to be.

So, what was her plan for tonight? Sleep on a park bench, or better yet, in a bomb shelter. She'd slept in worse places. Hot, sandy places where there was always the chance a sniper's scope was aimed at her head. A yellow brick road leading home was in her future. She could see the glittering gold, and a gate with a secret lock was waiting for her key. And if she met a wizard along the way who promised to rescue her, she wouldn't let him lead her astray.

Stay on the path. Stay smart. Stay safe.

With a plan and purpose, she took a moment to primp and fluff her hair as Molly had done. Kenzie didn't have any lipstick to apply, but she pinched her cheeks and straightened her clothes. She was now a soldier on a mission.

A breeze blew in through the open window, stirring her hair and caressing her skin.

Her buddy Trey whispered in her heart, *I've got your six.*

Whatever happened going forward, she knew he was looking down from above. She glanced up, acknowledging his presence, and missing him like crazy. "You'd like this adventure, wouldn't you, Trey? I'll do my best to enjoy a slice of it just for you." She couldn't imagine enjoying any of what lay ahead, but she'd find a moment in the madness to cherish on behalf of the friend who had saved her life. She owed him that.

7

London, England, Present Day

DAVID PULLED THE rental car up to the side entrance of the Ritz on Arlington Street, blinker flashing, and signaled to Jack, who was standing under the awning. Jack held up a finger, indicating he needed a moment. He wasn't talking on the phone, so what was he up to? A moment later a woman with long blond hair, a black mink and stilettos, walked through the door behind him.

If David hadn't been watching closely, he would have missed the slight movement of Jack's shoulders when he straightened them inside his leather jacket. David glanced across the street at a high rise. Jack and the woman's reflections were visible in the building's plate-glass window. Jack had obviously been waiting for her.

David rolled his eyes and placed his hand on the horn, but didn't sound it yet.

Whatever Jack said to the woman, she laughed. He then took her elbow and escorted her down the four steps to the sidewalk. A limo pulled up in front of David's Mercedes, and the Ritz's doorman opened the car door. Jack released her arm and plucked what had to be a business card from his jacket pocket. She gave it a quick glance, tucked it into her small clutch, and climbed inside the limo. Jack waited until the chauffeur pulled the car away from the curb before he turned toward David's vehicle, wearing the look of a man on a merry chase.

"Do ye' hit on every woman ye' meet, or just those in furs and stilettos?"

Jack closed the car door and buckled his seat belt. "I wanted to know where she was from."

"I could have told ye' that."

Jack regarded him a moment. "I'm all ears."

David pulled up to the stoplight at the corner of Arlington and A4 and turned right toward Piccadilly Circus. "The limo had a French diplomatic license plate."

"You don't miss anything, do you?"

"I only noticed the tag because he almost clipped me. I was checking out her legs. Did ye' get her number?"

"No, but she said she'll be at the Palm Court having afternoon tea. Wherever we're going, I have to be back in time for that."

"Ye'll have to put on a tie and ditch the jeans."

Jack studied a picture on his phone. "Appropriate attire is being pressed as we speak."

David weaved through traffic, an expert driver who knew the streets as well as any taxi driver. "Did she say tea at three-thirty or five-thirty?" Jack quirked a brow at his friend and David laughed. "She didn't say, did she?"

Jack peered at his phone again. "I doubt she'll be there. Her left hand sparkled with a diamond the size of the Starbucks' logo. But I'll make a reservation for both times. She might show up. Unlike you, I have to work for my dates."

"I wouldn't call lifting an eyebrow hard work, and that's all you have to do to get a phone number."

Jack wagged his finger toward the window. "Watch out for the biker."

"I see him. Ye're going to complain about my driving now?"

"Not unless you try to run someone off the road. And, just for the record, we both know that's a crock. The only thing you have to work at is remembering whose name goes with the dozens of numbers you have indexed under "sisters" in your phone directory. Women in every city in the UK are waiting by their phones for you to call. Hot women who would cancel an audience with the Queen to warm your bed."

"I didn't know ye' were gullible enough to believe Kevin's crap."

"Hey…" Jack held up his hands in mock surrender. "Kevin said Elliott confirmed it."

Elliott's body man/assistant gossiped more than any woman David knew, and he had reprimanded the lad on more than one occasion. Of course, Kevin generally blew him off, and Elliott let him get away with it.

"It's not true, and don't even joke about it around Alice. Comments like that upset her," David said.

"Only because they remind her of your womanizing father. You're not like him. He was a lazy son of a bitch who cheated on your mother with dozens of women. She didn't deserve that kind of treatment. And you didn't deserve a drunk for a father, but that's what you got. As for Alice, she wants you to find a nice girl, settle down, and give her grandchildren."

David had found the perfect woman, but unfortunately she'd been in love with someone else.

He pulled the rental into a parking space on Tavistock Place and cut the engine. Only two people in his life could get away with talking about his late father: Elliott and Jack. Jack was like a brother, and that gave him leeway to broach topics that would put lesser men on the floor with a broken nose or worse.

Jack glanced up the street and back. "Why'd we stop here?"

David pointed toward a two-story apartment building. "We're going in there."

Jack gave a wolfish grin. "Does this mean I finally get to meet one of your sisters?"

"Not mine. Jim Manning's."

"Oh, a real sister. Hmm. Is she tall like Jim? You like leggy women."

They opened their respective car doors and slid out. David slammed his side closed. "How would ye' know that?"

Jack rested his elbow on the top of the car and tugged at his chin while he mulled over David's question. "On the rare occasion I've seen you flirting in a pub, I've noticed the women have one thing in common. Legs to their armpits."

"Ye're full of crap. Ye' wouldn't notice a lassie's legs because yer eyes never go lower than their belly buttons."

"Okay, I'll admit to that. So what's up with Manning's sister?"

"Half-sister. He called this morning, said she's disappeared, and asked me to check it out."

Jack walked up the sidewalk toward the apartment complex entrance. "I don't know Jim as well as you do, but I've never heard him mention a sister of any kind."

"Don't feel left out. I hadn't either."

"Does this have anything to do with the Harvard-Cambridge program?"

"She's enrolled."

"Impressive. It's not an easy program. When I was at Harvard Law School, I knew a couple of students who were accepted. Top of the class, but socially boring. Jim's sister could have big boobs and long legs, but I doubt either of us would find her appealing."

"I don't know about ye', but I'd never hit on a friend's sister, even if I found her attractive."

Jack doubled over laughing. "Did you hear what you just said?" He continued laughing until tears streamed down his cheeks.

Incensed, David said, "I never hit on yer sister."

Jack's laughter slowed to a chuckle. "Keep believing that, but I was there. Remember? Well, except for the weeks I was incarcerated."

David glared at him. "Sometimes ye' can be the biggest dick."

"Yeah, you've told me that before. I think the first time was when the Yanks allowed you into my cell."

David took the steps two at a time. "I wanted to punch ye' for what ye' put yer sister through, and hug ye' because ye' were still alive."

"I'd rather not relive those days right now. What else do you know about Jim's sister?"

David stopped at the first landing. "She graduated from West

Point."

"Seriously." Jack caught up with David on the landing. "She would have had a five-year commitment following graduation."

"I don't have all the details, but I believe she went to Afghanistan."

"Jesus. That's even more impressive. What's her name?"

David headed up the next flight of steps. "Kenzie Wallis-Manning."

"I'm looking forward to meeting her."

"We have to find her first."

"What's her flat number?"

"Three-E."

"There it is." Jack crossed the hall to the door in the corner. "By the way, don't police generally handle missing-person cases in London?"

"They're investigating, but haven't found any clues so far."

"Have you checked social media sites: Facebook, Twitter, Instagram?"

David pulled a pick from his stainless-steel set and inserted the small tool into the lock. "She ran an endurance race on Sunday. Another participant tagged her in a Facebook picture."

A door to another apartment opened and a man in his mid-forties stepped out. "*What are you—?*" He grabbed his phone from the messenger bag slung over his shoulder. "I'm calling the police."

David stepped away from the door. "No need to do that. Are ye' Howard?"

The man's eyes narrowed. "Yes."

"Kenzie's father asked us to check into her disappearance. I read the police report. It mentioned their interview with you. Is there anything you can add?"

The man, about five-ten, average weight, and physically fit, put away his phone. "I'm so worried about her. She missed her six o'clock appointment for a massage on Sunday. She was so tight after that grueling race. She's not the type to disappear. Something has happened to her."

"We'll find her."

"You sound more positive than the police," Howard said.

"I was going to use a pick to get into her apartment—" David said.

"Do you have a key?" Jack asked.

Howard's eyes went to Jack, and he gave him a slow once-over. "No, I don't, but I can call the super."

Jack cocked his head and pointed toward David with his thumb. "He doesn't need one. But thanks."

Howard dug through the side pocket of his bag, pulled out a business card, and handed it to Jack. "If you have questions, call me. Or if you need a massage, I'll work you in."

Jack glanced at the card before tucking it into his pocket. "I'll be in town a few more days. Maybe I will."

"Great," Howard said. "And let me know if you get any leads on Kenzie. She's a sweetheart." He took one last look at Jack before heading down the stairs.

David picked the lock and shoved the door wide. "Did ye' really do that?"

"What?" Jack asked.

David flipped on the light switch and sniffed the air inside the apartment. "Give Howard yer book jacket smile."

"Sure, why not?"

"Because he was hitting on you."

Jack lifted his shoulder in a half shrug. "He had the number one New York Times bestselling novel in his messenger bag, and I would never offend a potential reader. Straight, gay, or even, God forbid, a member of the Republican party."

David rolled his eyes.

Jack entered the apartment behind David. "What's that smell?"

"Combination of empty Chinese food containers on the kitchen table, dirty dishes in the sink, and muddy running clothes on the floor."

"She's not a tidy person, is she?" Jack said.

David picked up a muddy sports bra, checked the size, and

dropped the garment on top of the pile. Small. Not Jack's type.

Jack picked up Kenzie's backpack. "I'll check this. You check the rest of the apartment."

David crossed to the bathroom, where he sniffed a pleasing, lingering fragrance. *Clover and lavender?* He pulled a few strands of hair from the hairbrush bristles. "She's a redhead."

"She's also a Mac user. There's a thirteen-inch MacBook Air in her backpack. I wonder why the police didn't take it."

"Jim Manning said they're checking the contacts and email on her phone. If she has the iPhone synched to the MacBook Air, the police probably didn't think they needed both. If she'd been suspected of terrorism, they would have emptied the flat."

David opened the medicine cabinet and mentally catalogued the items: large bottle of ibuprofen, spermicide, diaphragm, condoms, toothpaste, toothbrush, dental floss, deodorant, hairbands, and body lotion. All neatly organized, in stark contrast to the disorder in the other room. A folded blue towel hung from the shower curtain rod. Both the sink and the tub were clean, and a light green robe hung from a hook on the back of the door.

He sniffed the robe. *Lavender.* Clean bathroom, messy kitchen, unwashed clothes. Kenzie Wallis-Manning was a bundle of contradictions. "I saw a bookcase in there. What's she reading?"

"I'm sure your books aren't on her list." The thump of books hitting books resounded through the sparsely furnished flat until Jack laughed out loud. "I've gone through most of the titles, and I was right. Your books aren't here, but one of mine is."

David reentered the kitchen area. "Stop gloating. Ye've sold millions of books. Ye' also went to Harvard Law School." He crossed the room and stood in front of the bookcase, thumbing through a few of the titles. "Most are history books. D-Day and Churchill. She might be writing her thesis on a topic related to the war." He eased a book to the edge to match the ones Jack had left undisturbed. "Did you find anything else?" He turned to find Jack holding a brown paper wrapping. The color had drained from his face.

"What?" David asked. "Is there something dead in there?"

Jack puffed out his cheeks, and blew a long breath. "You're not going to believe this."

David took the wrapping out of Jack's hand. "Fucking Digby's at it again." The horrors of the Civil War invaded David's mind, complete with the clanking of swords. The months he had spent in Washington trying to win Jack's freedom would always loom large and foreboding, an ever-present canopy over the worst of times, including having his heart broken.

"If she's got a brooch, where'd she go?" Jack asked.

David set the wrapping down next to the computer. "Let's take her books, notes, and computer..."

"You might want to take that, too." Jack pointed toward the sofa. "It looks exactly like my sister's puzzle box."

David snatched it up and turned it over and around. "It's similar to Charlotte's, but the puzzle is different. It'll take me a while to open it."

"Anything in it?"

He shook the box. "Nothing rattles." Pieces of Kenzie Wallis-Manning's personality shifted and aligned themselves into one of four labeled columns: Warrior. Student. Athlete. Single-minded.

A shrewd glint in the depths of Jack's blue eyes zeroed in on David. "You suspect something. I see it in your face, in your eyes. You know where's she gone?"

"I might."

Jack gripped David's arm. "You're not going to keep me in suspense. You dragged me into this. Fess up. Where is she?"

David peeled back Jack's clawed fingers. "The MacKlennas raised Kit with an appreciation for pioneer life. She met Cullen on the Oregon Trail in 1852. Your sister, Charlotte, spent years participating in Civil War reenactments. She met Braham in 1864."

"So?" Jack prompted with raised eyebrows. "What does that have to do with Kenzie?"

David selected a book off the table next to the bed and tossed it to Jack. "D-Day. I don't know anything about Kenzie's parents, her life growing up, but I know she's intelligent, organized, and methodical."

Jack glanced toward the kitchen. "I wouldn't go that far."

"That mess is a reflection of her independent streak, and it's situated between a clean bathroom and a clean living area. My guess is that she's trying to break out of the mold that's defined her life."

Jack snorted and inclined his head with a mischievous glint in his eyes. "The only mold I see around here is on the leftover food."

David picked up a clothing tag from the kitchen table and read the description. Kenzie had paid £166 for a navy dress. He was willing to place a sizable bet that the dress was an extravagant purchase for her. Nothing he had seen so far indicated an indulgence in…

He blew past the bathroom door and snatched up a bar of soap sitting on the edge of the tub. He held it to his nose. Lavender. He spotted a soap wrapper in the trashcan.

"What are you looking for?" Jack asked.

David handed Jack the soap wrapper. "Inconsistences." He handed Jack the soap wrapper.

Jack sniffed the wrapper. "Penhaligon's in Covent Garden. This is expensive soap."

"We might have rushed to an incorrect conclusion." David left the bathroom and jerked open the closet's louvered door. Blouses and sweaters hung haphazardly on the hangers, and jeans were tangled up on the floor. He pulled back the collar on one of the blouses and read the label—J. Crew. Sensible, good quality, but not top of the line. He scratched his head. "I think I've got her figured out, and then she confuses me again. She took a bath with expensive soap and put on something new."

"You think she had a date?"

"Maybe. But she didn't plan to have sex. Her diaphragm is in the medicine cabinet, and, as messy as the kitchen is, I wouldn't think she'd bring a guy here. Would you?"

"If a woman brought me here for sex, I probably wouldn't notice."

David tapped a fist on the kitchen cabinet as if that would knock pieces of a puzzle into alignment. "We need to open the puzzle box, get into her computer, and study her notes and the books she's been reading. And I want to talk to her father."

Jack snapped open a paper sack and began to stack books into the bag. "What about the police? Shouldn't we check with them?"

"They don't have anything, and I doubt they'll find the answer in her cell phone."

Jack set the books, backpack, and computer next to the door. "What else do you want to take?"

"You've got the puzzle box?"

"Yep."

David took a long look around the room, letting his senses roam free, breathing deeply. The chimes of Big Ben rang in the distance, and he shivered.

He continued to let his senses breathe.

Air raid sirens. Bombs. Churchill's drawl sounding like a man with rocks in his mouth. Swing dancing. Screams. Soldiers. Gunfire. Cigarette smoke. Rations.

He shook his head to clear away the visions…or thoughts…or whatever had settled upon him. "We got it all. Let's go."

Jack stood in front of the door, barring the exit. "Before we leave, I want your best guess. Where has Kenzie gone?"

Intuition told David one thing. His good sense told him another. "If she'd taken her diaphragm, I could believe she was on a date. But her birth control is in the cabinet." David pressed his lips together, thinking. A moment passed and he quirked his brow. "I believe she's gone back in time, and right now she's smack in the middle of World War II."

Jack braced himself against the door, his face ashen. "Holy shit."

8

London, England, Present Day

WHILE JACK PACKED and checked out of the Ritz, David paid a visit to the police station, where he learned nothing beyond the names of the officers working the case. He spoke to the lead investigator.

"It's slow progress, Mr. McBain. We've interviewed all the contacts on Miss Wallis-Manning's phone, talked to her neighbor, her postman, and canvassed every hospital from Wolverhampton to London. No one has heard from her in the last four days."

David left his contact information with the investigator and drove back to the hotel to pick up Jack. Kenzie had vanished. The police's lack of leads, especially the absence of a hospital admission, confirmed David's every suspicion. He knew in his gut that a brooch had whisked her off.

So what would Elliott want to do about Jim's half-sister? Before David discussed the situation with him, he wanted to narrow the time frame. There was a six-year window—1939-1945. An event in Kenzie's past, or a topic she found of particular interest might affect her landing point, or more likely, it would coincide with the soul mate she was meant to find. What he might not be able to calculate was the probability of whether Kenzie would choose to stay in the past as Kit had done or return to her time as Charlotte had done. Too many variables at the moment, but if he looked deep enough, he would find the window of time.

Until David knew every detail of Kenzie's life, he couldn't make a prediction or recommendation to Elliott. And Elliott would want one before he spoke to Jim.

"Any help from the police?" Jack tossed his luggage into the backseat for the drive to Heathrow.

"None," David said.

"At least you know she's not in the hospital. What are you going to tell Elliott?"

"He and Meredith are spending the weekend at Louise's B&B in Edinburgh. I don't have to tell him anything, yet."

"You told him you were spending the weekend in London," Jack said.

David pulled the car out into traffic. "It won't be the first time I've changed plans."

"He'll be suspicious. Elliott knows everything, especially within his sphere of control. He doesn't have any control over us, but we fall in that sphere. He'll know you returned early. He'll also know I'm at Fraser House."

David checked the face of his iPhone for messages and missed calls. He had two of each. They'd have to wait until he boarded the plane and had time to respond. He pocketed the mobile. "If that happens, I'll tell him what's going on, but I'd prefer to wait until I have more information. Don't tell Charlotte where you are. She'll tell Meredith."

"Too late. Char called while I was checking out of the hotel. I told her I'd be at the castle for a few days."

"It's not a castle. It's a house. Don't ye' know the difference."

"To this Southern boy, it's a castle. It has a turret."

"Charlotte and Meredith text several times a day. That means Elliott already knows."

They rode in silence to the airport. As they were boarding the MacKlenna Farm jet, David's cell phone rang. "It's Jim. I don't think I'll tell him about the brooch yet." David answered, saying, "Jack and I went to her apartment, and I talked to the police. There's no trace of Kenzie."

Jim sighed heavily. "What should I tell her father?"

"That one's easy. I want to talk to him. Ask him to come to Inverness." David stretched out his legs and put his feet up on the chair in front of him. Damp days made his joints creak and groan. At thirty-four, his knees should be in better shape. Between falling off stallions and a grueling few years in the military, his joints had more wear than they should for his age. "I need to know who Kenzie is, inside and out, if I'm going to save—"

"You think her life's in jeopardy?" Jim asked in a voice that squeaked in the upper register.

David grimaced. The conversation was turning a corner that would take him in a direction he didn't need to go. "I don't know yet. But there are gaping holes that need filling, and her father can fill them. Why didn't ye' know about her?"

"Colonel Manning and I have been estranged my entire life. I'll tell you the entire story later," Jim said. "I have an appointment to get ready for right now. But tell me this. If you fill the holes, can you find her?"

The scent of lavender from the bag with Kenzie's belongings wafted over David and prickled his skin, unnerving him for a moment. "If I get the information I need, yes."

Jim's voice held a slight tremor when he said, "I'll tell the old man."

Fathers and sons and bad relationships had a way of putting trembles into voices. David had learned that lesson as a teenager. He sympathized with Jim, but he couldn't fight Jim's battle, any more than Elliott could have fought David's all those years ago.

"I'm sending the jet to Kentucky to pick up Kevin. Where does Colonel Manning live?" David asked.

"Close to Asheville," Jim said.

"I'll work it out with the flight crew. They can fly into Ashville and pick him up, probably late tomorrow."

"I'll let him know and send you his contact information," Jim said.

"Ye're welcome to come, too." David masked his feelings as

best he could. Unlike David, Jim's father was still alive. There was time left for them to work out their differences. Maybe they would, but David couldn't become embroiled in their dysfunction unless it impinged on Kenzie's welfare.

"You can manage extraordinary feats, David, but you'll never get the colonel and me in the same room. It's not going to happen."

David concluded the conversation with Jim and tossed the phone on the chair in front of him instead of putting it in his pocket. He needed a break from the constant vibration that announced his messages, emails, and calls.

"Your side of the conversation sounded interesting," Jack said.

"Dysfunction always does, doesn't it?"

Jack pushed his legs out in front of him, crossed them at the ankles, and hooked his thumbs in the front pockets of his jeans. "You, Elliott, Meredith, and I had a certain amount of dysfunction in our families growing up. Charlotte didn't."

"If ye' could go back again to 1865 and undo the changes ye' made to yer family history, would ye'?"

Jack shook his head. "Char and I don't have the same family history because of what happened in the past, but she's happier now, and not just because she's with Braham and has Lincoln. When the family dynamics changed, she changed, too, and I would never take that happiness away from her.

"If ye're looking for a happy relationship, look no further than Elliott and Meredith or Charlotte and Braham. They have what ye' and I both want, although we're both too stubborn to chase it."

Jack's eyes flashed, and then just as quickly the moment of reflection faded from his face. "So, what's up with Kevin? Why's he coming?"

David tossed back the last swallow of whiskey in his glass. "If Kenzie has gone back in time, I can almost guarantee Elliott will want me to go after her. I have to have a brooch to do that. Kevin knows about the box in Elliott's office at the farm. He can bring it and pick up the colonel on the way."

"We'll be landing in thirty minutes," the flight attendant said.

"Can I freshen your drinks?"

"Coffee, please." Jack turned in his seat to face David. "Look, I know I screwed up using the brooch when I shouldn't have, but I learned my lesson."

"You almost got your sister killed."

"I know that, and no one feels worse about it than I do, but you can't hold it against me for the rest of my life."

"Where are ye' going with this, Jack?" The memory of what he, Charlotte, and Jack had gone through still had the power to punch quite a large hole through David's stomach.

Jack tapped his index finger on the seat's armrest. "Hear me out." The flight attendant handed him a cup of coffee, and he sipped before he spoke again. "If Kenzie has gone back in time, she's gone back to meet someone, just like Charlotte and Kit. If Elliott wants you to go get her, you'll have to bring her soul mate back, too. Herding one time-traveler is a full-time job. Herding two is almost impossible. You'll need me."

David contemplated Jack's statements while he lowered the window shade against the dappled sunlight, but knowing Jack's request wasn't within his power to grant. "Elliott won't let you go, and neither will yer sister. Hell, she'd probably revoke my godfather privileges, and I'd never see Lincoln again. I'm not risking that. Not for ye'. Not for anyone. I love that kid."

Jack cleared his throat and leaned confidentially toward David. "If Elliott agrees, I'll handle Charlotte. I just need to know you won't go off without me."

David conceded the point with a nod.

9

Fraser House, the Highlands, Present Day

DAVID AND JACK sat at the conference table in the library, surrounded by Kenzie's books, laptop, notebooks, and a pile of receipts. David's decryption software had given him access to her email and stored files, and he was reading her correspondence. He doubted she'd take the news lightly that her privacy had been invaded, and would probably come after him with a cocked Beretta aimed at his ballocks. From the sketchy bio he had compiled, she seemed to be the type of woman to favor maiming a man before killing him.

The sweep of brisk footsteps on the stone floor announced Elliott's imminent appearance. He entered thumbing through a stack of letters David had seen minutes earlier on the table by the front door. "I thought ye' were going to London for the weekend. Did ye' even stay a day?"

"We decided to work on a new project here instead," David said.

Elliott strode over to the table, and with his free hand opened one of the World War II books. "Ye're writing another war story."

"Not exactly." David rubbed the back of his neck. He had hoped to have another day before telling Elliott about the appearance of the third brooch. He would ask questions David couldn't answer yet.

Elliott closed the book, eased into the closest chair, and crossed his legs. "What aren't ye' telling me?"

David slid a photograph of Kenzie toward Elliott, and poured a cup of coffee from a sterling-silver carafe. "Jim Manning asked me to investigate his half-sister's disappearance."

Elliott picked up the photograph and stared at it for several long minutes, then tossed it back on the table. "Can't see any of Jim in her. Ye' sure they're related? I've never heard him mention a sister."

"He's kept it a secret. I don't know why. Yet."

"What do ye' know about her?"

"She ran a marathon in England on Sunday. Went home, spoke to her father briefly..."

"Jim's father?"

David nodded. "Julian Manning. He's a retired Army colonel. The police are investigating, but no one has seen or heard from her since Sunday afternoon. Jack and I visited her apartment and found something of interest." David put a sack on the table in front of Elliott.

"What's this?"

"I think ye'll recognize it."

Elliott opened the sack and pulled out the puzzle box and wrapping paper. His face went white, and his hand shook when he shoved both items back into the sack. "Do *not* mention this to Meredith."

David dumped the box into a sack and shoved it under the table with his foot.

Elliott rubbed his hands together, then pounded a fist into his palm. "I tried squeezing Digby last time to give up the name of his client and got nothing."

"We can always try the rack," Jack said.

"He's the most tight-lipped son of a bitch I've ever met. I can understand attorney-client confidentiality, but he won't even agree to pass a message to his client asking the person to contact me."

"Maybe he's part of a secret society," Jack said.

"What? Like the Brotherhood of the Brooches?" Elliott said. "Anything is possible, but that doesn't jibe with the story Sean MacKlenna told Kit."

"If the MacKlennas can trace the ruby brooch back four hundred years, and the Mallorys can trace the sapphire brooch back to a similar time, then Kenzie's family should be able to do the same. That would validate Sean's story of three brooches gifted to three brothers for their part in rescuing the laird's lady," David said.

"Although if another brooch shows up, you've got a good argument for a brotherhood, or some sort of secret organization or conspiracy. But until that happens, all we've got is what we already know," Jack said.

"Then we're back to the original question. Who or what is Digby protecting so stalwartly?" David said.

"Don't get sidetracked with that question right now. Find Kenzie; then she can go after Digby."

"That tactic didn't work for me or Charlotte," Jack said. "What I can't figure out is why the brooches are passed on. They're dangerous. Kit was almost raped and murdered. Charlotte was threatened by General Sheridan and almost died during the fall of Richmond, and God knows what will happen to Kenzie."

Jack ran his hand over his hair as he marched to the window, where he stopped and gazed out over the terrace, the Loch Ness, and the hills beyond. The view was one of David's favorites. It probably was why he preferred working in the library, in spite of the drafty interior.

No one spoke for a few minutes. Like Jack, everyone seemed lost in thought. Elliott's inner circle had suffered as a result of the last trip to the past. But Jim Manning was Elliott's attorney and adviser. That made his sister, estranged or not, part of the MacKlenna Clan. And in Elliott's world, anything family needed, they received, regardless of the cost. Elliott had personally spent a half million dollars on research and preparation for Charlotte and David's rescue mission that took them back to the Civil War. Jack had repaid Elliott, but Elliott had financed the venture without expectation of repayment.

Elliott poured a cup of coffee, spooned sugar into his cup, and stirred. "What else do ye' know about the lass?"

"Our information is spotty."

Elliott narrowed his eyes. "I know ye're early in yer investigation, so give me the spots."

"Kenzie Wallis-Manning graduated seven years ago from West Point. She served five years in the Military Intelligence Corps, which included two tours in Afghanistan. Three years ago, she was almost killed in a bomb blast. After receiving treatment at Landstuhl Regional Medical Center in Germany, she was transferred to Walter Reed Army Medical Center, where she underwent additional surgeries and spent several weeks recovering.

"What were her injuries? Any disabilities now?"

David flipped his pen against the top page of his legal pad. "My medical contact has only been working on this for a couple of hours, so I have nothing. But if she was able to run a marathon last Sunday, I doubt she has any disabilities. At least not physical ones."

"What's that supposed to mean?" Elliott asked.

"She was severely injured in a war zone. Even those who aren't injured have emotional scars. I don't know if she suffers from PTSD, but I wouldn't be surprised if she did."

Elliott's phone beeped. He read the message and sent a quick reply. "What's Kenzie been doing since she recovered, and what brings her to London?" Elliott glanced at his phone again. The small lines in his forehead crinkled. It was a worried expression he often tried to hide.

Since returning from his deployment and going to work full-time for Elliott, it had been rare for David not to know the intimate details of Elliott's life. Why wasn't he sharing his problems now? Surely he wasn't drinking again. David would know if that was the case. Elliott had been free of his dependence on alcohol and pain medication since Meredith's bout with breast cancer.

Alarm bells went off like klaxons in David's brain. Elliott's distraction had nothing to do with his own health and everything to do with Meredith's.

Jesus Christ.

She was sick again. David didn't know how he knew, but he

knew. And he didn't dare ask for specifics. Meredith was an extremely private person. Ye' didn't invade her space. Ye' waited until she invited ye' in.

Composing himself, David said, "If ye've got to be somewhere, we can do this later."

"I've got a few minutes. Give me all the information ye've collected."

David cleared his throat of the knot of fear hanging unwanted and indissolvable and waited while it took a razor slide into the acid pit he called his stomach. The aftermath of his trip back in time to rescue Jack and writing the book had resulted in an ulcer. A doctor was treating him, but the sores never failed to flare up under stress. No one other than his doctor knew of his condition, and he took great care to hide his medication.

Publishing deadlines had become the bane of his treatment. And now this…

"Kenzie retired from the military," David said, diving back into his report, "and applied to Harvard Law School. During her second year, she was selected to spend her third year reading for an L.L.M. at Cambridge."

"That's impressive. Intelligent lass."

"Intelligent, no doubt. But she's a risk taker, and that makes her dangerous."

"I'll trust yer judgment on that. What else ye' got?"

"She's been in the UK since last September. She's currently working on an independent study titled 'What persuasive speaking skills can be gleaned from Sir Winston Churchill's war speeches that can make lawyers more effective advocates for their clients?'"

"If she intends to be a litigator, Jim should reconcile with her. He needs a new one in his firm."

Jack returned to the table and clicked on his laptop. "Kenzie grew up living on military bases all over the world. I don't see her settling in Kentucky."

"What countries?" Elliott asked.

David turned to another page of notes. "Germany, Italy, and

Japan. She's fluent in those languages, plus French."

"Any real surprises?"

"Two," David said. "She's renting a small flat in London, has few possessions, and buys clothes from Lululemon, Gap, and J. Crew. She has, however, amassed a small fortune through very risky investments."

"How small?"

"Over five hundred thousand."

"Gutsy."

"The second surprise is what I found on her calendar—a list of endurance races she intends to run. She's also a triathlete and rock climber. Among her marathons, she's run Paris, New York, Boston, Big Sur, and the Grand to Grand Ultra."

Elliott's eyes widened. "How many miles is that last race?"

"Six days and one hundred seventy miles," David said.

Elliott had once been an endurance runner, but an attempt on his life had put an end to his avocation. Now he only ran short races—5K and 10Ks. From what David could tell, Elliott seemed satisfied running those distances, and he always included James Cullen, pushing him along in a racing stroller when he was smaller, but now the lad ran with him.

During David's briefing, Jack, sitting next to David, had tapped, scrolled, pinched, and swiped his way through his files with multi-touch gestures, clicking open documents and pictures.

"A few years ago," Jack said, "I did a bit of research on women graduating from West Point. There's a prevailing attitude of indestructibility that comes with their commissions. I'm only an amateur psychologist—"

"Amateur sleuth, too," David said.

Jack cocked his head and continued, "And an expert on nothing. Anyway, back to amateur sleuthing and psychoanalyzing. Based on my research of West Point coeds, I believe Kenzie's injury destroyed her sense of indestructibility—"

"And let me guess," Elliott said. "She participates in endurance races in an attempt to reclaim that feeling."

"That's my two-cent analysis. Running endurance races and making risky investments are how she's trying to regain 'that old feeling.'" Jack sang a few lines of the song Frank Sinatra turned into a hit in the 1960s. "'Once again I seem to feel that old yearning…'"

"Spare us the Sinatra rendition. I prefer Judy Garland," David said.

"Would you two"—Elliott pointed fingers at David and Jack then rotated his hand and pointed the fingers at his eyes—"focus."

Jack straightened. "She lives on the edge. It makes her feel alive."

"My injury destroyed that for me, too," Elliott said. "I could ride an eleven hundred pound Thoroughbred forty-plus miles per hour without blinking an eye. Couldn't do that now. I'm too afraid of another injury."

"And that makes her dangerous," David said.

"If she's living on the edge, can she protect herself? How are her tactical skills?" Elliott asked.

David glanced at his legal pad. "She was awarded an expert qualification badge and a combat action badge."

"In other words, she's an expert shot," Jack said. "I wouldn't want to meet her in the dark."

Elliott drummed his fingers, thinking. "Kit could yoke a team of oxen and cook over a campfire. She believed she was equipped to cross the Oregon Trail in the mid-1800s. But her skills only gave her a false sense of security. If Jim's sister is well trained and finds herself in the past—"

"We believe she's gone back to World War II London."

"Damn," Elliott said. "I'd rather see her in the Revolutionary War than World War II. She'll be a danger, not only to herself, but the American Expeditionary Forces as well. What do ye' know about her family?"

"Her mother was a Wallis. Jim said the family lived near here. Do ye' know them?"

"Laurie Wallis?" Elliott eyes went hard, his face stern. David knew sternness well. It sat squarely and often on his own features.

Elliott's face then relaxed so quickly that if David hadn't been watching him, he would have missed it altogether.

"Ye' know her?" David asked.

"Aye, she was a bonny lass. We went to school together." His voice was reflective—almost sad—and then he flashed the look again, but less edgy this time. A moment later it was gone.

"If you knew Kenzie's mother, did you ever meet her father?" Jack asked.

"Laurie eloped with an American serviceman. Her parents were furious. They had plans for her to marry a wealthy boy from Inverness. Her father followed her to America, threatening to have the marriage annulled. Laurie was pregnant and very much in love. She wouldn't abandon her soldier. There was a ruckus, and she fell off the porch, and miscarried shortly afterward. She told her father to go away, and that she never wanted to see him or hear from him again. I don't think her family ever stopped grieving."

"What about the boy she was supposed to marry?" David asked.

"He went off to college and lived his life. That was at least thirty-five years ago." Elliott grew silent, lost in a moment's reflection. "So Kenzie's father is the American soldier."

"Are Laurie's parents still living?" Jack asked.

"Her father had a heart attack and died several years ago, and her mother passed last year, I think."

David scrolled through the emails on his computer, checking for the latest communication from Kevin. He found the email confirming Kevin's arrangements with the colonel, along with their estimated time of arrival. "Kenzie's father will be here tomorrow."

Elliott raised one eyebrow slightly and held his silence for a heartbeat. Then: "Why is he coming here?"

Elliott's tone told David nothing, but he had learned that whenever Elliott's mouth tightened down at the corners like it was doing now, he was being defensive. Why would he care whether Jim's father came for a visit? Must be a timing issue. Elliott was too busy or distracted to entertain company.

"I sent the plane to pick up Kevin and the colonel. I want to talk to him face-to-face, and I didn't want to go to him and lose research time."

Elliott stared again at the eight-by-ten glossy of Kenzie, this time with a softer eye than he had at first. "Why's Kevin coming? He has a list of projects at the farm and the winery to complete in the next few weeks."

David rolled his shoulders. "I needed the box out of the desk. I didn't trust anyone else to bring it. Ye' would have done the same."

"Ye've already decided to go after her?" The weight of Elliott's glare was surprisingly heavy.

David answered hesitantly. "Not necessarily. I want to talk to her father and narrow down the parameters before I make a final recommendation. But I will say, if I had been here when Kit went back in time, I would have gone with her. And if Jack hadn't accompanied Charlotte the first time she went back, I would have gone with her."

"Based on what I know of Kenzie, I would go if I could," Elliott said. "Go get her and bring her back before she can get into trouble."

"Wait a minute. Aren't you forgetting something?" Jack said.

Elliott and David looked at each other, eyebrows raised. "I don't think so," Elliott finally said.

"What about her 'soul mate?'" Jack emphasized the term with air quotes. "The brooch took her back in time to find the love of her life. You can't yank her out of there without bringing him, too. What if he's a soldier? What if he has a major role to play in the war? Bringing him to the future could cause a disaster. Maybe this isn't such a good idea."

David thought a minute. "We'll have a database created with as much information as possible about the war in Europe and the people involved. Hopefully, after we've identified Kenzie's soul mate, we'll find him listed in the records. If not, we'll have to make the best decision we can and hope we get it right."

Jack jumped to his feet, tossing a stack of clipped papers onto the table. "What? Then play God?" The paperclip popped off and the pages flew across the books and notepads and tumbled over the edge. "If Mr. Soul Mate only saved five lives during the war, we'll take him out…" Jack grabbed at the flying pages trying to catch them before they found their way into the open hearth's roaring fire.

David pressed a bent finger against his lips, surprised by Jack's outburst.

"…but if he saved twenty, we'll reevaluate." Jack caught the last page, but in frustration threw them all into the flames. "If he's a captain, he's expendable. If he's a colonel, he's not. Is that what you intend to do?"

"If it's too much of a moral dilemma for ye'…"

Jack leaned forward and thumped David's chest with a finger. "It should be too much of a dilemma for *you*…buddy."

"*Enough*," Elliott said. "We're dealing with hypotheticals, which will get us nowhere."

"I need a drink." Jack stomped over to the wet bar and sloshed whiskey into a highball glass.

"I suggest ye' go back, identify the man, return, and research him. Then make a decision based on what you discover. If he's driving a truck, while that's an important contribution, ye'd be safe enough whisking him away. If he's a fighter pilot, that's a different matter. What year are we dealing with? It might be close enough to the end of the war that it wouldn't matter."

"It could be anytime between 1939 and 1945. If she's studying Churchill, his 'We shall fight on the beaches…' speech was delivered on June 4, 1940. There's no way to know."

Elliott swept to his feet. "Keep me in the loop, but do what ye' have to do. Jim's legal advice has saved me millions. I'll pick up the tab."

David sat back, relaxing in his seat and flicking his pen on his notepad. "I'll have the rest of the reports this evening. Do ye' want to meet later for an update?"

Elliott stroked his jaw absently. "Meredith and I are leaving for Edinburgh and spending the night at Louise's B&B. Send me an email."

David pushed away from the table. Elliott hadn't said anything about leaving town. He was keeping his schedule under wraps for only one reason. He didn't want anyone to worry, and that only increased David's worry. "I'll drive ye'. Jack can work on the case while I'm gone."

Jack returned to his laptop with his drink and nodded. "Go. I'll call if I have any news."

"No need," Elliott said. "Meredith and I will manage." He left the room, calling for his wife, which reminded David he hadn't discussed the excavation of the cave with Elliott. Normally he would take care of an issue and advise Elliott later, but this involved Meredith, and Elliott would want to know her concerns were being addressed.

David followed Elliott. "When are ye' coming back? I want to talk about the cave."

"Meredith said she asked Ned to get rid of the bats."

"The problem is bigger than the bats."

"I can't deal with it right now. Take care of it."

"It needs to be excavated. I've put a call in to a mining engineer I've worked with before."

"*David. Stop.* Are we having a communication problem?"

David scratched his head. "Something is wrong, and I wish ye' would tell me."

"Hi, David," Meredith said, kissing his cheek. "Are you ready to leave, Elliott? Our bags are in the car, and here's your laptop."

"You didn't carry them out there, did ye'?"

"No, sweetie. Alice did. Come on or we'll be late."

Elliott swung the laptop strap over his shoulder and said to David, "We're having dinner with Louise and Evelyn. We'll talk about the cave when I return from Edinburgh, but I'm sure ye' have it under control."

"And ye' won't be back to meet—"

"We'll be gone at least two days. Hold down the fort."

David stood in the doorway and watched Elliott and Meredith drive off. His gut instinct was rarely wrong. He'd bet his next book's royalties that Meredith's cancer had returned. Kenzie's disappearance couldn't have come at a worse time. If Meredith was sick, David couldn't leave. He wouldn't leave. There was James Cullen to consider.

As he'd been reminded many times in his youth, the best choice was to "keep yer options open and yer powder dry." *I will, Auld Fraser. I definitely will.*

10

Fraser House, the Highlands, Present Day

KEVIN AND COLONEL Manning arrived at five o'clock the next afternoon. David seethed when Tate and Tabor, Elliott's golden retriever and Maine Coon cat, and normally permanent residents of MacKlenna Farm, bounded into the foyer, barking and screeching.

"I told ye' twice not to bring the animals. Why are they here?" David demanded, anchoring his attention on Kevin.

Kevin shrugged in his usual attempt to absolve himself of responsibility. "Mrs. Collins was sick. Tate saw my suitcase and ran out to the car. Tabor followed. What was I supposed to do? Lock them up?"

If Elliott didn't have such a soft spot for his body man, David would kill him. Elliott would be happy to see Tate and Tabor, but it wasn't the best time to add confusion to an already stressed household.

"Lexington has facilities to care for cats and dogs. Ye' should have tried one of those. Elliott isn't in the mood to deal with a turf war between Annabella and Tate."

At the mention of her name, a blue-gray Scottish deerhound thundered into the room and growled at Tate. Tabor took off up the stairs, her bushy tabby tail streaming out behind her like a bridal train, while Tate huddled between David's legs for protection.

"Take them both outside. And *don't* bring them back until the turf war is over."

Kevin grabbed both dogs' collars and hustled them out. David huffed out a breath of exasperation and turned his attention to the colonel, extending his hand. "David McBain, sir. I'm sorry about that. Annabella doesn't like having her territory invaded. They'll get along as soon as Tate is reminded he's on the deerhound's turf now. It's the reverse when Annabella goes to Kentucky."

The colonel gave a brief snort. "As for the cat, she thinks she's a person."

"She sees herself as a queen, regardless of the territory. I hope they weren't too much of a bother during the flight."

"Tabor jumped on my lap once. I set her down. She didn't try again." He brushed at his pants with the backs of his fingers as if removing cat hair. "I want to hear what you've discovered about Kenzie."

"Dinner will be ready in an hour. Would you prefer to freshen up or have a cocktail?"

"I freshened up before we landed. Like a good aide, Kevin saw to every need. I'll take a straight up, dry, gin martini, shaken with a twist. And conversation suits me fine."

David escorted the retired Army colonel into the library and mixed their drinks, taking time to assess the man while he studied Elliott's large collection of first edition classics, which were arranged alphabetically on the shelves circling the room. Without his slightly weathered face and thick gray hair, Kenzie's father could easily pass for a man twenty-five years younger. There was no curve to his square shoulders, and age probably hadn't shortened his over-six-foot frame. He appeared fit, trim, and athletic, with inquisitive hazel eyes, but he also had unsightly thread veins on his face, most likely from heavy alcohol use. Kenzie came from good genes. But what about Jim? He'd known Elliott's attorney for a dozen years, but yet he didn't see him in the colonel's face. Jim must resemble his mother, but he definitely inherited his father's height and body structure.

"Jack Mallory is working on Kenzie's disappearance, too."

"The author?"

"He's a friend of mine, and enjoys a good mystery."

"I assume this won't be a mystery for long."

"He's on a conference call at the moment, and he might have new information when he joins us. Shall we sit by the fire? This is a drafty room."

"Yes, it is. How long has Fraser lived here?"

"Fraser House has been in the family more than four hundred years. Elliott was born here." David pointed behind him. "I was born in the caretaker's cottage, and my mum has been the housekeeper since before I was born."

The colonel's pupils were pinpoints of distrust. "And your father…" He posed the question with an expectation of an answer that he would then use to judge David's character.

Prickly heat crawled over David's skin. He could sidestep and not answer the question, but the colonel probably already knew everything about him and was asking only to assess David's competence. Competence and character—two vital elements of leadership. "He was the caretaker before joining the Royal Scots Dragoon Guards. He went off to war, and when he returned, he didn't treat Mum well. Elliott's father kicked him out. I saw little of him, but through the years, I heard more than I wanted to hear. He died several years ago."

"And you never left?"

"Two tours in Afghanistan, but this is home. I travel extensively, but always come back."

Jack entered the room, cursing under his breath, and stopped. "Sorry," Jack said, approaching Kenzie's father. "I'm Jack Mallory. Just got off the phone with the police."

"Did they have any news?"

Jack's glance flickered to David, then back to the colonel. "She hasn't been seen since leaving the Starbucks three blocks from her flat Sunday afternoon. They are taking a closer look at what she did before returning to London. She was seen at the Wolverhampton train depot talking to a man dressed in running gear. He boarded a train to Edinburgh and she boarded a train to London. The Police are trying to identify the man, believing she might have met up with him later, or even taken a later train to Edinburgh. Nothing so far."

The colonel studied Jack with piercing scrutiny. "She wouldn't have gone to Scotland, and she wouldn't have disappeared on her own volition. She's too committed to her studies." He took a long drink of his martini. "She would have called by now."

"Why do you believe she wouldn't have gone to Scotland?" David asked. "Her mother is from nearby, right? Has your daughter ever been here?"

The colonel unglued his eyes from Jack and lowered them, watching the olive at the bottom of the glass. He pried his eyes from the drink and cleared his throat. "Laurie's family disowned her when we married, and the shattered relationship hurt my wife deeply. Kenzie knew her grandparents didn't want anything to do with her. Because of that, she would avoid setting foot in Scotland, even if she had to travel a thousand miles out of the way to get where she was going."

"Kenzie's mother died when she was young, right?" Jack asked.

"When Kenzie was ten, she spent the afternoons at the library four blocks from our base housing playing chess and solving puzzles. She was required to be home before dark, but sometimes the game dragged on and she wouldn't quit. One day when she didn't come home on time, Laurie went to get her. A car ran a stoplight and hit her on the driver's side. She died instantly. When I told Kenzie what happened, she blamed herself for her mother's death, claiming if she had been on time, her mother would still be alive.

"Kenzie understands, at least intellectually, that it wasn't her fault, but she can't reconcile that with a ten-year-old's emotions and beliefs. She believes a lie, and no one can talk her out of it. It doesn't impair her ability to function on an extremely high level, or solve complex problems, but it has caused her problems in relationships."

The colonel's story punched through David's ribs as if the colonel had hit him with the force of his full weight fused into his fist.

Damn the brooches. He hated them and the pain they caused. He refused to concede to the emerald and allow it to hurt Kenzie the way Charlotte and Kit had been hurt. He would find a way to short-circuit the process, snap the red tape, and go directly to the end result. Kenzie was a warrior. She had paid her dues with more than enough of her own blood.

"Did she get counseling?" David asked.

The colonel nodded. "She saw a child psychologist a few times and convinced the therapist she was coping just fine. She wasn't acting out, and continued to do well in school. I saw no need for more therapy when I was reassigned to a base in Japan."

The hairs on the back of David's neck stood on end. The colonel's tone of voice was layered with anger, and his story didn't mesh with Elliott's. Now wasn't the time to press. If he did, the colonel might clam up, and David needed Kenzie's father to be forthcoming.

"Jim said he didn't know about Kenzie until a few years ago. I assume that's when she found out about him."

The colonel's face turned a chalky white. "She doesn't know Jim exists."

"Why is that?"

"Personal reasons. I didn't want her to know I had abandoned my son. I couldn't risk losing my daughter, too."

"Jim didn't tell me how the two of you became estranged. Do ye' want to explain?"

The colonel set his glass on the table next to the chair and linked his hands in his lap, squeezing them until his knuckles turned white to match his face. "If you must know, Jim's mother and I were dating before I got drafted in 1962. She was pregnant before I shipped out for basic training. We married quickly. Several months after the baby was born, she asked for a divorce. I was in Vietnam and doubted I'd come out alive. I agreed.

"When I came home, I tried to see my son. My ex-wife had remarried a well-to-do lawyer, and didn't want me involved in our son's life. I didn't have anything to offer him at the time, since I intended to go to officers' school and make the Army a career. Fighting for visitation to see a child I would never be close enough to visit seemed pointless. I was young and didn't think of the consequences. I never missed a child support payment, even though she didn't need the money.

"Did you send birthday or Christmas presents?"

The colonel looked away. "For special occasions, I sent her extra money, hoping she would buy him a gift. I don't know if she did or not."

"Jim was an outstanding athlete. Did ye' ever see him play?"

"I had a friend in Lexington who sent me newspaper clippings about Jim's accomplishments, and when I could, I'd come to town and watch him play a game. But I never approached him. By the time he was a teenager, it was too late. By all reports, he was a well-adjusted young man. He didn't need me."

The colonel paused and looked down at his knotted hands. "I stood outside the church the day he got married. Sneaked into the hospital and visited the nursery when my grandchildren were born. I'm not proud of what I've done. I was a kid, surprised to be alive, and I made bad personal decisions."

"Jim has no idea, does he?" Jack asked.

"There's no reason he would know. I tried to do better with Kenzie. We've fought over her money decisions and career choices, but mostly we've argued over the personal risks she takes."

"She has a nice portfolio," David said.

"I saw a monthly statement a couple of years ago. She lost a hundred thousand dollars in one day. Almost wiped her out. That was the last time I ever looked at a statement from her broker until last week. We argued about it when we talked on Sunday.

"Kenzie could have a thousand dollars or a million dollars. You wouldn't know by the way she lives. For her, investing is more of a challenge than financial security. The market is her playground."

"Did she learn that from you?" Jack said.

"*No.* Kenzie's a risk taker."

"She sounds like an adrenaline junkie," Jack said.

"If ye' and Jim hadn't been communicating, why did ye' call him for help?"

"That's a fair question." The colonel drained his glass. "Kenzie's first deployment coincided with my retirement. In a weak moment, I went to Lexington and paid a visit to Jim's office. He was kind enough not to throw me out, but he told me I was, as the saying goes, a day late and a dollar short. Before I left, I told him he had a half-sister, and that I hoped they would meet some day. He told me if I raised her, she wasn't someone he wanted to know. That was the last time I saw him. When Kenzie disappeared, he was the first person I thought of who might be able to help."

"Why is that?" Jack asked.

"I've followed his legal career, and I know he represents Fraser. When Laurie talked about her home, she often mentioned the Frasers, both Elliott and his father. When the police asked if there was anyone in the United Kingdom Kenzie might visit, I thought of Laurie's family in Scotland, but I didn't mention them to the police."

"Why not?"

"I didn't want to waste the police's time searching dead ends. I covered my bases by contacting Jim and asking for help."

"Ye' got what ye' wanted. We're looking into Kenzie's disappearance, and the police aren't investigating her connections in Inverness."

The colonel stood. "I've reserved a room in Inverness. I'm rather tired. If I could trouble you for a ride to town."

"Ye're welcome to stay here," David said.

The colonel sighed. "Revisiting old wounds has worn out this old soldier. If you'll excuse me, I'll be on my way. If you have additional questions, you have my cell number. I'll be here for a day or two before taking the train to London. I'm planning to stay in Kenzie's flat until she's found."

David shook the colonel's hand. "Where is Laurie buried?"

"In Berlin. I've wanted to bring her back to the Highlands, but I don't think she'd be welcome in the family cemetery. Maybe in another decade or two, after I'm gone, Kenzie might be able to massage the situation, but first we have to find her."

"Kevin will drive ye' to town," David said, "and I'll call if we have further questions."

David and Jack walked with him to the foyer and met Kevin and the dogs. "They're great friends again," Kevin said.

"Will ye' take the colonel to his hotel in Inverness, and see if Alice needs anything from the market?"

"I'll meet you in the car," Kevin said to the colonel before dashing off to the kitchen.

When the colonel left, Jack and David reconvened in the library.

"He gives me the creeps, and he was lying about Laurie. Why?" Jack asked.

David's jaw muscles tensed. "I don't know. He might have concocted his own version to assuage his guilt for running off with her. I'll talk to Mum. She doesn't gossip, so I might not learn anything new, but there's no doubt we've been told two very different stories. I believe Elliott's version. He has no reason to lie."

Jack cleared his throat. "What if Elliott was the lad Laurie was supposed to marry? What if the baby she lost was actually Elliott's?"

David poured a shot of whiskey. "Ye've been writing fiction too long, buddy. Elliott said they were classmates. If they had been more to each other, he would have confessed."

Jack shook his head. "At any other time, he would have, but something is going on with him. He's distracted. I'll drop it for now."

David clicked his shot glass against Jack's. "Good."

David would table the discussion of a possible relationship, but that wouldn't stop him from trying to reconcile it in his own mind. Had Elliott followed the colonel's career? The man he had been jilted for. Did he know the colonel was Jim Manning's father? Did Elliott hire Jim years ago because Laurie had once been Jim's stepmother?

All the tired, sore bones in David's body yelled, "Hell, yes."

11

Fraser House, the Highlands, Present Day

Two days later, David sat hunched over the library's conference table jotting down notes and suppositions. Preparation for this trip back in time, although he hadn't fully committed to it yet, would be extensive, more so than traveling back to the American Civil War. More dangerous. More consequential. More challenging.

He flipped a pen back and forth, playing a light, rhythmic beat on the notepad. At the same time he mimicked the classic kick drum, letting the air vibrate between his lips. When he got going, he was a one-man band without a gig.

Tate growled from his spot under the table. He had claimed the patch of carpet the day he arrived, after sniffing around the room three times or more. David leaned over and rubbed the dog's neck. "What are ye' complaining about? At least I'm not farting like ye' are. What'd Mum feed ye?"

Tate rolled over so David could give him a good belly scratch. "Ask me how the investigation is going." he said to the dog.

The retriever gave a short bark.

"Since ye' asked, not so good."

David stood, circled round to the window, and leaned against the sill, deep in thought about the redhead warrior he was tasked with locating. How was Kenzie managing? She had no identification or money. Where would she go for assistance? The Red Cross? How could she ask for help and explain her presence in London when she couldn't possibly understand it herself?

David had been through the fog twice. It was disorienting even when you knew what to expect. But she was trained to cope with the unexpected. Her training would keep her alive in the short term. But what about later, when the shock wore off and reality set in? How would she handle being in a war zone again? A war zone seventy years in the past. A war zone with German bombs falling indiscriminately from the sky. Even a well-trained Special Forces operative would find the situation disconcerting.

What would Kenzie do in mid-twentieth-century London? If that's where she landed. She couldn't volunteer to fight. The Army wouldn't allow her. She could volunteer to serve coffee, type, or operate a truck, but that would drive her crazy. She was an action person.

David returned to his place at the table and stretched his legs out in front of him. He was in stocking feet and tickled Tate. The dog nuzzled David's foot, found it uninteresting, rolled over, and went back to sleep. Tabor, however, who had been sniffing crumbs around Jack's empty seat, jumped into David's lap.

"The Queen has come to visit. What do you think about Kenzie, yer majesty?" he asked the cat as he stroked her back. Tabor churred contently. "She's a competent and bonny lass, don't ye' think?" The Maine Coon churred again.

Tate crawled out from under the table and nudged David's arm. "Oh, now that someone else wants my attention, ye've come to bid for it, too." David stopped stroking Tabor and patted the dog's head. Tabor hissed at Tate and the dog backed down.

"After all these years, ye' still forget Tabor is the queen." David distracted Tabor with one hand and reached out to Tate with the other to stroke behind his ears.

"Now, both of ye' run along. I've got work to do if we're going to get Kenzie home safely." Tabor jumped down and scampered out of the room, Tate went back to his spot under the table, and David refocused on his warrior princess.

At the top of his notepad he wrote the word EXPERIENCE, and under EXPERIENCE made two bullet points. Point one: *Five years in the Military Intelligence Corps.* Point two: *Multilingual (French, German, Italian, and Japanese).* Below the second bullet point he drew a big question mark.

How could she put her expertise to use in World War II Britain?

With the tip of his pen, David coaxed books stacked haphazardly into a straight up-and-down alignment, making the spines easier to read. Of the ten or so books, one was on the life of Eleanor Roosevelt, heavily highlighted and tabbed. Five other titles were of particular interest: *Overlord, The Guns at Last Light, Churchill: The Power of Words, London's War, The Lost World of Bletchley Park, D-Day: The Battle for Normandy.*

He scribbled three more bullet points: *Complex Problems, Risk Taker, and Problem Solver.*

He narrowed his eyes, zeroing in on one book in particular that represented all three points: *The Lost World of Bletchley Park.* David's internal radar went off, clicking madly, like a Geiger counter at the mother lode. Tate stirred, whimpering in his sleep.

Bletchley Park.

David rapidly clicked the laptop keys. His search terms were *Bletchley Park* and *Alan Turing.* He had seen movies about the Park and Turing, so he was familiar with the man and his work. The Park would be a perfect environment for Kenzie. She'd be among hundreds of other multilingual puzzle-solvers. The Park was a safe distance from the bombing. But....

He continued surfing the internet, looking for Bletchley's security protocol. His hunch was right. Their security was formidable. Kenzie couldn't get a position, even as a cook, without proper identification. Every man and woman who walked through the gates at Bletchley, regardless of their assignment, signed the Officials Secrets Act. Violating any provision of the Act would land an employee in prison or in front of a firing squad. Kenzie had the credentials, but not the documentation necessary to secure a position, unless she found a back way in. David didn't doubt

Kenzie's resourcefulness. Quite the contrary. He just didn't think she could outwit Military Intelligence.

Now what?

The questions that had plagued his sleep and driven his mind down alleyways and roundabouts now flashed like vibrant neon lights.

Why would Kenzie stay in the past, and what would compel her to live in a war zone again?

Unlike Kit, who ventured into the past on a quest to solve a mystery, and Charlotte, who had to protect her ancestral home, Kenzie had nothing coercing her, or at least nothing David had considered so far. She had fought her war and then traded in her assault rifle for textbooks.

If she wasn't on a quest or coerced, there were three other possibilities. She was injured. She lost the brooch. Or, third, her risk-taking personality had overcome good sense, and she was using the time to complete her research firsthand, worming her way into a position on Churchill's staff. If that was the case, she would only need a few days, and should have returned by now.

Charlotte Mallory would have jumped right back into the fog for a return trip if the stone's clasp hadn't been broken. And Kit, according to the entries in her journal, would have given up and gone home if not for Cullen.

That left three likely possibilities: Kenzie had been killed or seriously injured, she lost the brooch, or she fell in love and decided to stay in the past, which David thought was highly unlikely.

David stood and stretched his shoulder muscles. The fire was burning low, and the room's temperature had dropped a few degrees. He tossed a couple of logs on the grate, and pointed the nozzle of the bellows on the low-burning flames until they ignited the dry wood.

He wasn't sure he could buy into the possibility that Kenzie lost the brooch. Charlotte battled war, fire, and interrogation and held on to hers. Kit dove into a raging river to rescue a boy and didn't lose the ruby. Jack, of course, lost his, but his trip back in time had been a disaster from the get-go. Kenzie was a soldier, and accustomed to maintaining her equipment. She wouldn't lose her brooch. The loss would be similar to mislaying her assault rifle in enemy territory. That wouldn't happen. He mentally drew a hard line through that option. The one remaining option didn't sit well.

Killed or injured.

Brisk footsteps sounded outside the library. The door opened and Jack entered, rubbing his hands together. "Burr. It's got to be sixty degrees in here. Didn't you notice?"

David waved a hand to show off black, half-fingered gloves. "The house is always cold. A fire helps, but these gloves make it bearable if you're writing. Do ye' want a pair?"

"I'd prefer heat." Jack gave him an obviously fake smile before tossing a log onto the flames. "I have on four layers and I'm still freezing. Doesn't the cold bother you?" He prodded the wood with the poker until the fire popped and sizzled.

"I grew up here. I'm used to the weather. Next time I chop wood, ye' can help. The exercise will warm ye' up quicker than a fire. Living in Virginia has made ye' soft."

Jack surveyed the hearth with a slow shake of his head. "I've never seen you chop wood or refill the wood box. Tell me the next time you pick up an ax. I want to post a picture on Instagram." He filled a coffee cup from the carafe, pulled his chair up to the table, and booted up his laptop, sipping the brew. "And, by the way, I don't mind cold weather. It's the constant damp and dreariness that gets to me."

David settled the bellows back into the tool stand and closed the fireplace screen. "I chopped a half cord of wood this morning. I'm sorry I didn't take a picture for ye' to show yer fans."

"Never mind," Jack said, waving him off. "I don't want a picture of you. I want a video of me. It might attract a whole new following."

David laughed. "Not that I don't think ye' could do it. But ye' wouldn't like having blisters. They wouldn't go with yer image, and ye'd snag a lassie's black lace stockings with yer cuts and blisters."

"Women don't wear stockings anymore."

"Sure they do. Especially, the ones ye' spend time with."

"You're right. I'd be humiliated if I snagged a woman's stockings because of rough hands." He kissed his palms. "I keep these appendages soft as a baby's butt."

"Ye're so full of crap," David said.

In response, Jack scooped up the football they'd been throwing back and forth while brainstorming and threw it at David.

"There's an art to removing stockings without snagging them with rough hands." David tossed the ball back. "When ye' can do that, ye've got the finesse of an expert."

Jack threw the ball again and David snatched it out of the air with his linebacker hands. "You're a piece of work. Is that in your book bio?"

"No, but it should be." He threw the ball back with just enough spin that Jack fumbled. The ball crashed into a lamp on a table between the windows and the lamp tipped over. David leapt up and barely rescued the antique before it hit the stone floor. Alice would have had his hide peeled in small strips if the lamp had broken. He rubbed his arse, thinking of her taking a switch to him and put the ball on a shelf.

"I've been thinking about Kenzie and her brooch and why she didn't turn around and come right back home," Jack said. "Do you think she could have lost it?"

"We've been thinking along the same lines. I considered that. But I think Kenzie would treat the brooch the way she would treat her weapons—with great care."

"Do you think she would protect it with her life?"

"Considering what could happen to the world if the Nazis had control of a brooch, yes, I believe she would."

"Then, if she still has it, and if she landed in London during the war, she could have been injured during the bombing."

"I thought of that, too. If she was killed, we'll never find her body. If she was injured, we might find her in one of the hospitals."

"We'll have to take pictures of her to pass around. No. Wait. I've got it." Jack scrolled through the contacts on his phone. "Just the person we need. He's done character sketches for me. I'll send him a text to see if he's available for a rush job. If he can do it, I'll send Kenzie's picture and ask him to give her a Forties look. He'll think he's drawing a character for one of my books."

David filled a cup with coffee and picked up a sweet roll. "We'll need a fast turnaround and dozens of copies."

"We'll need more than a few dozen if we intend to canvass the hospitals, Red Cross centers, restaurants, and hotels." Jack topped off his cup, but passed on the rolls. "I found something interesting in Kenzie's emails."

"Which one? I skimmed them, but they appeared to be all research-related."

"This one probably is, too, but to me it doesn't fit. It's a memorandum to Churchill from an agent with Military Intelligence, and ninety percent is redacted. The agent relates a shooting of a U.S. Army Ranger on June 5, 1944, and the escape of an IRA German spy."

David glanced up from his computer and gave Jack a half-interested shrug. "Any names?"

"None. So, why would this document interest her?"

"Print it out and let me see it."

The printer on the table spit out five sheets of paper. David whisked them up and perused them quickly. Jack was right. Out of an approximately twenty-five-hundred-word document, all but a hundred words were redacted. "How important do ye' think this document is?"

"You said everything she did in the days leading up to her disappearance is important."

David sat back and crossed his arms. He could get a copy of the original, but he'd be breaking the law to do it. Was it that important?

Jack scratched the scuff on his chin while staring deep into his coffee cup. "The Army Ranger mentioned in that memorandum is a significant player in this vignette."

"Are ye' reading tea leaves now?" David asked.

"No, coffee."

"I didn't know ye' could read coffee grounds."

"The art of tasseography includes reading tea leaves, coffee grounds, and wine sediments. A few years ago, I interviewed a Gypsy for a book I was working on. I learned quite a bit about the art. Give me your cup, and I'll read the grounds."

David swallowed the last of his coffee and then wiped the inside of the cup with a tissue from a box on the table. "Not a chance in hell." He set his cup down, none too gently, out of Jack's reach.

"I'd give my next book advance to read the original copy of the memorandum."

"Find me a connection to Kenzie, the Rangers, Military Intelligence, and the IRA, and I'll get you a copy of the original."

"I know you have unlimited resources, and people who skirt the boundaries of legality, but hacking into The National Archives for a classified document is further than I thought even you would go."

"Well, thanks. I didn't say I was going to hack into their system. Besides, you have to find the links first, and I don't think they exist."

"I'll find a link. Why don't you go to the dentist or something?"

"I did that this morning." David stood and snatched the coffee pot off the table. "I'll get a refill. Ye've got a long night ahead."

Jack clicked the laptop's keys. "Sixty minutes. Start counting."

David went to the kitchen, ate a sandwich, read the newspaper, and chatted with his mum. An hour and a half later, he refilled the carafe with fresh coffee and returned to the library. Jack was sprawled in his chair.

"How long have you been gone?" Jack asked.

David shot a disbelieving glance at his watch. "Ninety-three minutes, thirty-five seconds."

Jack straightened and hit a key to wake up his computer. "I've been sitting here thinking for the last fifteen minutes or so, putting pieces together and you," he said, pointing his index finger, "need to sit down and start hacking."

Surprises were mounting up for David, and he didn't like that. Jack was an exceptional investigator and researcher, but David never expected him to be able to connect the dots. "Which one did you connect to Kenzie? Military Intelligence, the Rangers, or Ireland?"

Jack gave him a smug look and cracked his knuckles. "The Rangers and Ireland, but there's more. You're not the only one with contacts. Sit back and watch the master at work." A piece of paper spit out of the printer. Jack sailed it across the table toward David. "Robert Julian Manning was born April 4, 1922 in Newport News, Virginia. He joined the Army and volunteered for the Rangers. He endured training designed to break men, but he made the cut. Manning's CO described him as a man with a gritty sense of competition, hardened like steel."

David anchored his attention on Jack and in a halting voice asked, "Robert Julian? Kenzie's grandfather?" Jack nodded and David barked a laugh. "Keen work."

"That's not all," Jack said.

Another piece of paper spit out of the printer.

David summarized aloud. "Manning sailed on the RMS *Queen Elizabeth* with Second Battalion's Dog Company on November 23, 1943," Jack said, summing up the document David was speed reading. "The ship docked in Scotland on November 30. A few months later, he met and married Della O'Brien from Belfast, Ireland. On June 5, 1944, he was shot at the New Inn at West Knighton. Why?"

"You'll have to hack into The National Archives for that answer."

An inkling of excitement inched up David's spine. Jack was right, and David's bones were telling him so. Call it intuition. Call it a sixth sense. Call it a hunch. There was still a large dot Jack hadn't connected. "What does Military Intelligence have to do with this?"

Jack let out a discouraged breath. "That part I don't know."

David would never hack into a government system, but he wasn't above hiring someone to do it for him. It was a slippery, fine line, but one he could justify. Before he made the call, he considered the possibility that an easier way to get the information existed.

"We could ask the colonel what happened to his father."

Jack did sort of a shimmy as if spiders were crawling over him. "Yuk. That old geezer gives me the creeps. I don't think he's as sincere as he wants us to believe. Hacking into a government system would be easier than getting information out of him."

Tabor jumped into Jack's lap. "Hello, girl." He focused on finger-combing the Maine Coon's hair while David called the colonel on the library table phone. David put the call on speaker.

On the second ring the colonel answered in an irritated tone. "Manning."

"Sir, it's David McBain."

"Have you found Kenzie?" The colonel's attitude brightened about as much as a lamp on the lowest setting on a dimmer switch. He was giving David the creeps, too.

"No sir, but I have a question I hope ye' can answer for us," David said, anticipating the colonel's resistance. "The day before Kenzie disappeared, she discovered a document in the National Archives written by Military Intelligence to Winston Churchill. The memorandum is ninety percent redacted."

"That couldn't possibly have anything to do with her disappearance."

"Bear with me a minute, sir."

"Continue, soldier, but make it brief."

"The document was originally classified, but a redacted copy was declassified in the 1970s. Kenzie had a copy emailed to her address, so obviously she considered it important."

"It must be related to her thesis research," the colonel said.

"Aye, that's what I thought, but Jack had a different view. He took the few clues in the memorandum and searched for connections to Kenzie. The memo referenced an Army Ranger, an IRA German spy, and a shooting on June 5, 1944. Jack discovered—"

"I don't give a damn what he discovered." Anger spiked in the colonel's voice. "The memorandum has *nothing* to do with Kenzie's disappearance. Drop it and move on, or get the hell off this case."

David had stepped one foot into a quagmire, but he didn't give a damn what the colonel thought or said. Well, that wasn't exactly true. David was a soldier, and he respected authority. The colonel was a senior officer, but the colonel's pigheadedness was putting Kenzie's safety at risk. If David forced the issue, he'd plunge entirely into that quagmire.

"What happened to yer father, Colonel? We know he died on June 5, 1944, but we don't know the circumstances surrounding his death. What can ye' tell us?"

A long silence ensued. A long, uncomfortable silence. Tension rippled through the connection.

"Sir, is Lieutenant Robert Manning yer father?"

The colonel huffed. "Delving into the lieutenant's case won't get you any closer to finding my daughter. I'm ordering you to move on."

David remained silent.

The colonel growled, "You might be a war hero, Major, but you're just another hotshot soldier to me. *Stand the fuck down.* And stay out of my business."

The phone went dead.

David steepled his hands, placing his index fingers against his lips. "I'd call that confirmation ye're on the right track," he said to Jack. "Where will it take us?"

"London in the 1940s," Jack said. "Maybe even to June 5, 1944. But first you have to get an unredacted copy of the memorandum."

David bounced the tips of his fingers against his lips. The subject line of the email to Kenzie contained the Hollinger box number and file folder number. Once his hacker got into the system, it was a simple matter of locating the box and file folder number. Due to the intense interest in World War II, all documents had been digitized. Although they were not accessible to researchers yet, experienced hackers could get in, retrieve a document, and get out without leaving footprints.

But it was illegal.

Jack continued to run his fingers through Tabor's thick coat, from her rhinestone-studded collar to the tip of her bushy tail, "Arrr, matey. I think me partner is second-guessing his grand scheme,"

Jack said in a pirate's gravelly voice.

David put his shoulders back and projected a pretense of confidence, which ricocheted right back and smacked him in the face. He stroked his clean-shaven jaw. Unlike Jack, he shaved every morning. He kept leaving razors in Jack's bathroom, but Jack refused to manscape his face more than a couple of times a week. His blond hair was always freshly barbered, but not his jaw and neck, and women found him irresistible.

To each his own.

The light was changing outside, brightening the gloom that had filled the room throughout the day. The blue world beyond the leaded windows turned a soft purple, with pink around its edges. It was an unusually beautiful sky for this time of year. An omen, perhaps.

"Let's take a break. I have a couple of calls to make." David took his phone and left the library without further explanation. If what he was about to do fell back onto Jack, his friend could honestly deny any knowledge of what he had done.

David walked the length of the terrace down to the loch, thinking. He was convinced the information in the memorandum was essential to finding Kenzie. The brooch might put lovers in the same location, but there were no guarantees for the rescuers, as he and Charlotte discovered during Jack's imprisonment. Without a date to narrow their search, they would be blind time-travelers.

By the time David reached the water's edge, he had justified his actions to his satisfaction. He placed a call. All he said was the National Archives of London, the Hollinger box number, and the file folder number. He disconnected the call and threw the burner phone into the water.

He walked along the loch for a couple of miles, sorting through what he knew about Kenzie. The woman intrigued him, and he was in a hurry to find her, but he wouldn't let his interest dictate his course of action. Until he was prepared to meet all contingencies, he wouldn't open the stone.

He left the shoreline and cut through the forest for the shorter trek home. An electronic file should be in his secure inbox by now, along with a high five-figure invoice. He would pay the invoice with untraceable funds from the offshore account of Elliott's that he established prior to Kit's disappearance. If his goddaughter returned in the future, she would have access to the money, regardless of the year.

David returned to an empty library, not a surprise, since he'd been gone for close to two hours. He logged into an email account that, other than himself, only Elliott knew existed. He rubbed his hands down his pants legs. Not because he had sweaty palms, but because he needed to do a gut check. Once he opened the email, the line would be crossed. Was this still what he wanted?

He flipped through his notes, searching for the graduation picture of Kenzie her father emailed to him. Looking at her in full dress uniform, red hair pulled back into a tight bun, and her hazel eyes dancing with delight, David had his answer. He would cross the Rubicon for her.

He looked out at the now inky sky and did just that.

Fifteen minutes later, Jack returned to the library with Tate and Annabella loping along at his heels. "When'd you get back?"

"Sit down."

Jack froze mid-step. "You know what happened, don't you?"

David deleted the file on his computer and shredded the document he had printed. The facts were burned into his brain. He didn't need the evidence, and he didn't need anyone else to have access to the document.

"*No. Don't do that.*"

David fed the last sheet into the shredder. "What are ye' yelling about? I shred all my notes. Ye' know that."

"You could have let me read them first."

The shredder ate the last few inches of the piece of paper. The evidence of his illegal activity was now cut into unreadable strips. "Sit down. I want to tell ye' a story."

"If you're telling me a story, I need a drink. You want one."

"Aye." A spark of tension ignited a flame in David's belly, but he ignored it. "Pour me a double." David moved away from the library table and took a seat by the fire. Jack handed him a drink and sat across from him in the matching smooth leather wingback. The fire crackled between them, making inroads into the room's top layer of chill. Annabella settled herself next to David's chair, and Tate settled down next to Jack's, as if each was guarding their own man.

David took one sip, then put the drink aside. He needed to get through his explanation without sparring with his burning belly. He should have taken his medicine first. Too late now.

"Ye' already know Lieutenant Manning was a Ranger, and that he married an Irish lass named Della O'Brien. After they married, Manning tried to get a visa for Della to immigrate to America to live with his mother. Because of Ireland's neutrality, the embassy staff stalled, and Manning's request was never put through the channels.

"In early 1944, he was approached by a Military Intelligence agent who offered to assist with the visa in exchange for the lieutenant's help in passing along information to IRA German spies. At first, Manning resisted. When his wife turned up pregnant, he realized he had no choice. If he was going to get the visa, he had to work for them.

"He met at least a dozen times with a member of the IRA who was spying for the Germans. Manning passed along the false information he was given. On June 5, the agent sneaked Lieutenant Manning out of a restricted area to meet with the spy to pass along information that General Patton intended to invade France at Pas de Calais. There was an altercation. Manning was shot and died from his wounds a day later. The information about Calais was so sensitive that Military Intelligence couldn't allow the spy to discover Manning was working for them, so they leaked the story that the lieutenant was working as a German spy. He died before he could be formally charged with sedition. I don't know for a fact, but I assume his wife lost the survivor's benefits she should have received."

Jack's red face reflected his outrage. "They threw him under the goddamn bus?"

David gulped his whiskey. The lie that had probably psychologically damaged two generations of Mannings sickened him. War he understood, but allowing the truth to remain hidden for more than seventy years went beyond the pale, and he intended to see it rectified.

"Colonel Manning grew up believing his father was a German spy."

"*Son of a bitch.*" Jack picked up the football and threw it hard at the sofa. It bounced and rolled onto the floor. "Son of a bitch." He snatched it off the floor, lined his fingers up between the tip and laces and went through the motions of throwing the ball, but not releasing it. "If Kenzie knows anything about her grandfather, it's that he was a spy for the Germans. So what would she do?"

David held out his arms making a diamond shape with his hands in receiver position and Jack tossed the ball. David tucked it in close and zigzagged across the middle of the library in a fake run. He pulled up at the window. "I don't know what she'd do—" He held his fingers on the laces, turned, squared his shoulders, stepped, and with an overhand release threw a perfect spiral at Jack. "—but I damn well know what I'd do."

Jack caught the ball, sidestepped, and jogged across the room. "I don't think I want to hear this."

David leaned against the windowsill. "The Second Ranger Battalion was marshalled at Broadmayne near Weymouth, which was the embarkation area for men landing on Omaha Beach and Pointe du Hoc."

Jack put the ball on top of the bookcase to keep it away from Annabella and Tate, who had ripped David's last football to shreds while playing a tug-of-war with the pigskin.

"Manning was shot at the New Inn at West Knighton, less than a mile from the marshalling area in Broadmayne," David said.

Jack sat on the edge of the heavy oak library table and crossed his arms. "If I was writing this as a scene, I would have the hero waiting outside the bar to stop the lieutenant from entering."

"And get him the hell out of there," David added.

"But you can't arbitrarily go back in time and change someone's history because you don't like the outcome. We're not writing fiction. These are real people. Real lives."

"I know they're real people, but have ye' seen a rulebook? If so, I'd like to read it."

"No, I'm using common sense."

David pushed off from the wall and crossed the room toward the table. "That'll be a first."

Jack tipped the ball off the shelf and threw it hard at David. David used his lightning reflexes and snatched it out of the air, then threw it back. Jack squeezed the ball a few times before returning it to the shelf. "Look, I know I made mistakes, but at some point we have to move on. Give me a break."

David waved his hand dismissively. "Ye' fucked up."

"You're an ass, you know it?"

"And ye're a dick."

They both laughed. Jack went over to David and slapped him on the shoulder. "A real ass, but a real friend, too." He returned to his work space at the table and flipped through a legal pad. "I found out a bit more about the Manning family."

David opened a document on his laptop titled with Kenzie's name. "Shoot."

"Della O'Brien Manning settled in Virginia." Jack looked up from his notes with a puzzled expression. "Was there any mention of Della in the memorandum you wouldn't let me read?"

"Aye. Military Intelligence sent her a visa shortly after D-Day."

"Well, at least the bastards did that." Jack flipped a page on his yellow legal pad. "When she arrived in Newport News, she went to work as a domestic, and died in a house fire in 1961. She was forty, never remarried, and had one son, Julian Manning."

David added the information to Kenzie's profile. "From the preliminary work-up I did on the colonel, I know he enlisted in 1962. That would make it the year after his mother's death."

David crossed his arms, tapping his fingertips against his biceps. "The colonel's had a lousy life. His father died dishonorably. His mother died tragically. His first wife divorced him. His second wife was killed in a car accident. His son won't have anything to do with him, and his daughter has disappeared. That's not much of a legacy."

"No, it's not. If his father had stayed on base and not attended that meeting, then he would have shipped out and fought on Pointe du Hoc and been a hero. Della's life would have been quite different as the widow of an Army Ranger."

"And so would Colonel Manning's," Jack said.

David stacked the loose papers together, paper-clipped them, and put them away in a file folder. "If it was my grandfather, I'd keep him on base, stick to him like flypaper, and make sure he shipped out on D-Day."

"Changing history didn't work out so well last time," Jack paused for a breath and played his pens as if they were drum sticks. "Call the colonel back. Tell him you know the story, or as much as you can tell him, and that you want to know if Kenzie knows the truth."

"He's not going to like it."

"Who cares?" Jack said. "We're not working for him."

A trickle of perspiration meandered down David's back beneath his shirt in spite of the chill in the library. Antagonizing a superior was never a smart move, even if ye' weren't currently serving in the military. Old habits don't like to die. He felt a tightening in his muscles and a strange sense of fear. Not fear of the colonel, but fear of war and death and dying. That's what this ultimately was about—war.

David dialed the colonel's number and he answered after two rings. "I have one question for you, sir, and I need the answer. Does Kenzie know what happened to yer father, and the circumstances surrounding his death?"

"You goddamn bastard. You couldn't leave it alone, could you?"

This was the last conversation he intended to have with this arse. If he had to deal with the colonel again, either the colonel or David would end up in emergency care. "I need an answer, sir. I can't explain how this will help find Kenzie. All I can tell ye' is that it will."

David didn't have to see the colonel to know his lips were pressed tight and his eyes were narrowed. The ragged breathing on the other end of the line said he was more than annoyed, but David didn't give a shit. He'd just as soon deck the son of a bitch.

"Her mother and I were arguing about it one night, and Kenzie overheard us. My father was never discussed again. She was probably about eight years old at the time. My guess is that she doesn't remember the conversation. This has nothing to do with her disappearance."

Simultaneously, the phone went dead and the front door slammed shut. The entry filled with the sound of barking dogs. Tabor shot out of from under the table and ran into the hall with her long bushy tail trailing behind her. David slapped his palms on top of the table before yelling, *"Kevin. Get those goddamn dogs out of here."*

Elliott sauntered into the library with Annabella and Tate trotting along beside him. "Kevin's down at the barn."

"I didn't know ye' were back. Where's Meredith?"

"In the barn with Kevin. She wanted to see the new mare delivered yesterday." Elliott poured a cup of coffee. When he sat, both dogs settled at his feet. "What's the latest with the search for Kenzie?"

"We've narrowed the time frame down to the spring of 1944," David said.

Elliott whistled with surprise and both dogs jumped to their feet. Tate bumped Elliott's hand with his nose, signaling he wanted his head scratched. Elliott rubbed both dogs behind their ears. "Sit." Annabella did. Tate didn't. He gave Elliott moon eyes instead. "*Sit.*" There was no misunderstanding the tone of Elliott's command. Tate turned in a circle before returning to the spot under the table where he had staked a claim.

"Around D-Day. Why then?" Elliott asked.

"Kenzie's grandfather, Lieutenant Robert Manning, a Second Battalion Army Ranger, was shot and killed with a suspected IRA German spy. He was actually working for Military Intelligence—" David said.

"But Military Intelligence gave him up to protect the information Manning was passing along to Germany," Jack said.

"The truth never came out. The colonel has always believed his father was a traitor," David said.

"Son of a bitch," Elliott said.

"Those were my exact words," Jack said.

Elliott picked up David's legal pad and read his bulleted list. "Why'd he go to work for Military Intelligence?"

"His wife, Della O'Brien, was from Ireland. The American embassy wasn't in a hurry to expedite her visa to America. Manning volunteered in exchange for help with the visa."

Elliott flipped pages scanning David's notes. "Did he get it?"

"Della got the visa within weeks of his death," David said.

Elliott tossed the pad onto the table and picked up his coffee cup. "Do ye' think Kenzie's set on changing what happened to her grandfather?"

"Her father doesn't believe she remembers the details of the argument she overheard when she was a child. She might not remember anything about the circumstances."

"According to yer notes, she read a redacted memorandum that might jog her memory. Turning her grandfather into a hero would be a lofty goal. Keep him from the meeting and make sure he's on his ship on D-Day, and her job's done."

"We know what happens when we fiddle with history," David said.

"Tinkering makes a mess of things." Elliott went quiet and looked at Jack with determined eyes. "I recommend you go get her before she has a chance to screw up her father's life worse than he was already screwed."

"What about the great love Kenzie's supposed to meet?" Jack asked.

Elliott gave him a suit-yourself shrug. "Bring him, too."

"What if he pulls a fast one like Braham?"

"According to what the first Sean MacKlenna told Kit, when the three stones come together, some sort of event might occur. Let's hope it means the magic will cease to exist. Her soul mate won't be able to go home."

"Or united they become more powerful," David said. "Maybe they open a permanent portal."

"Cool," Jack said. "We could come and go as we pleased, and solve the great mysteries of the universe."

"No thanks," David said. "I vote we bury the stones in the cave."

Elliott's hands trembled slightly. He folded one leg over the opposite knee and fiddled with the cuff of his pants. The only time David could remember Elliott trembling was when he was drinking. But he wasn't drinking now.

"Go get Kenzie and her soul mate," Elliott said. "Bring them both back, lock up the stones, and keep an eye on the couple so they don't run off and do something stupid."

"Like what? Have a press conference?" Jack demanded. "I can see Kenzie's boyfriend meeting with the press and claiming he was kidnapped by aliens and transported to the future."

"God forbid," Elliott said.

"What if they don't realize they're in love?" Jack asked. "Charlotte and Braham didn't know."

"We'll lock them in the cellar until they figure it out. Look, I don't have the answers. All I know is that ye' have to get them out before Kenzie changes lives. What if she changes the future and it impacts Jim, and he doesn't go to law school? Good God. The possibilities are frightening. When can ye' be ready to go? Tonight?"

David opened his calendar and counted days. "It will take four or five days to gather our gear, create identities, and devise a fluid plan. We'll be going into a battle zone. I'd say we could leave on Saturday."

Elliott's eyes darted from David to Jack. "Ye' went into a battle zone last time, too."

"Bombs weren't going off in Washington. At least not the type we'll find in World War II London," David said.

Elliott stopped teasing the cuff of his trousers and put both feet on the floor, hands on his knees. "Have ye' given any thought to yer identities?"

"Jack could pose as a war correspondent, and I'll pose as an intelligence officer with the Royal Scots Greys on special assignment. That identity should allow access to restricted areas."

Elliott knitted his brows. "Even Allied Headquarters?"

David nodded, slow and decisively. "And Bletchley Park."

"Why Bletchley?" Elliott asked.

David circled two bullet points on his legal pad and put a checkmark next to the words *problem solver*. "Codebreaking fits Kenzie's profile."

"It also gives us a place to search if we don't find her in London," Jack added.

Elliott shot to his feet and the dogs jumped in response, forgetting they were friends and barking madly at each other. "Shush." The dogs quieted and followed close behind when Elliott crossed to the door. "Thanks for your work on this. Keep me in the loop."

"What about Meredith?" David asked.

Elliott turned and a veiled expression crossed his face. "What about her?"

"Is she going to remain out of the loop? I'd like to have her team working on a possible connection to the MacKlennas. Since Kenzie's mother is from the Highlands, it shouldn't be as difficult to find the connection as it was with the Mallorys."

"I'll make the call, but continue to keep this situation under wraps." Then he was gone and so were the dogs.

"Whatever is on his mind isn't getting any better," Jack said.

"Let's get this situation resolved quickly so it won't add additional stress. But before we go any further, ye' have to talk to yer sister. Ye're not going if she's not on board."

"Now that we have Elliott's directive—get in and get out—another time-traveling adventure should be easier for Charlotte to swallow."

"I doubt it, but ye' can try. Call her," David said.

Jack sat down and squeezed the nape of his neck while he eased his head back and forth. He was either working out kinks or gathering courage. Finally he clicked on Charlotte's number and waited with a slight grimace on his face. His brother-in-law, Braham McCabe, answered the call.

"Braham, I'm putting you on speaker. David's here with me."

"Hey, buddy," Braham said. "Lincoln asked this morning if you were coming for his birthday party."

"I wouldn't miss it. Tell him to send me his wish list. Is he getting a pony this year?"

"If I don't get him one, Elliott will."

"Is Charlotte around?"

"She's resting," Braham said. "These days she falls asleep sitting up. I'll have her call you back."

David remembered the early months of Charlotte's last pregnancy and his bittersweet involvement with her care. He would have married her and raised the child as his own, but Braham was her true love, and she would have waited the rest of her life for him.

"Hey, don't hang up. I'll run this by you first," Jack said.

"Sounds serious."

Jack drew a deep breath and huffed. "It is. The third brooch has shown up."

"Aw, crap. You're not going back in time again, are you?"

Jack flinched, screwing up his face. "Jim Manning's half-sister disappeared. We found an empty puzzle box and the wrapping paper with solicitor Digby's name."

"Where'd she go?" Braham asked.

"Our best guess is London, 1944."

The phone went silent. David tapped the home button on Jack's phone to make sure they were still connected.

"I don't have full knowledge of the wars since 1865," Braham said, "but I believe there was a world war in the 1940s, right?"

"The world was at war with Germany and Japan from 1939 to 1945."

David moved away from the table. It wouldn't do any good to hover. Charlotte and Braham would agree or they wouldn't. David wouldn't campaign either way. He preferred to go alone, but had to admit having a partner would make extracting Kenzie and her boyfriend easier. But was that worth worrying about Jack getting into trouble again? He listened in on the conversation while scrolling through the emails on his iPhone.

"You know what Charlotte will say," Braham said.

"She won't like it, but the bottom line is that I don't need my sister's permission. I'm doing this as a courtesy."

"I'll talk to her."

Jack sat back and put his stocking feet up on the corner of the table. "Tell her Elliott wants us to go back, get Kenzie and her boyfriend, and bring them to the future without delay."

Braham hissed. "You'll end up with another situation like mine. You can't kidnap people and expect them to find happiness."

"Maybe not, but Elliott is distracted and doesn't want to deal with this. For his piece of mind, we'll do it his way."

"That might sit better with Charlotte. I'll tell her to call you."

"Thanks, buddy. I'd ask you to go, but you've probably had enough time travel."

"You're damn right. Lincoln will be in second grade, McCabe House is finished, the stables are full, the vineyards are thriving, and I'm going to have a daughter in a few weeks. I'm not going anywhere."

David slipped his phone into his pants pocket. He didn't begrudge Braham his happiness, but if he ever mistreated Charlotte, Braham would answer to him.

Jack's phone rang within seconds of disconnecting the call to Braham. "Hi, sis. I thought you were napping." He put the phone on speaker so David could listen.

"Braham said you want to go back in time to rescue Jim Manning's sister."

Jack dropped his feet to the floor and leaned forward in his chair. "Half-sister."

"I don't want you to go, but I can't stop you."

"We're getting in and out quickly. There won't be time to get into trouble."

She laughed, but it was more of a nervous laugh. "You don't need time to find trouble. You just need to show up." She let out a ladylike growl. "Let me talk to David."

Jack turned and his eyes drilled David's. Charlotte didn't like to be on a speaker phone when she didn't know who else was in the room. David should have announced himself at the beginning of the call, but he hadn't wanted to get pulled into a discussion with Charlotte about Jack's propensity to find trouble even at a Church social. David lifted a bottle of water to his mouth and took refuge behind it, sipping, as he prepared for Charlotte to blurt out exactly how she felt about the venture.

"You're on speaker," Jack said. "He can hear you."

"*Thanks* for announcing your presence," she said.

David darted a glance at Jack, one eyebrow raised, and Jack said, "Sorry, sis. My fault."

"You two are going to do whatever you want, regardless of how I feel about those damn brooches. I never want to see them again, but I appreciate the lure they have for thriller writers. Go. Be careful, and don't get hanged again."

"I think the firing squad was the preferred method of execution in 1944 London."

"Don't be flippant, Jack. You're going into a war zone. Anything could happen."

David put the water aside and ran a cocktail napkin over his mouth before setting out across the room to be closer to the phone. "Charlotte, if your brother doesn't do anything stupid, we'll come back with one hell of a story to write."

"The baby's due in six weeks. You might not get back in time," she said.

"We'll be back. Elliott's orders," David said. "And I won't miss my goddaughter's birth." At Lincoln's birth, David had been Charlotte's birthing coach. This time around, though, he'd be relegated to the waiting room with Jack, which would be bittersweet.

"Have you thought about where you're going to stay?"

"We're going back to 1944, Char. Not present day London."

"I know that, but the Dorchester, Savoy, and Claridge's were quite popular then."

"Probably the Ritz, if we can get in, since I'm posing as a war correspondent. The hotel was a favorite of Americans and journalists."

"If you see Walter Cronkite, be sure to interview him. I read his biography years ago. He flew on a bomber. I hope you don't do something so crazy."

"We're not sticking around long enough, Char. Don't worry."

"Don't worry?" she said, her voice rising. "I worry about everything. I'm having my second child, and my brother is going back in time—again—to another war. I won't be sitting around twiddling my thumbs and eating bonbons, waiting for your return."

David made a cutting motion with his hand at his throat. The conversation was not constructive, and was upsetting Charlotte.

Jack nodded. "We've got work to do. I'll keep in touch and will let you know how the planning is going."

They said their good-byes.

David laid his hand on Jack's shoulder and pressed down hard. "We're going in to recon and extract Kenzie and lover boy as quickly as possible. Nothing else. No interviews with Cronkite. No stories with your byline. No press fly-alongs. Got it?"

The infamous conspirator's hood Jack had been forced to wear during his arrest and trial in 1865 was a haunting memory for David as well as for Jack, but the possibilities of what could happen to them in 1944 were even more terrifying. The tactics used by Secretary Stanton were children's games compared to the tactics used by the Gestapo.

God help them all...

12

Fraser House, the Highlands, Present Day

TWO DAYS LATER, Meredith entered the library, stopped, planted her fists on her hips, and demanded to know what was going on. "Elliott denies he's keeping anything from me, and the two of you have been closeted in here for the last few days. I know David sent his book to his editor, and you're on deadline, Jack. Whatever is going on is pretty damn important. If I had to guess, I'd say another brooch has shown up. Am I right?"

David lowered his gaze to avoid direct eye contact, but not soon enough to miss her blazing blue eyes.

"If Elliott's trying to protect me, it won't work, and if you can't look me in the eye, then I know I'm right."

David picked up the house phone and punched the number to Elliott's office. "Meredith's demanding answers. Ye' best come in here."

Elliott's footsteps, plus the patter of trotting dogs, came from the long, stone-floored hall. He entered the room grim-faced. "David's handling this, Mer. We're staying out of the way."

"Fine," she said, massaging her temple. "But I want to know what's going on. You don't have to protect me." She quit rubbing her head and ran her fingers through the streaks of silver in her dark, shoulder-length hair. Even after the ravages of radiation, chemotherapy, and surgery, she remained an ageless beauty.

"One of you," she glared from Elliott to David to Jack, "is going to tell me."

Elliott threw up his hands in surrender. "Jim Manning's sister…"

"Half-sister," Meredith said.

Elliott's brow arched upwards and he gave her a fixed stare. "Ye' know about her?"

"Kenzie Wallis-Manning, West Point graduate? Yes, I know."

David tightened his jaw to keep it from dropping to his chest, but the word "*how*" squeaked out.

"A couple of years ago we had a girl's wine night. Judy Manning let the name slip. I plied her with enough wine to get the full story. After she told her husband's secrets, I had to promise never to reveal the information. There's always a price to be paid when you manipulate a person or situation. The price Judy extracted was silence."

This wasn't the first time in the years David had known Meredith that he'd heard of her uncanny ability to ferret out information. She rivaled the best intelligence officers he'd met while fighting in Afghanistan.

"And ye' didn't tell me?" Elliott asked. "Don't ye' think I have a right to know?"

Meredith turned her head slightly, giving Elliott a sideways glance. "The last time I looked at the definition of the word *silence*, it wasn't spelled E-L-L-I-O-T-T."

"Kenzie received a puzzle box from solicitor Digby."

Meredith turned her attention away from Elliott and focused on David. "Do you know where she went?"

"London, spring of 1944, is our best guess," David said.

"D-Day?" Meredith asked with an incredulous tone of voice. "That's worse than the Civil War."

"We have no control over where the brooch takes its victims," Jack said. "But if you're interested in history, you couldn't ask for a better historical period to visit. It's like stepping into our parents' and grandparents' lives and living in their shoes for a few days or weeks."

"I'm sure Kenzie would prefer not to relive her parents' or grandparents' lives in a war zone." Meredith's cell phone beeped, and she checked for messages. She sent a quick response and then said, "You're going to go back and interfere. Aren't you?"

"I wouldn't say interfere," David said.

"No? What would you say? You're going to snatch Kenzie and her soul mate from the throes of a world war and bring them here before they have a chance to fall in love. You'll make a mess like you did with Charlotte and Braham's situation. Didn't you learn anything? We can't interfere."

"Who says the couple has to go through hell and back to fall in love? What's wrong with a normal courtship?" David asked.

Meredith gave an exasperated sniff. "I don't think the four people in this room know what a normal courtship would look like. Do you?"

Jack glanced at the other three, furrowing his brow. Like others who hadn't been around when Meredith and Elliott met, Jack was finding it difficult to reconcile their perfect marriage with an unsettling courtship. David had heard it all before. Comments like, "They must have fallen in love at first sight." He knew they didn't. They couldn't put their cell phones down long enough to fall in love.

"Braham and Charlotte fell for each other immediately," Jack said. "The electricity generated when the two of them were in the same room could heat all the apartments in New York City for an entire winter. He would have stayed here if he hadn't felt obligated to save President Lincoln."

"Get him on the phone and ask him. I bet you're wrong," Meredith said.

Jack dialed Braham's number. "Hey, buddy. Meredith has a question for you."

"Braham, I assume you already know about Kenzie Wallis-Manning and what David intends to do. My question to you is this: would you have stayed here in the present if you hadn't felt responsible for President Lincoln?"

"I wanted to return to my time from the moment I woke up in

the hospital."

"Thank you," Meredith said. "I rest my case." She faced Elliott, leaving Jack to end the call. "You can't treat Kenzie's lover like a stray you can bring home to feed and love. You can't snatch them from the past and expect them to find happiness until they're ready. And they won't be ready as long as one of them feels responsible for the life they left behind. Tread softly."

Elliott put his arm around Meredith. "I can't and won't be distracted by time-travelers right now. David has my blessing to handle this situation as he sees fit to bring about the best possible outcome. I won't interfere." Elliott checked his watch. "We need to leave or we'll be late."

"I'll go, but not before I say one more thing. I trust you with my life, David. But Kenzie doesn't know you. She doesn't know you can do the impossible with one hand tied behind your back."

Elliott kissed Meredith's cheek. "Miracles require two hands and take a little while longer."

"Exactly," she said.

David shifted uncomfortably in his chair. He wasn't a magician, he couldn't perform miracles, and anyone who believed he could was setting themselves up for disappointment.

"From what Judy Manning said about her sister-in-law," Meredith continued, "the girl is strong-willed, tenacious, extremely intelligent, and will not accept failure. You're going back in time to rescue a soldier who is *exactly* like you. Be prepared to meet a woman who will not bow at your feet, and that will be a first for you. I'm sorry I won't be there to watch the fireworks." Meredith breezed from the room, leaving in her wake the energy of an approaching storm.

"That went well," Jack said after the tension settled a bit.

David smiled and played drums with his pencils. "Elliott didn't back down. The mission is a go. What do ye' have left on yer list?"

Jack flipped a few pages of his legal pad. "I'm waiting on press credentials and clothes from the tailor. What about you?"

"My credentials will be here in the morning. We're leaving day after tomorrow. Advise yer sister."

13

Fraser House, the Highlands, Present Day

THE NEXT EVENING, after Meredith retired, David and Elliott met in his office to review the specifics of the mission. David arrived first, popping a stomach pill to extinguish the brush fire in his belly. He headed straight to the bar, where he poured a shot of whiskey into a tumbler.

Elliott entered the room and closed the door. "We have an hour. Bring me up to speed." He sat in his desk chair and rolled across the stone floor away from the monitor to face his desk and a stack of papers in a folder. He opened it and picked up a sheet of paper. "Is this the memorandum from Military Intelligence?"

"Aye," David said. "I scrubbed the file from my computer and shredded the other copy. You have the only one." He took a seat across the desk from Elliott. "I need yer opinion. Should I give the colonel the information we've collected on the lieutenant and let him use it to clear his father's name?"

Elliott sat back in the chair and crossed his legs. "If Kenzie wasn't already in the past, I'd say let the colonel handle it. But Kenzie's actions are an unknown. Why tell him now, when she might change the events of the night the lieutenant was killed? I suggest ye' wait and see. It's been more than seventy years, it can wait a few more weeks."

"But what if Kenzie doesn't want to stop her grandfather from going to the meeting and ultimately changing history?"

"Ye' say 'fine, lass. If that's what ye' want, we'll go home now, and ye' can let the colonel handle things from this end.'"

"She's a soldier. She'll see the injustice and want to right a wrong."

"Maybe. Maybe not," Elliott said. "She gave up the Army for the courtroom. She might not want to get involved."

"Her grandfather was treated horribly, and it damaged her father. Why wouldn't she want to fix it?"

Elliott gave him a pained stare. "Aye, laddie. Ye're seeing yerself in Kenzie's story. If ye' could change what happened to yer father in Vietnam, he might not have come home an abusive alcoholic, but this isn't yer story."

David flinched as if slapped. Elliott was coming from another planet with that suggestion. David had never once considered possible similarities between his family life and Kenzie's. Their stories had no commonality.

"If Kenzie doesn't want to get involved," Elliott continued, "ye' have to walk away. If ye' can't, don't go after her."

Walk away? Leave Kenzie without support? David would never do that to a fellow soldier. "I'll do what has to be done."

"I trust ye' to do the right thing." Elliott collected David's notes and handed them back. "Keep these. Meredith will snoop around my desk. Best if ye' have them tucked away." He stood and his knees cracked. "God, I'm getting old."

"Ye're only sixty-one, and that's the new forty-one."

Elliott crossed the room to the bar and set his dirty glass in the sink. "If I'm the new forty-one, what does that make ye'? A teenager?"

David ambled over to the bar, laughing. "Something like that." He wanted another drink, but the intermittent pain in his stomach sent a less than gentle reminder that alcohol wasn't helping him. He put his dirty glass in the sink, too.

Elliott reached for the desk lamp and turned it off, leaving only the lamp by the door that normally remained on throughout the night. Elliott often woke long before sunrise to work in peace for a few hours. The lamp provided enough illumination to keep him from barking his shins on the carved furniture. "Why do ye' think Kenzie is staying in the past?"

"Kit stayed because she was in love. Maybe that's why Kenzie hasn't come home."

Elliott crossed the hall, past the flight of stairs, toward the master's suite that encompassed the right side of the house's first floor. "Kit stayed because that's where she belonged. Kenzie has no reason to remain there."

David followed, but stopped when the hall turned toward the kitchen. Elliott had offered him a room in the house, but David preferred his remodeled suite in the cottage. "Love's not a reason?"

"Love is always a reason to act stupid, but it doesn't fit Kenzie. Have ye' considered that she might have lost the brooch?"

"She's a soldier. She wouldn't lose it. It might be taken from her, but not without a fight."

"Maybe she's stuck," Elliott said.

"Aye, but of the four people we know who have time-traveled, no one has had a problem with the stones. And it doesn't matter why she's still there. I intend to bring her home."

"And her boyfriend?"

"He's Jack's responsibility."

The chimes in the main hall struck eleven. "I think I'll have a cup of tea before I turn in." Elliott followed David toward the kitchen. "Ye' trust Jack not to get in trouble again?"

"He has a history of acting without considering long-term consequences, that's for sure." David filled the teapot with tap water, turned on the gas stove, and then dropped a teabag into each of the two cups he'd pulled from the cupboard. "He's given me his word, and I need his help."

"But not his problems," Elliott said.

"Exactly." The teakettle whistled and David poured hot water over the teabags for steeping. He dunked his teabag, bouncing it again and again, trying to clear his mind. There was one problem he hadn't solved yet.

"What about Kenzie's identification?" Elliott asked.

David tossed the teabag into the trash and took a sip before replying. "I have a passport issued with a 1942 date. I also have credentials identifying her as a member of the Women's Army Corps assigned to the Supreme Headquarters as a cryptographer and translator." David stirred cream into his tea. "I've also collected several thousand pounds. Money wasn't as hard to come by for this trip."

"Looks like ye' have it under control. Anything else."

"Do you have a secret compartment somewhere in the house? A place where I can leave you a message?"

Elliott glanced around the kitchen. "This place is four hundred years old. There're several possibilities." He stepped across the room to the fireplace. "I've never tried to open this, but Da said the corbels beneath the mantel twist open." He pushed and pulled, but nothing moved. "Try the other side."

David gave the corbel on the right side of the fireplace a hard twist. It moved an inch. It took a few minutes of fiddling before the hand-carved oak corbel slid down a few inches, revealing a four-inch rectangular pocket.

"What do ye' intend to put in there?" Elliott asked.

"Maybe nothing. Maybe a status report and the name of Kenzie's boyfriend. It depends on how much time I have. The train from London and back will take two days. I doubt I'll want to leave Kenzie once I find her, but check daily just in case."

Elliott returned the corbel to its position. "If ye' see Granda, tell him who ye' are and where ye' came from. He won't believe ye' at first, but he'll come 'round."

"What about yer da?"

"In 1944 he was fighting with the Eighth Army in Italy."

David finished his tea. "When ye' get the name of Kenzie's boyfriend, check him out. If ye' find a problem…"

"I can't leave ye' a message," Elliott said. "It doesn't work in reverse."

"I know." He took Elliott's empty cup and washed both of

them. He didn't want his mum to find dirty dishes in the sink, which reminded him he should clean the ones he and Elliott left in the office. "I don't believe Kenzie's the sort of lass who would live in the past. Whoever the lad is, he's meant to come home with her."

"Ye' may be right, but don't close yer mind to being wrong. The brooches work in ways we don't always understand, but we can't doubt their purpose."

"I wish the brooch hadn't worked for Jack," David said.

"If Jack hadn't gone back, we might still be waiting for Braham to realize he couldn't live without Charlotte. The sapphire was working on Charlotte's behalf when Jack used its magic. If his traveling hadn't been part of the plan, it wouldn't have worked for him."

"If the stones work, or don't work based on whether or not the traveler is pursuing the stone's goal, it's possible the stones we have won't work if our goal is to interfere with the emerald's purpose for Kenzie."

"Ye're not interfering. Ye're only hastening the result."

"Sounds like interference to me."

"There's only one way to find out." Elliott reached into his pocket and pulled out two brooches. "Pick yer poison."

David eyed both brooches suspiciously. "I've traveled with both. I'll take the ruby."

"If the brooch believes ye're interfering, it won't work. Ye'll soon have yer answer." He pulled David into a hug. "Don't be gone long."

14

The Rainbow Corner Club, London, England, May 28, 1944

KENZIE STEPPED AWAY from the mirror in the ladies' room as flashes of being the new kid in high school boomeranged around in her head. Like so many other Army brats, she attended three different high schools in three different states. In each school, she stood in front of the restroom mirrors, exactly as she was doing now, and imagined how others saw her. A lanky redhead with inquisitive eyes, dressed in the newest fashions from the most popular teenage clothing stores. She never wore funky, gothic, or trendy. She wore appropriately ripped jeans and T-shirts without provocative statements on the front or back. It was important to get attention, but only from the *right* kids. Not necessarily the most popular, but the students with values and good sense.

Once she got their attention, she had to stand out. That was the tricky part.

In the classroom, she didn't raise her hand and answer every question, although she could have. She asked questions instead. Questions that indicated she had a grasp on the material and only needed clarification. Then, to avoid looking like a nerd, she used humor. She never made fun of people. She did, though, make light of situations and stereotypes. Blonde jokes became redhead jokes.

From her perspective, she wasn't being manipulative. Although in hindsight, she probably had been. But she didn't have time to wait for kids to befriend her. She'd be off to the next high school before that happened. She learned early on to get in, get it done, move on, and do it all over again at the next school.

Her current circumstances were similar to relocating to a new high school. She was out of place and out of time, but she wasn't without resources. She knew how to make people laugh.

She pinched her cheeks one last time and brushed the remaining dust from her navy dress.

Do it right, kiddo, or don't do it at all.

Her shoulders automatically squared.

Confidence guided her return to the smoky bar, where circumstances had thrown her into a familiar situation—a loud bar, dancing, and singing. The scene was not conducive to in-depth conversations. Until she had a convincing backstory, she would have to control the questions asked of her. If someone posed a question she couldn't answer, she'd deflect with a joke.

Her work in the intelligence field taught her to keep it simple and as close to the truth as possible. And avoid suspicion at all costs. Spies and moles infiltrated the highest levels of command during the war, and her fish-out-of-water scales could easily be spotted by a well-trained informant or agent.

The band had returned, and the club was smokier than a London fog. In her twenty-first century opinion, the Red Cross needed to declare the Club a smoke-free zone.

She waved her way through the stuffy air, composing a joke: What do you call a smoky bar? *The Coughing Lounge, the Unlucky Lung, the Cough & Sputter.* She snickered. Humor, it worked every time. Even on herself.

Her dance partner stood next to her empty bar stool. On his other side stood another tall, lanky pilot with his arm draped round Molly's shoulder. The two were having an eyes-lingering-on-eyes conversation. The man's polished wings sparkled in the lights shining above the mirrored wall behind the bar. Were all American World War II pilots tall and lanky?

The band was onstage to tune instruments, and a stag line circled the dance floor. She veered left to bypass the soldiers, but a young man with unruly, curly hair blocked her path.

"Dance with me, sugar?"

Another soldier brushed her arm. "I've got the next one." A third appeared with the same request. She'd spent four years at West Point, and five years deployed, and never once had a soldier got sexually aggressive, but these three men who smelled of beer had dangerous gleams in their eyes. They moved in close, crowding her personal space.

"Back off, soldiers," she said in her most authoritative voice. The men moved closer, unfazed. She anchored her feet and put her hands on her hips, letting her elbows give more breadth to her personal space. "Stand down, soldiers."

Her blue-eyed pilot barged into the center of the group and claimed her hand. "The lady's dance card is full tonight, boys."

"I don't need rescuing," she whispered. "I can handle it."

"I'm sure you can, but the Red Cross doesn't allow fighting in here, I suspect you would have had that jerk from New Jersey bleeding on the floor, and my dance partner would have been tossed out."

She hid a smile behind her hand.

The soldier who called her sugar got up into the pilot's face. "You don't even dance, Cavanaugh."

Cav smiled, flashing straight white teeth. "I do now." He pushed through the wall of soldiers, squeezing her hand gently, and ushered her back to the bar.

Her eyes remained fixed on him. Normally, she preferred her men rugged and muscular, ripped jeans and an easy T-shirt—more Gerard Butler than Jimmy Stewart. But after the way Mr. Tall and Lanky handled the rude interlopers, he was looking even better than before. The time-travel warp drive must have jiggled her genes.

"Is anybody hungry?" Molly asked. "I missed lunch and afternoon tea with my aunt. I'm about to eat my fingernails."

"We can't have that," the man with Molly said. "How about Italian? Bertorelli's on Charlotte Street is excellent."

Kenzie's stomach rumbled at the mention of Italian food. "I

don't think I've eaten this year. Sounds like a great idea."

With Cav's hand pressed against her back, she fanned her way through the smoke and soldiers toward the front door. Once outside she took a huge gulp of smoke-free air. "I have to confess, my bags were stolen from the carriage when I fell asleep on the train from Cambridge. I have no money or identification."

"That's horrible," Molly's boyfriend said. "I'm Rainer Hamilton, by the way. What were you doing in Cambridge?"

Time to start with the lies. Keep it simple.

"I came to England with my brother. He was studying at Cambridge until he got called up two years ago." She had to turn the questions away from her. "I can tell Molly's a Londoner and you two,"—she studied the men's patches and insignia—"are pilots with the 91st Bombardment Group." She pointed at Cav, "I'm pretty sure you're from Boston, and you"—she pointed to Rainer—"maybe Chicago."

"Moved to Chicago as a kid and never left until I enlisted," Rainer said.

"What about you?" Cav said. "You don't have much of an accent."

"My mailing address would be the hills of North Carolina near Asheville." Her father would be pleased she called his mountain retreat her home.

Cav stepped to the curb with his arm raised to hail a taxi.

"If we're going to Charlotte Street, it's less than a mile," Kenzie said. "I don't mind walking." London had moved out of winter and into a drab spring, and while it was cool, she'd rather be outside breathing fresh air.

"You sure you don't mind? There're too few taxis for all the passengers. We can get there faster on foot."

Her legs were tired, but she didn't want to sit. She might not get up again. "I don't mind at all." Cav held out his hand, pointing in the direction they should go, then took his place at her side, whistling a tune she didn't recognize. "Where are you stationed, or is that a secret?"

"Bassingbourn. Rainer and I came down this afternoon. What about your brother? Where is he now?"

More lies. Make it simple.

"He's fighting with the Fifth…Army," she stuttered, thinking back quickly to her World War II Military History class at West Point. She cleared her throat and sighed for effect. "The last I heard he was on a tiny, shell-raked beachhead at Anzio. He…uh… told me to go home, but I refuse to leave. He's the only family I have, and I'm not going home without him. I came to London hoping I could volunteer, but I have to find a job, too."

Good grief, Kenzie. You have diarrhea of the mouth. Shut up.

"The Fifth has had a brutal struggle in Italy," Cav said.

"Heavy casualties. I know." Never in her life had she purposefully set out to deceive a person. Every falsehood she concocted dragged her down another rung on her morality ladder.

They strolled down the street, passing piles of neatly stacked bricks and empty lots with deep, smoldering craters. Kenzie stared at the jagged, bombed-out gaps in the townhouse rows.

"Why are they stacking the bricks?" she asked.

"They're carted out of town to store until it's time to rebuild," Molly said. "One day the war will end and life will return to normal."

Except for the absence of pine torches and wax tapers shining through the windows, the night could be like any other in medieval London. The ruins of ancient churches, a low priority for firefighters during the Blitz, eerily resembled stone lace etching the sky.

"I heard a funny joke yesterday. I'll try to tell it right," Molly said.

Rainer covered his ears, laughing. "I'm not listening. You never remember the punch line, and you leave us hanging."

"You tell one, then," Molly said, teasing him in return.

"He never remembers punch lines, either," Cav said.

"Two redheads find three grenades," Kenzie said. "They decide to take them to the police station. One asked: 'What if one explodes before we get there?' The other said, 'We'll lie and say we only found two.'"

Cav guffawed and slapped Rainer on the shoulder. "Now, that's the way to tell a joke. Do you think you can remember it? The crew would like that one."

Rainer gave him a thumbs-up. "Two redheads, three grenades. I can remember."

"Tell another," Molly said.

Kenzie would be glad to tell as many jokes as they wanted to hear, so long as they didn't ask her any personal questions. "A redhead goes to the vet with her goldfish. 'I think it's got epilepsy,' she tells the vet. The vet takes a look and says, 'It seems calm enough to me.' The redhead says, 'Wait, I haven't taken it out of the bowl, yet.'"

Molly, Rainer, and Cav laughed hysterically. Soldiers walking in the opposite direction stopped to see what was so funny. Rainer tested his memory and retold Kenzie's joke to the delight of the gathering crowd.

"Tell another one, Kenzie," Rainer said.

"How do you sink a submarine full of redheads?" She gave the group a few seconds to guess. They looked at each other, then shrugged. "You knock on the door."

A request for another joke followed, and for the next several minutes, Kenzie told redhead, knock-knock, and pilot jokes. A few of the jokes had her audience looking askance. The context had been too modern to understand, but they laughed anyway. She was sure no one wanted to admit they didn't get the punch line.

"Don't stop," one of the soldiers shouted after she told the punch line to: "What happened to the redhead who got locked in a grocery store?" She pointed to her throat, and said in a deep, growling voice, "I need a beer. Second show starts at ten."

Cav took her elbow and guided her down the street. "The beer's this way."

"My ribs hurt from laughing," Molly said. "The last one was the funniest one of all. 'She starved to death.' I never saw it coming,"

Still chuckling Cav said, "I don't know when I've laughed so hard. After the week I had, it's a real relief."

He did laugh hard. The deep, robust sound had been a turn-on for Kenzie, and she kept telling jokes to hear him and watch his blue eyes crinkle at the corners. If her throat hadn't been dry as sand, she would have told several more.

"I've heard those bombing runs over Germany are harrowing," she said. "What you're doing in the skies is making a difference in the war effort, but I know it comes with sacrifice."

His lips twitched. She knew well the look of remembered terror. It must be hell flying at twenty-five thousand feet in a tin can with flak penetrating your thin-skinned, vibrating, smoking aircraft. On the ground, a solider could duck and run, but not in the air. She slipped her hand in his.

If you ask me to go home with you tonight, Cav Cavanaugh, I will.

"Tell another joke, Kenzie, before we all turn maudlin," Molly said.

Kenzie opted for a silly one. "Why don't ducks laugh when they fly? Because they would quack up." Then she groaned at her insensitivity, but Cav laughed.

"I'm telling that one to my crew before our next mission. It's so dumb they'll laugh and for a few minutes forget their fear."

"It's actually funnier later," she said. "Guys will make quacking sounds to remind their buddies of the dumb joke, especially during the next tense situation. It's just enough of a release to keep the edge of alertness without going over the top, if you know what I mean."

"Like letting just enough air out of a balloon before it pops," Molly said.

"Something like that," Kenzie said.

"You sound like you have experience in the field," Rainer said.

"I read a lot." Kenzie told another joke before the conversation became too personal. "Two redheads are on a plane flying from England to the United States. The pilot makes an announcement that one engine has failed and the flight will be an hour longer, but not to be concerned, because there are three more engines. An hour later, he announces that another engine has failed, and the flight will be two hours longer. Another hour passes and the pilot makes a third announcement. The third engine has failed, and the flight will be three hours longer. One redhead turns to the other and complains, 'If the fourth engine fails, we'll be up here all day.' "

Cav hugged her to his side "Never mind remembering the jokes, I'm taking you with me."

And I will go, especially if it includes sex.

What in God's name had come over her? She hadn't spent the last year living in a desert. She'd had sex recently. Hadn't she? It was either last month or the month before.

Think again.

She did, suffering a nasty jolt of recollection. Her dry spell had lasted a while, a long while.

"You could get a job as a stand-up comedienne at one of London's nightclubs," Molly said. "You could lift the spirits of hundreds of patrons every night. The war might even end sooner."

"If I can't find a regular job, I'll consider it," Kenzie said.

"Molly works at a radio factory in Bletchley," Rainer said. "Maybe she can get you on there."

Bletchley Park, home of the codebreakers, and Molly works there. Interesting.

"Without identification, I doubt anyone will hire me. A radio factory sounds interesting, but I'm not good with electronics. The only talents I have are working crossword puzzles and translating foreign languages."

"And telling jokes," Rainer said.

"What languages do you speak?" Molly asked.

"If the accents you used in your jokes are any indication, you speak several," Cav said.

"Japanese, German, French, Italian, and a few words of Russian."

Cav pushed open the door to the restaurant and held it while the other three entered the cave-like atmosphere of a dark eatery. The air was thick with the overpowering smell of roasting garlic and baking bread.

Kenzie licked her lips. "Hmm." If she wasn't drooling, she

should be. She'd had a late lunch, but the rare steak had faded from her stomach's memory.

"With your language skills, you could get a job at the War Department. They need translators," Rainer said.

Cav led the way to one of the leather banquettes along the wall. He scooted in next to Kenzie, brushing her shoulder with his and triggering a tantalizing assault on her spine. Rainer and Molly sat across from them. Kenzie covered her lap with a cloth napkin and kept her shaky hands hidden there.

"The War Department would be an interesting place to work. Starting tomorrow, I'll be knocking on doors. Maybe I'll knock on that one."

"I'd start with the American Embassy. They could help you get a new passport," Molly said.

"Do you have a place to stay tonight?" Cav asked.

She shook her head, giving him a closed-mouth smile. *Are you going to ask me to stay with you? I will. Just ask.*

"If you don't," Molly piped in, "my aunt and uncle have a home on Eldon Road, and they enjoy guests. You'll be welcome there."

Eldon Road? Those houses now sell for ten million pounds sterling.

Kenzie gulped a long drink of water, considering the offer. "I don't want to impose."

"It's no imposition, truly. In fact, I won't accept no for an answer, and neither would my aunt."

Kenzie didn't know if she was relieved or disappointed. "Then I'll say yes. Tomorrow I want to sell my earrings. Do you know where I could get a good price?"

Molly looked closer. "They're beautiful. It's a shame to sell them, but they won't buy food, will they? Uncle Clifford can help you. He knows many of the city's merchants. If he doesn't know the best jeweler, he'll know a colleague who does."

The straitjacket sensation that had been suffocating Kenzie since her collapse in the ladies' room loosened its straps, and she took a deep, uninhibited breath.

"Good. That's settled. Let's have a drink," Cav said.

After beers for the men and gin for the women, large plates of scialatelli with eggplant and mozzarella sauce arrived at the table. Kenzie ate too much too fast, and finally had to push back from the table, groaning. "That was delicious. After that long run this morning—"

Cav cocked his head slightly. "Run? How far do you go? A mile?"

She was usually in her second mile before she warmed up and hit her stride. "More than that."

"Two," he said.

She turned up her cocktail and drank the last few sips. "A few more than that."

"Five, then," he said.

"You're not going to quit asking until I tell you, are you? Okay, twenty-six."

Molly gasped. "Twenty—"

"Six?" Rainer finished.

"There's a man at Bletchley Park who runs long distances. If you get a job there, you could run with him." Molly covered her mouth and giggled. "He makes an annoying grunting noise when he runs."

Molly was talking about Alan Turing. Kenzie had recently read his bio, and had seen *The Imitation Game*, a movie about his time at Bletchley when he broke the Nazis' unbreakable Enigma encryption system. If Kenzie's running experience could get her past the front door, she would use it. "That would be great. Few people run long distances for the fun of it."

"I take long walks every day, but I couldn't run very far. Maybe you can teach me."

"Why would you want to?" Rainer asked.

"I feel good when I walk fast," Molly said. "I bet I'd feel better if I ran."

"You probably would," Kenzie said.

Cav picked up the check the waitress had left on the table. "Who's up for dancing? Let's go to the Ritz."

Rainer reached across the table for the check. "I'm buying tonight. Remember?"

Cav coughed, covering his mouth with his fist.

Molly rubbed up against Rainer's arm. "Sounds like Cav won a bet. What was it?"

Rainer lowered his head and kissed her cheek. "I told him I'd buy dinner if he danced one dance, and that I'd buy cocktails, too, if he danced more than once. I wouldn't have made the bet if I'd known Kenzie was going to walk through the door."

Molly winked at Kenzie. "I think that's a compliment."

Cav glanced down and away, blushing slightly. "The girls are nice. Don't get me wrong. They're just…"

"Not your type?" Kenzie asked, cocking her head slightly.

Molly leaned in and said conspiratorially, "Cav believes all the women who come to the club are looking for GI husbands."

Kenzie pointed to herself. "And I don't have that look?"

Rainer laughed. "I'm not sure what the look is, but if you have it, I don't think he cares."

With four long-legged people sitting at a small table, any movement under the table bumped someone's leg. From the leg jerks under the table, Kenzie suspected Cav had just kicked Rainer in the shins.

"When the GIs first arrived in 1942," Molly said, "English women believed American men ran around shooting Indians. The *Times* had to explain that GIs weren't Hollywood stars or two-gun Texans with five-gallon hats. Now Londoners know GIs are friendly and have more money than British soldiers."

"In other words, they're a good catch," Kenzie said.

"Very good catch," Molly added.

"I suspect there'll be thousands of GI brides moving to the States after the war. One of them won't be me."

"But won't you go back to America?" Molly asked.

"Probably," Kenzie said. "But not as a married woman."

Cav stood, scraping his chair against the tile floor. "Now we've got that settled, let's get out of here. We might beat the crowd to Claridge's."

Molly tucked her arm through Kenzie's as they left the restaurant. "I have an inheritance and intend to travel after the war. I'm not ready to marry and settle down, either. I want adventure."

"Isn't living in a war zone adventure enough?"

"Don't get me wrong. There's plenty of danger and excitement in England. That's not what I'm talking about. I want…" Molly gazed dreamily off into the distance.

"You want more. More life. More love, and time to visit places you've only read about." Kenzie said.

"That's it exactly," Molly said. "Don't you want…more?"

Kenzie wanted a fulfilling job, and eventually a husband and children, but most of all she wanted to live in one place long enough that her license would expire before she had to change her address. She wanted stability.

"Right now all I want is my bag and identification back. Everything else will have to wait."

"Uncle Clifford will help tomorrow. For now, put it out of your mind, and let's go dancing."

15

Claridge's, London, England, May 28, 1944

A SMALL SHUDDER of relief went through Kenzie when Cav signaled for a taxi to convey the group to Claridge's on Brook Street in Mayfair. Could she have walked the distance? No. Only a tiny bit of spring remained in the muscles of her post-race, lead-filled legs.

"Hope you're up for a few more dances."

"Slow ones, for sure." If all she had to do was hold on to him and sway, she could manage. If he tried to flip her again, she'd land on her butt. And while she had a firm one, she didn't relish using her ass to mop the dance floor.

Molly and Rainer jumped into the taxi's backseat and Kenzie and Cav scrunched in beside them. The air inside the cab carried an electrical pulse generated by four slightly intoxicated and sexually charged passengers. The glint in the cabbie's eyes reflected in the rearview mirror. She smiled, and he did too, before studying the street ahead and pulling out into traffic. Due to the blackout, the taxi, like all vehicles, was fitted with a slotted cover to deflect the beams down toward the ground. Kenzie could barely see the vehicle in front of them or the one behind.

Cav rested his arm cross the back of the seat, and Kenzie curled into the curve of his warm body, yawning. The lanky pilot had a muscular chest and arms. While dancing earlier, she'd been more interested in his twinkling eyes than the breadth of his chest. He wasn't bulked up like a weight lifter, but had an active man's muscles that molded to her and fitted comfortably, like pieces of a puzzle made of cloth, not wood or cardboard. Some men were so dang hard you couldn't snuggle with them unless you enjoyed resting your head on concrete.

In the quiet hum of the taxi, and warmed by the lingering effects of the gin, she breathed deeply, inhaling Cav's musky scent mingled with sweet tobacco and oregano. "You and Churchill enjoy the same brand of Cuban cigars." She'd always liked cigars, enjoyed an occasional puff, and paid attention to brands that pleased her, like the iconic medium body Romeo y Julieta with its smooth, mellow taste.

Cav rolled the tightly bundled tobacco leaves between his thumb and forefinger. "I knew the Prime Minister enjoyed several a day, but I didn't know what brand he favored."

"Eight to ten cigars a day, or so I've read."

Cav puffed. His lashes lowered as he obviously savored the flavor before blowing out a plume of gray smoke that snaked out the partially opened window. "You're a wealth of information. Tell me another tidbit."

"Where do you get your cigars?" Rainer asked.

"Good question." As was any inquiry that turned attention away from her. "I doubt your local tobacconist carries Cuban cigars."

The cabbie slowed as they approached a portion of the street narrowed to one lane by rubble from a smoldering building. A scorched sign had been dragged from the debris and set to the side—resembling a headstone for a tailor's shop. She looked away, hit by a flashback of Afghan faces stunned and heartbroken by horrific acts of violence, kneeling in the wreckage and clinging to salvaged property. She swallowed back the sting of tears. Tears that hadn't been shed at the time. Was she grieving for the Afghans in another time and place, or was she grieving for Londoners and the devastation from a war that had ended decades before her birth?

Kenzie watched the other passengers' non-responsive faces. Had bomb sites become so commonplace to Londoners that they had grown numb to the destruction, or was her own recent war experience painting her friends with a discolored brush? Five years of war could numb even the strong-hearted.

Cav reached out the window and tapped off the cigar's inch-long white ash. "Grandpa stuffs a box or two between the cookies and socks in my monthly care packages. I keep looking for the whiskey, but if my dad puts a bottle in the package, my grandpa takes it out. Guess he figures if I've got cigars, I don't need the whiskey."

The taxi stopped and waited while another taxi dropped passengers off in front of Claridge's. As the taxi moved forward, a black sedan cut in front and parked in the empty spot. The cab's tires screeched, and Kenzie was flung forward. The motion would have jerked her out of the seat if Cav hadn't grabbed her shoulder, pinning her in place.

"Idiot." He glowered at the other driver's recklessness and handed the cabbie the fare. "We'll get out here."

Kenzie stepped to the curb. From the corner of her eye, she watched the passenger in the black sedan alight and stand at the curb about twenty feet from her, adjusting his coat. She sized him up with a quick glance. Tall and stocky, with an aquiline nose, smooth cheeks, round, protruding chin, and pursed lips. A fedora hid the top half of his face. In shadow, he resembled a stereotypical English Intelligence Officer. Whether or not he was, she had no way of knowing. But she was struck with a burning chord of fear.

Why was she afraid? Simple. She was in enemy territory without backup, no identification, no weapons, and no way home. Although she wasn't an enemy of the United Kingdom, she didn't belong here, and couldn't explain her presence. And any attempt to explain who she was would only dig her hole deeper.

She inched closer to Cav with her head lowered and arms tight to her body. If she didn't get her fear under control, feeling paranoid would be the least of her problems. As soon as she sold her diamonds, she intended to catch the first train for Inverness. She couldn't stay in London. The bombs alone would keep her cowering in the corner.

Fedora Man preceded them into the hotel, and she quickly lost sight of him in the lobby crowd. Hopefully, he had gone to his room, and that would be the last they saw of him. She shoved down the creepy-crawly sensation and looked around the lobby for a sign to the restroom.

"I need to use the ladies'," she said to Cav.

"We'll be in the ballroom," Rainer said, ushering Molly toward the stairs.

"Save us a spot," Cav called to his friend. Then to Kenzie he said, "I'll wait by the fire. Take your time."

She kissed his cheek. "I can't thank you enough. You've been a lifesaver tonight."

He pointed to his other cheek, grinning. "Kiss this side, too, and that'll be all the thanks I need."

Instead, she kissed him on the mouth with soft, slightly parted lips. Desire was jumbling her thoughts when she needed a clear head, but she found kissing Cav more enjoyable than worry and fear.

She eased back a little, but her eyes remained fixed on his, which were dilated by arousal. "Don't go away. I'll be right back." Other men she had kissed unexpectedly always came back for another. Cav didn't. His lips twitched, and she could tell he wanted to kiss her, but he held himself back. She wanted to kiss his warm, full lips again, if only for showing such noble-minded restraint.

She was a soldier, trained for the unexpected, yet acting like a plebe. No, not even a plebe. First-year students at the U.S. Military Academy had more control over their emotions than she was demonstrating. If she were dressed in an army combat uniform, she'd feel more secure. Fedora Man wouldn't warrant even a second look. She would have pinned him with a stare. Instead she had clung to Cav's side like a helpless female. God, what had happened to her?

Her emotions were all over the board—flashbacks, panic attacks, and loose behavior. It was as if her anchor had been ripped from the sea floor, and she'd been cast adrift with three mutinous shipmates without a compass or captain's log. Fear, exhaustion, and guilt were steering the ship straight toward the rocky shore.

Then she chastised herself for being so overly dramatic. It didn't suit her.

The concierge pointed out the sign to the ladies' room, and she hustled to get there ahead of the flock of women descending the stairs from the ballroom. No one was waiting in line to use the toilet, and the room was empty. She shoved the door closed and the latch banged against the strike plate, creating a loud ping in the small facility. A bolt secured the door and guaranteed a few moments of privacy.

But not even the bolt could steel her against the roar of airplanes flying directly above the building. The century-old building couldn't muffle the sound. She dashed out of the stall and braced for an explosion, but nothing happened. Must be the good guys.

She slumped over the sink and splashed cold water on her face. Droplets rolled down her neck and onto the collar of the dress. She snatched a towel and dabbed her cheeks dry. A knife-sharp pain cut deep across her chest and she leaned against the wall breathing heavily.

Home. If she could only go home. She squeezed her eyes shut and clicked her heels. "There's no place like home. There's no place like home." She glanced up into the mirror. Her hands clasped prayer-like beneath her chin. "That didn't work any better than the brooch." A chill raced up her arms, and she rubbed shoulders to elbows with tight up-and-down strokes.

Fear. But why was she afraid? Because she thought she was going to die in an air raid.

Sure, that fear was colossal, but her greatest fear was someone discovering that she carried secrets with more destructive power than the atomic bomb. An insignificant slip could impact the future in myriad ways, and for decades to come.

Acknowledging fear was the first step in overcoming it. Fear could be her friend if she transformed it into positive energy. At least that's what her therapist had said. If Kenzie was afraid of a slip, then she would parse her words before speaking.

"Anyone in there?" a female voice sounded from the other side of the door.

"Just a minute." She couldn't hide out any longer, but before she left the room, she sipped a handful of water from the sink's faucet. She might not have a uniform to wear, but she'd worn one for many years. She closed her eyes and remembered the honor and pride she experienced when dressed in uniform. The illusion might be an easily pierced veil, but under the current circumstances, attitude was the only protection she had.

Cav was leaning against the wall near the fireplace with his booted heel propped against the baseboard. He was smoking a cigar, wearing a look of contentment as he chatted with another pilot. Watching him, she wondered two things. Did he smoke after sex, and did he have the same contented smile?

When he spotted her, he excused himself, tossed the remainder of the cigar in the fire, and hurried to meet her. He clasped her hand and gently squeezed her fingers. "Ready to dance?"

His boyish exuberance couldn't be denied, at least not by her. "Lead the way."

They stood at the edge of the dance floor, watching Molly and Rainer slow-dance. "Do you want a drink?"

"Sure," she said.

"Come with me. There are too many soldiers here. I want everyone to know the most beautiful girl in the room is with me."

Kenzie lifted her eyebrows. "You think flattery will get you another kiss."

"No, ma'am," he said. "It's a fact. Look around at the other women. You are an ethereal beauty, and I can't take my eyes off of you." He ran the tips of his fingers through the hair at her temple, pushing strands behind her ear. "Everything about you is delicate and otherworldly."

Jesus Christ. Was this guy for real? She leaned in to kiss him again at the same time the music ended and the noise level took a dive. She pulled back, and he winked. "I'll get the beers. Don't move."

She rubbed her finger along her bottom lip, watching Cav saunter toward the bar.

"I can't get any supplies anymore, but that will all change after D-Day, which will be before June 15."

Kenzie jerked her head to see who was speaking. Three men stood huddled close by. The words on a sign she had seen recently while doing research at Bletchley Park popped into her head: *Don't help the enemy. Careless talk may give away vital secrets.* The statement she had overhead had been made by a Major General. Her eyes widened when he put a glass to his mouth and flashed a 1915 West Point class ring.

Her hands went to her hips, turning her elbows into hard, pointed weapons. She considered smashing one into his Adam's apple. The man was an idiot.

"I don't think the invasion will take place for another few months," another officer said.

"Major General Miller went to West Point with Eisenhower. He probably knows more than the rest of us."

Kenzie sidled toward him, saying, low-voiced, "Sir, I don't know where your intel comes from, and I don't mean to be disrespectful. But you have disrespected the ring on your finger. German spies are everywhere. Probably even in this room, and your comments have put our men and women at risk. When General Eisenhower hears of this, he'll have your ass on the first flight back to the States."

The Major General's chin dropped, his face flushed, and he reached for his Colt Single Action Army.

Kenzie bolted toward the door, but Cav caught her before she crashed through the entrance to the ballroom.

"Wait. Where're you going?"

"You shouldn't be seen with me. I'll meet you outside." She raced down the stairs and exited the building. Once outside, she searched for a place to hide. No recessed doors. No shadows. No trees. No tall fences. No hiding in plain sight. The only option was ducking between two parked vehicles, an empty taxi and a catering truck.

She squatted and grabbed hold of the bumper of the lead vehicle. Beads of sweat peppered her forehead, but she didn't dare release her grip to wipe her face. Her legs shook, and she wobbled on unsteady feet. If she'd been in uniform, she probably would have been shot on the spot. There wasn't much he could do to a civilian female, but if he'd seen her with Cav, he could hold Cav responsible.

A man in a ragged overcoat stopped between the vehicles and stared at her, shuffling feet with clean but scuffed boots. "Do you have the time?"

She held her wrist up to show she wasn't wearing a watch. "I don't. I'm sorry."

"Do you have a shilling to spare?"

She patted her pockets. The only object of value she carried other than the brooch and her diamonds was her class ring, probably her most prized possession. She should throw it in the river. No one would understand the twenty-first-century date, and she couldn't guarantee its protection from prying eyes. Gold and onyx weren't worth her life. She could get another one when she returned home. But what if she never returned home? She might need to use the ring to prove she was from the future.

"I'm sorry. I can't help you," she said.

A flash of something dangerous appeared in his rapidly blinking eyes, and then it was gone. Both of his hands were jammed into his coat pockets. The right hand fidgeted with a pointed object.

He has a gun.

She had to get to her feet. Defending herself from a squatting position would be impossible.

Move slowly. Don't alarm him.

"I'm going to stand up." She held her hands easily at her side, keeping them in plain view. If he intended to rob her, he already knew she didn't have a watch, and she didn't carry a purse. Thankfully, her hair covered the diamonds in her ears.

"There you are." Cav waved from the entrance.

Mr. Ragged Coat turned a panic-stricken glance in Cav's direction, then back at Kenzie. His gun hand jerked, and he mumbled unintelligible words before scampering away.

"You okay?"

Her breath whooshed through her teeth. "No, but I will be."

His eyes followed the man as he plodded toward the corner. "What'd he want?"

"Money. He was shaking, and his watery eyes wouldn't focus. He has a gun in his pocket. I think he's on drugs."

"You think he's sick?"

"What? No. He was probably…drinking," she said, trying to cover her time slip. Drug abuse wasn't well documented in the 1940s.

Cav wrapped her protectively in his arms. "You're safe now. Let's go back inside before he comes back."

Tires squealed, and they both twisted where they stood to follow the sound. A black sedan had come to a stop at the corner and two men jumped out, slamming car doors. Mr. Ragged Man bounded off the curb and raced across the street, glancing back over his shoulder.

"Halt or I'll shoot," one of the men from the car shouted.

Cav pulled her closer into the shadow of the truck. "They haven't seen us. Don't move."

Mr. Ragged Man took cover behind a red-and-white sidewalk sign advertising ice cream and fired. He hit one of the men in the upper arm. The injured man dropped to his knees and returned fire. Ragged Man fired again. A third man exited the vehicle with a drawn weapon. He had a better angle to see Ragged Man behind the sign. He fired two quick shots and Ragged Man fell to the sidewalk.

Kenzie stood on tiptoe for a better view. The man kicked Ragged Man's gun away from his hand, then knelt and felt for a pulse at his neck. "He's dead," he announced to the others. "Come get him and put his body in the trunk. We'll search him later." The shooter returned to the sedan and opened the door. The interior light provided enough illumination to see his face. Kenzie froze in place, and her throat closed up.

"That man"—she pointed, saying with a harsh voice—"is the same man who got out of the car when we first arrived here. *Who is he?*"

A slight quirk of his mouth softened the harshness of Cav's taut jaw. "And who did he shoot?"

She swallowed the urge to flee as fast and far as possible. "If you hadn't come out when you did, it could have been me dead on the street." The words stuck in her dry throat. They stood tree-like in the shadow of the truck until the sedan drove away, tires squealing again.

They waited a few more minutes until they were sure the men weren't coming back for them. Cav glanced up and down the street. "Come on. Let's go."

They hurried across the sidewalk toward the hotel's entrance, with Kenzie shaded in the protectiveness of Cav's arm. She'd spent years protecting others, and now she clung to him as others had clung to her. The role reversal coated her mouth with an icky taste. She stuck her hand into her pocket and slipped her class ring on her finger up to the first joint. Wearing it was impossible. She understood the consequences. But the thick band, heavy on her finger, was a much-needed reminder. She was, and always would be, part of the long gray line. No one could snatch that away.

"Why'd you run out of the ballroom? What happened?"

She peered around him, checking to be sure no one could overhear her. "A general in the ballroom spouted off about D-Day being in mid-June. I told him German spies were all over London, and that repeating rumors not only disgraced West Point, but put men and women in harm's way."

"Ouch," Cav said. "What'd he say?"

"Nothing. But then I made it worse by telling him when Eisenhower heard what he said, he'd send the general back to the states. That's when he lowered his head like a bull about to charge and went for his Colt. I took off. I shouldn't have said what I did, but he was out of line. He *should* be sent home."

"Do you know his name?"

"Major General Miller. He won't be a Major General much longer."

"He's Chief of Material Command of the Air Force. You're right. He better not see us together. He'll kick my butt from here to the Rhine."

They stopped at the fireplace where Cav had waited for her earlier. "Stay here and I'll go find Molly and Rainer. And don't talk to any more strangers." He turned to leave and threw a parting comment over his shoulder, "Or generals."

"Ha. Ha," she said. "Send Molly down first. We'll walk out together."

Cav nodded. When he reached the steps he glanced back over his shoulder and winked. God, he was gorgeous, sweet, heroic, and she was aware of him as a vital, living, breathing man. The heat of his energy and sex appeal was palpable. His long legs took the stairs to the ballroom two at a time with ease and strength, and she couldn't take her eyes off him.

A multitude of events had occurred in the last few hours, spiraling her into survival mode. In a psychology class at West Point, she had learned that in wartime landscapes even conservative men and women gave themselves over to wanton carnal relationships. A biological reaction to stress didn't excuse her lust, but it did explain why she was ready to jump into bed with a sexy, desirable stranger.

The clock on the wall marked his absence. Five minutes became ten. Ten became fifteen. When he'd been gone for twenty minutes, she headed for the stairs, but spotted Molly coming down.

"I was worried," Kenzie said.

"Cav ran into his commander, who insisted on buying a round of drinks. He and Rainer couldn't leave, but Cav said they would call in the morning to make plans for the day."

Kenzie's heart sank, and a prickle of foolish tears clouded her vision. She blinked rapidly and avoided making eye contact with Molly. She had been in wartime landscapes before, but never alone and unprotected. She had Molly and Cav, but she couldn't trust them to cover her back, not like she could her Army buddies.

For the first time in her life, she was on her own, and she doubted a repertoire of jokes would help her fit in for long. The lies would multiply until she was caught in a web of deceit that could cost her more than a chance to go home.

Her emotions were a bale of tangled wire, and the only hope of untangling them was escaping London.

Tomorrow I'll sell the diamonds and devise a plan.

The bellhop hailed a taxi for them, and fifteen minutes later they were dropped off in front of Molly's aunt and uncle's house. Molly paid the fare, explaining to Kenzie, "Cav gave me money to see us home. He's so sweet. I'm glad he found you tonight. You're perfect for him."

"I don't know..."

Molly cupped Kenzie's cheek and gave it a little pat. "Trust me. You are. And the two of you look like movie stars."

The taxi pull away from the curb, and the low hum of a car's engine pulled Kenzie's attention toward a vehicle parked across the street. The sky provided minimal light, not enough to see inside the car, but intuition told her a passenger was not only inside the car, but watching the house. The house she was about to enter. She sniffed sweet, scented air.

Pipe smoke.

Whoever the pipe-smoking passenger was, he didn't know her. Was he spying on Molly? She worked at Bletchley Park, and while Kenzie didn't know what her new friend did there, she knew security was ultra-tight. But did that extend to spying on employees during weekend getaways?

Her research on Bletchley wasn't extensive. In fact, it consisted of watching one movie, Turing's biography, and reading a piece of primary source material on Churchill's influence. But even with limited knowledge of the workings of the Park's security, she doubted there were resources available to spy on the thousands of employees during holidays.

As long as Kenzie wasn't the target of an investigation, she wouldn't become unduly alarmed, but not having any identification was a nail-biting concern. If military police or the intelligence community wanted to verify her identity, it would take a few days, possibly a week or two, before they discovered she didn't exist, at least not in the twentieth century. And this close to D-Day, all resources were directed at one objective—the invasion.

Kenzie picked up the pace and followed Molly to the front door of a five-story white Victorian home in Kensington. Even an exclusive section of London wasn't immune from German bombs. Several townhomes on the street lay in ruins, with fragments of wallpaper still clinging to soot-covered walls. The randomness of the destruction left the pulse in Kenzie's throat throbbing.

She took one last look at the sedan. Not in a covert way, but an overt glance. She had nothing to hide. "Have you ever noticed—?"

"—My aunt and uncle probably won't be up. You'll have to meet them in the morning," Molly said over the top of Kenzie's question. "I'm sorry. What'd you say?"

The car pulled away from the curb, and Kenzie decided not to mention its presence, admitting her judgment had probably been skewed by the events of the day. "Oh, nothing. And I'll look forward to meeting them in the morning."

Molly unlocked and pushed open the door. They passed quietly through a wide foyer furnished with antiques. The entry had a damp, musty scent that reminded Kenzie of a friend's apartment after floodwaters had receded, leaving behind sodden floors and walls. She was too polite to ask, but she assumed when the house next door was bombed, the fireman sprayed water on the non-burning adjacent homes to protect the residences from flying sparks.

They found a snoring Uncle Clifford reclining in a chair next to the fire, which had turned to ash, leaving a chill in the room. The gray-haired man's slippered feet were propped on a stool. Wrinkled, veined hands held a pair of round-eyed spectacles, and a leather-bound volume of *Two Plays for Puritans* by George Bernard Shaw. An empty tumbler rested in a coaster on a small table alongside a low wattage reading lamp, the only light in the room, and the windows were covered with blackout curtains.

Molly patted his shoulder gently. "Uncle Clifford. Uncle Clifford."

He opened his eyes and beamed up at Molly. "What time is it, child?"

"After midnight."

Molly marked his page with a fringed bookmark and set the book and glasses on the table. "I brought a new friend home with me tonight. Her name is Kenzie."

"Just Kenzie?" he asked, sleepily.

The friendly inquiry of genuine interest tugged on Kenzie's heartstrings. She cleared her throat of the small knot triggered by the homey, affectionate scene. "Kenzie Wallis-Manning." Her emotions were stampeding. If sleep didn't rein them in, she'd be whimpering in a puddle of her own tears by tomorrow afternoon. The fog must have been thick with a chemical that attacked her limbic system and turned her body's ability to manage her emotions into mush.

He shared a wink with Molly. "American?"

Molly pushed the footstool out of his way, helped him to his feet, and handed over a cane. "Yes, sir, and you can quiz her about Mr. Roosevelt tomorrow."

"Are you a fan?" Kenzie asked.

"Don't get him started," Molly said. "He's FDR's number one fan. Once he starts telling Roosevelt stories, he can go on for hours."

Kenzie stepped aside so Uncle Clifford had a clear path to the door. "Then I'm his number-two fan. I'm quite fond of Eleanor, too. We'll talk in the morning."

"What brings you to London, Miss Wallis-Manning?"

Kenzie jumped right in with a request for help to sell her diamonds. "I need to sell a pair of diamond earrings. Do you know a reputable jeweler?"

"I know just the chap. He'll give you a fair price, and that's all we can ask for. Leave them with Molly, and I'll see to it first thing in the morning."

Kenzie and Molly followed him to the stairs. "Good night, Uncle."

Uncle Clifford climbed the first step, stopped, and said, "Will Roosevelt survive until the end of the war, Miss Wallis-Manning?"

"Please call me Kenzie." She wasn't expecting the question.

After only sixty seconds of interacting with Uncle Clifford, she knew him to be an astute English gentleman who would see through a lie before the last word was spoken.

"No sir, he won't survive to see the end. He's quite ill."

"Hmm," he said. "I'll sell your diamonds in the morning, and then we'll talk."

She lifted her brow, curious why he didn't ask how she could be so sure; nor did he ask when the end would come for either the war or Roosevelt. A prickling sensation played with the fine hairs on her neck, and she buried the urge to rub her hand against her nape. "Good night, sir. I'll look forward to it."

16

London, England, the Bradford Residence, May 29, 1944

KENZIE SAT WITH her legs curled under her hip on the sofa in the informal drawing room, fingering the hand-embroidered doily covering the rolled arm of the Chippendale antique. Molly's Aunt Sylvia, a genteel woman who looked too frail to survive an ordinary day, much less a drawn-out war, poured tea from a Royal Albert tea service while Molly combed through the daily news. She read out loud whenever she found an interesting post that wasn't about the war. Those she glossed over, shaking her head and tsking.

Antiques, tea services, and careworn but beautifully patched linen napkins.

Until eight months ago, Kenzie couldn't tell a Chippendale from a Hepplewhite or a Brown Betty teapot from a Royal Albert. That all changed when she began reading World War II diaries, which included inventories of destroyed personal property. The diaries hadn't been part of her initial research; she fell into it accidentally after reading about the chaos and damage to the Prime Minister's residence at 10 Downing Street.

Security had removed all the furniture during the Blitz. Only the Garden Rooms, Cabinet Room, and private secretaries' offices were left in use, and those rooms had been heavily reinforced with steel and anti-blast shutters. According to first-hand reports, the new quarters resembled "third-class accommodations on a Channel steamer."

The Germans had targeted the immediate area around Downing Street, and it suffered significant damage. After reading about Downing Street, she signed up for World War II walking tours of the Mayfair and St. James area. No amount of research, though, could have prepared her for the stark reality of the destruction she witnessed last night. How much worse would the burned-out, smoldering shells of residences and businesses look in the clear light of day? She had avoided glancing out the windows to save her psyche additional trauma, if only for a few hours. Although she couldn't remain holed up inside indefinitely; she knew what awaited her. Until she received orders to move, she would remain right where she was, listening to Aunt Sylvia, a walking almanac of London society.

"Would you like to hear my favorite George Bernard Shaw story?" Aunt Sylvia said.

Kenzie had a sneaking suspicion the story Sylvia intended to tell was one involving Winston Churchill, and it was a good story. She wouldn't ruin Sylvia's excitement by letting on that she was familiar with the anecdote.

"I'd love to hear it," Kenzie said.

Aunt Sylvia took a sip of tea. "Well…" She set down her tea cup and leaned forward with her hands clasped in her lap. "Shaw sent Churchill an invitation to attend the first performance of his new play. 'And bring a friend if you have one,' Shaw wrote at the bottom of his invitation.' " She tittered. "Churchill replied, 'I'm sorry I can't attend the first performance, but I will attend the second performance, if you have one.' "

Kenzie laughed, not at the story, but at Sylvia's childlike telling of it. "Don't you love a man with a good sense of humor?"

"I've never met one," Molly said. "English men are emotionally constipated."

Kenzie wiggled her eyebrows. "And American men…?"

Molly's eyes brightened. "Not at all. At least the ones I've met."

The front door opened and closed, and the tap-tap echo of Uncle Clifford's walking cane preceded him into the drawing room.

Exertion had turned his cheeks rosy. Sylvia lifted her chin and Uncle Clifford kissed her cheek. "Good morning, mi' lovely."

She giggled, and Kenzie had a sense that Sylvia had giggled every morning of their marriage that, according to Molly, had spanned half a century. Kenzie's parents had been deeply in love. Would they have been, in their old age, still in love, like Clifford and Sylvia? A knot under Kenzie's breastbone ached for what she had lost so many years ago. She took a deep breath before dabbing at the corner of her eye where a tear balanced precariously on her bottom lashes. Damn tears. Damn emotions. And while she was damning things…damn the fog.

Uncle Clifford handed Kenzie an envelope. "I got a hundred pounds for the earrings. The jeweler was impressed with the quality of the diamonds. He asked if I had more." Uncle Clifford tilted his head in a conspiratorial fashion, waiting for her response.

She pressed the envelope to her chest, and her shoulders slumped. "I wish I had more, but I don't. Thank you so, so much." The tear dropped onto her cheek, and she swiped it away. "We have an expression in America, *the cavalry saved the day.* You certainly saved mine." And he had. She glanced up, sensing that Trey was looking out for her.

Uncle Clifford poured a cup of tea and sipped. "I heard Mrs. Apley is finally selling her daughter's clothes. It might be worth your while to pay her a visit if Kenzie needs to replace her wardrobe."

"Becky was killed in an air raid during the Blitz," Sylvia added. "She attended a social function almost every day, and had such beautiful clothes."

"Worn remains of a time of graceful living." Uncle Clifford smiled sweetly to his wife, and she attempted a smile in return, but it didn't reach her eyes.

What memory were they sharing, Kenzie wondered? Most likely a joint memory of London's glorious days before the deprivation of a city at war. Quite often the only way to survive loss and devastation, as she had discovered, was to hold tight to the memory of the way things had been.

"Oh, that's perfect," Molly said. "Kenzie will be going on job interviews and will need an appropriate interview dress."

Sylvia cocked her head one way and then the other, studying Kenzie with inquisitive blue eyes. Kenzie squirmed under the older woman's gaze, imagining herself captured in a net and sealed in a jar for observers to ogle at.

"You're about the same height as her daughter, and she wasn't any bigger than you. You're so tiny," Sylvia said.

"Let's pop down the street and see what Mrs. Apley is selling," Molly said.

Kenzie had washed her underwear in the sink and spot-cleaned and pressed her dress before going to bed the night before. During her tours in Afghanistan, she had spent days wearing the same uniform, but, for some reason, now the thought of wearing dirty clothes made her skin crawl. "Since I don't have a coupon book, it's the only way I'll get a new dress. Let's go."

An hour later, Molly and Kenzie returned, each carrying an armload of clothes.

"Come in here, girls," Sylvia said. "Show me what you found."

"Two sweaters, two skirts, a pair of full-legged trousers with cuffs, three blouses, a jacket, a dress, a black clutch purse, and two pairs of stockings," Kenzie said breathlessly. "And the *pièce de résistance* is this..." She held up a pair of white Keds. "They fit, too." They weren't the best shoes for running, but she could make them work.

"And don't forget this," Molly said, dangling a black-and-white checkered scarf. "It goes well with both sweaters and the jacket."

Kenzie folded the clothes into a pile. "I would have bought another dress, but Mrs. Apley wouldn't sell anything else. From the look on her face, every garment she parted with ripped out another of the few remaining pieces of her heart."

Molly glanced out the window and said in a raspy whisper, "Try laughing after you fall down and hurt your leg."

"What darling?" Sylvia said.

"Oh, nothing." She made a motion with her shoulder and then

said, "I was imagining what it must be like living with grief every day. If you fall down and hurt your leg, you might be able to laugh again, but if you fall down repeatedly, you'd find it hard to even smile."

"I doubt Mrs. Apley even tries to stand these days. So many have lost so much."

The phone rang and Uncle Clifford answered, saying, "Hello? Yes. She's here. Just a minute." He turned the receiver toward his chest and pressed it against him, saying, low-voiced, "An American named Rainer is asking for you."

Molly jumped to her feet, knocking over the stack of clothes Kenzie had folded with great care. "Oh, sorry."

Kenzie lunged for the clothes. "Sh…" She caught herself before spewing profanity, but the blouses and sweaters toppled to the floor and all the tight, wrinkle-free folds came undone.

"Hi, Rainer." Molly bubbled like a teenager on her first date while Kenzie gathered up the only possessions she had in her new world. "That sounds like fun. Let me ask her." She held her hand on the mouthpiece. "Rainer and Cav invited us to the matinee of *The Wizard of Oz*. I've been *dying* to see the movie."

Kenzie had seen it dozens of times, and had memorized most of the lines. "Sure. That sounds like fun." Watching Molly's face brighten with excitement, Kenzie realized it would be fun watching the film with three Oz virgins.

"No need to do that. We'll meet you there at three o'clock." She replaced the receiver. "Rainer and Cav have to report to the War Office at one o'clock for a meeting. I told them we would meet them at the theatre. It's in Piccadilly, not far from here."

Kenzie finished folding the clothes and set the pile away from the edge of the sofa. "That gives us two hours. Did Rainer say what they wanted to do afterwards?"

"No, but I'm sure we'll have dinner and go dancing."

"Then I definitely need a nap." And before she rested, she intended to try the brooch again. Maybe it only worked every twelve hours, or every twenty-four hours. She had traveled around the world and heard fairy tales, mythology, and folklore in a dozen different languages. Never once had she heard a story about a magic brooch that could whisk a person into an alternate universe. As old as the stone appeared to be, why weren't there stories about it?

That was as much a mystery as the brooch itself. She found it impossible to believe that she was the only person to ever hold it in her hand and say the magic words. Had Mr. Digby time-traveled? If so, why had he sent the brooch to her? She wanted answers, but they would have to wait until she found the answers to the bigger questions: How and when could she go home?

17

London, England, May, 29 1944

MOLLY AND KENZIE were standing in front of the theater in Piccadilly, chatting like long-time friends and watching people come and go, mostly soldiers, when Molly pointed toward a taxi pulling to the curb. "There they are."

When Cav alighted from the car, for a moment, for just a heartbeat, time stopped for Kenzie. From the top of his thick head of hair to the bottom of his long, narrow feet, the confident and handsome pilot oozed sexuality.

Cav Cavanaugh was, in the daylight, not a President John Kennedy lookalike. Nope. He was a John Kennedy, Jr. lookalike.

Drop-dead gorgeous and a personality to match. What was there not to love? And, while her mouth watered, so did the rest of her. His million-dollar grin was directed her way. Forget going to Oz. *Take me to bed, or lose me forever.*

He kissed her cheek. "Did you sleep well?"

She nodded, licking her lips—dumbstruck. What in the hell had happened to her? The fog had happened, and she was not herself. Men didn't affect her this way. She was always the one to keep emotions under control. She got horny, sure, but never like this; never this rip-your-clothes-off kind of horny. She swallowed hard and tried to squeeze an answer to his question past the knot blocking her vocal cords.

"Ah," she said. *That's a start, Kenz. Can you do any better?* "Once I fell asleep, I slept like the dead. Molly had to shake me to wake me up this morning."

"That's the truth." Molly threw back her head and arms in an exaggerated pose, mouth agape, and then she straightened, saying. "I came close to calling the mortician. I thought for sure she'd passed during the night. I didn't know whether to blame the dancing, the food, the twenty-six miles she ran, or—" Molly raised her eyebrows, "—Lieutenant Cavanaugh."

He winked at Kenzie. "Must have been the jitterbug flip." Then he gazed at her with intensity and focus that made her want to kiss him. "You're beautiful, and your eyes look true emerald green in this sweater than the navy dress you wore yesterday."

Hold that kissing thought.

This was weird. No man, other than her gay guy friends, ever mentioned the color of her eyes or clothes.

Her face must have reflected her confusion because he added, "I notice color. Even shades of gray. I pay attention."

"Oh, like changes in the clouds." Relief swelled in Kenzie's voice. Of course, he was a pilot. He would notice color changes.

"Come on, let's go," Molly said. "It's time to follow the yellow brick road. I read the book years ago, and I'm so excited."

Yes, Kenzie had to admit, she was, too. Even in the midst of a war, with all the worries they had, her companions were teeming with excitement over a silly movie that in Kenzie's time had been out for more than seventy-five years.

She tucked her hand in the crook of Cav's elbow and they entered the theater. Within moments, even before the film started, the hype swept her away, too.

Rainer and Cav brought popcorn and Cokes, and they found seats toward the back of the crowded theater. Cav and Kenzie bumped knuckles every time they simultaneously dug into the popcorn. The first time, her knuckles tingled. The second time, the tingle went up her hand, the third time, the tingle reached her neck. At this rate, she'd be making out with her sexy pilot before the movie started.

Her?

Really? When had Cav become *her* sexy pilot? Honestly, she didn't know. Maybe it was the whiff of his snug-fitting leather jacket, sweetly scented by his cigars. Would she stay in the past for him? No. She had had enough of war and wanted to go home. Period. But while she was stuck here, she would make the most of it.

She dug her hand into the bag and scratched the bottom. There was no more popcorn. Only a long, slender hand touching hers. She glanced up at him. One corner of his mouth curled wryly. She homed in on his lips. They were neither too big nor too small. Perfect shape. Perfect size, and she longed to feel them against her own. Her lips parted, and she pulled the corner of her bottom lip between her teeth. The hungry look in his eyes told her he would prefer to be searching for the closest hotel instead of watching the movie.

Molly elbowed her and whispered, "I've wanted to see this movie for several years but could never get tickets. Cav did this for you."

"Then let's enjoy it," Kenzie said. She laced her arm with Cav's and snuggled up to him, touched by his thoughtfulness.

"Do you want more popcorn?" he asked.

"Depends on where we're going after the movie."

"We have dinner reservations at the Savoy."

And after dinner...

She didn't ask. She didn't need to. "I'll pass, then. I don't want to spoil my dinner."

The lights flashed, indicating it was time for everyone to take their seats, and a man stood up in front of the theatre. "If an air-raid warning is received, you will be informed from the stage. For those wishing to leave, you will have seven minutes to find shelter. For those who wish to remain, the show will go on. Please walk, do not run, to the exits. Do not panic. Remember, you are British."

Kenzie leaned over so Cav, Molly, and Rainer could hear her loud whisper. "I don't know about you all, but if there's an air raid, *I'm* leaving."

"Let's be sure to hold hands so we won't get separated," Molly said. They all clasped hands as if to practice, but Cav didn't let go of Kenzie's until Dorothy, the Tin Man, Scarecrow, and the Cowardly Lion succumbed to the slumbering scent of the pretty poppies. After he let go of her hand, he draped his arm around her shoulder and tugged her closer.

The man was impossible to resist.

He pressed the tip of his finger against her jaw and turned her face toward him. Then he leaned down and fitted his mouth over hers. His gentleness was in no way tentative, and it held a promise of power tightly leashed, and she kissed him back in a way that said *I am yours for the asking.*

18

London, England, May 29, 1944

AFTER THE MOVIE, Cav hailed a taxi and they toured the city, including a visit to the Old Curiosity Shop that inspired Dickens to write the novel by the same name. The building had some bomb damage, but was still standing. Some blocks, however, were completely gone. Kenzie had difficulty staying oriented, but when she saw Buckingham Palace she gaped in soundless horror.

"Oh, my God."

"It's had nine direct hits," Molly said.

"I heard King George and Queen Elizabeth work there during the day, but spend their nights at Windsor," Cav said.

Kenzie's gut churned at the sight of the damage. She'd seen pictures, of course, but pictures never conveyed what reality revealed. "Thank God they have Windsor Castle to retire to at night. But why isn't Windsor bombed as well?"

"If it was located in London, I'm sure it would be." Molly squeezed Kenzie's hand. "They've been such an inspiration to the people, as has the Prime Minister."

"Hitler calls the Queen the most dangerous woman in Europe," Rainer said.

"Why?" Kenzie asked.

"It's her spirit," Molly said. "The English people rally around her."

Kenzie sat back in her seat and glanced out the other window, hiding the shock she knew was obvious on her face. It wasn't so much the bomb damage itself that shocked her, deeply and indelibly, as much as the realization that nothing was spared in this war. No place was truly safe. No day could be taken for granted. A pilot had no guarantee that he would return from his next mission. Her throat felt thick and sticky as glue.

My God. This could be Cav's last weekend in London—ever.

19

Green Park, London, England, May 29, 1944

DAVID AND JACK arrived on the other side of the fog, smartly dressed in double-breasted wool suits, and carrying two bags apiece. When the peat-scented cloud dissipated, they found themselves in a dark, vacant lot, possibly a park, without identifiable landmarks and bearing no resemblance to Green Park in London, where they had departed.

"What's that smell?" Jack asked.

The smell assaulted David's nose, instantly alerting him. He tensed with alarm as he did a quick visual surveillance of the immediate area. Empty, including the craters dotting the landscape like a pockmarked face. "It's the smell of war."

Jack smirked. "Can you be more specific? Am I going to step over dead bodies?"

"You're smelling a combination of dust, wet plaster, burned bodies, and smoke from dirty coal."

Jack turned in a slow circle. "Doesn't look like London. Do you know where we are?"

"My limited experience with the brooches has been ye' land where ye' leave from. That would put us somewhere in Green Park, near the London Ritz."

"But we *could be*"—Jack's voice held a worried undertone—"hundreds of miles away from there."

"Aye. But let's hope not. That would put us in occupied

France." David paused a minute, then said with a slight chuckle. "Save yerself the worry. We're in London."

"How do you know?"

"Because I'm *listening*, and I've never heard those distinctive chimes anywhere else."

Jack spun in the direction of the ringing. The chime of bells rang resolute in the otherwise silent night. "Big Ben?"

"Or its clone," David said. "Come on. Let's go."

They exited the park and encountered crowded sidewalks and a busy street with passengers, mostly soldiers in a mix of Allied uniforms, hopping in and out of taxis and double-decker buses. Blackout curtains covered shop windows along the street, and faint light flashed when patrons pushed aside curtains that hung over the doors. Stained sandbags were piled along the sides of the buildings, and only the peeling paint on the walls of the old wooden residences showed vestiges of former glory. In time it would all be rebuilt, but for David, the shock of seeing the destruction went bone deep.

"Look," Jack said, pointing to the side of the Ritz. "What'd you suppose happened here?"

"Shrapnel. Come on. Let's go inside and see if they have rooms available."

"They always have room for me. I'm a regular," Jack said.

Reminding Jack he was a regular in another century wouldn't dampen his enthusiasm.

They entered the Ritz and made their way to the registration desk. "We need adjoining rooms for a week," Jack said.

David scanned the faces of several dozen people idling about in the smoke-filled lobby. Mostly soldiers, a few reporter types, and several well-dressed young women on the arms of American officers. But no Kenzie Wallis-Manning.

"I'm...sure we can accommodate you." The clerk's attention was riveted on the wad of notes in Jack's hand. He peeled off several and the clerk palmed the bills. Their accommodations were more important to Jack. David had only one concern. Finding Kenzie.

"What's the date?" David asked.

The clerk's eyes widened behind his wire-rimmed frames. "May 29."

"Nineteen—"

"Forty-four," the clerk added.

Jack leaned over the edge of the counter and whispered. "You'll have to excuse my friend. He's forgetful..." Jack made a circling motion with his index finger at the side of his head. The clerk scooted himself and the guest register away from David.

David checked himself before he could roll his eyes.

"Show him Kenzie's picture," Jack said, elbowing David in the arm.

David removed a three-by-five flier from his inside jacket pocket and flipped it around to face the clerk whose nametag identified him as Neil. "Have ye' seen this woman, Neil?" He let the lilt in his voice give the question a casual tone. If word got back to Kenzie that two men were searching for her, it was imperative she not feel threatened. If she left London, he would still find her. But it would take longer. And he didn't have *longer*.

Neil peered closely at the black and white photograph printed on vintage-looking paper. Instead of doing a drawing, Jack's artist friend had Photoshopped a picture of Kenzie, styling her hair and clothes into a 1940s look. The result was a professional image of a woman who could easily be a model or actress.

"She hasn't been a guest of the hotel. I'd remember that face." Neil tapped the photograph with his index finger several times. "She's an American movie star, isn't she? You got an extra copy? I'll show it around. Maybe someone's seen her."

A man about forty years old and dressed in civilian clothes stood on the other side of Jack. His head jerked at the mention of a movie star, and he stretched his neck to see the picture. "Can I see that?"

David slid it across the counter, watching the man's face closely for any sign of recognition. His eyes widened slightly. "Does she look familiar to ye', then?"

The man waved to an Army lieutenant with comically bushy brows who was lounging near the front door smoking a cigarette.

"I'd like to show this to that fella. Do you mind?"

"Be my guest," David said.

The man scurried across the room with the flier flapping in his hand, and when he reached the lieutenant, held it out for him to see. Recognition flitted across the junior officer's face. He bobbed his head up and down repeatedly.

David mumbled under his breath to Jack, "He's seen her." The fear that had crunched in his veins like ice thawed in an instant. Kenzie was alive. His warrior instinct had told him she was, and he had relied on his instinct to keep hope alive, but now he needed a visual, or reliable first-hand intel to locate her.

The lieutenant snuffed his cigarette out in a receptacle and then strode jauntily over to where David and Jack waited at the registration desk. He slapped the flier against his palm. "If this woman has red hair, then I've seen her twice. She's got a cupid's bow mouth like my sister. Noticed it right off. Beautiful girl. And that red hair…"

David leaned casually against the desk. "Where'd ye' see her?"

"You're not going to cause trouble for her, are you?" the lieutenant asked.

"Trouble? No." Adrenaline created additional alertness, but David remained at ease.

"'Cause she's beautiful and funny and a great dancer. I tried to get in line for a turn on the dance floor…"

David forced a congenial smile and rested an elbow on the desk, adopting a non-threatening posture. If he could keep his hands from fisting he might be able to pull it off. "Go on," he said casually.

"A flyboy from the Mighty Eighth made it clear she wasn't dancing with anyone else."

Jack was signing the guest register and without looking up said off-handedly, "That must have been disappointing."

"I wasn't the only one disappointed. I thought a young ensign, who had probably spent the day at the pubs, was going to start a fight. But a buddy took him outside."

David leaned in closer in a confidential sort of way. He needed a date, time, and location. His heart raced, yet he softened his face, and nodded his understanding. "I'm David McBain. I heard Kenzie, my cousin, was in London. I want to visit her before I ship out. Any help ye' can give would be appreciated. How long ago did ye' see her?" If he made his voice any friendlier, he'd be kissing the lad.

"Cousins, huh? She doesn't talk like you."

"Aye," David said regretfully, giving a slight shrug. "I'm from Inverness, where her mother's from. Kenzie didn't grow up in Scotland." As multilingual as she was, David didn't want to pin her down to a specific region and contradict any story she might have told.

The lieutenant tilted his head back, eyes narrowing a bit while he appraised Jack. "Are you a *cousin,* too?" The tone he used indicated the story hadn't passed the lieutenant's hundred percent believability test.

"Not me." Jack extended his hand. "I'm Jack Mallory, war correspondent." He poured on the charm, giving the man what Jack's sister called his book jacket smile. "Kenzie and I were classmates. I met David through her."

David's gritted his teeth while his toes clenched inside his Army boots. Jack was at least fifteen years Kenzie's senior. Why didn't he say his sister was her classmate?

The lieutenant squinted, studying Jack, and David's foot itched to kick Jack's arse back to the twenty-first century. In Jack fashion, he had taken the helm and immediately sailed them into unrehearsed, mine-infested waters.

What would Kenzie do if she heard two men were looking for her, claiming to be her cousin and a former classmate? He knew what he would do. Surreptitiously seek them out, and if he didn't like what he saw, he'd either leave town or…

It was the *or* that sifted unpredictability on top of his skin like a fine layer of sand. If he couldn't predict what she would do, he could lose her.

The lieutenant tapped a pack of unopened Camels in his palm, then opened the end of the package and withdrew an unfiltered cigarette. A lighter burst into flame, and he bent his head to light the cigarette dangling between his lips. He blew smoke upwards, no longer tilting his head as if mentally weighing the evidence. Kenzie must have made a whopping impression on the young man for him to play the gallant now. Did he truly believe she needed protection from a reporter and a Scot?

David willed his breathing to a normal rate. "We need to find her. And I don't have much time. I'm shipping out in a few days."

The lieutenant took another draw and said, "The first time I saw her was about eight o'clock last night at the Rainbow Corner Club."

David held his smile in place and nodded for the soldier to continue, while his heart raced wildly.

"That's where she was dancing with the pilot. I believe his name is Cavanaugh. His buddies call him Cav. I saw them again around nine-thirty walking down Piccadilly."

"Where were they headed?" Jack asked.

"Don't know. But your cousin was telling the funniest jokes I've ever heard. I must have stood on the corner—"

"What corner?" Jack asked the question in a reporter's urgent fashion, but for some reason, perhaps his pleasing Southern accent, the lieutenant didn't tense up. He remained engaged.

David stood by, letting Jack take the lead, hoping he didn't screw it up.

"Not sure. About a block from here, I reckon. Anyway, I must have stood there listening for ten minutes or more until she said her throat was dry and she needed a drink."

"What happened next?" Jack asked.

"They headed down the street, and my buddies and I went to a pub on Piccadilly. We didn't see the four of them again."

"Four?" David couldn't believe their luck. The lieutenant's information was spinning threads to follow. "Do you know the other two?"

The lieutenant flicked the ash into the ashtray before taking another draw. He blew out the smoke, picking at a piece of tobacco stuck on his tongue. "Your cousin was with Molly Bradford and another pilot. I've seen Molly with him before. His name is Rainer."

"Does he have a first name?"

The lieutenant's smile was brief, to match his nod. "That's the only name I've heard him called. Could be first. Could be his last."

Jack produced a small notebook and pencil, flipped over a few pages, and prepared to jot down some notes. "What can you tell us about Ms. Bradford?"

"What does she look like?" David jumped in. His cheeks held a quiver, and he couldn't keep the good-natured smile going much longer.

"Soft brown eyes, blonde, knockout figure, and glamorous like your cousin. If there was a woman for every man, Molly would still have a line waiting."

"English or American?" Jack asked.

"English. Born and raised in London. Brains and beauty. She studied at Oxford."

"Do ye' know where she lives?" David asked.

"Her aunt and uncle own a big old Victorian house on Eldon Road. I know because I gave Molly a ride home one night a few months ago. She only stays there when she's in town. She works at a radio factory near Bletchley."

David was fairly vibrating with tension. From the information they had thus far, it was possible they could snatch Kenzie and Cavanaugh and return home tonight. "Do you know what other clubs Molly visits?"

"No, I've only seen her at the Rainbow Corner Club. Sorry. If I see her again, I'll let her know you're looking for her."

David held up his hand in a stop gesture. The lieutenant flinched. "Sorry." David lowered his hand. He had to squelch the idea. He didn't want Kenzie to know who he was until he was ready to make his move. The introduction had to be on his terms. "If you tell her, the news will ruin my surprise. I'd be grateful if you would leave a message here at the desk."

The lieutenant commented with raised eyebrows. He butted his cigarette in the ashtray and smashed it against the side several times more than necessary. He obviously needed an explanation, or he would charge off to rescue a damsel in distress.

David took a bold step out onto a ledge, hoping it would support the weight of his lies. He lowered his head slightly and sighed. "The last time we saw each other, we didn't part under the best of circumstances. She might still be miffed with me. But family is family, and ye' can't pick and choose who ye're related to."

The lieutenant chuckled. "I've got a few family members I'd like to disown. I'll keep quiet, then. She'll show up again. She likes being with people. You can tell."

The man who had first seen Kenzie's picture scurried across the crowded lobby to join them. "I just heard from a reporter who was at Claridge's last night that a young woman with red hair insulted a major general and told him he was a disgrace to the U.S. Military Academy."

Nobody moved for the span of several heartbeats.

Colors in the room became murky, and David clenched and unclenched his fists. If Kenzie told off a major general, David might have to break her out of the stockade before he could take her home.

Jack slapped David on the shoulder, laughing. "If that was Kenzie, it's a good thing your cousin's not a soldier, or we'd be visiting her in the stockade."

The colors in the room shimmered bit by bit back into coherence. Jack was right. In this day and time, Kenzie wasn't a soldier. A civilian could unwisely insult a general without fear of repercussions. Maybe that's why she'd spouted off, because she knew she could get away with it. But why? The woman had been somewhat of a mystery since the first time he had heard her name. And from the current reports, she was holding true to form.

"Did the reporter happen to mention why she insulted him?" David asked.

"The general made a comment about the date of the invasion."

"How'd he know?" Jack asked.

"I heard he's a friend of Eisenhower's."

Jack chuckled. "I bet he's not a friend today."

"That's just it," the reporter said. "Eisenhower busted him in rank and sent him stateside. That redhead is somewhat of a legend today."

David's ulcer picked that moment to act up and turned into a three-alarm fire.

Jack took possession of the proffered room keys from Neil. "If you hear any more news about our mysterious redhead, please leave a message with the desk clerk."

David shouldered his duffle bags and thought of one last question. "Where's the best dancing tonight?"

"Check the Savoy," the lieutenant said.

David and Jack reached the lift in silence, and, other than confirming the appropriate button to push, kept their comments to themselves until they reached their adjoining rooms.

"What the hell is she up to?" Jack asked.

David tossed his duffles onto the bed. "From what I remember of Charlotte's trip back in time by herself, she didn't stay under the radar, so to speak, and neither did Kit. Time travelling to the past is empowering, because knowledge is empowering. But it's a false sense of empowerment. What yc' know of the future impacts yer decisions, and ye' can make bad choices. Charlotte's decision to rescue Ramseur at the Civil War Battle of Cedar Creek resulted in her capture by the Yankees."

"If she hadn't been captured, she wouldn't have been sent to rescue Braham, and he would have died."

"Not necessarily. She might have found her way to Richmond anyway. We'll never know."

Jack unlocked the adjoining door and tossed his bags into the room. "Are you sure the woman he was talking about was Kenzie? It doesn't sound like the woman we've investigated."

David stepped to the window and gazed down into a city that lay in total blackness. "The colonel didn't mention her joke-telling skills or that she loved to dance. Either he didn't think they were worth noting, or we've got the wrong woman. Only one way to find out."

Jack's mouth opened slightly and his eyes slightly more. "Go dancing?"

"Aye. Put on yer dancing shoes."

Jack's face split into a grin. "I don't know how to jitterbug, and Kenzie is your assignment, not mine."

David leaned against the windowsill, pursing his lips. "What will ye' be doing, then?"

Jack's blue eyes now glinted with humor. "Standing at the bar drinking beer with a pilot."

20

The Savoy, London, England, May 29, 1944

Kenzie had just finished a run of jokes when the waiter brought another bottle to their table in the Lancaster ballroom at the Savoy.

"We didn't order this," Cav said, "but since it's here, we'll drink it."

"Compliments of the gentlemen sitting behind you," the waiter said.

Kenzie turned to see two extremely handsome men, one was blond with green eyes, and the other was a dark-haired, brown-eyed regiment officer with the Royal Scots Greys, dressed in a black Stewart tartan and a civilian dinner jacket.

Kenzie had met a few Royal Scots Dragoon Guards during her deployments. One night she'd been offered free beer by a couple of them. After a few drinks, she asked about the history of the regiment. Not that she cared, but after all the beer, she feigned interest. An hour's explanation boiled down to the fact that The Royal Scots Greys were amalgamated with the 3rd Carabiniers in the 1970's, and the formation was christened The Royal Scots Dragoon Guards. She tucked the information away in a mental cubbyhole and never drank beer with them again.

She glanced away, surprised by the intensity of the look in the soldier's whiskey eyes. It lasered through her skin, her muscles, straight to her heart. She took a deep breath and said, "Thank you."

"We're enjoying your jokes and didn't want you to quit," the blond said with a strong Southern accent, one she'd heard often when her father was stationed in Washington, D.C. Molly had commented earlier that American men in London were either soldiers, reporters, or businessmen, all with money they were eager to spend. So far, Molly's assessment proved true.

"Join us for a glass," Molly said.

Kenzie wanted to kick her under the table. The four of them had been getting along famously, and they were no longer asking her perilous get-to-know-you questions. Introducing two more men into the mix would invariably lead to those kinds of questions. Superficial but intrusive. She didn't want to tell more lies, and was afraid she wouldn't remember a past lie and answer the same question with a new one. A slow, pounding headache sprang to throbbing life in her temples.

Cav put a possessive arm around her shoulders. "Bring your chairs and we'll make room."

The Dragoon squeezed his chair in next to Kenzie, and she became aware of his wide shoulders and his scent, a combination of soap and tension, and oddly, sawdust—which reminded her of a neighbor's woodshop where she spent delightful hours as a child making small objects with cedar shavings. The fresh soap smell was also familiar, yet hard to place.

As soon as they were all settled, Jack Mallory introduced himself and his friend Major David McBain. Then the waiter popped the cork and filled six glasses.

"To the end of the war," Jack said.

After clinking glasses, Kenzie started in on another joke, not wanting to give them time to ask where she was from and why she was in London.

"A pilot has engine trouble," she began, "and lands in a field. As he walks around the plane to check out the problem, he hears a voice behind him say, 'You have a clogged fuel line.' Looking around, he sees only a cow. Startled, he runs across the field to the farmer's house and pounds on the door. When the farmer appears, the out-of-breath pilot stammers that his cow has just talked—and even tried to explain what was wrong with the airplane.

"The farmer drawled, 'Was it a brown cow with a white patch on its forehead?' The pilot says, 'Yes, yes, that's the one.' The farmer says—' "

Something flickered deep in McBain's eyes before he said, "That's okay, it's just Flossie. She knows nothin' about aeroplanes."

Kenzie gave a tight smile that did little more than bare her teeth. She didn't care that people told her punch lines. It so rarely happened. But McBain's Scottish accent grated on her nerves. Not the sound, but the fact that it originated in Scotland.

Scotland? Wasn't that where she intended to go? If she could put her prejudices and hurt feelings aside long enough to talk to him, she might be able to find out where wills and inventories were kept. That would give her a head start in her search for the origins of her mysterious brooch. If the records were held at local parishes, she could start in Inverness, where her mother was from, then spread out from there.

Was she capable of putting her prejudices and hurt feelings aside, though? If she wanted to find a way home, then yes. She would put on big-girl panties and do just that. It might be like scratching fingernails on a chalkboard, but she could do it. She'd done much worse and survived.

Molly clapped her hands. "You're the first person to tell the punch line of one of her jokes. Tell another one, Kenzie. See if he can do it again."

Cav refilled her glass. She twirled the crystal champagne flute, studying the bubbles for a moment, then took a big gulp, reviewing her repertoire of riddles. It took two smaller sips to come up with one.

"Here's a riddle. 'I have two arms, but fingers none. I have two feet, but cannot run. I carry well, but I have found I carry best with my feet off the ground. What am I?' "

"Two arms?" Molly asked.

"And two feet," Rainer said.

McBain contemplated Kenzie as he sat back in his chair. Then one brow quirked up. "A wheelbarrow?" He didn't change expression, but something nameless passed between the two of them.

Kenzie turned her back to McBain, facing Cav, and pointed over her shoulder. "I bet he's heard *all* my material. Let's dance."

Cav stood, and McBain followed suit, saying, "I won't tell any more of yer punch lines if ye'll dance with me." His arms were relaxed at his sides and his voice sounded like the comment was bantering, but the tension around his eyes told a different story.

Then Jack shot a hot glance at McBain. Was it a curious reaction to his seemingly impulsive gesture? If so, Jack wasn't the only one reacting. There was a tensing in her own chest, and Cav jerked his head in McBain's direction, pressing his lips flat. McBain was a soldier, and didn't seem the type to do anything impulsively. So what was the deal? Was he testing Cav, and if so, why?

She found McBain unsettling…and Jack, too, especially the way his mouth quirked up at the corners. His face was familiar. Like McBain's scent, the familiarity of Jack's smile was as ephemeral as a moonbeam.

Not that she'd tried to catch any moonbeams lately. But she had spent childhood summer nights with her mother, enjoying the garden while balmy breezes heavy with the scent of night blooming flowers cooled off the heat of the day. They had caught twinkling fireflies and attempted to bottle moonbeams. And when they failed, they laughed and hugged and tried again.

Damn fog and the chemical it contained that continued to play havoc with her memories and emotions.

She summoned up a polite smile for McBain. "I'll put your name on my dance card." Then she linked her fingers with Cav's. "Come on. Let's jitterbug on this famous oak parquet floor."

"I didn't know it was famous." Cav threaded a path around the tables, leading her toward the dance floor.

"It will be after we dance on it." The buzz of war swarmed in an ever-increasing expectation of an invasion of Europe. She kept walking, holding her secrets close, and the truth even closer.

Cav swung her onto the dance floor to the music of Benny Goodman's "Swingtime in the Rockies."

They sidestepped to the music until they got their footing, and then added side bumps, spin bumps, and turns. The spotlights hit the green of her dress, and it shimmered as it inched up her legs every time Cav spun her around. Dancing and music filled her soul, and she shoved fears and concerns into a closet, locked the door, and tossed the key, if only for a few hours.

After a half dozen Glenn Miller and Benny Goodman songs, her head was spinning from the combination of a sexy dance partner with ultra-smooth moves and several glasses of champagne.

"I need a break," Cav said. "Do you want to dance with Major McBain or take a rest?"

"I'll keep dancing. You'll come right back, won't you?"

"I'm just going to the men's room," he said.

She caught McBain's eye and waved for him to join her on the dance floor. Dancing with him would give her a chance to ask about Scotland. A look of restrained surprise crossed his face.

Cav kissed the back of her hand before stepping back and allowing McBain to take his place. "I'll be right back."

"Take yer time." David slid his sporran over to his hip, out of Kenzie's way, before spinning her around.

Her ears perked up. She was a military brat and a soldier, used to hearing and taking orders. McBain had merely said, "Take yer time" in a joking sort of way, but to her ears, the words had been delivered as an order. How had Cav heard them?

McBain's intense energy was evident even in his hands. Where Cav's were long and slender, McBain's were big and powerful and slightly warm to the touch. She gazed up into his eyes and nearly passed out from the raw need she saw there. He wrapped her in an embrace as startling as it was comforting. No, there was nothing comforting about it. The combination of animal magnetism and alcohol reached an almost orgasmic level.

"I need air." She gasped and fanned her face. Her body was betraying her.

Was?

Who was she kidding? She had been invaded by aliens. She could out-drink and out-dance almost everyone she knew, but the fog had turned her into a wimp. If she didn't get home soon, there would be nothing left of the woman who had just run the Tough Guy Marathon.

McBain parted the crowd saying, "Step aside," and led her to an alcove with an open window behind a blackout curtain. She lifted the fabric. With the breeze came a soft expulsion of a pent-up breath that seemed to take forever to leave her body. She sat on the ledge and opened the top button of her blouse before passing her palm across her sweaty forehead.

"Sorry about that. Too much champagne and fast dancing."

He handed over his handkerchief. "Use this."

She didn't bother checking to see if it was clean; of course it was. "Thank you." She folded the creased and monogrammed handkerchief before returning it. "What do the Ms stand for? One's for McBain, right?"

He slipped the folded square back into his breast pocket as neatly as it had been before he took it out, taking his time, and she wondered if he intended to ignore the question. Finally, he said, "MacKlenna. The handkerchief was a gift from a friend who didn't know I dropped the name from my signature years ago."

"MacKlenna, huh? Sounds familiar. Is it a family name?"

"My grandmother was a MacKlenna."

The name rambled round her brain, searching for trailing ends of a severed memory. The memory loss was becoming more than annoying. "I don't know where I've heard it before."

"Do ye' enjoy horse racing? That's what the family is known for."

"I love to ride, and enjoy the track, too. Although I have a strict rule when it comes to betting. I only place money on horses that normally come in last."

He pressed his palm flat against the wall slightly above her head. The fresh scent she had noticed earlier was still there, but it was now layered with musk. He sidled up beside her. "Sounds like ye're a risk taker."

She finger-combed her damp hair away from her face while her heart lurched in a ramshackle rhythm. How could he have pinned the tail on that donkey so quickly? She had only just met him and, as far as she remembered, she hadn't said anything about running, climbing, or investing.

"I've been known to take a few," she said.

He leveled a steady look at her while a taut smile played on his lips. "I have a buddy who can pick the winner of nine out of ten races. I've asked him how he does it. He's explained his process. It doesn't work for me. I believe it's magic the lad has, and the horses talk to him."

"You believe in magic, then?"

"Gaelic is a magical language."

She came up off the window ledge, bumping his arm, but he didn't step back. The inscription was written in Gaelic. Was it possible the secret to returning home was hidden in the words? She softened her voice to control the rising excitement. "Do you speak the language?"

"Aye."

There was an awkward silence as she considered how to broach the question.

"Come, I'll take ye' back to the table. Yer pilot will be looking for ye."

She dug in her heels. "Wait. I need to ask you something." Outwardly he appeared unruffled, but a tic in his jaw gave him away. Her training told her to be wary and ease into her questions. After all, she didn't know if she could trust him. He was a Scotsman. She cocked her head, pursed her lips, and jumped in with both feet.

"Where in Scotland are you from?"

He squinted thoughtfully, as if mulling over the question, and said with a slight bit of hesitation, "Inverness."

She suppressed her shock by forcing a swallow to rid her throat of the thickness suddenly lodged there. "Y-you are?" she stammered through the word. He probably knew her mother's family. She wasn't sure if that was a good thing or bad. "Then you might know if the wills and inventories are kept in the parishes or sent to a central location."

"They're in the General Registry House in Edinburgh, and packed to the rafters. I've never done any genealogy research myself, but I know people who have. Is there anything in particular yer searching for?"

"Wills, mostly."

His eyes turned steely at the same moment a deep, Boston-accented voice said, "There you are."

She jumped and whirled around, arms raised defensively. "Jesus Christ, you scared me."

Cav held up his hands, guarding his chest, until she lowered hers. He glared at McBain and then softened his expression. "I've been looking for you. Another pilot said you left with a guy wearing a kilt."

She flinched at the iciness in his tone, but recovered quickly, refusing to sanction his jealousy. "I needed air. He was gracious enough to escort me to the closest window."

"Molly wants to go to the Covent Garden Opera House. She said the music is better there."

"Well, she knows the hot spots. Let's go."

Cav placed his hand beneath her elbow and escorted her back to the table where Molly, Rainer, and Jack were milling around their chairs. Kenzie collected her purse, glancing over at McBain. "You and Jack are welcome to join us."

McBain's movements were slow and deliberate, yet there was no tension. His chin and head were up and his back was straight. Cav, Jack, and Rainer were alpha males, but McBain was the top dog in this group. He reminded her of the Army Rangers she knew. There was no shortage of testosterone flowing through those veins. On the flip side, though, it was not all rainbows and vanilla ice cream with protective, loyal, and oversexed Rangers, and putting up with their idiosyncrasies was a test of one's patience. A test she had never taken. Too much work for a small return on investment.

"Thank ye', but we have other plans," he said. "We'll meet again, I'm sure."

She nodded, knowing it would never happen. He had given her two important pieces of information, and she now knew where to start her search. She also knew the key might be hidden in the brooch's inscription.

She extended her hand to him. "Thanks for the champagne."

He clasped his other hand over the top of their joined hands, and the sensation that had rocked her world earlier now scored a ten on the Richter scale. She withdrew her tingling fingers. "Good-bye, McBain."

Cav slipped her sweater over her shoulders, gently brushing her cheek with the back of his hand. "You ready, Kenzie?"

Jack flashed his familiar grin, and McBain nodded.

"Lead the way, flyboy," she said to Cav.

As she walked away from McBain and Jack, she experienced a breathtaking sense of emotional loss, as if she was about to be permanently separated from lifelong friends. She had no lifelong friends. So how could she possibly know what it felt like to lose them?

She cupped her elbows with her palms and tucked her arms inside the drape of her sweater. The remnants of the fog were messing with her mind again. How else could she explain lusting after a Scotsman? Was she lusting? If not, what would she call it? Cav and McBain were at opposite ends on the man-meter. How could she be simultaneously attracted to both? Was she? It seemed that way. But it wasn't a big deal. Not really. After tonight she'd never see either of them again.

On the way out of the Savoy, Cav said, "Rainer and I have to be on the train back to base by two o'clock. That gives us a couple of hours before we have to take you girls home."

"Then let's hurry. I don't want to waste a minute of the time we have left." Last night she would have said they shouldn't waste their last couple of hours dancing. But tonight she wasn't as eager to jump into bed for casual sex. Why? She didn't know, didn't intend to analyze it, but suspected it had something to do with McBain.

The Opera House was packed with soldiers and sailors and their dance partners. The pub had to be violating a fire code regulation to allow so many people jammed in together. If there was an air raid, only those closest to the exits would survive. Everyone else would be trampled. If the laughter was any indication, though, no one minded the crowd or the conditions.

Although his furlough was coming to end, Cav was smiling, too.

She found herself searching faces for Jack and McBain. What was it about those two that kept their names fresh on her mind? Fresh. That was it. McBain's clothes smelled like the Downy Unstopables she used in her wash. She stared off into the room, trying to puzzle it out.

He did *not* smell like Downy. That was impossible. It was a twenty-first century P&G product. If she wasn't convinced before, she was now. She had lost her mind in the fog, and her emotions and memories had become hopelessly entangled.

21

London, England, the Bradford Residence, May 29, 1944

TWO HOURS LATER, Kenzie stood on the Bradfords' front porch saying good night to Cav. Rainer had returned to the taxi, and Molly, after telling Kenzie to take her time, had gone inside the house.

"You have my address," Cav said. "Write when you can."

She looked at him, choking with gratitude while she tried to find words to express her appreciation. "It's been a wonderful two days. I'm so happy I met you."

He leaned forward, tall and easy. "I want to see you again, but I don't know when I'll get another leave."

"I don't know where I'll be. I probably won't stay in London." She was beginning to feel extremely uncomfortable about leading him on and making promises she couldn't keep.

He watched her now with a hooded expression. "If you return to Cambridge, I might have more luck slipping into the city for a few hours than getting a weekend pass." He removed his hat and threaded the brim through his fingers while gazing into her eyes. "The last forty-eight hours have been very special."

"I'm so glad you pulled me onto the dance floor. I would have turned you down if you had asked."

His chest rose as he took a deep breath. "I've always been known to go after what I want."

"Has it ever gotten you into trouble?"

He hung his hat on the edge of the porch railing and pulled her toward him. "I don't know. You tell me." He lowered his face to hers. The kiss started with a brief touching of their lips, but his mouth was soft and warm, and she moved instinctively against him. He skimmed the backs of his fingers over the exposed skin of her neck, erotically tickling her. She wanted him to stop and prayed that he wouldn't.

She whispered against his lips. "You're not in trouble, yet." His late-night beard stubble rasped her cheek, but she didn't care.

He threaded his hands up underneath her hair and cradled her head. The tips of his strong fingers massaged her scalp in seductive circles. This man knew how to please a woman. The kiss lingered, and he caressed her lips lightly with his tongue until a throat-clearing from the taxi interrupted them.

He pulled away slowly, stroking her hair and along her jawline with a light, gentle touch, "I'd better go." Instead of going, he hugged her waist and pulled her closer for one last kiss. Her mouth met his with equal demand. When he opened his eyes, they were full of regret.

He didn't want to leave, and she didn't want him to go.

He took her mouth again, and a faint moan escaped her. He was no longer gentle as he devoured her, ravenous against the curve of her throat and the flesh of her ear. Smooth palms grazed her arms, as if he thought she might be chilled, but the heat his hands generated made her feel anything but cold.

Another throat-clearing.

"I have to go. I don't want to lose future privileges and miss seeing you because I didn't return on time." He pressed his forehead against hers and slowed his breathing. "Go back to Cambridge. I'll get there as soon as I can."

"I'll write after I've made plans." She knew she wouldn't write, but she made the promise anyway. The only things soldiers and sailors had were memories and promises. She couldn't deny Cav either one after all he'd given her. "I've had a wonderful weekend. Thank you."

He set his hat on top of his head and straightened it, probably more from habit than need. "I'll see you again. That's a promise."

"I'll hold you to it, flyboy."

He smiled. "Good night, Kenzie."

She remained on the porch, stroking her tender bottom lip, until the taxi pulled away and disappeared. She turned to go inside and noticed a black car parked across the street. She didn't see anyone inside, and couldn't tell if it was the same car as the one from the night before. She shook her head, scolding herself for letting her imagination run rampant. The owner of the car likely lived there, and its presence wasn't sinister at all. Even as a child she had never feared shadows in the dark.

Why now?

Because for the first time in her life, she had *no* protection. No father. No classmates. No Army buddies. No one to protect her back. All she had was her training. And her training told her not to take anything for granted. Not an unidentifiable scent. Not a recognizable smile. And certainly not an unoccupied black sedan.

22

The Ritz, London, England, May 29, 1944

Jack rolled his jacket up in a ball and threw it on a chair in David's room. "What the hell was that about?"

They had agreed not to discuss Kenzie and Cavanaugh except in their rooms. There were too many war correspondents on every street corner and in every pub to risk letting their names slip, especially Kenzie's. Especially since her red hair was now famously associated with the insult to Major General Miller.

David shucked his jacket and unbuckled his sporran. "I don't know what yer talking about"

"*You don't?* Let me refresh your memory. You were all but screwing—"

"Don't be vulgar," David interrupted, digging through his duffle bag for a bottle of whiskey.

"*Vulgar.* Your behavior was vulgar. You were all but screwing her on the table in the ballroom."

David straightened quickly, feeling as if his heart had migrated up to his head where he could hear it pounding like a hammer hitting a crooked nail, over and over and over. "Don't be an arse." He closed his eyes to block out the visual, but that only made it more explicit.

Frowning, Jack said in a testy tone, "I've hit on enough women to know what it looks like. And, then you embarrassed the hell out of me when you stood up and said, "I won't tell any more of yer punch lines if ye' dance with me." Jack infused a tattle-tale voice with a Scottish inflection, imitating David remarkably well. "What the hell was *that* about?"

He snatched the whiskey bottle out of David's hand. "I need a drink." He poured a glass, gulped it down, and poured another. "What the hell did you do with David, and when are you returning him? Whoever you are, you aren't him."

Had he really acted like that? No, Jack had a history of embellishing. But David had to admit, the lass had turned him on, and that had surprised him. He overly prepared for everything he did, and Kenzie Wallis-Manning had figuratively sneaked up on him, grabbed his ballocks, and squeezed. He wouldn't be caught off guard again.

"We should switch assignments. You're too emotionally involved," Jack said.

"Even if I thought switching assignments was a good idea, I wouldn't do it. You're a reporter, and have the perfect cover to get onto Cavanaugh's base to interview him. Drag it out for a couple of days. Talk Kenzie up. See what he says, how he reacts. You're good at reading body language and facial clues."

"You've got credentials that allow you to go anywhere, including Cav's base. I don't trust you with Kenzie after tonight," Jack said.

"Nothing is going to happen." Now that he had found his Achilles heel, he would protect his vulnerable spot.

"Charlotte hurt you, and Kenzie can't be yours, either. Don't set yourself up for more pain."

David fell silent, staring at the floor for several moments before rousing himself. "Take the lecture and yer clothes and go to yer own room. I'm tired."

"Not only are you breaking all your own rules, but you're grumpier than hell. What's going on with you? You growled all the way back to the hotel."

"Nothing's going on." At least nothing a couple of antacids wouldn't cure.

"I haven't known you long, but I know you well. Either your ulcer's inflamed, or seeing Kenzie with another man pissed you off."

David took ten seconds to let his anger cool before he answered. "I don't have an ulcer, and why would it bother me to see Kenzie and Cavanaugh together?"

"I've seen the antacids, and you're hotter than a volcano about to erupt when you and Kenzie are within five feet of each other."

David plucked the whiskey bottle off the table. Right now he didn't care how much whisky irritated his stomach; let it fuel the fiery pain that matched his mood.

Jack grabbed for the bottle. "Don't drink that."

David swatted at Jack's hand. "Leave me alone."

"You told me Elliott disregarded doctor's orders and used alcohol and drugs to deal with his pain. You're trying to be just like him. Whiskey is destroying your stomach. Stop drinking it."

"You don't know what you're talking about."

"Go ahead. Deny it if you want to, but that won't cure you. You take your medication erratically and you drink too much caffeine and alcohol. Take your medicine and stay away from the whiskey, at least until we get Kenzie home. Then you can drink yourself back into the hospital."

David glowered at Jack. He hadn't told anyone about his stomach problems, not even Elliott.

"Kenzie needs you to be at the top of your game, and so do I."

"It was an outpatient procedure, and I'm fine. I'll make a deal with you," David said. "Play this straight. Don't do anything stupid that could get you locked up in jail or shot, and I'll lay off the alcohol."

"And caffeine," Jack said.

"And we don't mention it again," David said.

"Deal," Jack said. Then after pausing for a beat or two he said, "We should have taken them back to the future tonight and ended this. From what Molly said, Kenzie hasn't mentioned any family members other than a brother stationed in Anzio, of all places. It's possible her grandfather isn't even on her radar."

"Kenzie asked me if I spoke Gaelic and where I was from."

Jack's mouth dropped open in shock. "You didn't tell her, did you? She doesn't like Inverness or its people. If she can't trust you, we might as well go home right now."

"I couldn't lie. She'd see right through me."

Jack threw up his hands and collapsed into the nearest chair. "Damn. Since she's lying to everyone she meets, for sure she'd notice if someone lied to her. Is that what you're saying? So what did she want to know?"

"She asked if wills were kept at local parishes. I told her they were in the General Registry House in Edinburgh."

"Whose will is she looking for?"

David sat on the edge of the bed and removed his ghillie brogues and hose, and flopped back on the bed crosswise. "Cavanaugh showed up and I didn't get to ask."

"Do you suppose she's trying to find out where the brooch came from?"

David unbuttoned his shirt and pulled the shirttail free of the kilt. If Jack stopped talking for five minutes, David would fall asleep. "It's possible, but she could do that when she goes back home. Why take the time now?"

"You have to tell her who you are."

"The time's not right. There's a delicate balance here that we could easily upset."

Jack sat forward in his chair and pressed his hands on his thighs, elbows out. "You upset that balance tonight. I didn't see sparks flying between Kenzie and Cav, but I saw them between the two of you."

David rubbed his temples. The pounding was becoming noticeably worse. He needed to dig into his medical box. "I didn't notice."

"Of course you didn't. You were too busy trying to get into her pants."

"Don't be crude. Kenzie doesn't deserve it."

"You're right. She didn't do anything wrong." Jack sat back again and rested his head against the wall. "When Charlotte and Braham met, you couldn't be in the same room with them. They electrified the air. Kenzie and Cav didn't, but that doesn't mean it won't happen if we give them time…and *you* stay out of her way."

"If we told Kenzie we came for her and Cavanaugh, do you think she would take him home with her or leave him here?" David asked. He already knew the answer, but he wanted to hear Jack's opinion.

"Right now, she'd walk away. That's why we've got to give them time without interfering."

Sleep was pulling David under, stealing in to take him where he longed to go. "What do you propose?"

"We've got to get her closer to Cav so they can spend more time together. Cambridge is only about a half hour from his base, but I don't know if she would leave London."

"London has bombs. She won't stay…"

Jack stepped over to the bed and shook David's arm. "Wake up. We're not done."

"We'll bump into them tomorrow and…"

Jack shook him again. "Wake up and tell me how you propose to bump into them?"

"Stake out Molly's house. When they leave, we follow."

"Okay, but if you act like a dog chasing a bitch in heat, we're changing things up. Got it?"

David scrubbed his face with his hands and sat up. "Ye're not going to let me sleep. Are ye'?"

"Not until we work this out."

David crossed the room to the bathroom to brush his teeth and pour a glass of water. "How did ye' leave it with Cavanaugh?"

"I told him I'd be in Cambridge tomorrow or the next day and want to interview him for an article."

David stripped off his shirt and unbuckled the kilt. He tossed the tartan on the end of the bed and climbed in naked. "Do ye' have any research on the Ninety-First Bombardment Group?"

"Some, but I need his bomb squadron number."

"Didn't you see his patch? He's with the Three Hundred and Twenty-Fourth. Same as the Memphis Belle," David said.

"The Belle flew back home in 1943 to do bond tours."

David fluffed the pillow and rolled onto his side. "Search your database to see if Cavanaugh's name pops up."

"And if I find he was killed in action?"

"We'll save his arse."

Jack saluted the air with his drink glass. "Here's to changing history again."

"I don't like it any better than you do."

"From what I saw tonight, you like the mission just fine. So other than being turned on by Kenzie, what'd you think of her?"

David punched the pillow, trying to shape it for his head and neck. Sleep would come easily right now, but within an hour or two, he'd be up pacing the floor. "She's exactly what I expected."

"You lying son of a bitch. She blew you away. Admit it."

"She didn't...blow me away. Surprised me a wee bit. That's all."

"There's something sexy about the Forties style. Women are feminine. No jeans and T-shirts. Only dresses and nylon stockings."

"Ye' were hitting on Molly. Stay away from her. We don't need more complications."

Jack stood, gathered his jacket, and headed toward the connecting door. "She's beautiful and sexy, and I didn't get the impression she was serious about Rainer. I'll find out more when I go to Cambridge."

"Leave Molly alone. Managing Kenzie and Cavanaugh is going to be more than enough work."

Jack slung open the adjoining door. "I'll leave her alone if you leave Kenzie alone."

"My only interest in Kenzie is getting her home."

"Right. You keep on believing that." Jack hit the light switch, darkening the room. "You might regret not taking Kenzie and Cav home tonight. We could all go down in a blaze of glory."

David's eyelids slid shut, and he mumbled again, "God, I hope not."

23

London, England, the Bradford Residence, May 30, 1944

EARLY THE NEXT morning Kenzie was awakened by a knock at the door. Her eyes popped open to stare at ugly beige wallpaper with stripes and flowers. Why would she have walls covered in wallpaper as old as her grandmother? Well, if she had one. Where was she, anyway? She gripped her head, searching through the alcohol-induced confusion for the answer before whoever was knocking gave up waiting and barged in without an invitation.

There was no hollow, no indentation on the pillow next to hers. Good. She had slept alone. That eased her somewhat. Cav's face came to mind, along with the kiss they had shared, but why was he wearing a kilt?

McBain.

She squeezed a pillow over her face and attempted to end her suffering.

Another knock. More forceful this time. She tossed the pillow aside. Ending it all would have to wait until she faced whatever music awaited her.

"Come in." The words stuck on the roof of her pasty mouth. God, how many glasses of champagne had she guzzled? She needed water and ibuprofen, but doubted even a handful of pills would calm the team of lacrosse players celebrating in her head, thumping their sticks against her skull.

Molly opened the door and stuck her head in. "Are you awake?"

"I am now." Kenzie sat up. Big mistake. Her brain whirled, and the evening played in rewind mode. "You had just as much to drink as I did. Why are you so chipper?"

"I had a big dose of Uncle Clifford's elixir before I went to bed. If you hadn't stayed outside kissing Cav, I would have given you a swig. I don't know what Uncle puts in it, but I've never been hungover." Molly sat on the edge of the bed, very carefully. But even her petite body jostled both the mattress and Kenzie's head. "So how was it? Is Cav a good kisser? He's got the lips for it."

"Seriously?" Kenzie eased back down onto the bed, careful not to jar her head. "I feel like crap, and you wake me up, hoping I'll tell you about my make-out session. You're sick, Molly. Deeply, truly sick. I don't kiss and tell. Go away," she groaned. "Come back next week."

Molly patted Kenzie's shoulder, laughing. "You're funny even when you're hungover. Just tell me if he's a good kisser or not, and then I'll tell you *my* news."

"Yes, he is. Probably the best ever."

"I thought so. Was it just a good-bye kiss, or did he use his tongue?"

"Oh, gross. Go away."

"I wouldn't mind kissing that Jack Mallory. David was too serious for me, but Jack was…"

"*Molly.*" Kenzie was relieved her inquisitor had moved on, but fantasizing about multiple guys didn't seem to be Molly's forte. "Why are you thinking about other men? I thought you liked Rainer."

"Oh, I do, but I just met him this weekend."

Kenzie squeezed her eyes shut. Between her headache and Molly's enthusiasm and revelations, Kenzie's indiscretion the previous night didn't seem so…so inappropriate. "You acted like you had known him for a while. I just assumed…"

Molly stood and walked across the room, picking up Kenzie's discarded clothes, draping them over her arm.

Kenzie rose up on one wobbly elbow. "I'll do that."

Molly waved her off before opening the armoire. She hung up Kenzie's dress, then folded the sweater, turned inside out, and laid it on the dresser near the door. Near a suitcase that hadn't been there before. Or had it? The bedroom was furnished with beautiful antiques, but the Bradfords also used it for storage. Boxes filled every nook and cranny. It was possible Kenzie had missed it, but she didn't think so. She was a trained observer. And while she hadn't spent much time in the room, she'd spent enough. The luggage was definitely new, which meant Molly brought it in with her. A sudden rush of regret nearly staggered Kenzie. Her inappropriate behavior was getting her evicted from the Bradfords.

While Kenzie's brain was rambling on and pointing an accusatory finger, Molly said, "It's because of the war."

Kenzie backtracked through the conversation. What had she missed? "I'm sorry. What is?"

Molly set the tweed leather suitcase on top of a footstool and unsnapped the latches. "You know your time together is short. Dating customs have changed." She placed the sweater inside the suitcase.

I'm definitely getting evicted.

Kenzie hadn't had time to draft Plan B. Now it would have to happen on the fly.

"Before the war, girls dated a boy six months to a year before they kissed," Molly continued. "Now it happens much faster." She packed the trousers Kenzie purchased the day before neatly alongside the sweater. "You only met Cav two days ago, but last night you were kissing him like you'd never see him again."

I won't see him again.

"Before the war, you wouldn't have done that. That's what I mean. The war has changed us in so many ways." Molly added Kenzie's second pair of shoes to the suitcase. "It's eight-thirty. We need to hurry. You have an interview at noon, and we have to catch the ten o'clock train to Bletchley."

"Whoa. Wait a minute. We went from discussing social mores to catching a train to Bletchley for an interview. I'm hung over. I need a bit more transition time. Start at the beginning while I prop up my eyelids with toothpicks."

"*Eek*. Please don't do that."

Kenzie rolled her eyes, coming suddenly alert. "It's only a figure of speech. Would you tell me who is interviewing me, and what the job entails?"

"I called my boss yesterday morning and told him about you."

Kenzie stood up slowly and carefully, holding onto the bed post for support. "Why didn't you tell me?"

"I didn't want to disappoint you if he wasn't interested. Well, he is interested. Very interested. He just called and wants to interview you this afternoon. We can't be late. He's quite finicky."

"A job outside of London sounds perfect. I'll do anything. But I don't think I can get through security without identification."

Molly's eyes widened and color bleached from her face.

Oh, Jesus.

There's no way Kenzie should know about the high level of security at Bletchley, and the threat of being shot for treason that hung over every employee's head. "I mean…through an employer's application process. My identification card and passport were stolen. Remember?"

Molly visibly relaxed and a pink tinge returned to her cheeks. "I told him that, but he said if you impressed him, he would petition the American Embassy to expedite your replacement passport."

A job at Bletchley Park was the chance of a lifetime, and the facility was in the right direction—north. According to the train schedule she'd seen, a trip to Inverness would take eleven hours. Bletchley would be a fascinating place to spend a few days while devising a plan. It didn't require much soul-searching to know the closer she came to crossing the border into her mother's home country, the more she would be tempted to drag her feet. But she had never in her life given up on anything, and she wasn't about to start now.

Scotland would not defeat her.

24

King's Cross Station, London, England, May 30, 1944

TWO HOURS LATER, under a cloud-filled sky, the taxi dropped Kenzie and Molly at King's Cross for the fifty-mile train trip to Bletchley. From her prior research, she knew Bletchley Park was a Forties version of Silicon Valley. To work alongside the most gifted and quirky individuals of a generation would be a grand adventure. Heck, not only an adventure, but to play a part, albeit a very small one, in the work that would shape the coming computer age would be the equivalent of a runner's high, and an experience she would never be able to tell a soul, assuming she eventually found a way home.

Kenzie and Molly grabbed seats at the rear of the carriage and stowed their suitcases in the overhead bins. The luggage was a gift from Aunt Sylvia, and Kenzie felt awful for lying to the sweet woman, and being forced to continue lying to Molly. She had told so many lies in the last forty-eight hours that surely a path to hell was newly renamed Kenzie Lane.

"Hide your valuables in your pockets. You don't want to lose everything again."

The brooch was pinned to the waistband of her trousers. Her class ring and the Rubik's Cube were in one pocket, and the rest of her cash was in the other. As long as a robber didn't hold her up at gunpoint and demand she empty her pockets, her valuables were relatively safe. The keychain worried her, though. Its presence thirty years before its invention could mess with history, and she didn't want any part of that possibility. Leaving behind a trail of jokes was bad enough. Hopefully no one was writing them down.

Kenzie rested her head against the window and watched the people, mostly men in uniform, bustling by to catch one of the other trains leaving the station. A man in a leather jacket and tousled blond hair jogged by. She did a double-take. The man looked familiar. But it wasn't as if she knew a lot of people in the twentieth century. She craned her neck. It was Jack. It had to have been.

Tall, broad-shouldered, neatly trimmed blond hair—styled hair. Not a barbershop cut. Nicely dressed in quality clothes without stains or frayed edges. New shoes. Not scuffed and worn. Breeding, manners, wealthy, but understated. Easy on the eyes with a voice that would melt ice cream at a Sunday social. And a smile…A familiar smile? And that familiar smile she couldn't place was driving her nuts. She must have seen a picture of him in a book or an article. Usually, if she couldn't solve a puzzle or problem, the solution came during sleep, but not this one. It was like an apple on a branch too high to reach. She could see it, imagine its taste, but it remained frustratingly out of reach.

Answer that question, and she might get closer to the apple.

Okay. It was a genuine smile. Not plastered on, but full of spontaneity and sex appeal with a trace of mystery. That didn't help. What about McBain? Was there anything special about him, other than his Scottish accent? An inch taller than Mallory, probably six one or two. A random strand of gray in his chestnut-colored, short-cropped hair. Smoldering, whiskey brown eyes.

Smoldering? Really?

Okay, so she *had* noticed. How could she not? He had put his hand on the wall over her head and canted toward her. Close enough that she could inhale his musky scent and the whiskey on his breath. Close enough to notice his starched white shirt had no frayed collar or sleeves. That his ghillie brogues were made of supple leather, polished to a spit-shine, and the mink sporran—yes, mink—had a fine sterling silver cantle and chains. Like Jack, McBain came from family and breeding. But she couldn't forget the one label that tagged him unacceptable—Scottish.

Molly nudged her arm. "What are you looking at?"

"I think your friend Jack just walked by. All I saw was the back of his head, but he has memorable hair."

Molly almost fell into Kenzie's lap peering out the window. "Where?"

"He's gone now."

Molly grabbed hold of the window latch to steady herself, her cheeks flushing with excitement. "Which train did he catch?"

Kenzie shrugged. "I don't know."

"Hmm." Molly nibbled on her lower lip while she drifted back to her seat with her forehead pinched in thought. "Jack mentioned doing a story on Cav and Rainer. I wonder if he boarded the train to Cambridge. Was David with him?"

"I didn't see him."

"Jack said David was an intelligence officer with the Royal Scots Greys on special assignment. Did he say anything to you about where he was assigned?"

Kenzie shook her head. "Nope."

"Do you think we'll ever see them again?"

The casual question caught in Kenzie's throat with a sudden unexpectedness. "Probably not." She had met five people she enjoyed spending time with, but her entire life had been full of hellos and good-byes, and that wasn't likely to change.

Kenzie clutched her brow and must have moaned, for Molly turned and asked, "Is something wrong?"

"No, nothing," Kenzie said, "But I am curious. Are you interested in Jack?"

Molly raised her brows, obviously finding the notion intriguing. Evidently, it wasn't quite as insane as it sounded. "He's handsome and funny. I would go to dinner with him if he asked."

"What about Rainer?"

"Rainer's only interested in a dinner and dancing partner. After the war, he'll probably go home and marry an old girlfriend."

"Does he have one?"

A subtle flicker of amusement appeared in Molly's eyes. "He's a handsome man from a large family in Chicago. I'm sure he has more than one girl waiting for his return."

Kenzie was silent for a moment, thinking through what Molly had said. Something about the story rang a bell for Kenzie, but why? She shrugged it off.

"I didn't think you were looking for a husband."

"I'm not. And neither am I staying home waiting for a flyboy to receive a twenty-four-hour pass. A reporter like Jack has more flexibility. I like to go to the pubs and dance. If he asks me, I'll go."

The train jolted and trundled out of the station at a crawl, past water towers and small houses on cul-de-sacs with their backs turned in at odd angles to the track. Molly buried herself in the morning newspaper and mumbled incoherent comments as she rustled the pages, turning them at a speed-reader's pace.

The train swayed around a bend, and Kenzie wondered where Jack's train was, and where he was going on a Sunday morning. No, that wasn't true. She wasn't thinking about Jack. While the carriage rocked in a comforting rhythm of wheels on the track, side to side, she thought about Cav. If she was offered a position at Bletchley, she could see him again. If she did, did she want more than a serious lip-lock?

You mean sex?

She glanced up as soon as she heard Trey's voice, or imagined his voice. They had similar conversations while at West Point, and he usually talked her down off the ledge when she got excited about a guy's attention. "He just wants sex," Trey would say. "Is that what you want? Do you want him talking to his buddies? If not, stay away from him."

As hot as she had been for Cav over the weekend, the answer to whether she'd sleep with him or not should be a resounding yes, but now it wasn't. The aftereffects of the fog must have worn off.

The train picked up speed, the noise changing from a rattle to a rumble. And her thoughts became more disturbing. What about

McBain? He was a soldier in a war that wouldn't end in Europe for another year. The odds of them ever being in the same place again could be measured on the slim to none scale. For the last twelve hours, though, even in her sleep, she had been trying to understand why he disturbed her. Now she knew. When he looked at her, it wasn't her eyes, or face, or mouth he focused on. Instead, his gaze zeroed in on her heart, as if, like the answer to the punch line, he already knew all the surface stuff and wanted to get to the real Kenzie.

Kenzie, on the other hand, wanted to stick to the surface stuff. While they stood in the alcove, she had wanted to see beneath the wool of his jacket and the cotton of his shirt to the hard planes of his body, to his lightly furred chest. She knew it would be furred, and not because she was intuitive, but because McBain had an overload of testosterone.

The man was simply lethal.

25

Train to Bletchley Park, England, May 30, 1944

THE MILES PASSED quickly, but it wasn't until the train slowed while it clacked over the points in the track that Kenzie became aware of the Buckinghamshire countryside. If first impressions mattered, Bletchley in the Forties was a dump. The railway station was scruffy, and what she could see of the town held no promise either. The station teemed with activity, though. The platforms were crowded with travelers, mostly in uniform, waiting on trains heading west to Oxford and east to Cambridge, or to bases scattered near those cities.

She considered bypassing Bletchley altogether and going straight north. But she needed to take baby steps before she—you know—went to that *other* country. Bletchley was a good stopping point. She only needed a few more days, a week maybe, to further acclimate to her new reality. Thank goodness her emotions had leveled off. Those first twenty-four hours had been insane.

Molly nudged Kenzie's arm. "This is our stop."

Kenzie grabbed her bag from the overhead bin and followed Molly to the exit. The tangy smell of the town's chief industry, the manufacture of bricks, permeated even the inside of the carriage and hung heavily in the air. The stink didn't bode well for an extended stay at Bletchley.

They descended from the train and staggered up a rutted, narrow path toward an eight-foot-high chained fence topped by a roll of barbed wire. Kenzie's scratched shoulder still stung from contact with barbed wire during the marathon. After scrutinizing Bletchley's security, she decided she'd have to be running for her life before she would attempt to scale the Park's formidable fence.

Molly proffered her identification to one of the two guards. She pointed at Kenzie with her thumb. "Miss Wallis-Manning has an interview with Commander Travis. He's expecting her"—she glanced at her watch—"in five minutes."

"I need your identification card," he said to Kenzie, extending a disfigured hand. The scarring and finger contractures were probably from a burn, and likely a war injury.

"I'm Kenzie Wallis-Manning. My identification was stolen." If guilt from lying showed on her face, the guard would not let her through the gate.

Molly squared her shoulders and took a step forward. "I explained Miss Wallis-Manning's situation to Commander Travis. He said to come anyway. Call him. He'll tell you."

"I intend to." Kenzie's skin crawled from the guard's visual inspection of her. "Wait here." The guard entered the security hut and placed a phone call while the second guard stood in front of the gate with his rifle shouldered.

Kenzie's knowledge of Commander Travis, the operational head of Bletchley Park, was limited to a letter Alan Turing had written to Churchill, essentially going over Travis' head. In the letter, Turing complained that the work at Bletchley couldn't be done because of staff shortages, but he hadn't blamed Travis. According to her research, Churchill responded by directing his principal staff officer to see to it that Bletchley Park had all the staff it needed. Maybe they needed one more member—her.

The security guard returned and opened the gate. "Commander Travis is waiting for Miss Wallis-Manning at the house. Go directly there."

As soon as they passed through the gate and were out of earshot, Kenzie asked, "What'd you tell Commander Travis about me?"

Molly fixed her with a direct look. "I told him you were smashing and multilingual, and that he'd be utterly astonished by you"

Kenzie couldn't stifle her snickers. "Astonished?"

"Well, *I* was," Molly said. "Look at you. You're beautiful and funny and…" She trailed off, palms up with a helpless look, then dropped her hands. "Men simply adore you."

"The commander's not looking for a dance partner. So I don't think he'll care about my looks or sense of humor. There's a war going on, and he'll be suspicious of a woman who speaks German and Japanese and can't document her qualifications, experience, *or* national origin."

Molly linked her arm with Kenzie's. "He was suspicious, and getting you an interview wasn't easy, but I managed it."

Molly knew how to get things done in a bulldozer sort of way. From the moment Kenzie met her in the ladies' loom at the Rainbow Corner Club, Molly had barreled cheerfully through Kenzie's resistance and hesitation. Not one of Kenzie's acquaintances had ever done that before. So why now? Her charm? The situation? Or the fish out of water syndrome? It didn't matter. Kenzie wouldn't be around much longer.

They skirted potholes and followed the driveway to an eclectic redbrick mansion resembling many of the overblown Victorian villas dotting England's landscape. But this one, with its impressive array of parapets and tall chimney stacks, and a copper cupola awkwardly jammed on to one side of the house's roof, was unique among them all for the ultra-secret work that went on inside, work that would contribute significantly to the Allied victory.

The grounds continued well past the mansion, with acres of meadows dotted with dozens of Spartan-looking, single-story wood huts with chimneys coughing out thick, inky smoke. From Kenzie's twenty-first century tour of Bletchley, she knew most of the huts didn't survive after the war ended, but the museum of the future had diagrams and pictures of the way the property had been laid out.

How odd to think of Bletchley Park as a future tourist attraction, when armed guards stood at the gates, and men and women told their families and friends they worked at a radio factory. Those same men and women, dressed in civilian clothing, emerged from every nook and cranny. She paused to watch them. Expressions lightened within moments of stepping out into the fresh air and away from the huts' smoky interiors. Was it the air? Or was it being free of the stress, if only temporarily?

"Hurry, we're going to be late." Molly tugged on Kenzie's arm, almost dragging her through a vaulted, Gothic-style inner porch into a dark entrance passage with paneled walls and ceiling. To the right was a three-bay arcade with polygonal columns of gray marble that opened into a lounge hall with a stone and marble chimneypiece and paned glass roof, and to the left was the commander's office. Kenzie would soon discover how accurately the room had been restored.

She made the turn toward the office, but Molly pulled her back. "Wait a minute. I need to tell you something. I might have embellished your qualifications."

Kenzie's heart fell like a stone, thudding into her stomach. She wouldn't get to meet Turing after all, but she could catch a train north and get on with her business. "Might? Like what exactly?"

Molly chewed on the tip of her fingernail. "I knew if the commander took the time to meet you, he'd offer you a position, so I told him you came from a military family and were a personal friend of Eleanor Roosevelt."

I wonder what time the next train departs for Scotland.

"I'm getting out of here," Kenzie said.

Molly pulled her over to the corner. "I've seen you with people. You always know what to say. You'll easily handle the commander. Tell him I exaggerated slightly, and that you're not a personal friend of the First Lady, but you have friends who are friends."

Kenzie didn't personally know Eleanor Roosevelt, but she felt like she did. The Eleanor Roosevelt National Historic Site was only two miles from West Point. On spring and fall afternoons she used to run there and sit near the gardens and study. She was inspired by the former First Lady, and read everything she had ever written. Maybe she didn't *personally* know Mrs. Roosevelt, but she knew enough to win a First Lady category in *Jeopardy*.

As for a long family military history, it extended only to her and her father. She could lie about her father's military record and say he served valiantly during World War I, but right now there was too much at stake to create a viable backstory for him. She'd already lied about a brother, so she'd stick with that one.

Molly led the way down a hall with decorative plaster ceilings. "I couldn't sleep peacefully in this house. Could you?"

Kenzie rolled her eyes. "Not my taste at all."

Molly knocked on an open door, and they peeked into the room to find a man with a bulldog face behind a nondescript brown desk that looked as if it had come straight from surplus. He waved for her to enter. "Come in."

They set their suitcases near the door and walked across the threshold and into a sparsely furnished office with green carpet. The view of the lawn and lake from a bay window upped the value of his piece of real estate. It was a perfect location to watch the comings and goings of Bletchley employees. He had probably watched her and Molly approach the house.

The man came round the desk and greeted Molly first. Then to Kenzie he said. "Miss Wallis-Manning, Miss Bradford insisted I interview you. Please have a seat."

"Thank you for agreeing to meet with me. I know Molly can be persistent," Kenzie said.

The commander made a choked sound that could have passed for a laugh. He gestured abruptly toward a straight-backed chair stationed at the side of the desk, probably the most uncomfortable chair in the room. "She insisted I hire you before you accepted other employment. Are you as talented as she said?"

Molly backed out of the room. "I'll be outside."

Kenzie sat and straightened her skirt. "I'm sure Molly was fair in her appraisal." The tension that had been running though Kenzie's veins since they disembarked the train snapped like a cut wire, and she breathed easier. She had been through intense, competitive interviews before she was accepted into the joint J.D. / L.L.M. program. This would be a cakewalk in comparison.

The commander collected a pen and notebook and turned to face her. "I understand your identification was stolen on the train from Cambridge. How did that happen?"

Kenzie nearly shrugged, but caught herself. The commander expected a confident, intelligent woman, not one with a lackadaisical attitude that had resulted in a theft of her belongings. "Exigent circumstances. I left my case unattended while I went to the ladies' room. I was only gone a minute, but that was enough time for another passenger to abscond with my belongings. I told the porter, and he reported the theft to the station master."

The commander sat back in his chair and tapped his pen on the notepad while he studied her. "Did you apply for a replacement passport at the American Embassy?"

"That's on my list for tomorrow."

"Miss Bradford said you speak several languages. German, for one. Can you also read German?"

"Yes, sir. Along with Italian and Japanese, and a smidgen of Russian. I understand more of that language than I can speak."

His peaked brows made his bulldog face look more owlish. "That's a curious combination. Why'd you study those particular ones?"

What lie was she going to tell now? The commander's eyes held steady on her face. Whatever it was, it had to be convincing. Being an amateur standup comedian had taught her to be fast on her feet mentally, and after years of performing for her friends, telling stories came naturally. Now, lies were rolling off her tongue with the same easy stride. If she could stick to the basic truths, like the basic formula for a joke, she could embellish to make a lie relevant.

"My father dragged me to those countries. I didn't have anything else to do, so I studied the language. I'm a quick learner."

"What kind of business was he in?"

"He wouldn't discuss it, but I suspect he was spying for the American government." That wasn't too far-fetched. She had often thought as a teenager that her father's role in the Army was more clandestine than he wanted her to believe.

The commander gave her a look that strongly suggested he was reserving his opinion. "Do you think he's still spying?"

"He's been dead for ten years."

"What about your brother?"

"Brother." Her breath hitched on the word. She forced tears to her eyes to cover for her forgetfulness. Occasionally, her acting skills trumped her comedic skills. But fortunately neither trumped her warrior skills. Those were still expertly honed. "He's at Anzio. I haven't heard from him in weeks. Of course, even if he wrote, he wouldn't know where to send the letter."

"Did he travel with your father, too?"

"Not as much. He was in school."

The commander gave her a level look and then said tightly, "Do you know what we do here?"

She tilted her head slightly. "Make radios?" His expression didn't change, but his eyes darkened, and sudden goose flesh ran up her arms, lifting the fine hairs. She leaned forward in her seat with her fingers laced and resting on her knees. "I think it's unlikely, though, that Churchill would send a prized cryptologist to babysit a radio factory."

The commander looked surprised and rubbed a knobby knuckle beneath his nose. "You're perceptive."

"I don't know about that, but I am well read."

He opened his desk drawer and removed a sheet of paper. "Then read this."

She accepted a typed sheet of stationary, noticing the Royal Coat of Arms of the United Kingdom. "Is this something you want me to translate?"

"No. Just read it."

Kenzie scanned the document, recognizing it as the Official Secrets Act required of all people in the UK working with sensitive information. She'd seen copies of signed forms, and had thought it was silly that people had to sign a document promising to uphold the law.

She read the heading out loud, "*An Act to Amend Section Six of the*

Official Secrets Act 1920." She lowered her hands and the paper creased slightly in her lap. "I could debate the necessity of signing this amendment. It's the law of the land, not a contract between a signatory and the Crown."

"It will serve as a reminder that you agreed to abide by the restrictions of the Act."

"So you can't sue me for breach of contract, but you can shoot me for violating its provisions. Is that it?"

He stood and gripped his hands behind his back. "More or less."

She picked up the pen and scribbled her name. The K and Z in Kenzie, the W and Ls in Wallis, and the M and G in Manning were the only legible letters. It wasn't her usual signature. Evidence of her passing through couldn't remain in the twentieth century. From here on, she'd be backtracking at the end of each day to erase what she had done, like someone brushing away footprints in the sand.

She slid the paper across the desk. "Now if I talk, you can shoot me. What's next?"

He slipped the paper into the top middle drawer. "Your next interview is with one of our cryptologists. Miss Bradford will escort you to Block D."

It sounded more like a prison than a top-secret codebreaking center, and was probably just as restrictive. If that was the case, she was taking the next train to Edinburgh. If common sense prevailed, she'd be on the next train regardless, but her common sense seemed to be suffering from the same lapses as her memory. Everything was off kilter. She was a trained soldier. But you wouldn't know it from the way she was behaving toward superior officers.

The commander gestured for her to follow him to the door. As she passed the closed window, the faint scent of sweet, robust pipe tobacco wafted through the air, mixing with the smell of the messy and inefficient coal-burning fireplace. Unless the smoker was hiding behind the bulky curtains, the smoke had to be coming through the walls. She sniffed again to be sure her senses weren't deluding her. Someone was definitely smoking a pipe nearby.

The commander opened the door and Molly hopped to attention. "Escort Miss Wallis-Manning to Block D."

Molly appeared mildly surprised at the request. "Block D?"

"Nothing is wrong with your hearing, Miss Bradford. Good day." The commander shut the door, and the click of the latch resounded in the hall. Kenzie put her ear to the door, but no words passed through the thick wood paneling.

Molly grabbed Kenzie's arm, pulling her away from the door. "What are you doing?"

Kenzie kept her eyes riveted on the door, wishing she had X-ray vision. "I smelled pipe smoke, but no one else was in the room. I want to know if someone's there now."

Dragging Kenzie away from the door, she said, "Someone was probably smoking outside the window. Smoke rises, you know."

"The windows were closed. The smoke didn't come from outside."

Molly whispered. "I don't care where it came from. We're not going to spy on the commander. Let's get out of here."

Reluctantly, Kenzie picked up her suitcase and followed Molly toward the front door.

"Why would someone want to spy on you?"

That was good question, and one she couldn't answer. "Maybe they were spying on the commander."

Molly laughed in spite of her obvious agitation. "I think your discussion with Uncle Clifford at breakfast has you seeing spies in the shadows."

"Not only shadows, but street corners and parked cars. But even if I'm imagining spies in the shadows, someone was definitely smoking somewhere." Kenzie tugged at her bottom lip, thinking. "My guess is that it was Colonel Mustard in the conservatory with the candlestick."

Molly opened the front door and stood aside while four women entered the house. Molly made quick introductions, promised to meet the women later at the café, and then ushered Kenzie out of the mansion.

"Your Colonel Mustard with the candlestick sounds similar to the game *Murder*. Londoners like to play it during long air-raid drills. I've never played, but I've heard it's fun. Will you teach me?"

Kenzie had never heard of the board game *Murder*, but the game was probably the forerunner of the game *Clue*. "Sure, if we can find it."

"I'll ask around tomorrow. Bletchley is a hot spot for game players, musicians, thespians, and, hopefully"—Molly wiggled her eyebrows—"a new comedian. Come on, let's cut through here."

They skirted the mansion, heading toward a row of low brick buildings, and passing men and women on bicycles and others strolling and chatting. They all had at least one thing in common. They looked exhausted. Long, focused hours doing tedious work would give anyone a wan face and red-rimmed eyes.

She read recently that Eisenhower had credited the work at Bletchley, or the Park, as it was called, for shortening the war by two years, and saving countless lives. Codebreakers, WRENS, WAAFs, and posh debutantes worked together. And if the second interview went well, she would be part of it all—one of the women who made up three-quarters of a workforce that totaled ten thousand. She would be a Bletchleyette, and one of the thousands of women airbrushed from history.

But could she play second fiddle to the men? She would have to swallow her pride and be a worker ant. Sure for a few days she could manage, but then she had to make her way to Scotland. If she didn't get home and show up for class, she'd flunk out of law school. Wait a minute. Would she even return to the same day, month, or year? It was possible that years could have gone by while she was stuck in the Forties. That was a scary thought, and one she couldn't dwell on right now. It gave her that spider crawling on her neck.

"If you're offered a job, I'll call Rainer and ask him to let Cav know you're here with me. Maybe they can get a pass this Saturday, and we can all meet in Cambridge for lunch or dinner."

Kenzie glanced down at the shade-dappled path, counting a few dozen men in close proximity. "There are a lot of men here. Why go to Cambridge?"

Molly scrunched her nose. "Eccentric men aren't all that attractive. They're handsome enough, but their minds are too cluttered with whatever work they're doing to consider a woman's needs."

"Do you think men who put their lives on the line are sexier?" Kenzie asked.

"Rainer and Cav take risks every day. They go on missions and never know if they'll make it back. Men facing death give women their full attention."

"Women help them forget about the danger. If only for a little while."

"Does that come from personal experience?" Molly narrowed her eyes at Kenzie, obviously trying to guess the answer.

"Sadly, it does." She was remembering the rip-your-clothes-off sex with a contractor working for the Army after barely escaping an explosion.

Molly gave her a look of sympathy mingled with interest, but didn't ask for the clarification that would have forced Kenzie to lie again.

"While you're interviewing, I'm going over to the cafe"—Molly pointed toward the building across the drive from the mansion—"for a cup of tea. Go there when you finish. And good luck!" She gave Kenzie a one-armed hug and trotted off, suitcase in hand.

Kenzie stood in front of Block D alone, one hand gripping her suitcase, the other the doorknob. There were six small windows in the top third of the door, but they were covered with blackout curtains. So were the windows along the side of the hut. Even though she couldn't see inside, she knew what to expect when she opened the door—a smoky, dark environment. She took a breath, blew it out, and sucked in another, wondering how many lies she would have to tell this time.

When she stepped inside the smoke-filled hut, she coughed. Beneath the thick layer of smoke was the scent of percolating coffee. Would the Allies have won the war without cigarettes and caffeine? Soldiers now didn't smoke as much, but caffeine would never go out of style.

She walked down a long hall lined with offices illuminated by yellow lamplight. Inside each room were dozens of women working at wooden tables stacked high with trays of documents. The scratching of pencil lead on paper and the clacking of heels on marred floorboards resounded through the otherwise quiet room. Blackout curtains covered closed windows. If they opened them, a cross breeze would carry away the smoke.

She cleared her throat, but the women didn't look in her direction or offer assistance. They kept their heads down, focused on their work. Had she walked into a sweat shop? Because that's exactly what the room resembled. The train to Edinburgh was looking sweeter than chocolate.

She cleared her throat again, louder this time. A woman at the end of the closest table, without glancing up, pointed across the hall.

Kenzie stepped over to the door of a small office and peeked inside. A shabbily dressed man with thick, dark brown hair sat at a corner desk thumbing through a stack of papers.

"Holy crap," Kenzie muttered under her breath. "He's Molly's boss? Are you kidding me?"

26

London, England, May 30, 1944

DAVID SLUMPED BEHIND the wheel of a car parked down the street from the Bradfords' house. After spending the night in cramped quarters, he was grumpy and hungry. At least he hadn't had to conduct surveillance hiding in the bushes. Jack had saved David that inconvenience by borrowing the vehicle from a news correspondent he befriended in the bar at the Ritz. But the vehicle had to be returned by noon because the correspondent was leaving town for several days.

The joys of a stakeout.

All he knew so far was that Kenzie and Cavanaugh were hot for each other. Their make-out session on the stoop had been enlightening, and although he had tried not to watch, he ended up sitting transfixed, wishing it were him. David could taste her on his lips and feel the silkiness of her hair as it glided across his cheek when he twirled her on the dance floor. The woman bewitched him, but he had known that from the moment he stepped into her apartment.

Why was this happening to him again? Hadn't his feelings for Charlotte been punishment enough? Did the gods of the brooches want to extract another pound of his soul? Damn them. He had to put his feelings aside one more time. The three brooches would soon be in one place, and he wouldn't have to go through this again.

Cavanaugh obviously hadn't wanted to leave Kenzie. That was good to know. The next step was getting Kenzie to Cambridge.

Once there, Jack would bring Cavanaugh up from the base for a wee bonding time, and then the brooch would whisk them all back to the future.

The only information Jack had uncovered about Kenzie's pilot was that Christopher Joseph Cavanaugh had flown thirty-five missions and returned home after the war. Nothing spectacular about his service, other than he had survived the required number of missions, had been included in Jack's limited database. No heroics reported. But David didn't want to snatch Cavanaugh from his century and leave questions that would tarnish his reputation. It would take finesse to make his disappearance look legitimate.

A taxi pulled up in front of the Bradfords' residence. David reached for his camera to snap pictures of whoever was leaving. The taxi driver honked, and the door opened. An elderly man, leaning heavily on a cane, walked out onto the porch and waved. David took several pictures. A minute later, Molly and Kenzie came out, each carrying a suitcase.

David put the camera aside and slid down into the seat far enough to be unrecognizable, but not so far that he couldn't see the street. Where were the girls going? He would give his next meal for a working mobile. Jack was taking a train to Cambridge this morning en route to Cavanaugh's base. If Jack could be reached, David would ask him to escort the women to their destination first. Since David had no reason to travel, it wasn't logical for him to be the escort. Unless Kenzie intended to take the train to Scotland. In that case, he was the logical traveling companion.

The taxi driver put the suitcases in the boot and opened the door for the girls. They could also be traveling to Bletchley. Molly worked there, and Kenzie needed a job. The distance from Bletchley Park to Bassingbourn, where Cavanaugh was stationed, was only about forty miles. Cambridge was closer, but the security at the Park would keep Kenzie safe when David wasn't around.

After the taxi pulled away from the house, he made a U-turn and followed at a discreet distance, arriving shortly at King's Cross Station. After parking the car, he hid the keys under the seat, snatched his bags, and entered the railway station to find a phone. He had to call Neil, the desk clerk he had hired to perform small tasks, and ask him to pick up the car and return it to the correspondent.

Kenzie's red hair was an easy beacon, but he didn't know what train they were taking. To be on the safe side, he purchased a ticket to Bletchley, another one to Cambridge, and another ticket to Edinburgh.

Shortly before boarding time, David spotted Jack in the crowd and hurried to reach him before he passed through the turnstile. "Meet me by the newsstand behind us," David said before disappearing into the crowd. He waited at the side of the newsstand for Jack, who wove in and out through the crowd.

David filled him in.

"What's the plan, then?" Jack said.

"If they board your train, run into them accidentally. I'll board after you do. If they don't get off at Cambridge, you get off and I'll follow them from there."

"What if they don't go to Cambridge?"

"I'll board whatever train they take and stay out of sight. When I get a chance, I'll call Cavanaugh's base and leave a message for you. If you need to leave one for me, call the Ritz and leave a message with Neil at the front desk. He'll relay it to me."

"What'd you do with the car?"

"It's parked on the street. Neil will pick it up and return it."

"He's being overpaid for what he's doing, but in the dark ages you need to have a dependable communication system. You were right to hire him."

Kenzie's head came into view as she approached the turnstile. "Let's go before we lose them."

Jack and David followed a short distance behind the girls, but hidden in the hustling crowd.

"They're getting on the train to Bletchley," Jack said. "I'll head to Cambridge and on to Bassingbourn."

David slapped Jack's shoulder. "Stay out of trouble. If anything happens to ye', I could never face yer sister again."

"Whenever I have the urge to do something you'd consider reckless, I recall wearing that horrendous canvas hood during the conspiracy trial. That memory trumps an urge any day."

"Good. Keep that thought front and center."

Jack gave him a thumbs-up and hurried to catch his train. David waited long enough to see the girls climb aboard the third-to-last carriage on the train to Bletchley. He hopped on the fourth-to-last and encamped on the last row, near the door separating the cars. If he could come up with a plausible reason to be on the same train, he would march through the door and take a seat next to Kenzie. Nothing would please him more.

Not today, McBain. She's not yers.

He settled back for the hour-long trip, letting silky strands of red hair weave erotic thoughts he shouldn't be having.

When the train arrived at Bletchley, David hid inside the station, watching from a window as Molly and Kenzie exited the train and hiked up the path toward Bletchley Park. He followed, and when they stopped at the gate, he slipped into the trees and faded into the background, listening.

After a conversation with the two guards, one went inside the guard's hut for a couple of minutes before returning and opening the gate, admitting Kenzie to a classified facility.

Molly must have connections at the highest level.

He had new appreciation for the gorgeous young woman. He had underestimated her, and that rarely happened. She might prove be to be a reliable ally.

If Kenzie had an interview, she would be there for an hour or two. That gave him enough time to find accommodations. He needed a bath and shave. Then he'd infiltrate Bletchley Park. His credentials identified him as a major in the Royal Scots Greys, attached to Supreme Headquarters, Allied Expeditionary Force, a liaison position.

The artist David hired to forge his documents had come highly recommended. However, until the papers were scrutinized at the security gate, David wouldn't know the true extent of the forger's talent. Either David would be allowed to pass, or he'd be escorted to a detention area for a chat with Military Intelligence with a rifle pressed against his back. If that happened, he'd demand a full refund from the inept forger.

Unless Military Intelligence shot David on the spot.

27

Bletchley Park, England, May 30, 1944

KENZIE UNDERSTOOD THE expression "shock and awe" in military terms. But it also adequately described both the shock and the awe of discovering the identity of the man who occupied this little office in Hut 8. She tentatively knocked on the open door and waved a shaky hand in greeting.

"Excuse me, Dr. Turing. I'm Kenzie Wallis-Manning. Commander Travis sent me to interview with you."

Alan Turing screwed up his face and waved her in, but otherwise ignored her. Had Travis even notified Turing she was coming by? From his obvious disinterest, she guessed not. If he gave her the opportunity, she would have to sell herself on the spot. There would be no second chances.

She stepped inside the sparsely furnished office, which was thick with smoke. Turing wasn't a smoker, but the occupant of the adjoining room was, and the door between the offices was ajar.

The door to a free-standing closet also stood open. A coat and sweater hung from a rod, and a pair of white tennis shoes had been tossed on the floor. Next to the closet was a radiator. She chuckled to herself when she noticed a coffee mug hanging from a chain attached to the end of the radiator. Either a kleptomaniac or a forgetful eccentric worked in Hut 8.

There were no bells and whistles for the Park's premier codebreaker. In her opinion, he deserved at least a leather chair or a nice print. Instead he'd been given a rickety, secondhand straight-backed chair and a poster of Churchill.

Turing's eyes remained fixed on whatever held his attention. She put her hands in her jacket pockets. It wasn't unusual for commanding officers to keep junior officers standing at attention while they finished their business, but Turing wasn't an officer.

She fiddled with the miniature Rubik's Cube key chain and her class ring tucked in her pocket. If the interview went south, she'd entice the elusive mathematician with the greatest and most fiendishly manipulative puzzle of the twentieth century.

"Sit down, Miss Wallis-Manning, and stop fidgeting."

It wasn't her nature to fidget, so why was she doing it now? She lowered to the chair facing his desk and waited. He stacked papers, clipped them together, and set them in a wire basket on the corner of the desk.

She compared him to the pictures she had seen. He was broadly built, not long and lean like today's runners. She had read an article in *Runner's World* magazine that an injury had kept him, or rather, would keep him from competing in the 1948 Olympics. If he was an Olympic-caliber runner, she definitely wouldn't be going for a run with him.

"Do you know what we do here?" The impatience in his voice said he didn't have time for her.

She had only a second to sell herself. How was she going to handle it? In an off-handed tone, she said, "Either make radios or break German and Japanese codes."

"Who gave you that idea? Miss Bradford?"

"Molly only said she worked here. Not what she did. But if the Allies are going to win the war, someone has to break the codes. Why not a genius mathematician and cryptanalyst like Professor Turing?"

He rubbed his hand over his hair, making it stand up like a full head of cowlicks. "You've heard of me?" His voice went up an octave.

"I've also heard you're a runner. So am I."

His head popped up. "Why do you run?"

"It clears my head. Allows my mind to focus on solutions rather than problems, and it lowers my stress. What about you?"

He flipped his pencil back and forth between his thumb and index finger. "What stresses you?"

"For starters...whether or not I'll ever find a way home."

His brows knitted as he considered her answer. "Miss Bradford said I could use you, but she didn't tell me you were an American. Why does she think I need an American woman working for me?"

She set her mouth in a hard line. This was the question she'd been waiting for. If she didn't intrigue him now, she would lose the opportunity. She withdrew the Rubik's Cube from her jacket pocket, removed the keychain, and set the puzzle on the edge of his desk. "Besides being an avid puzzle solver, I am a student of military history, and multilingual."

He aimed his formidable focus on the cube, and his eyes fired like a perfect twelve-cylinder engine. "And Russian?"

"Not as well as German, but I get by."

"What's your longest running distance?"

She had run ultramarathons but distances longer than a marathon would be harder to explain. "Twenty-six-point-two."

"You've run a marathon?" His tone changed again, and he was definitely intrigued. "What's your best time?"

"My personal record is three-fifteen. Why?"

He looked up then, caught her eye, and gave her a faint, tired smile. "We focus every day on tasks of stunning complexity without letting the pressure undermine mental well-being."

"I'm not daunted." Though she might be if she took a moment to analyze what she was volunteering for.

"Do you know why I agreed to interview you?"

She held up three fingers and lowered one at a time. "My language skills, my passion for running, or my ability to tell a joke."

He chewed a fingernail with yellow teeth, watching her, but she didn't flinch. She wouldn't let him unnerve her. Finally he said, "We need humor infused into our lives. Do you know why I'm hiring you?"

She blinked. Did she hear him correctly? Yes. There was nothing wrong with her hearing. He was going to hire her. She widened her eyes and held her hands open in a questioning gesture. "Because you want a running buddy?"

"I enjoy the solitude that comes with running. I'm hiring you because you're not afraid."

She sat back in her chair, surprised by his comment. She managed fear well, but how did he know? What signals had she sent? "I'm afraid of some things, but not of you."

He shook his head with a wry smile. "Tell me about the cube."

She slid it across the desk toward him. "It's called a Rubik's Cube. There are twenty-six sub-cubes internally hinged. Rotation is possible on any plane. There are six distinct colors. The goal is to move the cubes until each side has a single color. A genius should be able to solve the puzzle within an hour."

His blue eyes twinkled above his small, odd smile. "How long did it take you?"

"I'm not a genius," she said.

"When does my time start?"

"When you say go."

Turing leaned forward, placing his elbows on his knees, staring at the cube. She glanced at the large clock on the wall and watched the second hand. After forty-five seconds he picked up the cube and said, "Start counting now."

After five minutes he set it down and spent the next twenty minutes writing cryptic notes in a notebook. Then he picked up the cube again and twisted the sub-cubes until he finished thirty minutes later. He set it down with huff. "What's the time?"

"Fifty-six minutes."

"What's the record?"

"About five point five seconds. Of course, that wasn't the person's first try."

He made a choked sound that could have passed for a laugh. "How come I've never seen this before?"

"It's a well-kept secret by its inventor, a Hungarian professor of architecture. He intends to sell it after the war."

"How'd you get it?"

She took an especially deep breath and prepared to tell another lie as coolly as possible, though her heart had taken a convulsive leap, and was now trying to burrow out of her chest, abandoning ship. She hated lying, and having to do so had lost any and all charm forty-eight hours earlier.

"I was given a prototype."

"Why show it to me?"

"I knew you'd like it, and I want to work for you."

"A bribe?"

"A bribe is payment for illegal activity. There's nothing illegal about this. I'd call it a hiring bonus." She paused, then added, "Although bonuses are typically given to the person being hired, not the one doing the hiring."

He handed her back the cube. "Next time I'll beat the record."

"Oh, I'm sure you will."

"Tell me, Miss Wallis-Manning. Do you think a computer could ever enjoy strawberries and cream or make you fall in love with it?"

Beneath the cranky, irreverent exterior, Kenzie saw a man of unworldly innocence, with a certain sensitivity, and maybe even modesty. She liked him a lot, shabby clothes and all. "I think you'll have to enjoy the strawberries and cream yourself, but I believe you can fall in love with a computer. Or, maybe fall in love with what one can do for you." She certainly loved her Mac, and would cry buckets if it crashed.

"Miss Bradford will show you to your billet and where to report to work once we have your identification papers. That may take a few days." He returned to the work on his desk, summarily dismissing her.

Did she still like him? If she hadn't had a dozen senior officers treat her just as rudely, she would probably say no, but he was a brilliant eccentric, and probably unaware of the effects of how he treated others. That didn't make his behavior acceptable, but it did make it forgivable.

Kenzie took her leave of Turing and Hut 8, and made her way over to the café to find Molly. Turing said she wouldn't be able to work until her identification papers arrived. She shivered, imagining the commander's reaction when he received the American embassy's report that Kenzie Wallis-Manning did not exist.

She needed to disappear before that report arrived.

There was no reason to stay any longer. She had met Alan Turing, and while she would never have a chance to work for him, she did get to watch him solve the Rubik's Cube. She'd never look at a cube again without thinking of him. The mental video she made of his facial expressions and body language while he worked on the cube's solution would keep her mind busy the next time she needed to mentally escape—like during the next conversation with her father.

There was nothing standing in the way of traveling to Scotland to find a way home. What was she going to tell Molly, though? Her friend would be terribly disappointed…and what about Cav? She would never see him again, either. But she already knew that.

She wandered down by the lake with her arms wrapped tightly around her while thoughts peppered her brain with options. Options? Really? What options? There weren't any. She had four or five days max before her identity—or lack thereof—was discovered. She could use some of that time to nose around and meet other famous Bletchley Park employees, but she absolutely could not linger.

Lingering could be her death knell.

Military Intelligence would be extremely interested in how a multilingual woman who didn't exist wormed her way into a high-security facility. Not only was she at risk, but Molly could be, too. If the commander believed Molly violated the Official Secrets Act, her friend could be shot. Of course, Kenzie would likely be shot first.

Lingering twenty-four hours might be too long. The memory of the London street shooting had a front row-seat in her brain. She could be next.

How long would it take employees at the American embassy to search its records? Without computers, it would take a day or two, even as a priority request. Employees would have to search several years' worth of records, plus census reports. The answer eluded her, but her gut told her every hour put her in greater jeopardy.

Tomorrow Kenzie would tell Molly that while she was waiting for her security clearance she would go to Cambridge to visit Cav. Instead, she would take a train to Scotland. Once there, she would cut her hair and become a blonde again. However, there was still the matter of proper identification. She would simply have to plug into the underground and find someone to forge documents for her. When she reached Scotland, she would put her skills to work.

A plan. Relieved, she marched toward the café with more confidence than she had when leaving Turing's office.

She burst through the café door with more exuberance than she intended, and spotted her friend. Molly jerked her head toward the door and said something. An American soldier glanced at Kenzie, too.

A Ranger?

When she was closer, her suspicion was confirmed by the black with red trim cotton insignia on his shoulder sleeve with the words 2ND RANGERS BN stitched in white. Kenzie's breath hitched. This man would scale the cliffs at Pointe du Hoc on D-Day—a hero immortalized by the words of Ronald Reagan in 1984. She owed him the thanks of a nation. Heck, not just a nation, but the world.

"Did you get the job?" Molly asked.

Kenzie pulled her attention away from the Ranger. "He said you'd show me where to billet and where to report to work."

Molly clapped her hands, her face glowing with an infectious grin. "I knew he'd be interested in you. I knew it."

The Ranger pulled a pack of Lucky Strikes from his inside jacket pocket and tapped out a cigarette, then flicked a lighter and touched it to the tip. He took a long drag before blowing the smoke toward the ceiling. "Your friend's been anxiously awaiting your return."

Kenzie doubted Molly had been too anxious, since she was flirting with an American soldier. "Thank you for keeping her entertained. I was being interviewed for a job to scrape barnacles off the bottoms of submarines." Kenzie glanced around the café and read the menus posted on the wall behind the counter. "I need a drink, and I'm desperate enough to guzzle warm beer."

"We'll have to go to the beer hut," Molly said, cocking her brow. "But don't you think it's a bit early?"

"Heck, no. It's five o'clock somewhere. We'll just pretend we're there." Kenzie headed for the door. "Are you coming?"

"Kenzie," Molly said a little sharply. "Have a cup of tea instead. When it's five o'clock in England, we'll go to the beer hut."

An inkling of annoyance caused Kenzie to squeeze the door handle while she sucked in a deep breath. "I guess I'll have tea, then."

"Let me get that for you," the Ranger offered, butting out his cigarette.

Kenzie looked up from his insignia to his face. She even took a step back to get a more comprehensive look at his six-foot-plus frame. There was something eerily familiar about him. Way too familiar. Her spidey senses jolted into high alert. Something was wrong, maybe even dangerous. But what that might be eluded her until she noticed the Ranger's name stamped onto a tailored label above his jacket pocket.

LIEUTENANT R. MANNING. A qualm skittered down her backbone like a mouse with icy feet.

No. Impossible.

"I'll get the tea," she said in a wobbly, barely audible voice, "but thanks for the offer." She hurried over to the counter, where she let out the shocked breath she was holding.

R. Manning? Could this man really be her grandfather? The Ranger's slightly wavy auburn hair and big hazel eyes resembled a picture she had seen of her father taken shortly before he was evacuated from Vietnam.

R. Manning. *No way.*

She ordered a cup of tea and held it tightly with chilled, shaking hands. She didn't know much about the man. Her father had only mentioned him once that she could recall. It had been during an argument with Kenzie's mother. He had called his father a traitor. Maybe that's why she had copied the document in Churchill's papers. The words *Ranger* and *traitor* had triggered a childhood memory.

What was she supposed to do now? Ignore him?

Molly sat at a table near the front window and the Ranger joined her. "Kenzie, bring your tea over here."

What? She couldn't sit with him. What would she say? "Hi, I'm your granddaughter."

Get a grip.

She glanced up, feeling Trey's presence. *What should I do, Trey? Talk to him. He's your grandfather. Trust your instincts.*

Ignoring her grandfather wasn't an option. Trey was right. She needed to trust her instincts. And her instincts told her to talk to him. The man would one day be her father's father. Her family had always been so small. Her Scottish grandparents had never wanted anything to do with her, and her grandfather's memory had been erased from her father's past. The brooch brought her to this time and place for a purpose, and maybe it was to meet this man.

If that was the purpose, then it had been accomplished. Maybe it would take her home now. The thought of twenty-first century England warmed her heart faster than the hot teacup had warmed her cold hands.

"Molly said you're also a Manning, but that you're from North Carolina. I grew up in Newport News, Virginia. Maybe we're related. We even have the same color hair."

Great. Thanks Molly.

"Totally random," Kenzie said. "Besides, my father's family lived in the Asheville area." Lie number one million, six hundred thousand, nine hundred and fifty-six, or thereabouts. She continued, "They're all gone now, and I've never heard of any cousins from Virginia with any color hair—blond, brown, black, or red." Her father had grown up in Virginia, too, and she had lived there for a few years when she was young.

Dang, she couldn't sit here calmly and continue to lie to him. It wasn't right. Nothing was right. The whole adventure had been one left turn after another.

Relax, soldier.

Easy for you to say, Trey. But I'm living the nightmare.

Not a nightmare, Kenz. A gift. Find a way to enjoy it.

Lieutenant Manning crossed his legs and leaned back in his chair, grinning. "We're not that far from each other. A distant relative could have crossed the mountains. You never know." When he smiled, the dimple in his right cheek deepened. A dimple identical to her father's. She swallowed hard and inched to the edge of her seat. She had to get away from Bletchley Park, from her grandfather, and from a moment without an explanation.

A familiar-looking black sedan, visible from the café window, headed down the driveway toward the security gate. A memory of the Saturday night shooting outside the Savoy replayed on fast forward in her mind, followed by snapshots of the car parked across the street from the Bradfords'. They had nothing to do with her, but collectively the events were disturbing.

The lieutenant lit another cigarette and let it dangle from the corner of his mouth while he put the Lucky Strikes and lighter into his pocket. "I saw an advertisement in the Chauffeurs' Hut advertising a cabaret show Thursday night. Are either of you performing?"

"I'm singing," Molly said. "You should come."

"You are?" Kenzie asked. Molly hadn't said anything about the show, and Kenzie had never even heard her hum a tune, not even a song from the *Wizard of Oz*. This sounded more like an inducement to see the lieutenant again. Something Kenzie didn't want to happen. This was all too surreal. "What are you singing in the show?" she asked with more sarcasm than she intended.

Molly sat up straight and folded her arms on the table top, with an annoying bob of her head. "Two of the Andrews Sisters' songs: 'Boogie Woogie Bugle Boy' and 'I'll Be with You in Apple Blossom Time,' and I thought I'd sing 'Somewhere Over the Rainbow,' too."

She winked at the lieutenant. "Will you come?"

Manning raised admiring eyes. "If I can wrangle a leave, sure."

"I hope Kenzie will join the cast, too. Her jokes will have you rolling on the floor laughing."

"A comedienne, huh? Have you heard the one about a British fighter pilot who was shot down over German-occupied airspace and captured by the Nazis? He was beaten up pretty bad in the dogfight and parachute landing, and they had to amputate his leg…"

"So he begged the Germans to drop his leg over Britain on their next bombing run," Kenzie said.

"And then his other leg had to be amputated and he asked the Germans to do the same thing with that leg," Manning said.

"And the German snapped, 'No, we think you're trying to escape,'" Kenzie said.

Surprise flushed his face. "You've heard it."

Kenzie smiled. "I ruined your joke. I'm sorry."

He stubbed out his cigarette then crossed his arms, challenging her. "You tell me one."

She had never lost a joke challenge, and she didn't intend to lose now. She ran a finger down a mental list of her repertoire, coming up with a World War II joke written in a similar vein to the one he had told.

"Hitler and Göring were standing on top of Berlin's radio tower. Hitler said he wanted to do something to cheer up the people of Berlin—"

"'Why don't you just jump?' suggested Göring."

Kenzie's jaw dropped. She recovered quickly and fired off another joke. The lieutenant spilled the punch line again before she could tell it, and he told another she spoiled. This went on through five jokes each, until they both were laughing hysterically.

"You are the—" Kenzie said.

"—first person to ever guess my punch lines," they said simultaneously, and that resulted in another round of laughter. Molly wasn't laughing, though. Her brows had snapped together following the first joke, and were now stitched tightly into what appeared to be a perplexed frown. Her attention shifted from Manning to Kenzie and back again, and each time the frown deepened.

A young man dressed in civilian clothes burst through the café's door, stopped, and scanned the room while breathing heavily. Heads turned, and voices quieted. He seemed to recognize Lieutenant Manning before striding over to their table.

"Excuse me, Lieutenant Manning," he said breathlessly. "Commander Travis's aide called the Chauffeur's Hut. He asked that you report to the commander's office immediately."

The lieutenant shot to his feet, scooting the chair aside. "It's been delightful to meet you ladies. If I can arrange leave, I'll come to the show."

Kenzie stood, and Molly pushed back her chair, too. She wormed her way around Kenzie until she stood, toying with a lock of her hair, directly in front of the lieutenant. While she gave him last-minute details, including the location and show times, Kenzie studied his face, taking stock of him. There was a strong resemblance to her father's Roman nose and high cheekbones. And like her father and grandfather, she too, had square shoulders, solid hands with short-clipped nails, and long legs. But most of all, the color and texture of his hair, and the depth of his hazel eyes, made the other similarities inconsequential.

Why hadn't he noticed the resemblance? Why hadn't Molly? Maybe she had. If so, that would explain her pinched expression.

Kenzie was the female version of him. It was his smile, though, that embedded in her heart. A smile she had not seen on her father's face, ever. Not even when her mother was alive. And the odd thing was that the lieutenant wasn't flirting with Molly, in spite of her charms. He was genuinely interested, but not in the way other soldiers usually were. He was a gentleman. She could almost picture him in a Confederate uniform. How could such an honorable man have betrayed his country? The few facts Kenzie knew didn't add up.

Molly finished her spiel and the lieutenant made a move to leave, but Kenzie couldn't bear the thought of him leaving just yet. "If you come to the show," she said, "you'll have to come onstage with me, share the spotlight, tell some jokes, too." She put her hands on her hips and sashayed for emphasis. "I can't have you out there in the audience heckling."

He took his hat off the table and casually fingered the wool. "I wouldn't do that, ma'am. It would ruin the show for others in the audience." He nodded good-bye and left the café.

Her eyes lingered on him until the door closed. And then, even though there was nothing more to see except a door with peeling paint, she kept her eyes glued to the spot where he had last stood. Old, familiar grief enveloped her. She plopped in a chair, crossed her arms, holding herself tightly to ease the heartache.

Catching a movement in the window out of the corner of her eye, Kenzie watched him walk briskly out of sight. Had she inherited her joke-telling skills from him? No. That wasn't a gene you could inherit. It was more of a personality trait. But didn't scientists believe some traits had a genetic basis?

Kenzie felt herself melting like the Wicked Witch of the West. She took a gulp of air, probably her last before sinking through the floor, leaving behind only a pointed hat and a puddle of clothing.

"That man," Molly said excitedly, wagging her finger toward the door, "not only has your name, but your hair color and eyes, too. You're related to him, aren't you? And he didn't even know it. Why didn't you say something?"

Kenzie glanced at the floor, expecting to see a pointed hat, and she mentally squashed the image. What in God's name could she tell Molly? She gulped in a lungful of the room's smoky air and coughed. The tightness in her chest was a noose around her heart.

Kenz. Relax. You have a brilliant mind. This is a puzzle you can solve.

She buried her face in her hands, thinking, or maybe she was praying for inspiration, when a punch line to a joke gave her an idea. Although creating another brother pushed the bounds of credibility.

Sell it, Kenz. You can do it.

"Several years ago, I heard a rumor that my father had an illegitimate child in another state. I never heard whether the child was a girl or a boy. I didn't care then, and I don't care now. If that man is related to me, I don't want to know. Please, let's not talk about it."

"But you got on so well. Why don't—"

Kenzie held up her hand, gesturing Molly to stop. "We did, but there's a war going on. If he survives, if I survive, then maybe after the war we can meet again. But I don't want to get to know him, then lose him permanently. Does that make sense?"

Molly took her hand, clasping it tightly. "Perfectly. Then let's get out of here before he comes back." Molly tugged her toward the door. "Wait here while I go outside to see if he's still around."

Kenzie leaned against the wall, trying to control her ragged breathing. If he was her grandfather, she knew little about him other than he was a Ranger, a spy, and was killed before D-Day. Period. That was it. Her father wouldn't talk about him. What were the odds that she would run into him at Bletchley Park?

Hell, what were the odds that she would travel more than seventy years back in time? Maybe that's why she was here. Maybe...

The door opened and Molly blew in. "He's gone," she said excitedly. "I watched him drive away from the Chauffeur's hut. You can come out now."

"Good. Let's go. I need fresh air." Kenzie waved her hand in front of her face as if she were swatting at flies.

They left the café and crossed the grass leading toward the driveway. The overcast sky gave way to patches of blue, and Kenzie scanned the tree lines toward the city. In another few weeks, when the trees were fully leafed, you wouldn't be able to see a smokestack or a rooftop.

"What shall we do now? Find my billet?" Kenzie was so befuddled, she wasn't sure she could find her way to the ladies' room. Prior to entering the twilight zone, she had never been befuddled, and always had a plan. One more thing to blame on the fog.

"You have a room at the Bletchley Inn until a local family has an opening. I hope you don't mind. I tried to work out arrangements for you to stay with me, but it would be too crowded."

"You're amazing. When did you have time to work out housing

arrangements?"

"While you were interviewing I sweet-talked the owner of the Inn into letting you have a room. I told him how funny you were and that you'd put on a show for his customers. He liked the idea, and since he had a couple of vacancies today, he agreed."

"If I ever need a manager, I won't have to look any further than Molly Bradford."

Molly slipped her arm around Kenzie's waist, a spontaneous gesture she had made several times over the last few days, and Kenzie found it surprisingly comforting. "Come on. It's time to line up another gig for you, and I won't even take a booking percentage."

Kenzie laughed, letting relief steal anxieties and befuddlement. "Good, because ten percent of zero is still zero. What do you have in mind?"

"I think we should sign you up for the cabaret and then go over to Hut 2," she paused and pointed. "It's the beer hut. We'll stop there after the audition, and before we go to the Inn."

"I think we should go there first." After the shock of meeting her grandfather, a beer would settle her a bit, even a warm one.

Molly tugged on her arm. "Not now. We'll come back later. It gets so crowded in there it's almost impossible to move down the corridor. If we get there before the rush, we can get a table."

"I bet if we have a table, others will buy our beers just for a seat."

"You catch on fast."

"Maybe, but what I still can't figure out is how you were so confident I'd get a job offer."

"I knew Dr. Turing would like you. I mean..." Molly paused, saying nothing but thinking hard behind her blue eyes.

Kenzie was tickled. Molly must have known Turing was gay and didn't know how to explain the situation to someone she didn't know all that well. Kenzie helped her out. "I know he's gay...I mean homosexual, and I liked him, too. His sexual preference doesn't matter to me."

If eyes could sigh with relief, Molly's did.

"If we don't go to the Inn now, will the innkeeper give my room away?"

"Not after what I told him about you. He was seeing pound signs."

Kenzie bent her arm at the elbow and raised and lowered it in a fluid movement, saying, "Ker-ching."

Molly wrinkled up her nose, and not for the first time. That was her tell when she didn't understand Kenzie's jokes. "Ker-ching is the sound a cash register makes when you ring up purchases."

"You always say the cleverest things." She gave a light flip of her hand. "Men like that in women."

Kenzie wasn't so sure. More than one man had told her to stop hiding behind her sense of humor. If pressed, she'd have to admit, *maybe*, that she had a habit of telling jokes during sensitive conversations. But if men couldn't handle lightening the mood to reduce stress, it was their fault, not hers. Never worked with her father, though. Nothing ever lightened his mood.

She followed Molly toward the security gate, watching the road for black sedans and Ranger drivers. "Where're we going?" Kenzie asked.

"To the Assembly Hall. It's that building right outside the gate. We passed it when we came in."

From the corner of her eye, Kenzie spotted a soldier walking with quick, determined strides toward the café. From where she stood, she couldn't see his face, but his tall, broad-shouldered body and agile gait stood out among the shorter men she'd seen so far at the Park...and in London, too, with the exception of one man—McBain. She craned her neck, checking out the soldier until he walked out of her line of sight. Nah. It couldn't possibly be McBain.

What if it was? Would she be glad to see him again? Not that she had to choose, but if she did, she'd choose Cav. McBain was too intense. Men like him were great sexual partners, but rarely stuck around afterwards, as if that would make a difference to her now. Hot, steamy sex followed by a quick good-bye was preferable to steamy sex and a complicated emotional attachment. The odds of seeing either man again were remote. The possibility of steamy sex was even more so. And there she was again, thinking about sex. It was becoming an annoying obsession.

Molly pushed open the door to the Assembly Hall, and they stepped into a beehive of highbrow activity—not surprising, given that the finest minds of a generation were gathered there.

Molly led the way and picked a path through the crowed hall. Along the far wall a platform had been erected with a microphone placed center stage. A man and woman with clipboards were directing people when they reached the front of a line, extending from one end of the room to the other.

"Is this the audition line?" Kenzie asked.

"It's only to register. It'll move quickly. Once they have your name and talent, they'll schedule an audition."

"I can't believe this many people want to perform."

"Any time we can get together and laugh at the institution we work for, we will. Some shows even go on the road to raise money for various military benevolent funds."

"This show won't go on the road, will it?"

"If it's well received we might play a few venues during the upcoming weekends. Come on. Let's get in the sign-up line."

This show would never go on the road. Once D-Day arrived, everyone would be focused on the invasion. It was so close now that Kenzie wondered if the brooch had opened a door to the past so she could get the scoop about her grandfather. Not a story distorted by her father's memories, the Army, or seventy-odd years. But could she afford to put off a trip to Scotland and a possible return ticket home to solve the mystery? Why not? It was possible she wouldn't be able to find a way home anyway, so why not try to fix the past while she was stuck here?

Fix it? Seriously? Changing the future could eradicate her life. She could go home to a world in which she didn't exist. She swallowed hard over that one. She liked her life. She liked herself.

Sorry, Grandpa. But I'm not in the market for a new me.

Molly waved to a young woman across the room. "That's one of my roommates."

Kenzie studied the slender brunette, who appeared to be about Molly's age. She was cute, but not beautiful like Molly. "How many do you have?"

"Two. That's Judy. Zoey is usually with her." Molly stood on tiptoe to see over the heads of people standing in line behind them. "I don't see her, but you'll meet her later. I'm sure she'll be at the beer hut. Zoey is such a flirt. She always has a new guy on her arm."

Kenzie almost cracked up. If Molly thought her roommate was a flirt, what did it say about Molly's behavior?

"Next," the woman with the clipboard said.

Kenzie stepped forward. "I'm Kenzie Wallis-Manning, and I tell jokes."

28

Bletchley Park, England, May 30, 1944

After David watched Kenzie and Molly pass through the gate unmolested, he was confident she'd be safe enough that he could return to town to secure accommodations. Not an easy task with the influx of out-of-towners working at Bletchley.

He rented the last room in the Bletchley Inn. From what the innkeeper said when he handed over the room key, David was lucky to find a room within an hour of the Park.

It took a bit of haggling, but David negotiated the use of a rusty bicycle with flat tires. With a bit of elbow grease, he'd have semi-reliable transportation. In an emergency, he could pedal faster than he could run.

He stowed his gear and went to work disassembling the bike. An hour later, he had a functioning bicycle, complete with a new basket strapped to the handlebars and a red paint job. He propped it against the wall near the back door of the Inn and chained the frame to the water pump. Leaving it untethered was a bicycle theft waiting to happen.

He washed his greasy hands at the pump, surprised by how satisfying it had been to repair the bike. He had learned handyman skills as a teenager out of necessity. His mum didn't have extra money for repairs, so he learned how to fix broken items around the cottage, and was even a halfway-decent carpenter. Nowadays he rarely picked up a hammer, much less a wrench.

The innkeeper came through the back door with soap and a towel. He handed them to David then gave the repaired bike a thorough inspection. "If you need to make a few pounds while you're here, the town could use someone with your skills."

David thanked him for the soap and scrubbed his hands again. "If I have extra time, I'll be glad to do what I can."

"Be sure to keep the bike chained up."

"I painted it red to discourage sticky fingers," David said.

"Won't matter. You could have painted it with pink polka dots and a poor soul sick of walking would lift it without thinking twice."

David rattled the chain to be sure the padlock was locked and held up the key for the innkeeper to see. "This baby's not going anywhere without this."

David excused himself and returned to his room for a bath. He had intended to rest for a while, but he'd already left Kenzie longer than he intended. It was past time to return to Bletchley.

For this visit he'd wear the brown uniform of the Royal Scots Greys. The decorations on his jacket were the World War II equivalents of the medals he had won during his two tours in Afghanistan. Elliott had insisted, saying that it gave David more credibility.

The transformation from novelist to soldier took him aback, and he growled at his mirror image. When he left the Guards, he swore he would never wear a uniform again, yet here he was. The whys and wherefores didn't matter. A job had to be done, and he was Elliott's logical choice.

He set his beret on his head, canting it left, realizing very quickly that he could take the man out of the uniform, but he couldn't take the uniform out of the man. He was a soldier and always would be, whether he was on active duty or not.

He secured the door tightly behind him with a concealed locking device. He couldn't afford to have a nosy landlord going through his gear.

Speaking of the landlord, David met him at the bottom of the steps. "I'm going out for an hour. Before I go, I need to place a call to a buddy at Bassingbourn Air Base."

The landlord nodded toward the phone on the registration desk. "Make it short."

David dialed the operator and was put through to the airfield where the call was then routed to the officer's mess. Jack came on the line.

"It's about time you called. Where are you?" Panic vibrated in Jack's question, and David fought a quiver of fear that tumbled into the abyss of his burning stomach. Something had happened.

"The Bletchley Inn. What's wrong? Where's Cavanaugh?"

"He's flying a mission. When are you coming here?"

"I don't have plans. But if ye' don't tell me what's going on wi' ye', I'll have to hire a car and make an unplanned trip."

"If anything happens to you, I won't be able to go home. You have the brooch."

"Is that why ye' sound like a wild boar's chasin' ye'? Ye're afraid of being stuck here, too." The adrenaline rush that had caused a mild cold sweat abated. Nothing had happened. Jack was only recalling the horror of his imprisonment in 1865, and how alone and helpless he had been. David had seen it twice before in the months following their return home. "Elliott won't leave ye' behind. He didn't last time, and he wouldn't now."

"He knew where I was then."

"I'm going to Inverness tomorrow to leave him a message about Cavanaugh. Relax. He'll know where ye' are."

"Are you sure?"

"Aye." Bringing Jack along was looking like a bad idea. David didn't have time to babysit.

"And what about Kenzie?" Jack asked.

"She had an interview at Bletchley. I'll confirm she has a job before I leave. If she's working, she'll stay put for a few days. Someone with her skills won't pass up an opportunity to work with the codebreakers."

"Turing's a big runner. She'll probably finagle a run with him."

The longer Jack stayed on the phone, the slower his breathing and the calmer his speech. A wee bit longer and he'd be back to normal.

"Does she know you're there?" Jack asked.

"Not yet. I'm going over after this call and have a look around. How's it going with Cavanaugh?"

"I told you, he's out on a mission. I'll talk to him tomorrow."

"Where's Rainer? Maybe ye' can talk to him."

"He's Cav's copilot. He's not here, either. Didn't you listen to the introductions when we met them?" Jack paused a minute. "Never mind. Forget I asked. You didn't take your eyes off of Kenzie."

David pulled the handset away from his ear and rolled his shoulders like a diver about to spring from the high board. Jack was right. He was so far off his game he might as well be in another country.

Blame could be placed on the distraction caused by stomach pain and a heavy dose of worry over Meredith, but he'd had pains and worries before and still functioned at a high performance level. The cause of his slipups cut deep. If he didn't get his shit together, the entire mission could easily become one colossal fuck-up.

"Get Cavanaugh to Cambridge on Saturday. I'll get Kenzie there." He didn't know how he'd arrange it, but he'd come up with something.

"He might not be able to leave the base."

"Make it happen, Jack. That's what ye're there for."

"Bring Molly, too."

"Not unless ye're bringing Rainer."

David didn't have to see Jack's face to know he was chewing his lower lip. Jack gave a small grunt of amusement, but said nothing else.

"Stay clear of the lass, or ye'll be going home shattered."

"It's not like we only have four reservations for a return trip. We can take more people with us as long as we're all holding hands."

David squeezed the bridge of his nose, squinting to ease the pain that had erupted in his temples. Jack had more than earned his reputation for acting without considering consequences. To him, managing three or four people wasn't significantly different from one or two. There was no point getting into a discussion about it now.

"By the way, when are you going to tell Kenzie who you are? She should know."

The innkeeper moved behind the desk, and David turned his back to him and said, low-voiced, "I'm not going to tell her. I'm certain she has an agenda. Until I know what she intends to do, I can't show my cards. If she disappears, it might take weeks to find her. We don't have that kind of time."

"I know we've talked about this, but I still think you're making a mistake. She'll be more cooperative if she knows who you are. You can't just throw her into the fog and hope for the best."

"Given a choice, I prefer to ask for forgiveness rather than permission. It's more efficient. I can't guarantee her cooperation, so why force a battle of wills if it isn't necessary? If she doesn't want Cavanaugh—"

"It doesn't matter," Jack said. "If they're meant to be together, the brooch will unite them somehow, some way, someday, regardless of what you or I do. So tell her the truth."

"Let it go, Jack. Kenzie's my responsibility." David had spooled Jack's panic and put it away, but now the man was being a dick. "I gotta go." Before he hung up, he gave Jack the hotel's telephone number. "Call and leave a message once ye've worked out plans for Saturday, and we'll need hotel rooms, too."

Following the call, David drummed his fingers on the counter top. He wasn't going to second-guess his decision. Kenzie was a soldier. She could take care of herself. If she set her mind on a task, she wouldn't give it up easily. But what had she set her mind to do? Go to Scotland? If that's what she intended, why not invite her along? He tapped his fingers again, as if playing the finger buttons on his sax.

On the bike ride to Bletchley Park, he made a decision to tell Kenzie he was going to Edinburgh so he could gauge her interest. If she was willing to leave England, then more than likely she didn't intend to interfere with her grandfather's life.

When David reached the security gate, he hung back and fumbled through his jacket pockets, allowing a group of men and women to be admitted ahead of him. If he entered at the same time, his identification wouldn't be scrutinized as thoroughly as it would be if he entered alone. Although he had authentic-looking creds, it didn't mean it was safe to swim with sharks. He always took precautions. And he always had a backup plan.

The guards waved him through, barely glancing at his ID. Just as he had predicted, the uniform trumped his papers.

He had studied the layout of the property, but he didn't know where Kenzie would be assigned, and he didn't want to draw attention by asking for her. With thousands of men and women on the grounds, no one would think it odd to see someone they didn't know, especially since contact with other sections was extremely limited. No one talked about what they did at Bletchley, so he wouldn't be asked which hut or block he worked in. He had to vary his schedule, though, to avoid seeing the same crowd gathering around the lake or at the café.

He made note of the time and his location near the yew tree maze flanking the lake. In another few weeks, Bletchleyites would be promenading around the water, avoiding the honking geese and the reported abundance of frogs. He and Kenzie would be long gone by then.

He made his way to the café for a cup of tea and sat at a table next to two women in WRNS uniforms. *Join the Wrens—free a man for the fleet.* Whoever came up with the slogan for the Royal Navy picked a winner. Normally in a café he would have sought solitude, but he needed information. A gaggle of women, if prodded, would reveal a lot in a short period of time.

Glancing covertly from the newspaper he picked up at the counter, he studied the women sitting next to him. Average age: early twenties. Both had mildly red-rimmed eyes. They might be tired, but they weren't by any means, glum. Amidst their buzzing conversation, one woman with abundant ash blond hair fluffed out on either side of her naval beret was brave enough to bat her eyelashes his way. He nodded acknowledgment, and she gave him a coquettish grin.

"We haven't seen any soldiers from the Royal Scots Greys here before."

"Just arrived. Came here right away for a cup of tea. Heard this was where the lassies were." He winked. "Ye' know Highlanders, always preening and peacocking to be noticed."

The woman crossed her legs casually, leaned forward, and extended her hand. "I'm Zoey Webb. You could wear a dirty, torn uniform and you'd still be noticed."

He shook her warm, slim hand and gazed into startling, steel-blue eyes, albeit tired ones. "Major McBain."

The other woman laughed. "Stop flirting, Zoey. We've got to go."

Thoroughly intrigued, he leaned forward, elbows on his knees. "Back to the grind?"

"We have the afternoon off for cabaret rehearsal." Zoey's voice was husky now, as if she'd been running laps.

The inference was clear. Zoey would skip rehearsal if he asked. He wouldn't ask. Not this time. He didn't need the complications, but he did need her help. "When's the cabaret?"

"Thursday night. Are you going?"

"Count on it," he said. "What part are ye' playing?"

She pointed to herself and then to her girlfriend. "We're doing a dance routine. But I bet you sing. You should join the cast."

He gave her his best mischievous grin. "I don't sing, but I play a wee bit of a tune on the saxophone."

Zoey touched him, fondling his forearm with fingers tipped with chewed, ragged fingernails. "No bagpipes?"

"I tried, but I was squeezing at all the wrong times. Gave it up, picked up the sax, and never looked—"

"—back." Zoey's eyes sharpened. Her telegraphed message was even clearer this time.

The girlfriend grabbed Zoey's arm and pulled her to her feet. "If we miss rehearsal, we won't be allowed in the show. You can see

Major McBain Thursday night."

Zoey pouted her red-painted bottom lip. "Do come, Major."

"Count on it." David watched Zoey sway out of the café. She was hot and available, but he wasn't interested. At all. Some lassies were born to cause trouble, and Zoey wore a warning sign scrawled across her forehead: TREAD CAUTIOUSLY, OR DON'T TREAD AT ALL.

He sipped his tea, thinking of the one woman who wore an even bigger warning sign. Kenzie was never far from his thoughts. Why couldn't he have bumped into her in London in the past few months? He'd been there often enough. The weak tea without lemon slid down his throat. So rationing had impacted even the most storied of English traditions. He pushed the cup aside and considered a cup of coffee, but the thick, overcooked brew would be too much for his stomach today.

He put his elbows on the table, steepled his hands, and propped his chin on his fingertips. Little Lincoln, Charlotte's son, called it David's thinking pose. He was thinking now. What was his next move? Find Kenzie and make sure she was well ensconced at Bletchley, make plans to visit Cavanaugh on Saturday, and then head to Scotland to leave Elliott a message.

He would return Thursday before the curtain rose on the performance. He was ninety-nine percent sure if there was a performance this week, he'd find Kenzie onstage, which meant she might be auditioning there now. He jumped to his feet and rushed the door, catching it before it closed behind the women.

"If ye' don't mind, I'll walk with ye'. Ye' can show me where to go."

Zoey ogled him from beret to boots. "We don't mind a bit. But you'll need a sax to audition."

He mentally kicked himself in the arse for mentioning the instrument. Zoey was the sort of lass to remember every word a man said and use it against him to suit her purposes. A trapped rabbit probably didn't feel as cornered. Reluctantly he said, "Do ye' know where I can find one?"

"I might…" Zoey sang the words, teasing him. "If you'll buy me a beer later."

"Aye." David forced a smile. He didn't want to encourage her, but she probably knew more people at Bletchley than any other employee. Asking a person for help following an introduction produced higher favorable results than asking the same question of a stranger.

They entered the Assembly Hall and David followed Zoey through the crowded room.

"My roommate should be here," Zoey said, dodging people right and left. "Oh, I see her now." Zoey waved. "Come on. I want you to meet her."

If she was a clone of Zoey, he'd beg off and do some reconnaissance around the Park. But the roommate wasn't a woman he wanted to run from. He spread his hands in a gesture of welcome and Molly kissed his cheek.

"I didn't expect to see you again," she said.

Zoey tossed her hair with a flip of her hand, then heaved an exasperated sigh. "You know him?"

Molly gave David a friendly smile. "We met Saturday night." And then to David she said with the lift of her brow, "Are you working here, too?"

He leaned in and whispered, "I can't say, but where's Kenzie? Have ye' seen her?"

Zoey crossed her arms, fidgeting, rocking back and forth on her feet while drumming her fingertips on her upper arms. Her eyes narrowed and darkened. "You could have told me you knew her," she snapped at David.

David didn't tolerate jealously in women he dated. It probably bothered all of them that he saw other women, but they never complained. When David spent an evening with one, she became the most important woman in his life, and he never gave her a reason to feel insecure. Jealous women were as determined as suicide bombers, and he stayed clear of potential threats.

"Is Jack with you?" Molly asked, glancing past his shoulder in the direction of the door.

"He's at the base with Rainer and Cavanaugh. I'm supposed to meet them in Cambridge on Saturday. If ye're interested we could make a day of it."

Molly placed her small, delicate hand on his arm. "Kenzie will be excited. I can't wait to tell her."

Would she be excited to see Cavanaugh, or him?

Stop being an arse, McBain. This isn't your story.

Zoey squared her shoulders, tried to smile, and failed. Then threw the weight of a glare on Molly. "*Who* is Kenzie, and why would she be excited?"

He twitched an ear and wisely did not answer.

She patted Zoey's hand affectionately, as if she were a child. "A girl I met over the weekend. I arranged an interview for her. Let's go find her."

"You go." Zoey fluttered lashes that enhanced her mink-brown eyes, but did nothing to dilute her surly disposition. "I promised Major McBain I would find a saxophone for him to use for an audition."

Sharp interest kindled in Molly's eyes. "A saxophone?"

David shrugged. "I didn't say I was any good. Only that I play."

Molly pointed a finger at Zoey. "You, find the sax, and you," she said, pointing at David, "come with me. I want to ask you a question." Molly dropped Zoey's arm, captured David's, and led him away. "Ignore Zoey. I do. She can be sweet, but…"

"When she unsheathes her talons, beware."

Molly laughed. She directed David's attention with quick nod. "Kenzie's over there."

David's gaze followed a path through the crowd in the direction Molly indicated. "Makes it easy to find the lass with that head of hair. It appears she's entertaining admirers." The undertone of jealously in his voice surprised him.

"She's auditioning. But as funny as she is, she's probably giving them more material than they need to judge her worthiness for the show."

"Hard to turn her off, huh?"

"She'll gladly turn off, but her audience won't let her. You should have seen her with this man we met in the café earlier. They swapped jokes, telling each other's punch lines."

"Did she tell the one about the wheelbarrow?" he asked curiously.

"She didn't tell that one. Matter of fact, as many of her jokes as I've heard, the ones she told the lieutenant were all new to me, but he had heard them before."

"I bet she was mad that he ruined her jokes."

"Like she was with you? No," Molly looked puzzled. "Kenzie laughed, and so did he. And then they made a kind of contest out of finishing each other's jokes. And get this..." Molly glanced around to be sure no one was listening. A group was within earshot, but didn't appear to be paying attention to them. Molly inched closer to David and lowered her voice. "The man's name was Lieutenant R. Manning. He had hair almost the same color as Kenzie's, but his eyes were a lighter hazel."

She pulled David closer to the wall and farther from the group. "After the lieutenant left, I mentioned to Kenzie how much they looked alike and asked if they could be related. I had to drag the information out of her. But finally she admitted it was possible.

"She said that several years ago she heard a rumor that her father had an illegitimate child. Kenzie never knew the child's sex. If R. Manning was her half-brother, she didn't want to know, and she didn't want him to know about her, either."

So Kenzie had met her grandfather and passed him off as a half-brother. David had to admit it was a good save on her part in what must have been a ticklish encounter.

David rubbed the back of his neck, wondering how hard to push. He didn't want to appear eager for information, but he had to know where to find the lieutenant. "Two Mannings working at Bletchley Park. That's a coincidence."

"He doesn't work here. He's a courier. He delivered a message to Commander Travis and was waiting in the café for a response to take back to his base. He got a message to report back to Commander Travis, and I saw him drive away a few minutes later."

"Did he say where he was billeted?"

"No, but he said he would try to come back Thursday night for the show. But I don't think Kenzie will talk to him again."

After Kenzie had time to let it sink in, David felt certain she would want to see her grandfather again. "If that's her decision, we shouldn't interfere." He had every intention of interfering, however. "Saturday night, Kenzie said she needed a job. Did she score an interview?"

"Yes, and she was offered a position," Molly said.

"There you are, Major. I found a sax for you." Zoey wormed her way in between David and Molly. "Come with me. I'll introduce you to the man in charge of auditions." Zoey laced her fingers with his and dragged him to the opposite end of the hall.

"Zoey said you want to play the sax," the man said, assessing David. "Get up on the stage and tell the band the name of the tune. They'll back you up."

What in the hell had he gotten himself into? Elliott would be pissed that he was attracting attention.

"What are you going to play?" the drummer asked.

"Summertime."

Standing several feet away, he saw the back of a woman who resembled Kenzie. There couldn't be another woman at Bletchley Park with hair the color of his fantasies.

29

Bletchley Park, England, May 30, 1944

KENZIE WAS REVIEWING her list of jokes with the clipboard man when the soulful, seductive sounds of a saxophone brought conversations in the Assembly Hall to a standstill. Every head turned toward the stage, including Kenzie's. Her breath hitched when she recognized the man with the sax.

McBain? Impossible.

She wove through the crowd, as if following the Pied Piper, mesmerized by the sound of angels transforming music into pure emotion. The tips of her toes bumped the edge of the platform, bringing her to a standstill mere feet from where he stood onstage.

Gifted was one of the few words that came to mind as she listened to his interpretation of the popular favorite. Other women gathered near her, and they all swayed with the soft, slow jazz. Her heart thudded in time with the music.

McBain didn't just play with his lips and fingers. He played with his entire being. He was a high wire act of musical textures, and both the sound and the man were purely erotic. He captivated the audience, and as the last note hung in the air, the crowd went wild.

Molly slipped in behind Kenzie and whispered, "I've never heard 'Summertime' played with so much emotion."

The music still reverberated in Kenzie's soul. "I"—words stuck in her dry throat—"haven't either."

McBain set down the sax and jumped off the three-foot high

stage, landing inches from Molly and Kenzie.

The stage manager grabbed the mike. "We hope Major McBain will be available for an encore performance Thursday night. Buy your tickets now to guarantee a seat."

A buzz erupted around the ticket table as it was swamped with purchasers. You would have thought news of a surprise performance by Paul McCartney or Bruce Springsteen had just been announced. Who *was* this guy? She'd never heard his name or seen his picture in any of her research. A jazz musician of his caliber would have been recognized at some point during the war. There would have been a recording of him playing at a venue, or a newsreel. His talent wouldn't have been lost to the ages unless...

Like so many other talented men and women, he must not have survived the war. The thought left her shaking.

A woman rushed up and wrapped her hand around his arm, suggesting a certain amount of familiarity between them. "Major, you were simply divine. I can't wait to hear more Thursday night." She fluttered thick lashes. "Let's go to the beer hut. You *did* promise me a drink."

He had a helpless, deer-in-the-headlights sort of look.

The woman was a Cruella de Vil type, probably very intelligent, but had all the earmarks of a woman pampered by a wealthy London family and used to getting her way.

"I don't know if I'm more surprised about encountering you here or listening to you play," Kenzie said. "You need to take that act on the road. Molly can probably line up a gig or two."

"That was my one and only wartime appearance. But thank you for the offer."

"But surely you'll perform Thursday night," the Cruella lookalike purred.

"About that..." McBain said, prying her fingers from a white-knuckle grip on his jacket. "I doubt I'll be able to stay until Thursday."

"Of course you can." The girl turned to Molly. "With all your connections, you can get the Major's schedule rearranged."

Molly's forehead puckered as she glared at Zoey. "I don't have control over Major McBain's schedule *or* anyone else's."

The woman gave Molly an obnoxious fake pout. "You're being modest." The woman turned her attention to Kenzie, and said with a dour expression, "You must be the girl Molly met over the weekend."

Kenzie extended her hand. "I'm Kenzie Wallis-Manning. Molly and I met at the Rainbow Corner Club Friday. We met Major McBain and his friend at the Savoy Saturday night. And you are…?"

"Oh!" Molly said. "I'm sorry, this is my other roommate, Zoey."

"Friend?" Zoey asked.

Molly jumped in, asking Kenzie, "How was your audition? Are you in the show?"

"The last joke sealed the deal," she said.

"Tell me the joke. What was it?" Molly asked.

"An actor calls the theatre office to talk to the director. 'I'm sorry, he's dead,' comes the reply. The actor calls back twenty-five times, always getting the same reply from the receptionist. At last she asks him why he keeps calling." Kenzie glanced at McBain and waited for him to tell the punch line.

He stared back, eyebrows raised. "Because I just like to hear ye' say it."

"Have you heard all—?"

Kenzie cut Molly off, determined to tell a joke McBain didn't know. "What does it say on a blues singer's tombstone?"

McBain smiled. "I didn't wake up this morning."

Kenzie turned to face him squarely and fired another joke at him. "I've got a new dog. He's a paranoid retriever."

McBain faced her, although Zoey maintained her clasp on his arm. "He brings back everything because he's not sure what I threw him.'"

Kenzie seethed. Why hadn't it bothered her when her grandfather blabbed her punch lines, while it irritated the hell out of her when McBain did? It took a moment for the realization to hit that it had been a fun game with her grandfather, but it was a battle of wills with McBain.

Molly jumped in again to cut the tension building between Kenzie and McBain. "Kenzie and I saw your friend Jack this morning at the train station."

McBain dragged his attention from Kenzie to Molly. "He didn't mention it,"

"We were already on the train. He didn't see us."

Zoey stuck her nose in the air. "*Well*, I can see I'm wasting my time here." She managed a well-practiced half-pirouette on the toe of one foot and flounced off.

Molly cocked her head, watching her roommate stomp off. "Zoey can be sweet, but she doesn't do well with competition."

"I noticed a restaurant a short distance from here. Could I interest ye' ladies in a bite to eat?"

Molly folded a square of paper and slipped it into her pocket. "I'm needed elsewhere for an hour or two. If you could take Kenzie and drop her at the Bletchley Inn afterwards, I would be grateful."

Kenzie's first thought was that Molly was being summoned for bringing Kenzie onto the Park's premises without the necessary security clearance. But that made no sense, since Kenzie had already met with Commander Travis and Professor Turing. Military Intelligence could have become involved, though. If so, Molly could be subjected to an uncomfortable interrogation.

"I can wait for you," Kenzie said.

Molly gave her an apologetic look "I'm not sure how long I'll be. A co-worker just slipped this message into my hand. I really must go right now."

"But—" Kenzie said to Molly before she quickly disappeared in the crowd. Kenzie chewed her bottom lip. It was too soon to get word back from the embassy. Her cover couldn't be blown, not yet. However, it did make her question her decision to wait a couple of days. Leaving town tomorrow seemed a smarter move.

"If ye're ready, we'll go now," McBain said.

"I need to get my suitcase. It's on the other side of the stage." McBain followed and collected the bag. "I can carry that," she said.

"I know ye' can. And so can I."

Kenzie left the Assembly Hall with McBain. On the way out, they passed Zoey in the company of two young men, neither of whom could have measured up to McBain. If looks could kill, yep, Kenzie would now be a squashed bug on the windshield. She sloughed it off. In high school, she had dealt with several girls with similar personalities and learned that they might have loud barks, but would quickly tuck their tails and run if anyone barked back. Zoey was harmless. When Molly returned to her billet tonight, she could easily turn down Zoey's temperature from a boil to a simmer with a few well-chosen words.

What left Kenzie confused was why she cared. If Zoey wanted to flirt with McBain, what difference did it make? Kenzie would only be at Bletchley for another day, maybe two.

It was hard to ignore the man walking beside her. His presence might not intimidate most women, at least those who only saw him as a cheetah who could only purr and run fast. Kenzie saw him as much more than that. He was a fully mature male lion, destined to dominate a large pride of females and cubs, and she had given up tangling with high-testosterone men like him when she left the Army.

But she had a question for him.

Thirty minutes later, they were seated in the dining room at the Garden Café & Restaurant in Bletchley. She ordered a beer and McBain asked for tea.

"I'll never get used to warm beer." She set down her glass, making a face. "What's the difference between light beer and having sex in a rowboat?"

McBain laughed. "They're both…Hmm. On water, nearly water, what?"

"Close to water."

He leaned forward with his elbows on the table. "You've got quite a repertoire. When'd ye' start telling jokes?"

She twirled a fork with her fingertip, studying the tines as the silverware turned round and round on the tablecloth, a distraction while she thought of an answer. "Forever ago. Ninth grade. My dad and I had just relocated to Texas. New school. No friends. I repeated a joke I heard the previous day. It got a laugh. The other kids were a little friendlier after that. I stopped at the library on the way home from school and borrowed a book on joke telling. The next day I told the ones I learned overnight. The next thing I knew, I was everybody's best friend. They wanted me around because I made them laugh."

"Why do ye' tell them now?"

She shrugged. "Habit. And I enjoy making people laugh."

"Do ye' write yer own?"

"Sometimes, but I pay attention and remember jokes I've heard. I recycle them, change them up a bit."

"Here's one ye' can change for whatever audience ye're playing to. A Scots boy came home from school and told his mother he had been given a part in the school play. 'Wonderful,' says the mother. 'What part is it?' The boy says, 'The part of the Scottish husband.' The mother scowls and says: 'Go back and tell yer teacher ye' want a speaking part.'"

Kenzie laughed, not only because the joke was funny, but because McBain's intonation and accent added a thick layer of humor—a Scottish layer.

Her enjoyment astonished her, but it shouldn't have. She had loved her mother's accent and the sound of her laughter. Those memories were deeply embedded in Kenzie's heart. Scotland hadn't hurt her. Only some mean people who lived there.

The waiter took their dinner order and returned with their plates within a few minutes.

She dug into the food with gusto, surprised by how hungry she was. "You're different from other men I've met here. Why is that?"

"Ye' probably haven't met many Scots."

McBain had impeccable manners, and ate at a leisurely pace. If she hadn't trained in the Military Intelligence Corps, she wouldn't have noticed he had his back to the wall, and although he didn't stare, his ears did it for him. Even when the door opened. He knew who entered the room without looking directly at the new arrival. He was a trained warrior. That should have made her more comfortable. It didn't.

"I've never been to Scotland," she said. "Never wanted to go, but I think I might now. How long does it take to get to Inverness?"

"About eleven hours. Why go now?"

"Just curious, I guess. I have a couple of days before I start work." She chewed on her lip. "Do you speak Gaelic?"

"Aye."

"Will you translate a sentence for me?"

There was a flicker of a glint in his eye, but it came and went so quickly she wasn't sure whether she actually saw it.

"Aye. Is it something ye' read?"

"It's an inscription on a family heirloom." She worried the cuff of her blouse between her fingers. Was she making the right decision? What if the words described the fog or time travel?

Ask him, Kenz. You have to know.

"I apologize in advance for mispronouncing the words. Gaelic is the most difficult language I've ever tried to speak. The inscription goes like this—" Before she said the first word, McBain's knee pressed against her, but she was concentrating on the Gaelic more than the Scotsman, and left her knee where it was. "—*Chan ann le tìm no àite a bhios sinn a' tomhais a' gaol ach's ann le neart anama.*"

He immediately removed his knee, and the absence of the pressure from his leg was even more noticeable than the pressure had been. She sensed more than heard his quiet sigh. After a moment he said, "Love is not measured by time or space. Love is measured by the power of the soul."

She repeated the words slowly, shaking her head, and then said softly, "I don't understand."

He gulped his tea, and grimaced as if in pain, but then quickly wiped the grimace from his face without further acknowledgement of any discomfort. "Scottish Gaelic can be traced back to the 4th Century AD. Depending on the age of the heirloom, the meaning of the words could be slightly different. I interpret it to mean: Love is birthed and nurtured by yer soul, and neither time nor distance can separate it from the beloved."

In a few brief words, he had outlined the puzzle she needed to solve. Somewhere hidden in those words was the answer to the riddle that would carry her home. Could the beloved be her grandfather? If so, then what did that mean for her?

"Do ye' intend to work at Bletchley until the war ends?" he asked, pulling her thoughts away from the ancestor she had met only hours earlier.

Stalling for a moment, she pushed away her empty dish, brushed crumbs off the tablecloth into her hand, and then dumped them onto the plate. The corner of McBain's mouth quirked up, as if he thought her tidying her place at the table was what? Cute? If he could see the way she left her apartment or the contents of her backpack, he would probably think she was a slob. She wasn't. It was a childish habit of asserting her independence.

Answer the question quickly and move on.

She lifted her eyes toward the ceiling briefly before answering, "As long as I can be helpful. But what about you? I know you'll go wherever you're sent, so instead I'll ask what you intend to do *after* the war."

"Jack and I have a writing project we're working on. We'll look around to see if there's interest in publishing our book."

"Fiction or nonfiction?"

"Fiction based on a true story, but a writer never talks about his work in progress, so that's all ye're going to get out of me."

Hoping for book information was not the reason she was staring at his mouth. *Stop thinking about kissing him. Tell a joke.*

"A visitor to a certain college paused to admire the new Fitzgerald Hall that had been built on campus. 'It's a pleasure to see a building named for F. Scott Fitzgerald,' he said. 'Actually,' said his guide, 'it's named for Robert Fitzgerald. No relation.' The visitor was astonished. 'Was Robert Fitzgerald a writer, too? Yes, indeed,' said his guide enthusiastically. 'He wrote the check.' "

McBain chuckled. "Do ye' have a joke for everything?"

"In most situations I can pull out a line or two."

After the waiter removed their empty plates, he asked, "Do ye' plan to see yer pilot again?"

"I wouldn't call him my pilot."

"I'm going to Cambridge on Saturday to meet Jack. He should be finished with his interviews by them. If ye' and Molly want to go, I'll ask Jack to get a message to Cavanaugh and Rainer."

"I'll mention it to her." Kenzie yawned. "Excuse me. I've had a long day. I need to report by oh-five-thirty, so I'd better go find my room."

"That's early."

"Dr. Turing sent a note over to the Assembly Hall asking me to run with him. I don't know how many miles he has in mind, but I sure hope he doesn't plan to run a twenty-miler."

"After all the dancing ye' did last night, I'm surprised ye' agreed to a run."

"Some people you can't say no to."

"Guess not." McBain set down his cup. "If ye're ready, I'll take ye' to the Inn."

He paid the check, and on the way out of the restaurant, Kenzie shivered in the nippy air, hugging her jacket snugly around her.

"How often do you get home, to Scotland, I mean?"

"I'm going tomorrow for a quick trip. Ye're welcome to come with me."

"It's tempting, but tomorrow won't work." He was the last person she wanted to travel with. Venturing into the middle of a lion's cage wasn't on her agenda. She sneezed.

"Gesundheit," a man said in passing.

She sneezed again. "Danke." *How odd to speak German on a street in England right now.* She glanced around but the man had disappeared into the darkness. "Either Bletchley's pollution or the damp air is bothering my nose."

"Ye' should spend time in Scotland and build up yer resistance."

"I'd rather go to a sunny beach and build up resistance to high humidity."

They strolled down the sidewalk. "If ye' change yer mind and want to travel with me tomorrow, leave a message at the Inn's front desk when ye' go out for yer run."

"Are you staying at the same place?"

"Arrived in time to book the last room in the house."

"I won't change my mind, but thank you."

"I might have to return again soon. I'll let ye' know. But fair warning. The weather is ne're good this time of year. For a favorable impression, ye' should wait a few months."

"I don't have a few months," she mumbled into her handkerchief.

30

Fraser House, the Highlands, June 2, 1944

DUE TO TRAIN delays, it took David a day longer to reach Inverness. Most of the time he was either cussing the railroad or staring out the window of the train, watching eagles and hawks soar above the rough, shaggy heather. The rugged landscape normally absorbed him, but not this trip.

Every moment away from his own time was anxiety-ridden. Every moment away from Kenzie was fucking hell. Although she had given him no reason not to trust her, he didn't, for the sole reason that he couldn't predict her behavior. Instead of lying low, she insisted on drawing attention to herself. Why? The only reason he could figure was that she didn't appreciate the danger she could be in. She had no identification and was working at a high-security facility. If that didn't draw the attention of Military Intelligence, then they weren't doing an effective job of protecting the United Kingdom.

During dinner Sunday night, he had the perfect opportunity to tell her who he was and why he was there, but he stubbornly stuck to his plan. He and Elliott had discussed this in depth, and Elliott insisted there be no repeats of the Charlotte and Braham escapade. David had to be sure Cavanaugh was the man Kenzie was meant to be with. There would be no second chances to get it right.

If David had asked her whether she had deep feelings for Cavanaugh, he knew in his gut the answer would have been no.

From what he had seen Saturday night, they were obviously hot for each other, but, as Jack implied, they hadn't steamed up the windows.

What troubled him was her recitation of the brooch's inscription. Even though she was a polyglot like Jack, could she have memorized the inscription from reading it only once? It was highly unlikely. Therefore, he had to assume she studied the inscription and memorized it. He had done the same. In the event of an emergency, or the absence of light, he wanted the words to roll off his tongue. Jack had the words memorized as well. But if Kenzie had spoken the words a second time with the brooch open, the fog would have swept her home. As far as he knew the brooch had always worked. Had Kenzie tried to use the brooch to go home and the incantation failed to summon the fog? That had to have been frightening for her to believe she was stranded. She wasn't stranded, though. He intended to take her home.

David settled into an easy stride for the jog to Fraser House. The Highlands were as familiar to him as the rabbits darting into the bushes as he clomped through the heather.

The stars provided enough illumination to guide him through the moors, but the combined brilliance of all the stars in the universe couldn't shine enough light on what was motivating Kenzie Wallis-Manning.

Her psychological profile corroborated his assessment that she was a risk taker. But his research and analysis showed that her risks were controlled. She didn't go rock climbing without a harness, nor did she trade on the market without the advice of a highly reputable broker.

David crossed another berm, climbed a rocky outcrop, and surveyed the surroundings. Spotting nothing alarming, he climbed down and jogged the remaining distance, with Kenzie once again occupying his thoughts.

The woman had gotten under his skin, and he knew he was setting himself up for another fall of mammoth proportions, but his heart didn't seem the least perturbed by the prospect of another crack the size of the Grand Canyon.

She wasn't his and never would be, but that didn't stop the wanting.

He settled her into a quiet corner of his mind and focused on his next steps, not just the ones through the heather, but what he intended to do once he reached Fraser House...and what he would do if he encountered Auld Fraser. Although Elliott believed his grandfather would welcome the idea of a time traveler, David wasn't so sure. He had been skeptical when he first heard about Kit's adventure back in time, but he eventually came around. He didn't believe Elliott's grandfather ever would. He was too much of a Fraser—translation: stubborn as hell.

David's plan was to sneak into the house through the cave, without alarming anyone, and leave a message for Elliott.

The berm with the secret entrance to the cave was hidden among the ancient Caledonian pines behind the house. He reached into his satchel, pulled out a pair of night vision goggles, and turned in a three-sixty to survey the terrain. London had changed since the Forties. MacKlenna Farm had changed. But in this part of Scotland, the land remained the same.

He climbed the berm and pushed aside the underbrush that concealed the entrance. The opening wasn't large enough for a man to stand, and would go unnoticed by passersby. Wild boars might find their way inside, and possibly back out again, but not humans. It was that well concealed.

The cave-in during the 1700s had left a rocky path from the entrance where he now stood to the heavy door leading into the wine cellar. The second cave-in, during the 1960s, completely blocked the path. Until Meredith took an interest in enlarging the wine cellar, no one had given a damn about the cave except the bats.

He switched on his flashlight and climbed through the cave's opening, startling the bats and rats. The creatures didn't concern him. The damp, moldy, enclosed darkness did. Despite the chill inside the cave, he started sweating profusely. A host of childhood memories assaulted him. He pushed them aside, or tried to, wiped his sleeve across his sweaty brow, and picked up his pace to get through the cave as quickly as possible.

As he neared the door to the wine cellar, the flashlight beam lighted up two pieces of squared timber framing the top of what must have been the opening to a tunnel, but the entrance was buried beneath heavy boulders. The second cave-in must have demolished the entrance entirely, because no one had ever mentioned it before. Having two escape tunnels made sense, and he wondered where the exit was hidden among the moors.

He made it through the debris piles easily enough and reached the door to the wine cellar. His hand shook and it took longer than it should have to pick the lock, but he did, and the door swung open. He stood still and listened. Other than the skittering rats and a trickle of water, he heard nothing else. The odds of Auld Fraser being in the wine cellar at this hour of the night were slim, but possible.

The lights were out. He flipped on the light switch and bolted the door behind him. If he left through the kitchen, which he fully intended to do, he didn't want an unlocked door discovered later.

The cellar was empty, at least of people. The centuries-old bottles of wine were stacked on shelves covered in dust, and would remain that way until Meredith appeared on the scene and modernized an already efficient wine cellar into a high tech one.

David still found it ironic that Elliott, who hated wine and never darkened the door to the wine cellar, fell in love with and married a vintner. His opinion of wine still hadn't changed, but he no longer harped on the stupidity of not selling off bottles of wine that had more than likely turned to vinegar. They could easily be auctioned off for something in the high six figures.

David treaded lightly across the dusty floor, but didn't bother covering his tracks. If his prints were discovered, Auld Fraser would likely believe the estate manager had been here, and the estate manager would believe the old man had been here.

The rickety, open-sided stairs to the kitchen were the same damn stairs he'd climbed for most of his life until Meredith had them replaced soon after she and Elliott married.

David climbed the stairs carefully, avoiding the creaks and groans that would announce his presence. He reached the top step and put his ear to the kitchen door, but heard nothing. He turned the knob and prepared to tuck and roll if Auld Fraser was standing on the other side of the door pointing a loaded shotgun.

A light flashed on, blinding him momentarily, and the sound of a rifle being cocked froze both the breath in his lungs and his feet to the floor.

"Don't move, ye' thievin' bastard, or I'll shoot ye' where ye' stand," a gruff voice bellowed.

David raised his hands, cursing at himself, Elliott, and Auld Fraser. "I thought I could get in and out and ye'd never know I was here."

Fraser kicked the door wide and it banged against the wall. "Who the hell are ye'? And how'd ye' get into the cellar?"

David's hands remained in the air and his eyes on the rifle. Although Elliott's grandfather was only in his mid-forties and appeared fit, David knew he could disarm him without hurting either of them. But he decided to let Fraser believe he was in control. Unless the situation escalated, David would play along for now. "I came in through the cave."

Elliott's grandfather jabbed the air with the rifle. "What the hell for? Ye' stealing the wine?"

David shook his head. "I'm not here to steal yer wine, yer jewelry, or yer rare books. Nor am I here to hurt ye'."

Fraser nodded toward the kitchen table and chairs. "Sit yer arse down. If ye're not a thief, why didn't ye' come to the front door?"

"It's complicated."

Fraser sneered. "I'm a pretty smart fella. Can't be that complicated."

David scrutinized the man in the glow from the table lamp. Nothing about him would lead anyone to believe he was the village idiot. His stature, strong facial features, and deep, thoughtful eyes appeared to be the much younger version of the quick-witted, intelligent, brutally honest, and respected man David had known as a lad.

"Keep yer hands where I can see them and start talking. If I don't like what ye're saying, I'll call the authorities or shoot ye' myself."

David eased into a chair. His heart pounded—not because he was afraid of the man holding a rifle pointed at his chest, but because he now would have to explain his presence, and even an intelligent man would find his story difficult to believe.

"I'm not a threat to ye', sir. Ye' can uncock the rifle."

Fraser hooked his foot around the leg of another chair, dragged it close, and sat directly opposite David, holding the rifle steady. "I'll decide whether ye're a threat or not. Ye' can start with how ye' got in and go from there."

David relaxed his upper body, but not his instincts. Those remained sharp and focused. He rested his hands on his knees, but his feet were firmly planted. He could spring forward at a moment's notice, quick as a cat, and disarm Fraser.

"I knew where the entrance was hidden in the embankment behind the house, and I picked the lock into the wine cellar."

"Why didn't ye' take the wine and skedaddle. Why come up here?"

The odds of Fraser believing his story fell somewhere between not at all and deciding that David was delusional and dangerous. In either case, David would have to disarm him, tie him up, leave the message for Elliott, and then run like hell. Unless…

"Did ye' know the corbel on the right side of the fireplace slides open?"

Fraser glanced at the low-burning fire. A quick glance, but long enough that David could have easily disarmed him. He didn't, though. Fraser might be more receptive to the story of the brooches if he believed he had control over the situation.

Fraser scrunched up his face and puckered his lips in a considering expression. A similar look to one Elliott frequently used.

"Once ye' slide the corbel down, ye'll find a secret compartment," David said.

Fraser's posture perked up, and he slid forward slightly in his chair. He couldn't hide his curiosity. "How do ye' know?"

"Do ye' want me to show ye'? David asked.

Fraser nodded and David stood slowly. "I'll need the knife in my pocket."

"Ye' try anything, I'll shoot ye'."

"Don't get nervous with yer trigger finger. This might be stuck pretty tight." David used his knife as he had done days earlier, but the corbel slid down easily, revealing the compartment."

"I'll be damned," Fraser said. "Now that ye' got it open, what do ye' plan to do?"

David closed his knife and shoved it into his pants pocket, then withdrew the note from his shirt pocket that he had written during the train ride. "Put this note inside and close it back up."

"Read it to me. And read it right, because I'll check it for sure."

David unfolded the note and read, "I found Kenzie. She's well and was hired on at Bletchley. Jack is at Bassingbourn Air Field Base with Lieutenant Christopher Joseph Cavanaugh. He's a pilot from Boston, currently serving with the Eighth Air Force. All we know about him is that he survived thirty-five missions. Kenzie appears to like him, but nothing serious yet. Pretty sure he's the right man.

"She met her grandfather at Bletchley Park. I don't know how much of his story she's aware of. She doesn't know who I am or why I'm here. Planning a weekend in Cambridge to get Kenzie and Cavanaugh together to see if there's a spark.

"She met a woman in London named Molly Bradford. Molly got her an interview at Bletchley even without identification, which Kenzie claims was stolen with her suitcase while on the train from Cambridge. Security will be checking with the American Embassy. I figure she's safe for several days before they discover she doesn't exist. Military Intelligence will be very interested in how a multilingual woman gained access to a high-security facility.

"She asked me to translate the Gaelic inscription. I did. She said it was inscribed on a family heirloom. She asked me where old wills were kept in Scotland. I told her they were at the archives in Edinburgh. I don't know why she wants to know, but she clearly has a plan in mind. If I tell her I was sent to bring her home, she could either run or accept my help. I don't know which, and I can't afford the time it would take to track her down if she bolts. If she knows I'm here because of her father, she would bolt for sure. Until I know more, I'm keeping my identity a secret.

"However this plays out, I plan to wrap it up within the next three days and be out of here before..." David hesitated and hedged his words. Instead of saying D-day, he said, "Before early June.

"I've also included contact information for the Ritz in London, Molly's relatives, the air base, and the hotel in Bletchley."

David refolded the letter and then held it out for Fraser. "Ye're welcome to read it."

Fraser tensed and slapped David's hand with the barrel of the rifle. "Put yer damn letter away. Ye're a disgrace to the Highlands. Ye're working for the Germans. I'd just as soon shoot ye' now."

"I'm *not* a spy," David said adamantly. "I'm from the twenty-first century, and so are Kenzie Wallis-Manning and my friend Jack Mallory."

It was time to put it all out there before Fraser got frisky with the trigger. David opened his other palm, revealing the ruby brooch. Fraser stumbled backwards. David took advantage of his stumble and snatched the rifle out of his hands. He set the brooch on the mantle while he removed all the cartridges, shoved them into his pocket, and hung the rifle in the rack near the back door.

Fraser gripped the mantel for support, shocked and ashen-faced. "Where did ye' get that stone?"

David's breath hitched. "Have ye' seen it before?"

"Nay," Fraser said softly. "I never believed the auld stories." He let go of the mantel and shuffled toward a cabinet in the corner. "I need a drink." He took a bottle of whiskey and two glasses to the table and collapsed into a chair. "Where did ye' get the ruby one?"

"From yer future grandson, Elliott Fraser."

Elliott's grandfather looked as if he'd been shot dead and hadn't realized it yet. Watching him recover his senses, David realized how much Elliott resembled him. Auld Fraser had the same lean runner's body, deep brown eyes, prematurely gray brown hair, chiseled cheeks. More rugged and weathered than Elliott, but just as handsome.

"I only have one child," Fraser said. "A son, Blaine Fraser. If he's going to have a son, that means he'll survive the war, come home, and marry. I want to know the lassie's name."

Of all the questions that must be running through his mind, the old man wanted to know the name of his future daughter-in-law. David almost chuckled, but maintained his composure and said, "Aileen McGregor."

Fraser poured one glass of whiskey and started to pour another. "None for me," David said.

"What kind of man doesn't drink whiskey?"

"The kind who's had a bottle too many." That was an easier explanation than trying to explain his stomach ailments. He filled the glass with tap water.

"She's a bonny lass," Fraser said. "I knew Blaine was sweet on her, but didn't know his affections were reciprocated."

They weren't reciprocated long enough, David thought sadly, remembering the trauma of Aileen's abandonment of her family for the love of another man. The scars that crisscrossed Elliott's heart from his mother's betrayal had taken years to heal. It had taken Meredith to put him back together.

David extended his arm, holding up the water glass. "To yer health."

Fraser stretched and clinked his glass against David's. "Slàinte." Fraser sipped and after a moment said. "My grandda told me as a lad: 'Some see darkness, but others see only the absence of light.' He told me to always keep my mind open. That situations will arise that will seem improbable, but they will be impossible only for the unbelievers.'"

"Yer grandda was a wise man. I've heard yer future grandson credit ye' with that saying."

Fraser emptied his glass and refilled it. "Where'd ye' come from?"

"I took the train from Cambridge."

"Don't sass me, laddie. Ye' know I'm not talking about trains."

"Aye. I left from London seventy years in the future."

"And the brooch, where'd it come from?"

David set aside the glass and placed his hands on the counter behind him, bracketing his hips. "Through the MacKlenna family. Thomas MacKlenna gave it to his daughter Jamilyn the day she married Donald McCabe in the early 1820s."

"How'd ye' come by it, then?"

"Jamilyn MacKlenna McCabe immigrated to America in 1826 with her newborn."

"They died on that ship during a storm," Auld Fraser said. "The MacKlennas live close by. I'm familiar with the story."

"The newborn didn't die," David said. "The baby was wearing this brooch when she appeared on the doorstep of MacKlenna Farm in Lexington, Kentucky, in the 1980s."

Auld Fraser's steely-eyed gaze held David in a vise. "That would be Sean MacKlenna's horse farm. Sean the fifth, I believe. Haven't seen him in several years."

"It was Sean the sixth who found the baby. He adopted her. He didn't know about the magic in the stone until several years later."

Fraser glanced over at where the stone rested on the mantle.

"The ruby brooch isn't the only one," David said. "We know there are three: a ruby, a sapphire, and an emerald. We believe the emerald was sent to Kenzie Wallis-Manning. She disappeared, and I was sent back to this time to find her. She's now at Bletchley Park near Cambridge."

"The note you read is for Blaine's lad."

"Aye," David said.

"Is she related to the Robert Wallises from Inverness?"

"Aye."

"Are ye' sure it's the emerald she's got?" Fraser asked.

"Has to be. There're only three, and Elliott has control of the ruby and sapphire."

Fraser gave a dismissive wave. "There're more than three. Possibly a dozen or so. The stones ye've mentioned, plus a diamond, and several semi-precious stones. A black pearl for one. Or, at least that's the story my grandda passed along to me."

David was tempted to put the cartridges back in the rifle and give the damn gun to Auld Fraser. Shoot him now and spare him decades of time-traveling histrionics. "Tell me anything, but don't tell me that."

Auld Fraser pinched his lips together and made an exaggerated twisting motion as if locking them with a key.

David rubbed the space between his eyebrows, which he'd been doing a lot lately, a habit he reserved for times of extreme stress, deep thought, or those what-the-fuck-am-I-going-to-do-now moments. In resignation, he said, "I'd be grateful if ye'd tell me everything ye' know."

Fraser didn't say anything for a beat or two, and then his breathing turned unsteady, a tinge of fear clouded his eyes. "My grandda was the only person ever to mention the stones to me. I was a lad of seven or eight." He stopped, glanced around, and lowered his voice. "He took me to the cave where we would be alone, and he confessed a secret he'd held for six decades. He made me pledge never to speak of it."

"Why tell me now?" David asked.

"You have a stone. You're part of the brotherhood."

"Was your grandda part of the brotherhood too?"

"If he was, he would have told…" Auld Fraser paused and scratched his scruffy cheek. "He must have been, but I've never seen one of the brooches afore now."

There was a prolonged silence in the room while David considered the pledge, or more importantly, the breaking of the pledge. He wasn't a member of anything other than a writers' guild and the local parish. But a brotherhood—whoa—he was the wrong man.

Auld Fraser took a swig of whiskey. "For centuries, or so my grandda said, there was a Keeper who held all the stones. Both the position of Keeper and the stones were passed down from one generation to the next until the mid-1600s, when Cromwell defeated the Scots at the Battle of Dunbar. The stones were disbursed among Highlanders for safekeeping soon afterward, and the four precious stones were given to a laird."

"That jives with the story told by Sean MacKlenna. Wait a minute. Ye' said four? I only know about three."

"Mayhap the laird kept one for himself. If it was also a precious stone, it would have been a diamond."

"So we can expect a diamond to appear one day."

Auld Fraser chuckled. "And the semi-precious stones, too. I don't envy ye', lad."

David was suddenly heartsick. After this mission, he didn't know if he could go back in time again. By then he'd likely be as gray-haired as Auld Fraser. "Where do ye' think the other stones are now?"

Fraser stared into his whiskey glass as if it contained the secrets of life. After a moment he continued with his thought. "According to the story, the Keeper gave them to Highlanders. The likelihood of the stones still being in Scotland, hidden among family heirlooms, is quite possible, but then," he shrugged, "they could be anywhere in the world."

"Where did the Keeper originally get them?"

Fraser shrugged again—this time, though, his shoulders almost reached his ears. "Guess he always had them."

The statement robbed David of wind and left him feeling his footing wasn't in a shallow stream, but planted firmly in the center of a trapdoor. He shoved his fingers through his hair, looking around the kitchen that he would one day remodel. Generations of Highlanders had lived in this room. Some had even conspired against the English Crown to restore the Stuarts to the throne of Great Britain. Some of them would have been given a stone.

More brooches surfacing at some point in the future made the fire in the pit of his stomach flare up hotter than hell. He wasn't going to add that bit of information to the note to Elliott, nor would

David tell Jack. When life had settled down for everyone, David would share the news, but not until then. Maybe not until another brooch showed up on Elliott's doorstep.

Auld Fraser stood and picked up the bottle and his glass. "I suggest ye' hide yer note, then join me in the library. I want to know everything that's going to happen in the next seventy years. Then it will be time for ye' to catch yer train back to Cambridge."

David shoved the note into the small space and raised the corbel. "Are ye' sure ye' want to know the future?"

"Everything but the date of my death."

"Ye' can pick my brain for the next twelve hours, but if ye' ask me information that I don't think ye' should know, I'll pass on it, and ye' have to respect my decision."

"Fair enough," Fraser said. "Now, ye' can start with telling me when this blasted war will end."

31

Fraser House, the Highlands, June 3, 1944

Before leaving Fraser House the next morning, David used the black phone in the foyer and called the operator to put a call through to Jack at Bassingbourn.

After a few minutes, Jack came on the line. "Molly called and told me about the cabaret. I worked it out. Cav and I are coming to the show."

"You're doing *what*? How'd ye' convince Cavanaugh's Commanding Officer to give him the night off?" A prickle sparked at the back of his neck. Aye, he wanted to get Kenzie and Cavanaugh together, but he hadn't planned on it being so soon. He had intended to take her to a late dinner after the show. He could still host an after-party, but Cavanaugh would have her attention.

Ye' dumb arse.

Jack broke into David's self-censure, saying, "I told him it would be great PR. Travel arrangements have been made, and unless the war takes a turn for the worse in the next few hours, we'll be at the Assembly Hall."

"I shouldn't be surprised at yer persuasive skills. Ye' did convince John Wilkes Booth to give ye' an interview with the expectation of a favorable review."

"Well...thanks. You didn't have to remind me of that one."

"I only wanted to remind ye' of how yer great ideas often sink ye' into a crap hole, leaving others to dig ye' out."

"Are you reminding me of Washington again?"

"Only because it nearly killed yer sister."

"This time is different. Give me a little credit."

"Show me ye' deserve it." David paused, waiting for a reaction, a murmur, or grunt of understanding, but he got nothing. Feeling the edge of an approaching storm, he said, "If Kenzie and Cavanaugh hit it off, we're going home after the show."

"I know this is a bitch of a favor to ask, but can we wait until this weekend? Cav has worked it out with his CO to let me go on a milk run."

"Haven't ye' been listening to this conversation? Clean out your goddamn ears. Ye're *not* flying in Cavanaugh's B-17."

"There's no danger. We'll be in Allied territory…most of the time." Jack tried mumbling the words, but David heard "most of the time" quite clearly. "If there was a possibility of encountering enemy fighters—" Jack continued, speaking distinctly now, "—the CO wouldn't have agreed."

"But *yer* CO says no."

There was extended silence and then Jack said. "I'll see you at show. And get some sleep. You sound like you've been on a drinking binge for a week, and I thought you quit drinking." Jack hung up, leaving David glaring at the handset. If Jack had been within five feet, David would have punched him.

Hang up on me, but ye're not gettin' yer way this time. I'm hauling yer arse on the first fog ride home.

David replaced the receiver and considered how to handle the upcoming reunion. If there was an attraction between Kenzie and Cavanaugh, David would see it in their eyes. Unless there was nothing there, which he seriously doubted after witnessing the make-out session on the Bradfords' doorstep, he'd whisper the magic words and have them all home before breakfast. Jack didn't even need to know what he planned.

He would need to do some explaining to Kenzie and Cavanaugh, he knew that, but explanations would be easier to make afterwards. After he locked up the three brooches or—better yet, threw them in the ocean. And then he remembered what Auld Fraser had said about the existence of other brooches. If Cavanaugh or Kenzie ever wanted to return to the past, they would find a way. David wearily dragged his hands down his face. He'd had little sleep for days, and had talked so long he was hoarse.

Fraser had given him as much history about the past as David had given him about the future. A fair trade. When David returned home, he would give the information to Elliott a bit at a time until whatever crisis he and Meredith were facing was resolved.

Fraser stepped out of the library and met David in the foyer. "Did ye' reach yer friend?"

David nodded. "He's bringing Cavanaugh to the Assembly Hall for the performance. If all goes well, we'll return to the future after the show."

"I wish ye' well. If it doesn't work out, and ye' need a place to stay, ye're welcome here."

"Thank ye', sir. I'm looking forward to telling Elliott about our conversations."

"Just so ye' know," Fraser said. "I'll never say anything about the brooches, our meeting, the future, or the past. I will, however, take an interest in yer life and provide whatever guidance and discipline is appropriate. Ye're a fine lad."

David laughed. "I hope I'll listen to ye'."

They embraced. A tear trickled down Fraser's cheek and he swiped at it. "Thank ye' for letting me know my son will come home alive."

David's eyes also watered. He didn't want to tell Fraser that his son, Blaine, would have a hard time coping later in life, so instead he gave Auld Fraser a testimonial about his grandson. "His son Elliott is the finest man I've ever known. He's highly regarded by not only the Thoroughbred industry, but by kings, queens, and sheiks all around the world, and gives the credit to ye'. I thank ye' for the way ye' shaped him. He's a man I'd take a bullet for."

Fraser opened the massive front door, and said, "*Mar sin leibh.*"

"*Mar sin leibh,*" David said good-bye in return and set out on his hike back to the train station. Only this time he wasn't weighed down with worry about entering the cave and sneaking into the house. Instead, the heavy weight on his shoulders and on his heart came from the knowledge of centuries of Gaelic lore that, if true, would change the direction of his life forever.

32

Bletchley Park, England, June 3, 1944

KENZIE WAS PACING backstage, going through a list of jokes, when someone hugged her from behind, squeezing her shoulders as only a lover would do, and then warm lips pressed against her neck. In a Boston accent, a man said, "I've been dreaming of doing this for days."

Smiling, she leaned back into Cav. "I didn't know you were coming." She turned in his arms and wrapped hers around his neck. "What a wonderful surprise."

"Jack Mallory convinced my CO that part of the interview should include an evening out enjoying local entertainment." Cav's tone was reminiscent of the one he used the last time she'd seen him. His voice, and the private smile they exchanged, put her right back on the Bradfords' steps, where she had nestled against the muscular planes of his body from her knees to her collarbone. Even now, the heat between them was palpable.

"Let's get out of here," she said.

Near them, two stagehands dressed in black pants and shirts stood in the wings waiting for the next set change. Simultaneously, they pressed a finger to their lips. "Shhh."

Ignoring them, Cav said, "We can't leave. You're on next, and I came to watch you perform. After the last few days I've had, I need a good laugh. I need several good laughs."

She rose on her toes and kissed him lightly on the lips. His eyes brightened before he bent his head and claimed her mouth with his, pressing into her with unmistakable implication. She went soft against him, giving him complete access to her mouth. His tongue was stormy and tempestuous, and she wanted him. They could be in her room at the inn stripped naked in ten minutes. He gentled, but passion quickly replaced tenderness. The movement of his tongue became less aggressive, more intimate. She moaned when he lifted his head, taking the warmth of his mouth from hers. She tossed her hair back and it fell silkily over one side of her face. He ran his fingers through the strands, tucking them behind her ear.

"Ms. Wallis-Manning, you're on now," one of the stagehands said.

The words registered, barely, but she didn't care.

Someone tapped her shoulder. "You're on. You have to go. You can pick up where you left off later, but the audience is waiting."

She and Cav stayed the way they were, tightly wrapped, until the second stagehand tugged on her arm. "They're clapping for you. Go."

Cav pulled away. "You can't keep your fans waiting. Molly has front row seats." Cav kissed her one last time. "I'll be the one laughing the loudest." He then gave her a light push in the direction of the curtain.

As she prepared to step onto the stage, she spotted McBain waiting in the wings on the opposite side of the stage. He mouthed the words, "Break a leg, Kenz." The idiom was enough to bring the present back into focus. She pressed her fingertips to her lips to seal Cav's last kiss. Then she took a deep breath, slipped on her performance face, and strode confidently out to center stage to rousing applause.

She started with a few redhead jokes and finished with her favorite pilot jokes, altered slightly by changing an F-16 to a B-17.

Thirty minutes later, after two encores, and sweating from the heat of the stage lights, she took her final bow and joined Cav, Molly, Rainer, and Jack in the front row.

Cav put his arm around her shoulder and pulled her close to

him, beaming. "You were brilliant. I hadn't heard any of those jokes. My sides still ache from laughing so hard. The crew will love hearing the ones I can remember."

She pulled a piece of paper from the sleeve of her blouse where she had tucked it earlier. "Here's my list. It might spark your memory."

He unfolded the sheet of paper and glanced at the punch lines of fifty jokes. "This will help. Thanks." He tucked it into his jacket pocket.

Jack, sitting on her other side, said, "Your delivery and timing were spot on. You're a natural. You could take your act on the road, and I bet every performance would be a sellout. If you need a manager, let me know. I've got a fantastic agent."

"Molly beat you to it," she replied. Something about his vernacular seemed odd, and his smile still tugged at her memory, begging to be recalled.

"Hell," he continued, "you can take it to Hollywood and become the measuring stick for all comedians."

She shook her head. "Not me." To her thinking, Eddie Murphy, Jerry Seinfeld, Robin Williams, Chris Rock, Jimmy Fallon, Ellen DeGeneres and others were the yardsticks. She moved the laugh meter only slightly when compared to the giants in the industry.

Onstage, the members of a three-piece band took their places for the next act, which she knew was McBain. The rendition of "Summertime" he played for his audition had probably sent ninety percent of the women in the audience to their lovers' beds or a cold shower. An encore performance would likely cause a similar reaction. She didn't want to listen. The soulful sounds from his saxophone would distract her from the sensual feelings Cav's kisses had already ignited.

But what excuse could she use to leave the hall? *Let's go before I swoon like hundreds of other women?*

She fidgeted in her chair. Cav took her hand and kissed the inside of her wrist. "Jack said he didn't even know David played the sax, and Molly said he's the best she's ever heard. I've been looking forward to this."

Damn. She was stuck.

McBain strode toward center stage, and a collective sigh seemed to sweep through the room. Kenzie glanced around to see women literally sitting on the edges of their seats.

Animal magnetism.

He adjusted the neck strap, then set the sax in proper alignment with his body while his long fingers hovered over the keys. He nodded at the members of the band, and the pianist began the interlude before he put the mouthpiece to his lips. When he blew into the instrument, the sound that came out was as soulful, sexy, and breathtaking as any music she had ever heard. The drummer added explosive backbeats and together they raised hairs on the back of her neck. McBain's rendition of "Smoke Gets in Your Eyes" sizzled with electrifying surprises—personal, eloquent, and revealing.

Sitting still while listening to his soft, sexy music was impossible. "Smoke" had been one of her parents' favorite songs. Images of them dancing across the living room filled her mind. She squeezed her eyes to make them go away. They did, sort of, but dancing people remained. Their faces however, were not her parents.

They were her and—God, no, say it ain't so—McBain.

"What the f—" Jack squashed the expletive before it fully formed. "I didn't know he could even play an instrument." Jack crossed his legs and plucked at his chin, shaking his head in wide-eyed astonishment. "If Char had known, this might have been a game changer."

McBain's ability to express himself musically could win over any available woman's heart. "What's a game changer?" Kenzie asked, knowing what the reference would mean in the twenty-first century, but unsure of its meaning in the twentieth.

"Nothing." Jack's explosive exhale surprised her. He was either deeply moved by his friend's talent or pissed that he hadn't known the talent existed.

They asked me how I knew...." She mouthed the lyrics, haunted by the visual that wouldn't let her go.

Several of the more brazen women rushed the stage. What? Were they trying to sneak a peek under his kilt? She could assuage their curiosity easily enough. The testosterone-overdosed Major would go commando. The image of what she would call his junk in Army vernacular was overly stimulating her imagination. She whispered to Cav, "I've got to go to the ladies' room."

Cav frowned, and disappointment darkened his eyes. "If you leave, you'll miss David's set."

How could she disappoint a man who looked at her with such fervent blue eyes? She couldn't, so she anchored herself firmly in her chair, and forced herself not to fidget, but the soft jazz unsettled her. She made it through "Smoke Gets in Your Eyes," barely, but after McBain hit the first few notes of "Somewhere Over the Rainbow," she sat transfixed with her heartbeat on pause while he held a single, emotionally charged note. When her heart finally beat again, she said, "I have to go to the ladies' room now. I'll hurry back."

Cav glanced at the stage and then at her. "I'll go with you."

Kenzie put her hand on his shoulder, pressing him back into his seat. "Stay. I won't be gone long." She didn't stick around to give him a second chance to be gallant. She ducked to avoid blocking the audience's view and dashed toward the exit, only then realizing she had left her purse in her chair. The emerald brooch, her class ring, and the Rubik's Cube were wrapped in tissue in a zipped pocket, along with some of her cash. Cav would take care of her bag and, as the gentleman he was, he wouldn't go through her belongings without an invitation.

She had no intention of reentering the Assembly Hall until McBain left the stage. If the gaggle of women who were all but throwing their underwear at him was any indication, he would be up there until he'd gone through his entire repertoire at least twice. The guy certainly had moves, and with lips that could produce sounds like that, he had to be one hell of a—

Stop it, Kenz. She put thoughts of McBain's lips on the back burner to dissect later, when he wasn't within a century of her.

She followed the path to the side of the building and leaned against the wall, sucking in the clean, crisp, slightly chilled night air. Cav was a sweetheart. If she was permanently stuck in the twentieth century, would she follow him to Boston? She might, but he would want a stay-at-home spouse and a house full of children, not a trial-lawyer wife.

What about McBain? That was easy. He would return to Scotland. End of that story.

"Good evening, Miss Wallis-Manning."

She jerked her head to see who had spoken her name and gasped when she recognized Fedora Man from London. He was smoking a pipe, holding the bowl in one hand. The other hand was in the pocket of his overcoat. Although she couldn't see the outline of a handgun, she would wager one was there. The familiar scent of the man's sweet tobacco filled the air between them. He took a step closer to her. She held her position, but since she was slightly shorter she had to tilt her head to look up into a face with the coldest gray eyes she'd ever seen.

Show no fear, Kenz.

"Is that your real name?" His voice carried a deep, sinister tone that made her wince. He was dangerous, she knew that. And he wouldn't hesitate to kill her if it suited his purpose. Should she scream? She could, but who would hear her? The Security gate was too far away, and she wouldn't be heard above the cheering crowd inside the hall.

"It's the only name I've ever had," she said, "although my parents considered naming me McKenzie instead of—"

"Who are you working for?"

"No one, yet. They're waiting for my new passport."

"They're not waiting any longer."

"Oh, good. It arrived then." She made a move to step around him, but he blocked her path. "If you'll excuse me, I need to find out where to report tomorrow." She tried again to pass, but he kept in step with her.

His eyes were as dark as dirty coal and as deadly as the dust that filled miners' lungs. "Who are you?"

"Who are you? I can't keep calling you Fedora Man, the nickname I invented when I noticed you in London."

"Who. Are. You?"

"Kenzie Wallis-Manning. I'm an American citizen."

"So you say. We need to talk."

"No, we don't. I don't know you. I'm going back inside."

"I'm with Military Intelligence, and I have a few questions I hope you can clear up for me."

"Ask them," she said. "I've got nothing to hide. I'm an American citizen with a valid passport."

"That's the problem Miss Wallis-Manning. You don't have a passport. Not even an expired one. How do you explain that?"

Show no fear.

"A mistake on your researcher's part. A thorough investigation couldn't possibly be done so quickly. I suggest you try again."

I didn't say to be cocky.

"Look," she continued. "I understand you have a job to do, but harassing me is only wasting your valuable time."

He withdrew his hand from his overcoat, revealing a Colt .45. He would shoot her and dump her body where no one would ever find her. But who would look for her? Cav? He would worry about her, but he had to report back to his base. McBain? No. He wouldn't either.

Fedora Man gestured with the pistol. "Let's go."

"Where? Who do you think I am?"

He barked a laugh and pointed the pistol at her face. "I know exactly who you are, and you underestimate my powers of persuasion."

"You underestimate my powers of self-defense." She ducked, getting out of the line of fire and reached up for the weapon. It discharged. She kicked him in the balls, then attacked, bringing the gun to his belly. She rotated the gun and yanked it out of his hand. Immediately, she stepped back, opening the gap between them, put a fresh round in the chamber, and wondered what the hell she was going to do now.

It had taken less than four seconds to disarm him, and his eyes were bulged from the shock.

Then three things happened simultaneously. A woman on the other side of the fence surrounding Bletchley Park shrieked and darted through the bushes.

Zoey?

A black sedan squealed to a stop a few yards from where Kenzie stood.

Someone from behind her bashed her head with an object hard as iron.

And Kenzie Wallis-Manning crumpled to the ground.

33

Fraser House, the Highlands, Present Day

MEREDITH WAS SITTING in her second floor office at Fraser House, reviewing Montgomery Winery spreadsheets and memos from the winemaster. The harvest months earlier had been fantastic. All the grapes had come in before the October rains, had ripened slowly, and showed good fruit quality. The white wines were already on store shelves, and the reviews were good. The reds were aging in oak barrels.

On rare days, she missed her job as President. Today was one of them. Probably because she was waiting on the results of a CT scan. It was reminiscent of almost ten years earlier, when she received the news she had breast cancer. Her second. Was she facing a third cancer?

Elliott was convinced she only had the flu, but when the chest discomfort and muscle aches didn't go away, he insisted on a chest X-ray. The radiologist ordered a CT scan after noticing suspicious spots. Now she waited. She checked the time on her Apple watch. The doctor had promised he would call by ten o'clock. It was ten-fifteen. Elliott was caught on a conference call negotiating a ten million dollar syndication deal, or he would be pacing the width of her office.

Her cell phone rang. The display flashed a number she didn't recognize, although the first digits were +44, Scotland's dialing code. She'd had a long-standing habit of taking calls from unidentified numbers. Vintners from around the world often called her to discuss wines. Elliott had pleaded with her to let unknown calls go to voicemail, but old habits were hard to break.

Her hand shook when she pressed the accept button. "Meredith Montgomery." Although her legal name was Meredith Montgomery Fraser, she continued to use her maiden name for business purposes.

"Ms. Montgomery, this is Dr. Mark Wilson at Edinburgh Regional Medical Center. Your reports came back today. You had asked me to call you directly instead of scheduling an appointment to discuss your diagnosis."

"I've been awaiting your call." She glanced at the door, expecting Elliott to walk in to hear the news with her. But he wasn't there.

"I wish I had better news," Dr. Wilson said. "The CT findings are consistent with malignancy. There are three two-centimeter lesions in the lung fields, two on the right and one on the left. The next step—"

"Excuse me, Dr. Wilson, are you telling me I have lung cancer?"

"The findings are consistent with cancer in your lungs, yes."

Meredith's heart thudded against the wall of her chest and her mouth went dry. "Consistent?" She picked up the bottle of water on her desk then slammed it down. Nothing would relieve the dry fear coating her tongue. "That means it's possible I don't have it, right?"

The news was a mistake. Montgomery was a popular name in the Highlands, so the results belonged to someone else. This couldn't be happening to her again. She pushed away from the desk and stood, but her legs were shaky, and she collapsed back into the swivel chair.

I ran ten miles this morning. I'm not sick. I refuse to be sick.

"With your history of two previous cancers," Dr. Wilson continued, "the specialists I consulted with believe a biopsy will most likely show metastatic breast cancer in the lungs."

Metastatic? The word was as sharp as a steel, plain-edge blade. "It's been ten years," she said, more to herself than to the bad news messenger.

"I know that, Ms. Montgomery, and I know this is difficult to hear. Is yer husband about?"

"Yes, I'll tell him, but please email a copy of the report to me. He'll want to read it." She swiped at the tears streaming down her face.

"We'd like to schedule an outpatient surgical procedure to biopsy one or more of the lesions to confirm the diagnosis. If the biopsies show metastatic breast cancer in the lungs, we'll schedule more scans to see if the cancer has spread anywhere else. We'll recommend a highly trained oncologist."

Outpatient surgical procedure. She'd been that route before. A knot the size of an orange lodged in her throat. She would suffocate before cancer had a chance to kill her.

"I have an oncologist," she managed to say. It had been so many years. How many members of her team were still practicing? "At least, I had," she corrected.

Her vision was too blurry now to even distinguish the features of her son's angelic face on her laptop's screensaver. She couldn't live without lungs like she could live without breasts. The plastic surgeon couldn't fashion new lungs out of fat and tissue and silicone.

God could, but not her surgeons.

God, take my hair, my hands, my feet. Take my vines, but please don't take my life. Don't take me away from Cullen and Elliott.

She couldn't talk anymore. The news had to be absorbed by her brain and analyzed before she could tell Elliott. A sense of hope had to accompany the news, but first she had to find the hope within herself.

She would survive. She would see her son marry and have children of his own. She would grow old loving and being loved by Elliott. Hope. That's all she had now.

"I have to go," she said. "Email the report, please."

She punched the disconnect button and tossed the phone onto the desk, glaring at it, wishing she had Superman's heat vision to melt the device and with it all traces of the call.

In her mind she retraced her early morning run. She was a marathoner and had logged thousands of miles during her running career, but this morning, like the last several runs, it had been hard to catch her breath. She had kept going, though, not because she was miles from home without transportation, but to quit would have been to admit what she had been trying to deny.

She was sick, and she didn't have the flu.

She had been lucky to beat the prior reoccurrence; another one was likely to kill her. She had read that somewhere. If it was in her lungs, it was probably in her liver, too. She stepped over to the window and looked out over the paddock. Kevin was giving Cullen a riding lesson.

I survived last time for you, Cullen, and for your father. I will again.

She would do whatever had to be done. Surgery, chemo, radiation. She had to stay alive.

She slid to the floor in the corner of the room and hugged her knees to her chest. Could she endure the sickness and pain? Could she endure the look of hopelessness on Elliott's face when the chemo no longer worked and the options had all run out? Could she tell her son good-bye? Could she kiss Elliott one last time?

Courage? No. She didn't have an ounce of it.

Fear and sorrow and anger assaulted her and she wept for all she would leave behind.

"Meredith. My God. What's wrong?" Elliott dropped to the floor and pulled her into his arms. "What happened?"

"I have lung cancer."

He squeezed her to him. "No, ye' don't. They're wrong. Ye' caught a bug. That's all."

"Dr. Wilson," she said, sobbing, "said the CT findings are consistent with malignancy."

"Consistent doesn't mean ye' have it. We'll get more tests. More opinions."

"There are three two-centimeter lesions in the lung fields, two on the right and one on the left."

"But they could be something else."

"He believes a biopsy will show metastatic breast cancer in the lungs."

"We'll leave today. We'll go home and consult the doctors who healed ye' last time."

"I don't want to die." The words came out as a wail.

"Ye're not going to, sweetheart. We'll get through this." He rocked her, saying over and over, "We'll get through this. We'll get through it together." His hot tears mingled with hers. "Whatever it takes."

She didn't know how long they sat on the floor and wept, but as her tears turned to hiccups, Kevin knocked on the open door. "I'll make the arrangements at the University of Kentucky."

"Call the flight crew first," Elliott said, "then see who's still on the oncology team at the hospital."

"Kentucky's gone through several changes, but I'll see who's at Markey Cancer Center. I'll tell Cullen we're going home."

"Did he hear me crying?" Meredith asked.

"I heard you first and asked Alice to keep him entertained while I came to see what was wrong."

"Thank ye', lad," Elliott said.

"Tell him I need to go home to see my doctor," Meredith said.

"He'll ask if you have cancer again. He always asks that when you get sick," Kevin said.

"Sometimes I think it was a mistake to tell him, but it was the only way to be honest with him about why he'll never have a sibling."

"It was the right decision," Elliott said. "I'll never second guess it." He pulled Meredith to her feet and held her in his arms.

"Boss," Kevin said. "One more thing. What about David and Jack?"

Elliott buried his face in Meredith's neck and his warm tears dampened her skin. After a moment he said, "They're on their own. There's nothing I can do."

"No." Meredith pushed away from him. "We can't leave them behind. We have to bring them home now."

Elliott framed her face with his hands and kissed her. "There's no way to communicate with them."

"Yes, there is. We have the sapphire brooch. Go get them, Elliott."

Elliott held her gaze intently. "No. If David was here, he'd say ye' have to come first, and ye' do. We're not abandoning them.

There's nothing we can do but wait, and we can do that in Lexington as well as we can do it here."

"But what if he leaves a message? We won't know."

Elliott paused, glancing around, then shook his head. "Kevin, ye' have to stay behind and check daily for a message from David."

Kevin leaned against the doorjamb and crossed his arms. "That's what I get for opening my mouth. How about if Alice checks for messages, and I go with you? I'm a paramedic. I know the docs. I know the staff. They're used to seeing me at the hospital. I'll be more helpful there than here."

"Alice doesn't know where David is, ye' know that. There isn't anyone else I trust with the truth. It has to be ye'."

Kevin dropped his arms and plopped into a chair near the door. "You'll leave me out of the loop, and I won't know what's going on. What if you get so distraught that you have a drink? Who'll take care of you while you take care of Meredith?"

Elliott released Meredith and rubbed Kevin's head. "Ye'll never be out of the loop, lad. Call Louise and Evelyn and ask them to come to the farm. Ye' and Louise gossip like high school girls. Ye'll never be out of the loop."

Kevin chuckled. "You're right about that, boss. I'll call them. Louise will have to get a friend to manage the B&B, but the University of Edinburgh is on break, so Evelyn isn't teaching next week. The timing is good. Okay, I'll stay behind. But David will owe me big time."

"When ye' call Louise, see if they're available to leave today. If they are, we'll fly to Edinburgh and pick them up. Also notify the flight crew we want to leave this afternoon."

Kevin left the room, quietly closing the door behind him.

Meredith kissed Elliott, ignoring his sandpaper whiskers. In their decade together, their love had grown stronger and deeper, irreplaceable and unbreakable. "The worst part of my last cancer was not being able to tell you. As soon as I had you fighting for me, I knew I'd win. I have that same faith now."

"And together we'll beat it again."

34

Bletchley Park, England, June 3, 1944

THE HAIRS ON the back of David's neck bristled, and something coiled in the pit of his stomach like a snake ready to strike. The bristling hair was a warning sign he never ignored. The coiling sensation he chalked up to several things, the least of which was Kenzie's absence. She had left following his first set, and when she didn't return by the end of his second, he quit playing, thanked the audience, and signaled to Jack as he hurried off the stage.

David handed the sax to a stagehand and motioned to Jack to follow him to a corner where they wouldn't be overheard. "Where's Kenzie?"

Jack pointed over his shoulder. "She went to the ladies' room."

"That was thirty minutes ago. Why didn't ye' go look for her?"

The edge of Jack's mouth curled up, showing only a small degree of tolerance. "Are you serious? How many times have you told me Kenzie was your responsibility? If you hadn't been onstage strutting like a peacock, you'd know where she is."

"What are ye' talking about? I was only doing what I was asked to do—play a sax to entertain a hardworking crowd."

"Sax? Would that be the instrument you forgot to tell me you even played?"

"Something's rubbing ye' the wrong way, and it's not about me playing a sax."

Jack ran his fingers through his hair, leaving it spiky and unruly.

"This mission feels off somehow. Ever since we got here, you've acted weird. You're sitting on the sidelines, and you need to get back in the game."

David was more in the game and more invested in the mission than any he'd been on during his deployments. "I *am* in the game."

"No you're not. If you were, you wouldn't have been up on the stage trying to impress her."

"Her?"

"You weren't playing to the dozens of women standing in front of the stage. If you had been, you'd still be up there. You're so hot for Kenzie, I can feel the heatwaves. This isn't *your* story. Even though I have reservations about this whole deal, our job concerns Kenzie and Cav, not Kenzie and David. The McBain I know wouldn't be out of control and ready to crash and burn. If you'd been guarding her back, you'd know where she was now."

David thought back to his performance. He had played from memory while he watched the rapt attention on Kenzie's face. Her blissful expressions had turned his insides out, and his imagination tortured him with vivid images of making love to her. "I should have stopped after the first set."

"You're not even listening to me!" Jack raked his fingers through his hair again, smoothing down the spiky ends. "There shouldn't have been even a first set."

David pushed aside a nearby window's thin layers of cotton blackout material and gazed out in the inky night. There were no chinks of light from nearby buildings or red glows from cigarettes, only dim starlight hidden by thinly veiled clouds. Were his feelings for Kenzie also so thinly veiled?

Jack tugged the cottony fabric back into place. "She's here somewhere. She's wouldn't go off without Cav. Let's go find her."

"Where's Cavanaugh now?"

"Are you looking for me?" Cavanaugh asked, walking toward them.

"Did Kenzie say she was going anywhere other than the ladies' room?" David asked.

"I tried to get her to wait until you finished playing, but she wouldn't. She told me to stay and that she'd be right back."

The prickling on David's neck was as bad as he had ever experienced. "Was anything wrong? Did she appear worried or scared?"

Cavanaugh shook his head. "She was fidgeting, but so was every woman in the Assembly Hall. You were a hit, Major."

Molly ran up to them, breathing hard. She wiped perspiration from her forehead with the back of her hand that held a small clutch bag. An identical one was in her other hand. "She's not in the ladies' room, and no one has seen her. I'm worried. I haven't known Kenzie long, but she wouldn't go off without telling someone."

"Does one of those bags belong to her?" David asked.

"Sure, this one." Molly held out the bag for David. "She left it in her chair."

He opened the clutch and fingered through the contents: lipstick, handkerchief, money, a comb, and a cube keychain. He unzipped the pocket and felt inside—the brooch and a ring, probably her class ring. If anyone discovered the items, questions would be raised that Kenzie couldn't answer, and neither could he. He snapped the bag closed. "If Kenzie was going to run off, she would have taken her money."

He tapped the bag lightly against his leg while he considered next steps. "Cavanaugh, you and Rainer walk through the audience. Ask people if they've seen her. Molly, there's a group of girls standing at the rear of the auditorium. If Kenzie left through the front door, they would have seen her leave. Jack and I will go outside and search the grounds."

He pushed open the backstage door and hurried from the building with Jack trailing behind him. "Kenzie's brooch and class ring are in her purse. If she was leaving, she wouldn't have left them behind."

"So where is she?"

"I don't know, but at least we know she hasn't disappeared into the fog. Do ye' have yer wee flashlight? There's something else in here." Jack pulled the golf-pencil size light from his pocket and opened his jacket to shield the beam while David unwrapped the tissue paper. "The brooch is an emerald."

"Did you doubt it?" Jack asked.

"Since I talked with Auld Fraser, when it comes to the stones, I'm not sure of anything." David dangled a key chain in front of Jack. "A Rubik's Cube? She should have destroyed this. Why hang onto it?"

"It has her house key?" Jack said.

"House keys can be replaced. Having an item that won't be invented for years is a much bigger problem."

Jack snapped off the light. "Put those things in your sporran before Molly or Cav come looking for us."

David stashed the ring, emerald brooch, and keychain in his sporran, but left the few pound notes and other items in the purse to return to Molly. "Let's walk around and see if we find any signs of a struggle. If someone took her—"

"Who would do that?"

"Since she's working in a secure facility without proper identification, Military Intelligence is the likely candidate. But whoever took her, assuming someone did, she wouldn't have left without putting up a fight."

"Unless she was surprised or knew the person. Do you think Molly turned her in?"

"If Molly had been suspicious, she wouldn't have brought Kenzie here."

"MI wouldn't hurt her? I mean…not like the Gestapo," Jack asked.

"It's wartime. Even the British did things…" David let the possibility pass without reflection, only acknowledging the reality. "Kenzie would have been trained to endure torture, but even the toughest Navy SEALs can only last so long. She'll hold out, and if she confesses, they won't believe her, and they'll escalate whatever pressure they're exerting."

"What's there to hold out for? She'll believe she's all alone, that no one is covering her back," Jack said.

Meredith's haunting words came hurtling back at David. *Kenzie doesn't know you. She doesn't know you can work miracles.* He wasn't a miracle worker by any means, but he had resources, and wherever MI had taken Kenzie, he would find her. She just had to believe she wouldn't be left behind. Without that belief, a soldier in captivity had nothing.

"David, where are you?" Molly called from the darkness. "I know what happened to Kenzie. Zoey saw it all."

"Zoey? Yer roommate?"

"Yes, you met her the other day. Cav and Rainer are trying to comfort her. They're sitting on a bench in front of the Assembly Hall. The poor girl is so distraught she's incoherent."

David took off in a lope with Molly and Jack running behind him. He found Zoey sitting on a bench between Cavanaugh and Rainer, weeping into her hands.

David went down on one knee in front of her. She was shaking harder than a leaf in a hurricane, and he doubted she had the wherewithal to provide reliable information.

"Zoey, lass. If we're going to find Kenzie, ye' have to tell us what ye' know. We don't have much time."

Between sobs, Zoey said. "Kenzie…fight…"

"Who'd she fight? Do ye' know?"

"She called him F-f-fedora Man."

"What's she talking about?" Jack asked.

"If it's the man I'm thinking about," Cavanaugh said, "he's dangerous. We saw him Saturday night at Claridge's. He shot a man on the street and dumped his body into the trunk of a sedan. Kenzie called him Fedora Man."

"Can ye' give me a description?" David asked.

"It was too dark to see his features clearly. Tall, thin, long face, heavy brows. He wore an overcoat and a fedora, and he was smoking a pipe."

Molly gasped. "Kenzie said when she was interviewing with Commander Travis she smelled pipe tobacco, but didn't know where it was coming from. Do you think the commander knows this man?"

"Possibly. But where did he take her?" David asked.

"Car," Zoey sobbed. "H-h-hit head."

"Fedora Man hit her on the head and put her in a car?" David asked calmly. Although he wanted to yank the answers out of the useless girl, he waited, fisting and un-fisting his hands.

"She...kicked him. Boom. T-took his gun." Zoey flung her hand wide, accidently smacking David. "*Boom.*" The small ruby ring she wore on her right hand scratched his jaw.

"Did Kenzie shoot Fedora Man?" David asked, blotting a trickle of blood with his fingers.

Zoey barely turned her head right, then to the left, while her body jerked and breath hitched with sobs. It wasn't exactly a shake of her head, but the intent was clear. Kenzie didn't shoot him. "Another man..." Zoey smacked the back of her head. "Kenzie d-down. Puh-puh-put in car."

David gathered Zoey's hands together then nodded at Rainer to hold them. "Ye' did well, lass." He stood and the joints in his knees cracked, sounding like big old trees felled by a lumberjack. He shook out his legs, taking a moment to piece the information together.

"Here's what I believe happened. Kenzie went outside to get some air, where she was accosted by a man she recognized from the street shooting in London."

"Maybe she recognized him inside the Hall and ran from him," Cavanaugh said.

"Kenzie's a..." David stopped before he said more than he should. "She's too smart to go where she would be in more danger. She had to already be outside, which means he either recognized her while she was performing, or he was stalking her and intended to grab her at the first opportunity. She used self-defense. The weapon discharged. It could have hit one or both of them. A second man hit Kenzie on the head and knocked her out."

"And they drove off, taking our Kenzie with them," Molly said, sniffling. "If he knows Kenzie saw him shoot that man in the street, she's a witness and could report him."

If David was going to get their assistance, he needed to offer them a plausible explanation. "I believe the man was with Military Intelligence."

"What could they want with Kenzie?"

"She's working in a secure facility without identification. She speaks German, Japanese, Italian, and some Russian. Military Intelligence might be…shall we say…concerned."

"Oh," Molly said.

"I have connections with some people who have connections with people in the Black Market. I found Kenzie's passport today, but didn't have time to give it to her. But she is who she says she is."

"Give it to Military Intelligence, then," said Cav. "That should help get her back."

David frowned. "It's not that simple. Number one, we don't know for sure who took her. And number two, if Military Intelligence did kidnap her, where did they take her? The address is not likely to be in the telephone directory."

"Maybe Commander Travis can identify the man. He might have been at Kenzie's interview, smoking his pipe in an adjoining room, listening to the conversation."

"Travis is in the Assembly Hall. I'll go ask him," Molly said. "Wait here."

David didn't like waiting. He was ready to throw some weight around, but he'd give Molly a chance first. One of Molly's other roommates came to get Zoey, and they trudged off, leaving a sobbing trail in their wake.

Five minutes passed, then ten. At the fifteen minute mark, David said, "I'm going in. Molly might need help."

Rainer jumped to his feet. "Here she comes."

Molly was out of breath and teary-eyed. "Sorry it took so long. I had to wait until he wrapped up a conversation before I could approach him. He said he didn't know the man, and that I was to stay out of it. That I was a valuable employee, but any involvement in what he called a *messy business* could lead to my being prosecuted for violation of the Official Secrets Act."

"He validated what I suspected. Here's what I want everyone to do. Jack, take Cavanaugh and Rainer back to their base and finish your interviews. Molly, go home and calm Zoey. Tell her what the commander told you, and tell her it applies to her, too. Report to work tomorrow as usual."

"What are you going to do?" Jack asked.

"I'm going to the War Department in London. I'll find her."

Molly hugged him. "Thank you, David. I know you will. Stay in touch."

"We'll drive you back to your billet, Molly," Rainer said.

"Thank you. My legs are so wobbly, I don't think I could walk far at all."

Rainer took her arm. "Come on. We'll go to the car and wait."

Cavanaugh clasped David's shoulder. "If anyone can find her, I believe you will. Please call the base as soon as you have news."

"I will," David said.

Cavanaugh walked away with Molly and Rainer, leaving Jack with David. They huddled so their voices wouldn't carry. "Tell me the truth," Jack said, "What are odds of Kenzie's survival?"

"She's been through SERE—"

"English please," Jack said.

"Survival, Evasion, Resistance and Escape. Each military branch has its own version of the program to teach soldiers, sailors, and aviators how to survive hostile environments, evade and resist the enemy, and, if necessary, escape."

"I take it the resist part is how to withstand punishment in captivity?"

"Kenzie went through additional training. It's harsh, but she did it. I have to trust her to stay alive until I can get to her."

"You found Charlotte."

"I got lucky."

"It was more than luck. You were prepared for all contingencies. I know you, McBain. You have a plan. You'll find her."

"Thanks for the confidence. Now, there's something I need you to do." David reached into his sporran, withdrew the ruby brooch, and placed it in Jack's hand. "If you don't hear from me by the 5th of June, go home."

"What about Cav?"

"Leave him here."

"Are you sure?" Jack's voice was low and hesitant, and even with only light from the night sky, fear was visible in his eyes.

"Aye. If ye' haven't heard from me, don't come looking. Go home."

"I can't leave you."

David took a deep, unsteady breath and blew it out all in one whoosh. "Ye' can if I'm dead."

Jack winced. "What about Kenzie?"

"If I'm gone, it's only because she was killed first."

35

London, England, June 3, 1944

KENZIE WOKE WITH her cheek pressed against a cold hardwood floor. She remained motionless, although she did peer into the darkness while she assessed the situation.

There was a coppery taste in her mouth, possibly from blood, but she didn't remember being hit in the face. Maybe she bit her tongue. And she had an excruciating headache. Her vision might be blurry, but in the dark it was impossible to know for sure. Either blackout curtains covered the windows or there were no windows. Flashes of memories sparked like a dying plug, sending bits and pieces of a nightmarish scene outside the Assembly Hall.

A fight. A gun. Fedora Man.

Adrenaline surged through her, making her heart pound. She breathed through her nose to calm herself. She had gone through specialized training to learn how to survive in captivity. She could do this.

She continued her inventory.

Her hands were bound with rope. She tried to twist them, but the knots were firmly tied. There was no wiggle room. She had no socks, stockings, or shoes. Her jacket had been removed, and she wore only a thin cotton blouse and a pair of beltless wool trousers. Her shoulders ached from the hunched position and the hard surface beneath her.

Strong odors almost made her gag. Body odor, excrement, urine, but the strongest odors were fear and death. The smells hadn't come from her...yet. She knew in her gut they would eventually. Wherever she was, she wasn't likely to leave alive. Not from this hellhole. No one knew where she was. No one cared. Who would bother to look for her? Cav couldn't. He had to return to base. McBain? No, he might make an effort for Molly's sake, but he wouldn't find her.

Don't give up, Kenz.

She managed a small smile. That sounded like something Trey would say, even in an apparently hopeless situation. Giving up wasn't in her genes. Resisting was, though, and she would resist as long as possible.

If she was interrogated, and that was likely the next move, how she answered the questions would predict the severity of the punishment. Name, rank, and serial number. That's all she could give. But she wasn't in the Army now, and they wouldn't believe her if she said "Captain, United States Army, Retired."

So what should she say?

The truth, Kenz, or as close as possible.

A door opened and dim light spilled into the room. Then a switch was flipped on and an overhead light cast another dim glow throughout an empty room, maybe fifteen by fifteen feet with stained rosebud wallpaper.

Two men dressed as English soldiers entered. One carried a straight back chair. The other grabbed her arms and yanked her to her feet, almost dislocating her shoulder. She hissed. They dropped her onto a chair set in the middle of the room, untied her hands, and then wrapped a rope around her chest, tying her to the chair.

"Where am I?" she asked.

Neither man answered.

"How long am I going to be here?"

Silence

"Why am I here?"

Silence.

"Guess you're not going to tell me."

One of the soldiers backhanded her so hard her head snapped to the right and she saw stars through teary eyes. She had been punched in the face once during training when she didn't duck quickly enough, but she'd never been backhanded. It wasn't as bad as a punch. Her cheek stung and the coppery taste returned. She flicked tongue over her back teeth, checking to make sure none of them were loose.

Stay calm, Kenz. Show no fear.

This time she glanced up. *Stay with me, Trey.*

A middle-aged, gray-haired man wearing the British uniform of a colonel and black circle glasses stomped in with a tall, burly soldier at his side.

"Wie heißen sie?" the burly soldier asked.

"Kenzie Wallis-Manning," she answered in German.

"Wie alt bist du?"

She stopped to think. Was it June yet? If so, she had turned thirty. "Dreißig."

"Bei welcher firma arbeiten sie?"

What company do I work for? Really? "Ich bin student."

The guard leaned down and the colonel whispered into his ear. He straightened and said. "Was studieren sie?"

"Do you mind if we switch to English? It's taxing my brain to think in German. I'm reading law at Cambridge." They weren't going to believe anything she said, so she might as well stick to the truth as much as possible.

"That's not what you told Molly Bradford," the colonel said. "You told her your brother was studying at Cambridge. A brother who's now serving at Anzio. We don't believe you have a brother."

"What's your name?" she asked. "I want to be sure I remember it correctly when I testify at your court martial for kidnapping an American citizen and subjecting me to these horrible conditions."

"Lt. Col. Alexander Paterson Scotland," he said.

She had read about him, and what she had learned chilled her to the bone. "Commandant of the London Cage, a Military Intelligence prisoner of war facility. If my memory serves me correctly, this facility was the subject of frequent allegations of torture."

Scotland jumped to his feet, his face beet red. "*Where did you hear that?*"

Kenzie pretended to think hard. "I read it on Wikipedia, I think."

Stop it, Kenz. You're only going to make it worse for yourself.

She glanced up quickly, then returned her focus to Colonel Scotland. If she was thankful for anything, it was that she didn't have the brooch with her. She could admit to coming from the future, but they wouldn't believe her. Now, if they found the brooch…

There was too much at stake to admit the truth. The brooch might not work for her, but it might work for another user.

"Who do you work for?" Scotland asked.

"As soon as my new passport arrives from the American Embassy, I think I'll be working for Dr. Turing."

"The American Embassy couldn't find any record of Kenzie Wallis-Manning ever being issued a passport. To them you don't exist."

"Your source is wrong," she said calmly, although she was anything but calm. She had enough adrenaline in her system to lift a car. "I've had a passport since I was old enough to need one. There's a war going on. I don't have to remind you of that. The American Embassy is swamped. They couldn't possibly have done a thorough search. Are they still looking? If they are, they will find my file."

Kenz, you're being an idiot.

She grimaced. Trey was so unimaginative sometimes. "Look," she said to Scotland. "My father was in the Army. We moved around. I'm in the system. I'm a loyal American. I wouldn't do anything to harm the Allies, Dr. Turing, the work at Bletchley Park, or my new friends. Whoever you think I am, or whatever you think I've done, you're wrong."

Scotland took a position directly in front of her and put his hands on his hips. She was eye level with his polished brass belt buckle, which had an Army insignia she didn't recognize.

"You were first spotted at the Rainbow Corner Club, where you met Molly Bradford and Lt. Christopher Joseph Cavanaugh. You were later seen standing on a street corner telling jokes. You then imposed upon the Bradfords to stay at their house, and convinced Miss Bradford to recommend you for a position at a high-security facility. Then you insulted a general at Claridge's. Before Friday night, no one had ever seen or heard of you in London or in Cambridge. How do you explain that?"

"You didn't ask the right people," she said.

"Give me names and addresses, and we'll ask them." The smirk on Scotland's face said he knew she was lying. She could give him the name and address of the sweet lady who owned the B&B near King's College. Kenzie had considered renting a room there short term. During her visit to the B&B, the lady had chatted for over an hour about her grandparents who had owned the house during the war and had rented rooms to students.

"The address is 68 Canterbury Street and is owned by the Finch family." The Finches would probably tell whoever called that they had so many students they didn't remember all the names. If pushed, which inevitably would happen, they would say they didn't remember her.

"Untie her from the chair, retie her hands, and let her stand."

The stand until you drop torture treatment. During training, she stood for twelve hours. She peed her pants, but she had done it. She doubted she'd have to go twelve hours this time, but she'd succeeded in getting what she hoped for—time, and she'd been untied from the chair. If she could find a window, she would dive through it. Well, as long as she was on the first floor and there was grass outside the window.

The big-neck guard stood well over six feet. When he sat in the chair he pulled her out of, it creaked. He tilted it back on its rear legs and glared. The man didn't look like the brightest kid on the block. Maybe it was the crossed eyes. She'd read that guards were selected for duty at the London Cage based on their size alone.

"I need to use the ladies' room." She didn't need to go, actually. It was only a test to determine the extent of their intent to humiliate her. She had peed in front of men—while not something she did every day—several times, both in the field and while on long distance runs. Granted, the men always turned away to allow her privacy, but it never bothered her.

"Pee where you're standing."

She was right. Humiliation was first. They would probably strip her next, and possibly rape her, but her goal was simple. Stay alive and look for a chance to escape. If they could humiliate her, they could weaken her. If they could weaken her, they could pressure her to say whatever they wanted or sign any paper they put in front of her.

Stay strong, Kenz. You can survive this.

36

London, England, June 3, 1944

DAVID BOUGHT A barely functioning vehicle off the innkeeper's brother, a farmer with too many children to feed. He needed the money more than he needed a vehicle he couldn't drive without petrol.

The innkeeper also knew a man who bought and sold items on the black market, and for a large fee, made the introduction. David purchased two jerry cans of petrol for the same price he paid for the vehicle.

Whoever had taken Kenzie had over an hour head start on him, it had taken so long to procure transportation. He could have taken the train, but he would need a car in London, and there were no guarantees he could use the one he borrowed before.

He tossed his gear in the boot and turned the key in the ignition. The engine hesitated, and he momentarily second-guessed his decision to drive. On the third attempt, the engine fired and rattled, a sure sign of its age.

The small slits of the headlamps' covers allowed only a pinhole of light to shine down on the empty streets of the darkened village. The vehicle puttered along with little power and insufficient brakes, but the ancient vehicle worked, thank God, and that was all that mattered.

Although a ban on private motoring had been imposed for some time, if David was stopped by local authorities, his forged identification papers would clear him to drive.

The long drive back to London gave him plenty of time to plan. While he was researching Kenzie's grandfather he had come across a story of the London Cage. The facility was run by Military Intelligence, and was located in a couple of houses at Kensington Palace Gardens. Enemy prisoners were taken there for interrogation, and few outside the War Office even knew of its existence. It was a torture chamber run by Colonel Alexander Scotland. According to sketchy research, over three thousand German officers were interrogated at the facility, which held sixty prisoners at a time, and had five interrogation rooms.

If Kenzie's abductors believed she was a spy working for the Germans, she might be taken there even though she wasn't an officer. According to testimony from criminals at the war crimes trials held after the war, prisoners at the Cage were forced to stand at attention for hours, stripped, threatened with execution, beaten until they begged to be killed, subjected to waterboarding, sleep deprived, given cold showers, and starved. There was no record, as far as he knew, of female prisoners.

Throughout history, women were always threatened with, and usually subjected to, rape. It sickened him to think the English would be capable of such tactics, but during wartime reliable information made the difference between victory and defeat. He didn't know if the people who had her also knew about Lieutenant Manning's work as a spy. That could make it even more tenuous for both of them.

But Manning was working for the British. If they believed there was a connection between the two, did they now doubt his loyalty because of Kenzie's sudden and inexplicable appearance? David had no answers. But he intended to find them—and her.

Kenzie was one tough soldier, but was she tough enough? Humiliation wouldn't be her Achilles heel, nor would physical abuse. It would be abandonment. She would hold on as long as she thought she had a chance to escape, but if there was no hope…

He wouldn't let himself go there. He would find her before hope died.

The War Department would be his first stop. He had to learn the identity of the agent Kenzie called Fedora Man. With a name and the right connections, David could track him down.

The trip to London along narrow, dark roads was irritatingly slow, not because of traffic, but because of the sputtering vehicle. When he finally reached London, the damp air, rank with coal smoke, once again irritated his nose.

St. Paul's Cathedral rose naked above the ruins, ghostly in the moonlight, and stood majestically among the jagged outlines of bombed buildings with foundations exposed to the elements. After five years of war, the Cathedral was a testament to London's resilience.

There was an undercurrent of sizzling energy in the city, but the troops were noticeably absent. He hadn't even thought about the date. *It was what? June 3, 1944.* No wonder the streets were empty. The troops were now sealed in their camps, all leaves were cancelled, and final briefings were underway. The invasion was three days away.

He pressed his foot to the floor, and the decrepit vehicle wheezed and chugged along at thirty-five miles per hour while he drove along Fleet Street. He passed Ye' Olde Cheshire Cheese, a favorite watering hole for war correspondents who swapped stories over tavern ale.

He slowed, pulling over to the curb. He reached for his pocket to grab his mobile to call Jack. "Damn." Neither of them had cell phones, and they would have been useless anyway. There was no way to get in touch quickly. Now he regretted sending him back to Bassingbourn. Jack could easily leak the story of a beautiful American woman abducted by Military Intelligence because her passport was stolen and she couldn't prove her identity.

Would that help Kenzie, or make her situation worse?

If the war correspondents did their own investigation, they would reach the same conclusion as Military Intelligence: Kenzie Wallis-Manning didn't exist.

No, best to stick with his original plan to go to the War Office. If he was unsuccessful there, he'd call Jack and ask his opinion. If the press could help find her, the brooch would take care of the rest.

David parked on Horse Guards Avenue and entered the trapezium-shaped, Baroque style building. He glanced up at the figure perched along the roof, symbolizing peace and war, truth and justice, fame and victory. All he was interested in at the moment was the truth part.

As he entered the main entrance, with its grand hall and staircase, he looked up toward the principal rooms located on the second floor, including the office of Secretary of State Sir Percy Grigg. David needed admittance to the Secretary's private office.

Guards stopped him at the door, and he flashed his credentials. "Is Secretary Grigg in his office?"

"Yes, sir," a private said, returning David's identification without asking if he had an appointment. Once again, his credentials proved to be beyond reproach. When he returned home, he would give his forger a bonus. "His suite is directly above us."

David jogged up the four flights of the open double staircase, where he found another set of guards. Once again he showed his identification. "I'd like to see Secretary Grigg."

The guard looked at his identification, then gave David a thorough visual inspection. Satisfied, he said, "Down the hall."

David reached the suite above the main entrance and opened the door, entering a reception area. A lieutenant shot to attention.

"I'm Major McBain," David said, returning the salute. "I've come from Supreme Allied Headquarters to see the Secretary."

The lieutenant's eyes widened. "If you'll wait here, I'll advise the Secretary."

The lieutenant entered the interior office, closing the door behind him, and then returned a moment later. "The Secretary will see you."

David entered a large office adorned with oak paneling and a marble fireplace with a roaring fire that reduced the chill in the room.

The Secretary glanced up from the paperwork on his desk. "What can I do for you, Major?"

David approached the desk and placed Kenzie's passport on the desk. "I'm searching for an American citizen who was abducted from outside the Assembly Hall in Bletchley." David had to make the search worth the Secretary's time and attention, so he lied. "The woman, Miss Kenzie Wallis-Manning, is a personal friend of Mrs. Roosevelt. She was to start working at Bletchley Park with Alan Turing.

"I believe," David continued, "that she's been abducted by Military Intelligence. Her travel documents were stolen recently, and she has no identification with her. I was able to find her passport. She's fluent in German, Italian, and Japanese, which makes her valuable to the work at Bletchley.

"Why the SIS is interested in her, I don't know, but I intend to find her before the First Lady gets involved. If it's believed she's a German spy, Colonel Menzies' operatives would want her as part of the double-cross system."

The Secretary sat back in his chair and tapped his fingers on the arm of his seat. "You're well informed, Major."

"I know there's a network of cages around Britain run by the Prisoner of War Interrogation Section, which operates under the jurisdiction of the Directorate of Military Intelligence. If Military Intelligence has Miss Wallis-Manning, they would have taken her to one of those cages. Their Gestapo-like tactics could kill her. I have to get her back immediately."

The Secretary picked up Kenzie's passport and reviewed it. "She's traveled extensively, but not for the last few years." He closed the passport and slapped it against his palm. "I heard a story yesterday about a young American woman having words with a general at Claridge's. That wouldn't be Miss Wallis-Manning, would it?"

"Aye, the lass speaks her mind. She thought the general's careless remarks would put the Allies' men and women in jeopardy."

"Obviously General Eisenhower agreed with her. The major

general was recalled to the United States the day after the incident." The Secretary returned the passport to David. "What's your interest in this girl?"

"She made quite an impression on an American pilot serving with the Mighty Eighth, stationed at Bassingbourn. Lieutenant Cavanaugh can't leave base to look for her. I told him I'd be in London preparing for the invasion and would do what I could. Don't want to let the chap down. Not while he's flying dangerous missions over Germany."

"Very gallant of you, Major. We don't want our pilots distracted. I'll do what I can. Where can you be reached?"

"I'll be sitting right outside yer office, sir."

37

MacKlenna Farm Jet Somewhere Over the Atlantic, the Present

THE MACKLENNA FARM corporate jet was halfway across the Atlantic before Elliott had a few minutes to himself to read the note he retrieved from the hidden compartment just before they left the castle.

He had hidden it from Meredith, because if it contained bad news, he didn't want her to know yet. As soon as Elliott found the note, though, he told Kevin he couldn't go off without him and to pack his bags. Changing plans was a common occurrence in the Fraser household.

Elliott's breath rushed out in an excited hiss. David had hit all of his milestones. He found Kenzie, met her soul mate, had an exit strategy in place, and had kept Jack, so far, out of trouble. If all went as planned, Elliott could expect David, Jack, Kenzie, and her Lieutenant Cavanaugh to arrive in the future any day now. Hopefully before Meredith's next procedure and the delivery of Charlotte and Braham's baby.

This report from David was worth opening a bottle of champagne, though—or, in Elliott's case, sparkling water. Although he couldn't wait to tell Meredith the news, because it would relieve some of the worry troubling her, he wouldn't wake her. The news could wait. Besides, he wanted to do a wee bit of research first.

Meredith would ask about Kenzie's soul mate, and he should have answers.

Elliott opened his laptop and pulled up the database David and Jack had created. Now that he had a name to search, he could learn everything he needed to know about Lieutenant Christopher Joseph Cavanaugh.

He went to the index and searched for a listing of the Mighty Eighth pilots. In that list he found the lieutenant, along with the names of his crew members, his B-17, and the number of missions he flew. Elliott then Googled the lieutenant and got several hits.

"God damn! This is impossible."

His finger actually shook as he clicked the top link, one of several with a similar headline: *World War II Flying Ace Lieutenant Christopher Joseph Cavanaugh Loses Grandson Captain Christopher Joseph "Trey" Kelly in Afghanistan bombing.*

Elliott read every word twice, trying to make sense of it all. The glee he felt earlier evaporated so quickly he couldn't say for sure it had ever existed. He sent the document to the printer along with two others he wanted to reread, word by word.

He slammed the laptop's lid and tossed the computer onto the sofa. Cavanaugh couldn't be Kenzie's soul mate. David had it all wrong. If the lieutenant didn't go home and marry his high school girlfriend, he wouldn't have the grandson who saved Kenzie's life.

For the next hour, Elliott stared out the window, reviewing what facts he knew and the possible ramifications if David and Jack successfully completed their mission. The message system David devised didn't work in reverse, but he had to get a message to David to let him know the role the lieutenant would play in Kenzie's future. But how could he do that?

There was only one answer. Elliott had to go back in time. His heart raced now—pounded actually, like a deep base drum. Could he leave Meredith when she needed him most?

Kit's adventure had been heartbreaking, Charlotte's a disaster from the get-go, but this situation made both previous adventures pale in comparison.

Kevin came through the cabin with a coffee pot. "Thought you'd like a refill, Boss."

"Thanks, lad."

Kevin filled the mug. "I've been reading emails from my contacts at the med center. A consultation team is being put together to meet with you and Meredith day after tomorrow. A couple of the docs were on the previous team, but her needs are different this time. They're bringing in a pulmonary specialist, pulmonary oncologist, and a thoracic surgeon."

"Good. In the meantime, set up appointments at Anderson Cancer Center in Houston, Memorial Sloan Kettering Cancer Center in New York, and Mayo Clinic in Rochester. After we get the biopsy results, I want as many opinions as we can get."

"I'll get the ball rolling right now."

Elliott watched Kevin pick up the empty cups and glasses and put trash in a bag he carried draped over his arm. Since David and Jack left, the lad had been in the doldrums. He wanted a taste of adventure, too, but David had closed down any discussion of Kevin going with them, saying, "Elliott needs ye'. We can't both be gone. Not at this time."

Elliott sipped his coffee, thinking. Could he send Kevin? The lad was immature in many ways, but he was resourceful, and knew how to handle himself in tough situations. Not like David, of course, but probably better than Jack.

Elliott would put it out there, test the waters, and see what the lad thought of the idea, without telling Meredith. Her reaction would be similar to David's. *When hell freezes over.*

"As soon as yer emails have gone out, I'd like to talk to ye' about something."

"Sounds serious."

Elliott shrugged. "We'll talk later."

"Whatever you need, I'm your man."

Elliott took the last sip and handed over the coffee cup. "Get Meredith's appointments arranged, then we'll talk." He reclined his seat and closed his eyes. Kevin would wake him in time to talk before Meredith and Cullen woke from their naps. The lad knew his habits, likes, and dislikes better than his wife, and she knew him damn well.

Elliott was dreaming of running the hills on Old Frankfort Pike in Lexington when Kevin whispered in his ear, "Boss, wake up." Elliott raised his seat, scraping cobwebs from his brain, and took the cup of coffee Kevin offered.

"The emails have gone out with copies of Meredith's reports. I asked them to communicate with you directly, but to copy me on all correspondence. She's still asleep. So are Louise and Evelyn, but it's about time for them to wake up. If you have something you want to talk about, we should talk now."

Elliott pointed over his shoulder with his thumb. "There should be three reports in the printer in the galley. If you haven't already read them, go get them, please."

"I saw them, but I haven't had time to read them."

Kevin knew everything going on in Elliott's life. It had taken Meredith a while to get used to the idea, but now she found Kevin's knowledge of Elliott's calendar and business dealings so beneficial that she shared her own calendar with him. Kevin often found conflicts in their schedules and straightened them out long before Elliott and Meredith were even aware of a problem. This was a bad time for the lad to leave them, but they would manage.

Kevin returned shortly, reading as he walked down the aisle. He leaned against the top of the chair directly across from Elliott, nodding his head as he flipped to another page. "Are you sure about this?"

"Yes," Elliott said. "I double-checked."

"You can't kidnap Kenzie's soul mate now. If Trey isn't born, Kenzie would probably die in Afghanistan."

Elliott put his finger to his lips. "I don't want Meredith to hear about this."

"What are you going to do? You can't let this happen."

"Shhh," Elliott said, he paused a moment, checked behind him and whispered, "I need ye' to take the sapphire brooch, go back in time, and give David these reports."

Kevin plopped in the chair. "Seriously?"

Elliott blew out a long breath. "Aye."

"David won't like it."

"Ye' work for me, not David."

Kevin rolled the papers into a tube and tapped his palm repeatedly. "But it's my ass he'll kick to the other side of the pond when he sees me."

Elliott chuckled. "Ye' think he'll shoot the messenger?"

"Probably."

"I thought ye'd be more excited."

"I *am* excited. But nervous, too. I'm as afraid of running into David as I am the Gestapo."

"I don't think ye'll see any Gestapo in London."

"What should I tell David?"

"Not a damn thing. Give him the papers and leave. In and out. He won't have time to yell or kick yer arse."

"Okay," Kevin said, and then paused, thinking. "How will I find him?"

Elliott gave Kevin the note from David. "Here's the information he left at Fraser House. It lists everyone's location. Jack is with Lieutenant Cavanaugh in Bassingbourn, and David is with Kenzie at Bletchley Park, along with a friend of Kenzie's named Molly Bradford. There's more information about contacts in London and at Bletchley."

Elliott handed Kevin a folder. "These are David's business contacts. Call the man listed on the top sheet. He'll prepare your credentials. I suggest ye' go back as a war correspondent, like Jack. That will give ye' the most freedom to travel."

Kevin glanced toward the back of the plane. "Meredith's awake."

"We don't have much time to talk." Elliott leaned forward, lowered his voice, and placed the sapphire brooch in Kevin's hand. "As soon as the plane is refueled and a new crew arrives, take the plane to London. If ye' email David's contacts right now, they should have everything ye' need as soon as ye' land. Find David, give him the research, and return immediately. I need ye' here to help with Cullen and run interference if we get crossways with the medical team."

Kevin chewed his lowered lip while staring at the brooch. Then he glanced up and looked Elliott in the eye. "I won't let you down, Boss."

"I know ye' been waiting for an adventure like this, but there hasn't been a need for yer skills until now."

Kevin's forehead creased. "And what are those?"

"Doing exactly what ye're told to do. Ye' have only *one* mission. Get in, get it done, come home. If I had any other options, I wouldn't send ye'. Ye're like a son to me." Elliott's eyes watered. "Don't take any risks, lad. Don't flirt with the English lassies. And if asked, don't give David yer opinion about what he should do, or what ye' think I think he should do. He has to make decisions based on what he knows of the past and the present."

"Hi, Meredith," Kevin said, a bit too cheerfully. "We'll be landing in about twenty minutes. Do you want to wake Cullen, or do you want me to do it?"

"I'll let you and Elliott finish plotting...and then I expect one of you," she glanced from Kevin to Elliott and back again, "to fill me in on the details."

Kevin jumped to his feet. "I need to secure the galley." As soon as Meredith walked away, Kevin said, "Please don't put me between the two of you."

Elliott's mouth twitched. "Ah, laddie, it's so much fun to watch you walk the line."

"For you, maybe, but it's hell on me."

38

London, England, June 3, 1944

KENZIE HAD BEEN standing for several hours when a guard she hadn't seen before stomped in, sneering. His brown eyes were sharp and penetrating. His absurdly large forehead and bald head made his facial asymmetry more obvious. He'd probably been ridiculed as a child, and now he enjoyed inflicting pain as payback. That kind of man could be deadly.

"Has the prisoner peed herself yet?"

The guard, who had been watching over her, and who looked like a simpleton, dropped the front legs of the chair to the floor, crossed to Kenzie, and grabbed her crotch. "Not yet." He smelled of onions and garlic. She controlled her anger and stifled her impulse to spit at him.

"She will," Baldy said.

"I'm right here," Kenzie said. "You can ask me."

Stop antagonizing them, Kenz. You know the tricks of the trade, and you have secrets to hide.

He placed the chair beside her. "Sit."

She did and stretched out her ankles and calves. "The past, present, and future walked into a bar. It was a tense situation."

Baldy slapped her face in the same spot the guard had slapped her before. Her head jerked so hard she almost fell out of the chair. Her cheek stung, and the pain brought tears to her eyes.

"I've heard your jokes and have yet to laugh at one."

"No sense of humor, huh?"

He slapped her again and this time she did hit the floor, hard. The guard yanked her to her feet and tossed her back into the chair. He dug his fingers into her shoulders, locking them there. If Baldy slapped her again, she wouldn't fall out.

"Who are you?" Baldy asked.

"And what have you done with my friend?" she asked, repeating the old cliché.

Baldy slugged her in the gut. The punch knocked out her breath in a loud hiss. "That...wasn't nice," she said in a shaky whisper. "I'll...have...bruises."

He punched her again, but this time she had a split second to clench her abs. It wasn't as bad, but she couldn't catch her breath.

"Who are you?"

"Kenzie. Wallis. Manning. American. Citizen." Each word came out slowly, between gasps.

Baldy stood in front of her, hands on his hips. "Where's your passport?"

"Stolen."

"When did you learn to speak German?"

Pain surged through her. But she'd been hurt worse. After a few moments her breathing returned to normal...or as normal as possible, considering her circumstances. "When I was six."

He paced, slapping a leather riding whip into his palm. "And Italian?"

"About eight."

She sensed his action only a second before he slapped her breasts, ripping the cotton blouse. Unlike her well-developed stomach muscles, she couldn't prepare her fair skin for the brutal sting. It would leave a mark, but it didn't cut her. Yet. He would do it again and again until he drew blood.

"When did you learn Japanese?"

She willed away the tears welling in her eyes. "A couple of years later."

"How long have you been spying for the Germans?"

"Nazi Germany and Hitler are despicable. They've murdered millions of Jews, stolen precious works of art, and terrorized most of the world. They'll lose this war because of Hitler's stupidity and egomania. I would never work for them."

"If you disagree with Hitler so strongly, why are you assisting him?"

"I'm not. Why do you think I am?"

Baldy handed the whip to the guard holding her. "Strike her anywhere you want when she gives me the wrong answer." Baldy leaned against the doorjamb and crossed his arms. "What do you know about Lieutenant Manning?"

Was this all about her grandfather? Did her captors believe she was a spy because he was? If so, she had to disabuse them of that notion immediately. "I met him Sunday at the café at Bletchley. I'd never met him before."

"How is that possible?"

"Have you ever been to America? It's three thousand miles from coast to coast. This year, the population is one hundred and thirty-eight million people."

"With that many people, how can two look so similar and have the same last name?"

"My last name is Wallis-Manning. Not Manning. And red hair occurs naturally in about two percent of the population. That would mean there are," she paused and mentally calculated, "almost three million people with red hair. I don't know who they are. If you want to know the odds of two redheads with similar last names in a population of—"

Baldy gave a quick nod and her guard snapped the whip across her shoulders.

"You were saying?"

"Before Sunday, I had never met him."

She caught the signal a split second before Baldy lunged and punched her in the gut again at the same time her guard slashed the whip across her breasts. She leaned forward and vomited on Baldy's shoes.

He plucked the whip out of the guard's hand and slashed back and forth across her legs, her chest, her arms. Her body jerked and she screamed, "*Stop*."

He didn't. Baldy was out of control.

Scotland came to the door with another guard. "Step back," he ordered Baldy. "You two," he said pointing to the new guard and her old one. "Take her into the other room."

It was the emphasis on *other* that got Kenzie's attention. Stinging from the whip attack, nauseated from the gut punches, and scared, she gathered her reserves and what little dignity she still had.

The guards pulled and twisted her tied arms and dragged her out of room and down a hall. The wallpaper was peeling, and the smell of bodily fluids was worse, and she realized that before the building had become a torture chamber, it had been a residence. Big Ben chimed, and she took some comfort in knowing she was at least in London, and not some hideaway outside of Bletchley.

Based on the design of the long hall and side rooms, she surmised she was in a row home, which usually had back doors and windows. Since the hardwood floor creaked and had a bit of spring, she knew she was on an upper floor. That ruled out throwing herself out the window and expecting to survive.

The *other* room was identical in size to the one she had been in, except for a few furnishings. Her heart rate escalated. A door had been placed across two tables. The hinges had been removed, and large iron rings were bolted to the sides of the door. Next to the table, sitting on the floor, were a bucket of water and a rope.

"If you don't mind. I'll skip the wash and go back to the other room," she said.

Baldy stepped to the head of the table. "We have methods to make people talk."

"And admit things that aren't true? Like the Spanish Inquisition? I'll save you the time. I'm a United States citizen. A retired captain in the United States Army, and I demand you release me."

"You must think I'm an idiot. There are no female captains in the United States Army."

"I seriously doubt you're an idiot. But you are misguided. I am not a spy. I'm a loyal American. I have done nothing wrong."

"Why did you single out Miss Bradford?"

"I didn't. Captain Cavanaugh asked me to dance. Molly was with his friend. I didn't have anywhere to stay, so she offered her uncle's home. But you know all of that, too. You were in a black sedan down the street from the residence spying on us."

"You're observant."

"I saw you several times, including the day I interviewed at Bletchley. You get around."

"So do you, Miss Manning."

"Wallis-Manning. What do you want from me? I'd be in the middle of this fight if the Army would give me a gun. One day they will, and women will serve honorably."

"Is spying for the Germans your way of getting back at the Allies because the Army won't give you a gun?"

"Nazism is evil and the state-mandated genocide has to stop. What's happening is profoundly inhumane."

"And what is happening?"

"The extermination of millions of Jews. It's despicable."

"Are you Jewish?"

"I'm as WASP as they come." He glared as if he didn't understand the acronym. "White, Anglo-Saxon, and Protestant." To lighten the tension she said, "What's an American WASP's idea of open-mindedness?"

He glared.

"Dating a Canadian." She paused. If she kept it up, he might at least twitch his lip. "How can you tell when a WASP is dead? He lets go of his wallet. What happens when four WASPs find themselves in the same room? A dinner party. Why did the WASP cross the street...?"

Rage tightened Baldy's jaw.

"...to get to the middle of the road. What's a WASP's favorite song—?"

"Enough of this. You have been lying from the beginning. You have no identification. You don't have a brother. You haven't been living in Cambridge. You used Molly Bradford to spy on Bletchley Park. I don't know where you came from, or who you report to, but you are not who you profess to be. And I *will* discover your identity."

They tossed her onto the door table. One guard held her while the other tied her hands and feet to the iron rings.

She wrapped her fingers around the rings and worked to control her breathing. She wasn't a strong swimmer, but she could hold her breath for almost three minutes. She tried once more to distract him, to win him over, to stop him. "Did you hear the joke about the woman—?"

Baldy whipped her violently across the chest, shredding her blouse and bra completely. "I will hurt you every time you speak when it's not to answer my questions." He tossed the whip aside. "What a shame to have scars all over your beautiful body. Why are you in London, and who are you working for?"

"You brought me here."

He rubbed his fist, and his face reddened. Baldy had doubts about her, and she didn't think he would kill her, but he would make her suffer. He picked up the bucket and tossed a cloth to one of the guards.

"This is in violation of the Geneva Convention," she said. She took deep breaths to fill her lungs. Deep, deep breaths. They ignored her, adjusting the angle of the board so her head was lower than her feet. "Britain prides itself on fair play. This is not…"

A cloth was placed over her face.

"I demand to be treated humanely." She tried to turn her head to the side, but they held her still, holding down the sides of the cloth, smashing her face and immobilizing her.

In training, she had gone thirteen seconds before she tapped out. Cold water in her sinuses was horribly painful and gave her the sensation of drowning. She would start flailing after two or three seconds. At that point she could tolerate another ten.

A strong stream of cold water, poured from a bucket, splashed on her face, and she snapped her mouth closed. Her nostrils quickly filled with water. She immediately fought back the panic of *Holy God, I'm drowning* until her training kicked in. She thrashed around to confuse her captors, and within a couple of seconds the water stopped and the board was raised. She gasped and coughed and tried not to groan.

"Who are you? Where did you come from? Who do you work for?"

"Kenzie Wallis-Manning. Retired Captain, United States Army. Service Number 512-78-6549. Date of birth April 4, 19—"

"The *truth* Miss Wallis-Manning. Now."

"Kenzie Wallis. Retired Captain, United States Army. Service Number—"

"Do it again."

They lowered the board, covered her face, and poured more water. She thrashed after two seconds and they continued for another four, well below her level of tolerance. Then they raised her.

"Who are you? Where did you come from? Who do you work for?"

"Kenzie Wallis-Manning. Retired Captain, United States Army. Service Number 512-78-6549. Date of birth—"

"Again."

This time she thrashed about immediately. They poured water for almost eight seconds before they stopped. "Who are you? Where did you come from? Who do you work for?"

"Kenzie Wallis—" She was shivering from the cold, but still under control.

They poured water on her face again—eight seconds, this time—and then stopped.

"Strip her, leave her on the board. We'll give her time to imagine how she'll feel after we do this a dozen more times."

The guards raised the board and proceeded to cut off her clothes. First her shredded blouse and bra. They pinched her nipples and laughed. Then they cut off her pants. One of the guards ran his hand down her leg, over her scars.

"What happened to you?" Baldy demanded.

"Grenade," she said.

"Where?"

"Afghanistan."

"What were you doing there?"

"Representing the United States."

Baldy stormed out of the room. "Give the colonel what he wants," one of the guards said. "He'll break you if you don't."

"I have, but he doesn't want to believe me." She closed her eyes to block out the terror, but it still stared her in the face.

"Tell him, Miss Wallis-Manning."

"There's nothing to tell. I'm not who he thinks I am."

They left her shivering for what could have been thirty minutes to an hour. Then the two guards and Baldy returned. Her heart raced in her throat as they covered her face with the rag. Cold water splashed on her and, once again, filled her sinuses with agony and the terror of drowning. She thrashed, pulling on the rings with her hands and feet, but her head was held too tightly to move.

She was going to drown this time. They didn't stop the water. She couldn't see anything but she could see everything. Her life, year by year, flashed before her eyes. And then the water stopped and they raised her head. She coughed and vomited.

"What's your name? Who do you work for?"

"Captain Kenzie Wallis, United States Army, Service Number—"

"Do it again."

"No," she wailed. "I've told you the truth."

They lowered the board and poured water again. She couldn't take it much longer. They stopped.

"What is your name? Who do you work for?"

"Captain Kenzie Wallis-Manning, United States—"

"Again."

"No," she screamed. But it did no good. No one would rescue her. No one knew where she was. *I'm going to drown.* Her mind approached a catatonic state. She knew she was going to die. Then a benevolent darkness washed over her.

39

London, England, June 3, 1944

DAVID PACED OUTSIDE the Secretary of War's office. He was not one to sit around and wait; plus, if the Secretary called Supreme Headquarters to check his credentials, someone would discover that, like Kenzie, he didn't exist. If he was arrested, he wouldn't be able to help her.

He marched over to the Secretary's assistant's desk, and the young soldier sprang to his feet. "Yes, sir."

"I can't wait any longer," David said. "If the Secretary discovers Miss Wallis-Manning's whereabouts, leave a message for me at the Ritz."

David hurriedly left the War Department and sped over to the Ye' Olde Cheshire Cheese. He didn't know London's wartime back streets and had no resources in place. He needed to change that in a hurry. With two or three competent men, hungry men willing to scrounge the city, he would locate Kenzie within the next twelve hours. He doubted the Secretary could do it any faster, assuming he would even try.

He whipped the car into a parking space down the street from the pub and trotted the short distance to the entrance. The pub was noticeably quieter than the ones he and Jack visited over the weekend, as if expecting an event at any moment that would change their lives. Even if the war correspondents didn't know D-Day was only a few days away, their instincts smelled a story.

At a round table near the back wall, Walter Cronkite and Andy Rooney sat with a handful of other reporter-looking types. It would be easy to pull Cronkite aside and tell him Kenzie's story, but David didn't know if that would help her case or not. He would give his investigation a few hours, then make the call. Cronkite wasn't going anywhere, at least not tonight.

David sidled up to the bar, looked around the room again, then eyed the barman, saying quietly, "I'm looking for information and am willing to pay." He opened his hand to show a wad of pound notes.

"What kind?" the barman asked.

"I need the name of a detective." David peeled off a few notes. "A man not afraid to get his hands dirty, but also loyal and trustworthy. Nothing illegal or against the Crown. And I need a name right now."

The barman's steely gaze went from the pound notes on the bar to David's eyes, where he stared hard. David didn't flinch under the harsh glare, nor did he blink, but held steady, measuring the barman as he himself was being measured. If the man decided to give him information, David felt certain it would be reliable.

"Head over to Piccadilly. There's a bobby who works down there. Name's Ryan. Tell him Qualls sent you."

David nodded, peeled off another note, and then hustled back to his car. At Piccadilly, he parked and walked down the street. At the Rainbow Corner Club, now empty of soldiers, he found a burly copper. "I'm looking for Ryan. Do ye' know him?"

"Depends. Who's asking?"

"Name's McBain. A barman named Qualls told me to ask for him. I need a good detective."

"Qualls, huh? Good bloke. Best in the business is a man named Teasdel. Can usually be found at the Old Bell Pub on—"

David hissed. "Fleet Street." He set aside his displeasure at Qualls for sending him the long way 'round.

"If you came from Fleet Street, I'd go back a different way. Especially if you want to keep your business private."

"Good advice."

David returned to his car, but instead of parking on Fleet Street, he found a spot two blocks over and walked to the pub. Once inside, he asked the barman, "Looking for Teasdel. Is he here?"

"Over in the corner," the barman said.

"What's he drinking?" David asked.

"Ale."

"Send a round to the table." David dropped a couple of notes on the bar and approached the corner table where a fifty-ish, slightly overweight, balding man nursed a half empty beer glass. "Ryan said ye're the man I need."

Teasdel barely glanced up. "Depends."

"Mind if I sit?"

Teasdel shrugged. "Suit yourself."

David placed a picture of Kenzie on the table and, with the tips of his fingers, slid it across to the man with the beer. "I need to find this American woman. Military Intelligence abducted her from the Assembly Hall in Bletchley about a few hours ago."

"If she's helping the Germans, I hope they put her on the rack."

"If she was helping the Germans, I'd buy us both a ticket to watch."

"Why don't you go to the War Office?"

"Been there, and they're looking for her. I don't think she's a high enough priority. I need more people on the street. People who know what's going on that can't be learned in a newspaper." David palmed a fist of notes. "I've got to find her. She's in trouble, and I don't know how long she can resist an interrogation before she agrees to whatever they ask."

"You sure she's innocent?"

"I wouldn't be doing this if she wasn't." David peeled off several notes. "I'm staying at the Ritz. Name's McBain. I'll be out on the street as well."

"If Military Intelligence has her, it might take twenty-four hours or longer to find her."

"I need a visual confirmation within the next six hours. I'll pay a bonus to the person who locates her." David tapped Kenzie's picture. "She has red hair. You can't miss her."

"Peel off a few more of those notes. I've got contacts to pay," Teasdel said.

"If ye' come through, I'll have more work." David slapped the wad into Teasdel's hand. "Her name is Kenzie Wallis-Manning. She's a strong woman, but she can't hold out forever against Gestapo-like interrogation. Find her quick. One more thing. She tells jokes. If ye' hear anyone telling jokes ye' haven't heard before, ask them where they came from."

"Meet me here at noon tomorrow," Teasdel said.

"Too late," David said. "I'll be here for breakfast."

David walked across the street, stood in the shadow of a closed store, and waited. Five minutes later, Teasdel limped out. David was generally a good judge of character, and he had no doubt the investigator's connections extended into the very dregs of the city. If Kenzie was here, he would find her.

David returned to the Ritz and stopped at the front desk for messages. There were none. If ever he needed a drink, it was now. But he'd sworn off alcohol and caffeine, and he had to admit his stomach hadn't bothered him in hours.

Once inside his room, he stood in front of the window and looked out into the blackened city. "Where are ye', Kenzie, lass? Don't give up hope. I'll find ye'. Ye' don't know me well, but ye' can trust me. I won't give up, and ye' can't either."

40

The Ritz, London, England, June 3, 1944

WHILE TEASDEL SCOURED the streets, David settled in for a long night of research. He had a jump drive full of information; finding a starting point was his biggest problem. He kept tossing around two key words: spies and torture. He paced, repeating the words. Then the connection clicked. *War crime trials.*

If he started with the trials, he might find a link between German officers charged with war crimes and those who claimed to have been tortured by the British. Their testimony might lead to an address in London.

After several hours of work, David closed the computer and stretched. Military Intelligence would want every asset they controlled to be reporting false information back to the Germans in preparation of the D-Day landings. If MI believed Kenzie was a spy, they would torture her until she agreed to join the double-cross operation. Many of the German officers who were "turned," according to the trial testimony he read, were interrogated at the London Cage.

David pulled up the file on the interrogation centers. There were ones at Doncaster, Kempton Park, and Lingfield. Another one at Preston North End Football Club. But the most notorious was on a tree-lined street a stone's throw from Kensington Palace, on Kensington Palace Gardens. He followed the link and pulled up a report on the Kensington locations. The center consisted of three attached mansions, Numbers 6, 7, and 8. Number 8 was where the worst excesses were reported to have been carried out.

He couldn't go to Number 8 and knock on the door. He needed intel. And the only way to gather that was to stake out the building. Until time to meet Teasdel, he would have his eyes and ears on a former residence on Kensington Palace Gardens.

41

London, England, June 4, 1944

DAVID SET UP a listening station on the roof of an abandoned residence directly across the street from Number 8. Anguished screams, shrieks, and curses, mostly in German, came though his earphones. He had witnessed and participated in interrogations while in Afghanistan, and they had never bothered him. But this was different. Listening to terror-filled screams while searching for one particular voice was gut-wrenching, and it was all his own damn fault.

When they returned to the future, Kenzie and Cavanaugh would become part of Elliott's inner circle, and they would hear the entire story of the mission to bring them back to the future. If he had only taken them all home Saturday night when he met Kenzie and Cavanaugh at the Savoy, none of this would have happened. When she discovered he could have prevented MI from capturing her simply by identifying himself and handing over the identification papers he brought for her, she would never forgive him.

And he would deserve her anger.

He was lying on his back, eyes closed, with the earphone cups pressed to his ears when a scream, one of many, rose to the top of the cacophony. It was a woman's scream. He was certain. While he didn't want her interrogators to inflict more pain, he needed just one more scream for confirmation.

He rolled over on his belly and picked up his thermal image

goggles. He couldn't see through the walls of the building, but he could watch the guards. One was stationed on the roof, marching back and forth like a palace guard. Another was stationed at the front, inside the fence. Once an hour, that guard left his position near the door and walked from one end of the wire fence to the other. He didn't go down the unattached side of Number 8, but a rear guard met him at the corner. The two talked while smoking cigarettes, then returned to their positions.

A weak link in security? Yes, but did the same men have guard duty every night, or did they rotate? Before he went in to extract her, he would have the answer.

It was almost dawn when he heard the scream again. Definitely female.

Hold on, soldier. I've got yer back.

If he could, he would have barged into Number 8, thrown around his credentials, and marched out with her in his arms. But if one of their agents called Supreme Allied Headquarters to confirm his identity and discovered there was no record of him, he would make it worse for Kenzie, and possibly get them both killed. And if he was dead, there would be no one else to rescue her.

He checked his watch and glanced at the horizon. The sun would be up in thirty minutes. He had to clear out before he was spotted. Suddenly, he was filled with venomous rage that froze the breath in his lungs. When Charlotte was kidnapped, he would have killed the men who took her. They were evil, but the men who had Kenzie were his countrymen. They weren't the enemy. It took a moment to rein in his temper. It wasn't easy, but he did. There would be time later to beat himself up. Kenzie should probably have first crack at taking a piece of him, though.

He packed his equipment and gear, rappelled to the ground, and returned to the hotel for a bath and short nap before meeting with Teasdel.

Shortly before eight, he walked to the pub on Fleet Street. It hadn't opened yet, and there was no sign of the detective. As long as Teasdel was working the case, David didn't mind his tardiness. He did a quick gut check to confirm his confidence in the man, and Teasdel passed. The investigator had integrity; it was clear in his eyes.

David bought a newspaper at a market, sat on a bench in front of the pub, and waited. He knew how to wait, how to be patient. He would have been dead ten times over without that particular skill.

At eight-thirty, Teasdel arrived. "How long have you been here?"

"Long enough to read this rag three times."

Teasdel wagged a keychain. "Come on. I'll open the door."

"Do ye' have the key because ye' spend so much time here, or do ye' have an interest in the place?" David folded the paper and left it on the corner of the bench. Someone would pass by and pick it up. Nothing went to waste in wartime Britain.

Teasdel unlocked the door and held it for David to pass through. "Belongs to my brother. I often open for him. We'll get a cup of tea and talk."

With tea and a plate of crumpets, David and Teasdel took seats at a table near the window with the best morning light. The detective poured a splash of cream into his cup and stirred.

"I know a lad who delivers groceries to a handful of military facilities every morning. He sees things. They pay him extra to keep his mouth shut. Occasionally, I pay him more."

"Aye, nice arrangement. He's a real entrepreneur."

"This morning he delivered vegetables…" Teasdel paused to bite into a crumpet, then he continued as he chewed. "…to a place on Kensington Palace Gardens."

David's throat went dry as his body clenched with abrupt, intense fear. He knew what was coming, and while it was the confirmation he needed, he wasn't prepared to hear news of Kenzie so soon. "Number 6, 7, or 8?"

"Number 7. Food for all three buildings is prepared there," Teasdel said. "The lad said two soldiers he had seen earlier coming out of the rear door of Number 8 were in the kitchen talking about a woman with more courage than any German officer they had ever interrogated. A redhead who kept saying she was a captain in the United States Army."

David sat forward, balling his fists. "That's as good as a visual."

"The lad also said the guards mentioned they were relieved she didn't have to be interrogated today. They said she would die before she told them what they wanted to know. Their instructions, according to the lad, were to begin again in the morning."

"Let her spend the day terrified of what's to come. Psychological torture can be worse than physical."

Teasdel looked down at his crumpet, shaking his head.

There was more, but Teasdel was holding back. David's chest was so crammed with worry and fear for Kenzie that pains radiated across his chest and down his arms. "What is it? What aren't ye' telling me?"

Teasdel sipped his tea before clearing his throat. "The last comment the lad heard was that the soldiers were glad she was on the second floor, because the sun came through the window and warmed the room. I'm sorry to tell you this, Major McBain, but Miss Wallis-Manning has been stripped naked."

David slammed his fist on the table, rattling the tea cups. "If they raped her, I'll kill every son of a bitch in there."

"Now, hold on," Teasdel said, with a note of warning more powerful than his words. "Those are British soldiers doing what they believe is necessary to win the war. They might be sadistic, but I won't be party to killing our own. You got that?"

David kept his eyes fixed on Teasdel for several beats and then moved on, letting his second anger attack of the day drift for a few minutes, knowing it would find its way back.

Teasdel didn't push for an answer. Instead he said, "I don't believe they would rape her. That's going too far even for MI, but they would hurt and humiliate her to get what they want."

Then Teasdel gave David a small smile that triggered a jolt of hope. "The good news is, I got a copy of the house plan."

Teasdel opened his jacket and pulled out a set of drawings from his inside pocket. "This only shows the layout when the residences were built." He spread the plan on the table top. "My source couldn't find any other plans. If the configuration of the rooms has been altered, there is no way for us to know."

"Did you ask the lad?"

"He's only been making deliveries for the last few months, and he's not allowed to go farther than the kitchen."

"Has he been in Number 8?"

"No." Teasdel pointed to the drawing of the rear of Number 8. "There are two rooms on the back of the residence on both the second and third floors. On the second floor, one window is boarded. The other is not. If you factor in the comment about sun coming into the room," Teasdel tapped the plan with his finger, "this is where Miss Wallis-Manning is being held."

"Are there bars on the window?"

"Yes, and one guard on the roof, one in the backyard, and one near the front door. There's also a high fence topped with barbed wire surrounding the entire complex."

This was not news to David, but he let the detective believe it was. "I'm not worried about the guards in the front or rear. The one on the flat roof presents a problem." David studied the drawings. "A distraction on the street could pull the guards' attention away from the back long enough for me to reach the building and scale the wall to the second floor."

"What kind of distraction would keep them entertained long enough for you to get in, get your woman, and get out?"

"Only one that I can think of," David said, grinning. "Ladies of the night."

42

London, England, June 4, 1944

DAVID SPENT THE afternoon hidden among the rubble behind Number 8 with his listening device trained on the second floor, trying to filter all other noises but those coming from the room with the barred window. An occasional groan was all he heard in six hours of listening, but it had given him time to visualize the plan he and Teasdel cobbled together.

When it neared sunset, he packed up his gear and headed back to the pub to meet Teasdel, who had been tasked with recruiting characters to play in their tableau. David had broken the plan down into several steps, each with a specific task, much like the planned, coordinated attack in the movie *The Dirty Dozen*. It was a dangerous mission, and he and Kenzie could both be killed, but he had to get her out. She'd been in MI's clutches for twenty-four hours, and it would be another six before he could extract her.

Teasdel was sitting at the same corner table smoking a pipe when David arrived.

David sat opposite the detective. "Everything in order?"

"Two women. Two men. Just as you requested."

David signaled the waitress for a round of beers. "How reliable are they?"

Teasdel leaned his back against the wall, folded his arms across his chest, and took a long draw on his pipe. "They're hungry, tired of the war, and would like to spend the rest of it not groveling for their next meal. They've all spent time in jail for petty crimes or prostitution. They'll do what they're told."

"What time will they be here?"

"They're in the backroom. Let's drink our beers, talk a bit, and then you leave."

"And go where?"

"Take a walk around the block, cut through the alley, and use the pub's back door. We'll be waiting."

When David finished his beer, he dropped money on the table and left. Kenzie's life depended on the reliability of prostitutes and petty thieves. He hoped the day would come when she found that humorous. But the odds of hell freezing over were ten times better.

He followed Teasdel's instructions and slipped through the back door thirty minutes later.

"In here," Teasdel said.

David entered a smoky room not much larger than a closet.

Teasdel pointed to the four people gathered there. "Carla, Nancy, Harry, and Tim."

Carla and Nancy had lived through more than a few rough years, and every one had left a noticeable scar or wrinkle. Both women were probably in their thirties but looked late forties. Teasdel must have given them instructions about what to wear. They were both showing lots of cleavage and leg. The men, both in their early fifties, were dressed in black shirts and trousers. Hard living, alcohol, and tobacco had aged all four of them, but David didn't smell alcohol on their breaths.

"Is everyone clear on their assignments?" David asked. "Or do you need a dress rehearsal?"

Nancy giggled. "Not unless you want me to…ah…" She pointed toward David's crotch, "…take care of you…"

David stepped back out of her reach and both women giggled behind their hands. "As long as ye're sure what to do."

"Honey, I learned what to do when I was thirteen. I don't need practice." Nancy bumped Carla with her shoulder, teasingly. "You don't need to rehearse, do ya, luv?"

"If I get to rehearse wit' 'im," Carla said, nodding her head in David's direction, "then, yeah, I do."

Teasdel turned and faced both women. "This is a dangerous mission. The Major and Miss Wallis-Manning could be killed. Take this seriously."

"Then let's go through the plan," Tim said. "At 1:00 I'll climb to the top of the building across the street, get into position, and notify the major."

"Nancy and I will walk down the sidewalk, laughing, and drinking from a bottle of whiskey," Carla said.

Harry stood taller as he took his turn. "I'll get into position at the rear of the property with my wire cutters, cut the fence for the major, and then prepare for the retreat."

"I'll crawl beneath the fence and wait for a signal from Tim," David said.

"Nancy and I will share the bottle of whiskey with the front guard and the rear guard, who should have arrived at the fence," Carla said.

"As soon as I see the girls entertaining the two guards," Tim snickered, "I'll signal the major." David glared at Tim and his face reddened. "No disrespect intended."

"At the signal, I'll cross the yard, throw the grappling hook, and climb the wall."

"When the men start moaning, I'll signal the major to blow the window bars."

"I'll then enter the room and grab Kenzie."

"Then I give status reports every minute the major is in the room, but that's the part I don't understand. How do I give signals? Wave my arms?"

"I'll get to that shortly." In order to get the job done, David needed to interject twenty-first century technology into the mission. The ramifications were impossible to calculate, but being in a hostile environment without reliable communication could doom them all. He had no choice.

"When I get the signal from Tim," David continued, "I'll exit the room, scale down the wall, and cross the backyard."

"I'll have the fence lifted and ready for your escape," Harry said. "And as soon as you crawl through, I'll notify Teasdel to be ready."

Teasdel puffed on his pipe. "I'll back the car into the alley and wait at the rendezvous point."

"Then we'll all return to the pub to celebrate," Nancy said, and the girls clapped with childlike excitement.

In the sternest of voices David said, *"This is not a game."* He had been on dozens of missions, and this one was a clusterfuck waiting to happen.

Nancy touched his arm lightly. "Major, we've lived in London all our lives. The last five years have been a living hell. If anyone understands this is not a game, it's those of us who live on the street. This is our one chance to get out of here, go to the countryside, and breathe again."

"I never married. Never had children," Carla said. "No one has ever depended on me before. I won't let you down, Major McBain. If I have to strip naked in the street, those guards won't catch you."

For the first time in hours, a wee bit of tension, like a leaky tire, seeped out of his mind and his muscles. He patted Nancy's hand, which was still clasping his arm, the only sentimentality he could afford at the moment.

He stepped away from her, dug into his duffle, and pulled out a PCS with four wireless headsets. "I have a portable communication system. It is experimental and highly classified. Harry, Tim, Teasdel, and I will be able to communicate with each other. Military Intelligence would be extremely interested in you and the device, so don't get caught with it in your possession." He watched their faces blanch and their jaws tighten, especially Teasdel's. "I did nothing illegal to obtain them, nor am I jeopardizing Britain's ability to win the war. I only want you to appreciate the seriousness of using this technology."

Teasdel nodded his understanding, but his confrontational stance indicated otherwise. He was astute enough to know he was getting only half the truth. If David didn't throw him a bone, he might walk out. "This is my team's invention, and we're field testing the range of reception. The signal might not reach Tim's position on the roof. These kinds of tests have to be performed before our men can use the devices in the field."

Teasdel scratched the back of his neck with a cynical look on his face. Then he relaxed his stance and took an interest in his headgear.

David unbuttoned the top button to his shirt. It was damn hot in the little room, and damn hotter standing under the light of Teasdel's smoky scrutiny. He had given the investigator all he could give for now. Either he was in or out.

"I'll demonstrate how to use it." David put on his headset, threaded the cord to the radio through the back of his shirt, and clipped the radio on his waistband. The others followed suit. "Tim," David said into the microphone. "Signal me if either the rear guard or the roof guard goes to the back of the residence."

Tim gripped the sides of his head, covering the ear cups, his eyes bulging. "Yes, sir."

David removed the headset and let it dangle around his neck. The others did the same. "Ye've got yer ladder in place ready to use?" David asked.

"Yes, sir. Right where you told me to hide it."

David looked at his watch. "Let's synchronize. It's 8:32."

Nancy and Carla extended their arms and nodded confirmation…before pausing to once again admire the fancy timepieces Teasdel had purchased for them on the black market. The men shoved up their sleeves and proudly showed their wrists. David wondered how long it would be before they pawned them. He didn't care what they did with them, as long as they did what they were supposed to do, when they were supposed to do it, for the next several hours.

"Any questions?" he asked.

They all shook their heads.

"If we get Kenzie out as planned, each of ye' will receive enough money to see ye' through the rest of the war. Good luck."

They left the small room one by one until only David and

Teasdel remained. The investigator still had reservations. David could either tell him the truth or a bigger lie. He decided to go with the lie. "I didn't want to tell the others but this is a joint top secret project with the United States. I checked the equipment out for twenty-four hours. I have to have it back at the lab early in the morning. Let's get this job done."

The creases that had been visible in Teasdel's forehead since they had all entered the little room vanished, and David's tension eased a wee bit more.

Teasdel opened the door and looked out, then glanced back at David. "Only a Scot could come up with this harebrained idea. And damn, I believe it might just work."

"You have Jack Mallory's contact information if this all goes to hell, right?"

Teasdel patted his pocket. "You've taken care of all the details, including the letter to Auld Fraser."

David shook his hand. "Ye're a good man, Teasdel, and I thank ye'. And I hope to hell it works. We won't get a second chance."

43

University of Kentucky Medical Center, Lexington, Kentucky, Present Day

ELLIOTT AND MEREDITH stopped by Dr. Lyles' office at the University of Kentucky Medical Center. The visit wasn't a professional one. The doctor had been Elliott's surgeon and friend for almost twenty years, and Elliott wanted a short consult with him before he and Meredith met with the team of specialists. Lyles didn't have office hours this morning, so it was a perfect time to meet.

"This place brings back wicked memories," Elliott said, holding the waiting room door for Meredith.

She slipped her hand into his. "I don't have any fond ones at all."

A receptionist looked up. "May I help you?"

"I'm Elliott Fraser. We have an appointment with Dr. Lyles."

"He just called, Dr. Fraser. He's finishing rounds and will be here in five minutes."

Meredith and Elliott took seats on a small sofa in the empty, subdued waiting room. They immediately scrolled through emails and text messages on their iPhones. Their fingers moved quickly across the small keypads, as if they were racing each other to complete one last message before more bad news brought their world to a standstill.

Meredith dropped her phone into her purse and snapped it shut.

"Cullen asked me at breakfast if I was sick."

Elliott's head jerked up, and he slipped his device into his jacket pocket. "What'd ye' say?"

Meredith dabbed at the corner of her eye with a knuckle. "That I was going to the doctor because I hadn't been feeling well lately."

"What did he say?"

"He was so bossy and determined it was hard not to laugh. He was too cute. He said the door to the cave must be locked and the key thrown away. Apparently, he blames the cave and the bats for making me sick, because I haven't felt well since I spent the week working down there."

"Did ye' tell him David already took care of the lock and key?"

"I did." Meredith's eyes flashed dark blue and angry. "I didn't appreciate it at all when Ned told me I couldn't go back down there. I hightailed it straight to David."

"Did he tell ye' he called an engineer to study the feasibility of excavating the cave and enlarging yer wine cellar?"

"He did, and I told him he could have talked to me about it first."

Elliott laughed. "Haven't ye' been around enough Scotsmen to know—"

"And he's been around me long enough to know that I would have appreciated being included in the decision."

Elliott kissed her. "Ye' were talking about Cullen. How did we get to David?"

Meredith chewed on her bottom lip. "I guess he's on our minds."

"Aye, he is. But if I stop to think about him, I get overloaded with worry. I want to focus only on ye'. So, back to Cullen, I wish ye' hadn't told him."

"You wish? Really? Well, he's your son, too."

He tilted his head and eyed her closely. "What do ye' mean by that?"

"He's intelligent and very sensitive. Even if no one says anything, he feels it in the air. We've never lied to him before. I'm not going to start now."

Elliott blew out his cheeks. "Ye're right. I'm sorry. I'm not handling this well, Mer."

"I'm not either."

The door opened and Dr. Lyles walked in wearing his white lab coat. He shook hands with Elliott and kissed Meredith's cheek. "Come on back."

He led the way down a hall past empty exam rooms, a small lab, and a consultation room, until they reached his cookie-cutter utilitarian hospital office with prefabricated furniture and light green walls. Diplomas lined one wall, and a large, signed photograph of the Kentucky basketball team holding the NCAA Final Four Tournament Trophy almost filled another.

Lyles thumbed through several loose pages on his desk. "I've studied your file, and I personally know all the doctors on your team, and I believe you will receive the best care possible." He stacked the pages, set them aside, and looked at Meredith. "Elliott asked me for an honest opinion about treatment options here versus other facilities." Lyles stopped and took a breath before continuing. "If a biopsy confirms you have metastatic breast cancer in the lungs, I would recommend you stay here, close to home."

"Why?" Meredith asked. "Why not search for the best treatment options?"

"Meredith, this is a matter to discuss with your oncologist once you have a diagnosis."

"I understand that. What I want to know is why that is your recommendation. You're not answering me."

"Once you have a diagnosis—"

"Ye've said that already," Elliott said. "Whatever ye're not saying, spit it out. Tell us the truth. We're big kids. We can handle it."

Lyles leaned back in his chair and clasped his hands in front of his belly. After a moment he said, "If the biopsy confirms you have metastatic breast cancer in the lungs, there is no surgical option.

The color drained out of Meredith's face. "Radiation?"

Lyles leaned forward and glanced at the notes in front of him.

"You've already had two cancers, and have received the maximum radiation to the chest."

Elliott scooted to the edge of his seat. "Chemo?"

"Possible, but the metastases will probably only partially respond to chemotherapy."

Meredith reached for Elliott's hand and squeezed. "Can anything be done?"

"Meredith, if a biopsy confirms you have metastatic breast cancer in the lungs, the goal of your treatment will not be a cure, but palliation."

She blinked at Elliott, her breathing fast and irregular. "Which means what exactly?"

Lyles shuffled papers, his eyes glistening. "Your doctors will keep you comfortable and as pain-free as possible."

Meredith's face twisted. "How long?"

"I'm not sure."

She pounded her fist on the arm of the chair. "*Tell me, damn it.* I want to know."

"If the biopsy confirms—"

"Stop it, Wayne." Meredith shot to her feet, put her hands on the desk, and looked him in the eye. "Tell me the truth. How long?"

"Maybe six to nine months."

"Less than a year?" Meredith's voice was soft and thready. "That's not possible." She put her hand to her forehead and wavered.

Elliott jumped to his feet, grabbed her, and eased her back into the chair. "Ye're wrong, Lyles. Ye're way off base. I've read the research. There're experimental treatments. We'll try them all."

"Elliott, sit down. You fought me for years over your own health. Let me finish."

Tears burned the backs of Elliott's eyes. Without Meredith, he didn't know if he could go on. He knew he would have to for Cullen's sake, but… "Ye've said enough."

Meredith leaned over, clutching her belly in anguish, shaking uncontrollably, and sobbing. "I don't want to die."

Elliott knelt in front of her, wanting to be brave, afraid that he couldn't. He kissed her head, and held her. "Ye're not. Not this year. Not next year. If we have to travel around the world, we will. We'll try every experimental drug. *I won't let you die.*"

Her deep wails were a knife to his heart.

"If not for you, I wouldn't have survived cancer ten years ago," she sobbed.

"And ye'll survive this time, too. Whatever we have to do, we will." Elliott glared at Lyles. "Let's go, Mer. We'll find a doctor who believes in ye' and has the power to heal ye'."

He pulled her to her feet and held her close. Her body jerked and shuddered against him, her sobs ripped his heart out, and her tears wet his shirt to the skin. "I won't ever let ye' go. Yer last breath will also be my own."

44

University of Kentucky Medical Center, Lexington, Kentucky

WAYNE LYLES STOOD at his receptionist's desk and watched the door slam in Elliott's wake. Through all their years together, they had fought over surgery, recovery, abuse of pain medication, and physical therapy, until finally he had fired Elliott as a patient and sent him to New York for treatment. It didn't last. Elliott was back in his care within two weeks, and since then they had worked together and finally healed his leg while Meredith healed his heart. Elliott wouldn't be able to function without her. Six months. The thought made Lyles physically ill.

"I'm so sorry," the receptionist said. "I know they're friends of yours."

"Elliott's been my friend and patient for almost two decades."

The receptionist turned in her chair and glanced up at Lyles. "How old is their son, Cullen?"

"Ten, I think. Time has gone by so quickly. Why?"

The receptionist shrugged. "Mrs. Fraser was telling Dr. Fraser a story about their little boy blaming the cave and bats for her sickness."

"What?" Lyles said.

"Evidently, Mrs. Fraser had been working in a cave with bats. The little boy said that's why she got sick and he wanted the door locked and the key thrown away."

"A cave? With bats?" Lyles said.

The phone rang and she reached for it. "That's what I heard," she said before answering.

Lyles hurried back to his office and thumbed through the pages of Meredith's reports. He sat back in his chair and rubbed his tense shoulder.

He had only seen one case of histoplasmosis in his career, but the respiratory infection was common in Kentucky. Meredith had been in the UK, specifically Scotland.

Was it possible she didn't have cancer at all?

He picked up the phone and called the Chief of Cardio-Thoracic Surgery. Elliott wouldn't speak to him again anytime soon, but at least Meredith's surgical team would know about their spelunking patient. If they thought she might have cave's disease, they could tell her. Meredith needed to trust and have confidence in her team. Giving her hope would go a long way toward establishing that bond.

45

London, England, June 5, 1944

DAVID CRAWLED INTO position at the fence behind Number 8, adrenaline pumping. The smell of ashes and soot from the grass battered his senses, and he had to pinch his nose to keep from sneezing. Although he had been on dozens of life-threatening missions before, this one was different. Instead of being armed to the teeth, he had no weapons other than the blade he carried in his boot. Teasdel had been adamant. The guards were British soldiers, and he could not shoot them. Incapacitate them if necessary, but they were not to be permanently harmed.

If the guards got in David's way, whatever the girls were doing to them would more than make up for a bump on the head. He didn't like going in unarmed. Un-armed? How appropriate. That was exactly how he felt—like his arms were tied behind his back.

His lips curled back in a snarl. He couldn't go in with that attitude.

Fake it 'til ye' make it.

Confidence was the only weapon he had. Well, that—and a fear of failure as powerful as a tsunami.

He had spent years at the race track watching feisty Thoroughbreds waiting for the gate to open and the race to begin, their hot demeanor calmed by the jockey's gentle encouragement. David calmed now by a voice in his head he had never heard before.

You're a good man, McBain. You got this. Save our girl.

I will.

A peace he had never experienced before a mission washed over him. The tsunami-sized fear retreated, leaving him free to focus solely on the second floor window.

I got your back.

David wasn't sure who had his back other than his team of misfits, but someone did, and he knew he could rely on the man behind that voice.

With preternatural calm, he went through the litany of steps the team would take. He glanced over his shoulder. Harry stood nearby, wire cutters in hand. The time: one o'clock exactly. The girls would be coming down the street guided by a bomber's moon and a starlit sky.

He had only one pair of thermal goggles, and had debated about who needed them more, and decided selfishly that he did. If he had to evade the guards after he extracted Kenzie, he would need them.

"Both guards are at the gate. Go."

Harry snapped the pre-selected wires. David belly crawled under the fence and shot out like a cannonball before hurling himself across the fifty feet to the rear of the building. He dropped one end of the rope and stepped on it to hold it taut. Then he began to whirl the end with the attached grapple. When he got a nice spin going, he let go. The hook hit the roof and grabbed.

A few quick tugs told David all he needed to know. "Going up," he murmured into the microphone to his team members. He grabbed the rope and climbed. Before he cleared the first floor window, his arm muscles bulged. Halfway to the second they burned, but he pushed on until he arrived at the window of Kenzie's prison.

Dangling on the rope, he molded PE-4 around the tops and bottoms of all eight bars and set the detonator to blow. When he heard moans from the front of the house, he said, "Blowing the bars now." He turned his face aside, held his breath, and detonated the charge. A flash of light and then darkness. If the light was spotted, the game was over. When no one came running, he took a deep breath.

Go.

The command from inside his head forced him to ignore possible repercussions and get back to the task. He removed the bars and slipped them one by one into a slotted sack hanging from the belt Teasdel had specially made to keep the metal bars from clanging together.

David then lifted the window, pushed the partially opened blackout curtain aside, and peered in. The door was closed. The room had no furniture, no light…nothing but a naked form curled in the corner. His throat became painfully tight.

Get her out now, soldier.

He swallowed hard at the command and climbed through the window.

David approached the form without making a sound. He put a hand over her mouth. "Kenzie, it's McBain. I'm getting ye' out of here." She moaned behind his hand, and he whispered again. "Be still, lass, and very, very quiet. I'm taking ye' home."

He'd realized she would need a wrap of some kind, and had stuffed a thin blanket in the back of his shirt. He pulled it out and wrapped it tightly around her, mummy style, then slung her over his shoulder. She moaned again.

"Shhh, lass."

He reached for the rope and looped it through the locking carabiner attached to his rappelling harness. He sat on the window ledge and glanced around the yard. The only person he saw was Harry. Good. There was one last thing to do before he rappelled down. He dropped Kenzie's passport on the floor. If MI had confirmation she was an American citizen, the agents might not come looking for her.

Footsteps pounded the floor in the hall outside the door, followed by a man's scream, "*Nein. Nein. Nein. Nein Wasser. Bitte. Bitte.*"

David waited until the footsteps passed, wondering only briefly what was in store for the German prisoner. "Hold on, lass. I'll have ye' down in a wee bit." He pushed off and rappelled to the ground.

"I'm on the ground," David told the team members.

"Guards are moving," Tim said. "The girls are clearing out."

That was David's cue to get the hell out too. He darted across the yard toward the corner where Harry had the fence raised and ready. David shifted Kenzie's position and held her in his arms protectively as he hit the ground hard on his hip and shoulder. Kenzie yelped. The jolt rattled him, too. Her cry, while small and weak, seemed loud in the quiet night.

Suddenly doors slammed and soldiers barked orders. "Find her."

"I'm through the fence," David announced as he jumped to his feet and ran. Teasdel wasn't at the rendezvous spot. "Where the hell are ye'?" David had a backup plan in the event Teasdel was a no-show, but he hoped to God he wouldn't have to use it.

After a few agonizing seconds Teasdel answered, "I had to circle around. I'm almost to the alley."

"Tim. Harry. Abandon your positions," David said into the microphone.

David tossed Kenzie back onto his shoulder and sprinted, heart pounding. Teasdel's tires screeched as he turned into the alley twenty yards away.

"Stop," a voice yelled from behind David. A rifle cocked and fired. The bullet hit a tree to David's right. "Stop."

He ran in a zigzag pattern, as if dodging opponents on a football field. Fortunately, he could see where he was going, while the guards behind him would be shooting blind. A bullet whizzed by, followed by another. Two, maybe three men were in the alley running behind him.

Duck.

David dropped, bent-kneed, as a bullet flew over his head. He nodded his thanks to the disembodied voice, and hissed, "Hurry, Teasdel. They're trying to kill us." If David hadn't ducked just when he had, Kenzie would have been shot in the head. He pushed to his feet and ran like hell.

Push it, soldier.

Teasdel was closer, but so was the second barrage of bullets. David continued running in a zig-zag pattern. Teasdel was speeding backwards with the rear door swinging open, back and forth. David hit the door with his arm and pitched Kenzie onto the seat. He followed, slamming against her. "Go! Hit it," he yelled.

A bullet shattered the rear glass, the shards pelting David, and several bullets pinged the side of the car as it sped out onto the street.

"We've got two cars on our tail. We'll lose them in the park. Stay down," Teasdel said.

The car rocked back and forth as the detective jockeyed in and out of the narrow streets. Twice David toppled onto the floor, but immediately climbed back up to cover Kenzie with his body.

Just when David's breathing was nearing a normal rhythm, Teasdel abruptly pulled the car to the curb and stopped.

David raised his head and looked out the back window. "Why are ye' stopping, for God's sake?"

Teasdel slid down in the front seat. "They'll drive past a sitting car, but will chase a speeding one."

David grabbed Teasdel's shoulder, trying to pull him back up. "If they see a car with a shattered window, they'll be suspicious. Drive man, drive."

"Not in London, they won't. Stay down."

David's heart rate ramped back up, and another surge of adrenaline poured into his bloodstream. Just in case, he reached into his pocket and clasped the emerald brooch. He wasn't prepared to leave. His gear was stashed at the hotel with information that could alter history, and he couldn't leave it behind, but if he had to choose between Kenzie and the future, he would choose her.

Two cars sped past. David lifted his head high enough to see men hanging out of the windows of the two sedans, flashing guns, reminiscent of the 1940's gangster movies he watched as a kid.

"We'll sit here another minute or two, and then we'll go back to the hotel. Did you leave anything behind that would identify you and lead them to the Ritz?"

"I left Kenzie's passport. Now they'll know her identity for sure."

Teasdel laughed. "I hope you have a plan for getting her home without one."

David stroked Kenzie's head lightly as he curled her shivering body closer to his. "I definitely have a plan for the lass, but first we need a doctor."

46

Bassingbourn Airfield, England, June 5, 1944

"Mallory, wake up."

Jack opened his eyes to find Cav leaning over him. He closed them again. "Go away."

Cav cuffed his arm. "I can't. I have orders. Get up."

Jack had fallen asleep in his bunk at Bassingbourn, propped against the wall while writing in his notebook. Now he had a stiff neck. He hauled himself up and massaged his neck and shoulder muscles to work out the kinks. "Did you bring food? I'm hungry."

"You're always hungry, and no, I didn't bring food, but I got something better."

Jack stretched his neck side to side. "I can't think of anything better than—"

"Going on a mission?" Cav interrupted.

Jack jumped to his feet, knocking the notebook to the floor with a thud. He raised his hand to give Cav a fist bump, but when Cav only looked at him awkwardly, Jack thumped him on the shoulder instead. "How'd you manage that? I thought the colonel had withdrawn his approval." This close to D-Day, the colonel's decision hadn't surprised Jack, but it had disappointed him.

"I thought so, too. But it doesn't matter why he changed his mind, does it?"

"Not a damn bit."

"Get dressed."

Jack checked the time. "It's three A.M."

"Breakfast at four, briefing at five. Let's go."

"At least I get to eat first." He should leave a message at the Ritz for David, but Jack's inner voice suggested that would be a mistake. David was occupied with Kenzie, and Jack's responsibility was to stick to Cav like glue.

He would go on the mission and tell David about it afterward.

"I'll meet you at the mess hall in ten minutes," he told Cav.

Jack passed on a shave, shoved his legs into trousers, yanked a shirt over his head, and ran out of the room shoving his shirttail into his pants. Then he remembered his notebook, backtracked to get it, and still beat Cav to the mess hall. He'd been lobbying for a ride since he first arrived, and had been told no, then yes, then no again. No way would he wait around for a second yes to turn into a third no.

"Do you know the target?" Jack asked Cav when he joined him at the door of the mess hall.

"We'll find out at the briefing," Cav said.

Breakfast wasn't Southern cooking, but Jack filled his plate while he walked through the mess line. When they finished eating, they headed over to the briefing room.

Cav's radio operator, nicknamed Static was ahead of him. "Hey, Mallory. Heard you were tagging along today. Glad to have ya'."

"Thanks, Static. Hope you'll show me around. Maybe I'll get to see that picture of Vivian Leigh you fly with."

Static shrugged. "Maybe."

"The boys might rib you a bit, but don't pay attention to them," Cav said.

"I can take the hazing." Jack would take a lot more than that for this opportunity. He hadn't been so excited since Charlotte agreed to return to 1864 to stop Braham from changing history.

Jack and Cav entered the briefing hut and took their seats toward the front of the room. The smoky air was thick with tension, but the airmen seemed to ignore it, telling jokes and teasing each other. The majority of the ribbing focused on Cav's navigator—a shy, skinny kid from Minnesota who fingered a crucifix when he got nervous, like now—and a young girl who worked at a local pub. The poor boy's fair skin turned beet red, which only fueled more jokes.

The door at the front of the room opened and the colonel entered. "At ease, men." The airmen relaxed in their seats and riveted their attention on the front of the room.

"Your target for today is a marshalling yard in Osnabrück, and will require maximum effort. There'll be two combat wings converging on this target. Weather en route will be fine, visibility good, so you'll have fighters on your tail and heavy flak. Any questions?"

Heavy flak? Jack wondered how much flak that was. Light, moderate, heavy were all rather abstract terms until he had firsthand experience.

"Our observer, Jack Mallory, is tagging along with Cavanagh's crew. Go easy on him. This is his maiden voyage."

Someone from behind Jack tossed a roll of toilet paper into his lap. The recognizable Texas drawl of Cav's bombardier, Deke, said, "Be sure to take that. You'll need it."

The reference to Jack's bowels drew the loudest roars of laughter. He took it in stride, letting the laughs reach a peak, then he tossed the roll back over his shoulder. "I won't need that, Deadeye Deke, I borrowed a diaper from your locker." He had given the bombardier the moniker shortly after meeting him. He was the son of a U.S. Senator from Maryland, and Jack thought he was pompous.

The guys absolutely lost it, their guffaws lasting for another minute or two until the colonel reined them in. "Make sure Mallory gets three pairs of socks and a parachute."

"Aww, colonel, do we have to give him a chute? I want to see him bail out and float to the ground on all that hot air he spouts."

Jack recognized the voice of the right waist gunner, Willy, who, before joining the Army, had never left his family farm in Tulsa, Oklahoma. Jack eased to his feet and said, exaggerating his Virginia drawl, "Please, give me a chute. If I bail out without one, my hot air will take me all the way to Tulsa. I'd rather spend the rest of the war as a POW."

Uproariously laughter started up again. The left waist gunner, Jeff, sitting next to Willy punched him in the arm. "Don't think Mallory wants to go to Oklahoma. I don't blame him none."

The colonel tapped his pointing stick against the map on the wall in another attempt to get the group's attention. "Settle down, now."

Cav leaned over to Jack and said, low-voiced, "You sure you want in on this one?"

Jack didn't pause for a heartbeat. "I wouldn't miss it for the world." And then he remembered his promises to David and Charlotte…and promptly ignored them. "I'll never get another chance."

Cav puffed on his cigar. "This might be the one you *should* miss."

Jack heard Cav's reticence clearly. "We'll be fine." Jack's reassurance was based solely on his experience with the brooches. The magical stones were in control. Cav was Kenzie's soul mate, ergo Cav's plane would not be shot down.

Jack turned his attention back to the colonel and scribbled in his notebook about the briefing, the attitude of the crewmen, and the smoke and rumble in the room.

"Drop your loads on target, boys," the colonel said, "Take the photographs, then shove the nose down and pedal home as fast as you can."

The briefing continued a while longer before the airmen broke up into groups for special briefings for the pilots, navigators, gunners, and bombardiers. Jack tailed Cav to his second briefing, where Jack endured another round of hazing.

He studied the group, searching the men's faces for clues to their emotions. Whatever they were feeling, they kept it to themselves now. This was business. Whoever coined the phrase *the greatest generation* must have known these particular men.

Edgy anticipation accompanied Jack for the next two hours while he prepared for the bombing run. He hadn't lied when he told the colonel he had previously flown on a B-17. But he let the man believe it had been a combat situation. In reality, the flight had been a safe, low-level excursion around present-day Richmond Virginia on *Texas Raiders*, a restored B-17 owned by the Commemorative Air Force.

Shortly before dawn they met for their final briefing, then gathered their gear and rode out to *The Shamrock*.

"Hey, Mallory, come with me. I'll show you around," Willy said.

"Good idea," Cav said. "Rainer and I have a visual inspection to do. Get settled. We'll leave shortly."

At five o'clock, the flying fortresses lined up for takeoff. Unlike the occasional hour-long wait on the tarmac at the Atlanta airport, B-17s took off within seconds of each other—a smooth lift off the ground. Wheels were up and the crew quickly settled into their preparations. Since all Jack had to do was watch, he did just that, making notes about the roar of the engines and the frigid air.

After about an hour, he made his way to the cockpit. "Is it as quiet up here as it is back there?"

"Second pilot, why don't you let Mallory sit down for a while?" Cav said.

Rainer climbed out of the seat. "I'll be with the navigator."

Jack strapped himself in, took out his notebook, and started sketching a loose depiction of the cockpit. He wasn't an artist by any means, but his drawings got the point across. When he had returned from his Civil War adventure, he had so many pictures in his mind that he had to get them out somehow. Charlotte suggested he take art classes, partly as therapy, and partly to develop his skills. His drawings weren't saleable art, but the people weren't stick figures either.

Cav pointed out the window. "Those are the Dutch coast searchlights I told you about."

Jack incorporated the cross-beamed lights into his sketch. "What happens next?" he asked into the intercom.

"We'll pick up some flak or a fighter or two, but not much action until we hit the rendezvous point."

As Jack continued to sketch he noticed a girl's picture taped to the dashboard. "Who's the girl?"

Cav tapped the picture with his finger. "That's Susan O'Shay.

My high school sweetheart. I thought we'd get married after the war, but she got engaged to my best friend. By the time I found out, I'd already flown a dozen missions. Didn't want to jinx my luck, so I kept her picture."

"Did you love her?" Jack asked.

Cav nodded. "Probably still do."

Jack sketched Susan's likeness into the drawing. Beautiful girl with striking eyes and kiss-me lips. No wonder he'd never seen sizzling sparks between Kenzie and Cav. The pilot wore a sign that read: "For sale, broken heart. Mending required."

If he had to guess, that was Kenzie's role in this drama. Funny thing about women. Some were born healers. Charlotte was one, but based on what he'd read about Kenzie, she wasn't. So what did the brooch have in mind for these two? Only time would tell. His job was to put Cav on the playing field. Magic would do the rest.

He patted his pocket. The brooch was easily accessible in case of an emergency. If Cav had bad luck and the plane was damaged and couldn't return to base, Jack intended to take the whole kit and caboodle to the future. That wouldn't happen, though. The brooch didn't work that way.

The stone had protected Kit during a water rescue, a buffalo stampede, and an attack by bandits. And Charlotte's stone had protected her during the Battle of Cedar Creek. Maybe it hadn't protected him so well, but he couldn't blame what happened to him on the brooch. It was his own stupidity that got him into trouble. This time, though, he had both a stone and the hero of the story. He sketched in more searchlights. *Bring on the fighters. This plane is gold.*

Cav's fighter group rendezvoused on schedule, and Jack sketched dozens of B-17's in formation. When the vast armada turned toward Germany, he gave up the second pilot's seat.

The inside of the plane lacked all creature comforts. There were sharp metallic edges and no clear path from one end to the other. There was a six-inch-wide fabricated gangway over a cavern that housed the bomb bay. He had to watch where he stepped and what he touched or he'd be bloodied for sure.

The skin was as thin as a tin can, easily pierced by enemy fire.

He returned to his jump seat near Willy and Jeff's waist gunner positions, but before he buckled himself in, Cav announced over the intercom, "Don your flak suit."

Jack put on a suit and steel helmet before buckling himself in. For a moment, he stopped to consider the danger he was in, but just as quickly dismissed it, as he had done earlier. Nothing would happen to him.

Within moments, he fell into his writer's zone and wrote like a maniac. The thick gloves made his writing look like a three-year old's, but he could decipher the scrawl later.

They reached the initial point and entered the bomb run. Then all hell broke loose as Cav flew the plane through a gauntlet of flak. Jack wrote furiously, jotting down, in shorthand, the conversations as they came across the microphone.

"Pilot to bombardier," Cav said. "Your ship."

"Bombardier to pilot, roger. Hold level," the bombardier said.

"Bombardier to crew. Bomb bay doors open. Radio Operator, cameras on. Steady. Steady."

"Bombs away on primary." Deadeye's voice boomed through the intercom.

Jack unbuckled his seat belt and looked out the window in time to see the explosion when the bombs hit the target. Within seconds, a massive ball of fire erupted, and so did Jack and the crew. He didn't think he would ever forget dodging the explosions and fires in Richmond, Virginia at the end of the Civil War, but he knew with certainty he would never forget the sight below him now, especially after his firsthand experience in bombed-out London. The fires in Richmond were an accident. The intentional bombing he was now part of was to save the world from a tyrannical dictator.

"Close bomb doors," Cav ordered.

Jack buckled himself back into his seat and wrote a couple of paragraphs, wishing he could write...*the bombs we dropped destroyed Hitler's command center.*

When he felt the plane veer unexpectedly, he looked out of a gunner's window to see a horde of about two dozen German fighter planes speeding toward them out of the clouds. Their shells burst directly in front of the *The Shamrock*.

A surge of enemy gunfire made a direct hit on the number-three engine, and flames shot out. The stink of the explosives clogged his nose while vibrations hammered *The Shamrock*, sounding like a roomful of off-balance washing machines.

A blast of wind shoved Jack forward until he hit the limits of his restraints, and shrieked through the main part of the aircraft in a powerful maelstrom, carrying with it everything not bolted down.

Another explosion, and pieces of an ME-109 German fighter collided with *The Shamrock*. Flaming metal blasted into the B-17's number-one engine, and the propeller flew off, scattering debris through the thin metal skin of the plane.

The plane tilted and zigzagged, jerking Jack side to side, and the waist gunners' machine guns spit out spent shells, but he kept writing. As long as he remained lost in his writer's world, he was able to pour his fear out onto the page.

"Number three engine's been hit," Cav said.

One engine out, Jack wrote. *The crew is focused on their jobs*. He forgot about the engines and the flak and approaching enemy fighters.

"Eleven F-Ws at two o'clock," the right waist gunner said.

"Four at nine o'clock," the left waist gunner reported.

Machine gun casings pinged constantly, littering the floor as the gunners went through rack after rack, moving with efficiency, swinging their guns up and down. The men knew their jobs. If they were afraid, their fear didn't show.

Jack checked the time. Somehow two hours had sped by since *bombs away*. He had filled almost an entire notebook with the briefing and the mission, and the excitement was mostly over. Enemy fighters could still be a problem, but *The Shamrock* was on its way home.

"Number one engine's throwing oil. We're losing altitude. Navigator, chart our course to these coordinates…" Cav said.

Jack didn't have a chart, and didn't know where they were going.

He glanced at Willy and Jeff, the waist gunners. Mild concern filled their eyes.

"I sent out a Mayday," Cav said. "And Air-Sea Rescue has been notified. They have a fix on us now. We'll ditch in the Channel."

Ditch. Jack's leg muscles tightened, ready to run, but there was nowhere to go. His breathing accelerated. *Calm down. You're with the hero of Kenzie's story. You're okay, man.*

"Mallory, come help us jettison loose equipment," Static, the radio operator said. "And get out of your flak gear. We'll need to jettison that, too."

Jack jotted one more thing in his notebook before shoving it into his pocket. He was okay. Cav was okay. They would come through this, and his next book would have one hell of a climax.

"Throw out everything not bolted down," Static said.

Jack gathered armloads of equipment and threw everything out the waist gunners' open windows, where they were jettisoning guns and ammunition. On a mental white board he scribbled down descriptions of the controlled expressions on the faces of the crew, the items he pitched, and the commands from the pilot.

"We're fifty miles from England," Cav said. "Air-Sea Rescue will keep a constant fix on us all the way down. Keep to your training." There were six short rings, and then Cav said, "Prepare to ditch."

"Second pilot ditching."

"Navigator ditching."

"Bombardier ditching."

"Flight engineering ditching."

"Radio operator ditching."

"Ball turret gunner ditching."

"Right waist gunner ditching." Willy removed his parachute, loosened his shirt collar, and removed his tie and oxygen mask.

A knot lodged in Jack's throat until he remembered he was an observer, and he had to keep writing. He made mental notes about the ditching procedure.

"Left waist gunner ditching."

"Tail gunner ditching."

Willy nodded to Jack. It was his turn. His mouth was so dry he wasn't sure he could speak. "Mall...ory ditching." He removed his parachute. *I'm with Cav. He'll survive. So will I. This is a hell of a story.* Call him stupid, but he threw the damn parachute out the window.

Jeff and Willy's faces were tense, but there was no terror in their eyes. They partially inflated their life vests, and Jack did the same, brushing his hand against the pocket holding the brooch.

Am I doing the right thing?

Cav was preparing to ditch a plane in the English Channel. He would survive, but there were no guarantees the crew, including Jack, would be as lucky. If he didn't use the brooch in the next few seconds, they would crash into the English Channel.

The landing was as controlled as it could be, just five miles from the coast with rescue on the way. He would never have another chance to live this experience. He dropped his hand and folded into crash position. If he did survive, David would kill him for taking such a risk.

God, I pray for courage to accept what's about to happen. I might not like it, but if I have courage, I can deal with it, and if you don't mind, will you keep the plane afloat? I bet some of these kids aren't strong swimmers.

There was a mild jolt when the tail struck the choppy waters of the English Channel. A second impact came as the nose hit the water, sending a severe shock throughout the plane. A fierce spray of icy water took Jack's breath. When his head bounced against the side of the plane, he knew nothing more, except total darkness.

47

The Ritz, London, England, June 5, 1944

A BLOCK FROM the Ritz, David's breathing finally eased. Teasdel had crisscrossed the streets of London and returned to the hotel by a circuitous route, pulling to the side of the street every few miles and ducking below the windshield. Throughout the drive, Kenzie had remained motionless beneath him. He rolled off of her now, and she groaned. She had probably been groaning, and he'd been so preoccupied with their escape he hadn't noticed.

"How's she doing?" Teasdel asked.

"She'll need a doctor. Someone ye' can trust."

"I have one waiting in the lobby. Take Miss Wallis-Manning to your room, and I'll go get him."

"Ye're a step ahead of me. Ye're sure he can be trusted?"

Teasdel slowed the car as he turned into the alley leading to the back of the hotel. "Major," the detective said with a bit of testiness in his voice, "I haven't gone through all this to sabotage the rescue by using an unreliable physician."

"Ye're a good man." David poked his head above the seat "I told Neil to have the hotel's back door open by one-thirty. Is it?"

Teasdel stopped the car. "It's propped open."

David tucked the blanket tightly around Kenzie and picked her up. Her shivering hadn't slowed much, if at all.

"I'll find the doctor and send him to your room," Teasdel said, and headed toward the front of the hotel.

David bounded up the back steps, adrenaline still pumping. He reached his room, unlocked the door, and pushed it open. A hot bath would warm her, but the thick bed covers would have to do until after the doctor examined her.

He laid her down and turned on the bedside lamp. Careful not to jostle the bed, he sat on the edge and pushed away knotted hair to get a look at her. A fading handprint covered the left side of her face from her jaw to the corner of her eye. Both shoulders had purple finger bruises, probably from a soldier holding her from behind. Both of her wrists had deep rope burns.

David's adrenaline spiked again with a surge of raw fear.

He unwrapped the thin blanket. Blue and purple bruises dotted her skin from the top of breasts to her belly. Fear turned into rage at the sight of tooth marks surrounding both nipples. The thought of a sadistic guard with his mouth on her heated his rage to a boil. The boil spilled over, sizzling, when he saw her pubic hair was matted with semen. Bile rushed to his throat, but he swallowed it back.

His hands shook while he covered her with a thick down comforter. He understood war. He'd been in the middle of battle and seen the worst of it, but what England, in the name of war, had done to Kenzie made her torture personal.

A knock on the door heightened his thoughts of revenge. He swung open the door with anger boiling, almost hoping the soldiers had tracked them down.

Teasdel stepped back, holding his hands stiff-armed in front of him to ward David off. "You're safe. Miss Wallis-Manning is safe. No one is here looking for you."

David was too angry to speak. He nodded and stepped aside for Teasdel and the doctor to enter to room. Then he glanced out into the hall, half hoping to see soldiers rushing toward him. All he had was a knife, but he could take down two or three before they subdued him.

"This is Dr. Sterling," Teasdel said.

The doctor moved toward the bed, setting his bag on the nearby table.

"How is she?" Teasdel asked.

David's barely controlled anger seethed between each word "They. Hurt. Her."

Teasdel squeezed his eyes shut for a moment while he ingested the news. Then he steeled his features and said, "We got her out, Major McBain, and by now MI knows they had an innocent civilian. Let Sterling do his work, then take her to Scotland. I'm going back to the pub to check on the others. You know where to reach me."

David pulled a handful of bills from his pocket. "This is for the bonuses. I'll never be able to thank ye' enough for what ye've done for the lass."

Teasdel pocketed the cash. "It was a well-planned mission executed without violence. Don't go back seeking revenge. Whatever was done to Miss Wallis-Manning might have been done in error, but the intent was to gain information to win the war."

"The goal may have been morally important, but torturing an innocent civilian can never be condoned."

Teasdel crossed his arms, his jaw tightened, and a vein throbbed visibly on his neck. "In this case, my countrymen were wrong, but I would rather they make one mistake than overlook a situation they shouldn't."

Arguing with Teasdel was futile. In the detective's defense, though, David had to agree with him. The blame for Kenzie's abuse had to be heaped not against MI, but at David's feet.

He shook hands with Teasdel, and the detective left with a promise that he would return later in the day unless David called him first.

David took a deep breath and crossed the room to the bed where he stood, still as stone, and watched the doctor's examination. Watching was a complete invasion of Kenzie's privacy, but he had to know exactly what they had done to her. He schooled his features, locked down his anger, and didn't avert his eyes. The knowledge was part of his penitence. Knowing she had been tortured was punishment enough. Knowing exactly what they had done would feed his nightmares for the rest of his life.

The doctor lowered her legs and covered her. "Her lungs are congested. She has a slight fever, and possibly two or three bruised ribs. There is semen in her pubic hair, but no signs of recent sexual activity."

"You're saying she hasn't been raped."

"No, she has not. They must have masturbated on her. Maybe threatened her with rape. From the extent of her rope burns, she resisted. I'll bandage her up, but rest is what she needs most. Her body will recover."

"Why won't she wake up?" David asked.

"Sleep deprivation. Probably no food since her abduction, and constant cold, fear, and trauma exhausted her." He wrapped bandages around her ribs, wrists, and ankles. "She needs to rest for a few days." The doctor snapped his black satchel closed and headed toward the door. "I'll be back later in the day to check on her."

"Will she be all right?"

The doctor's hand rested on the doorknob. "Major, you know what war can do to a man. It's often the wounds we can't see that are the hardest to heal." He glanced back at Kenzie. "I've never seen a female patient so physically fit, in spite of the old injury on her hip and thigh. Do you know what happened to her?"

"Shrapnel."

The corner of his lip curled up in an appreciate slant. "She had a good surgeon."

"But she'll recover?"

"Yes, her body will recover."

But what of her mind?

David locked the door and leaned against it. When they returned to the future, he would see that she had the best mental health treatment he could find. She had endured her mother's death, her friend Trey's, her own injuries, and now this. He squeezed his fist into his palm. He didn't know how he was going to make it right, but he would never stop trying.

He showered, dressed in a T-shirt and kilt, and then pulled a chair up next to the bed. As tired as he was, his mind wouldn't rest. He would call Jack later in the morning. It was time to take Kenzie and Cavanaugh back to the future.

48

The Ritz, London, England, June 5, 1944

Toward dawn, Kenzie stirred, waking David. He leaned forward in the chair, bracing his forearms on his knees, and watched closely to see if she would go back to sleep as she had done an hour earlier.

She was more beautiful and desirable than any other woman he'd ever known. Damn his weakness, his longing for her. He deserved whatever torture awaited him for wanting her for himself. He hadn't been in the habit of falling for women he couldn't have, but he had done it twice now. He had thought falling for Charlotte put him in hell, but he'd been wrong. The present was hell, and it would only get hotter.

Her breathing accelerated, and she thrashed around in the bed. *"Water. No. Please. No. I'm Captain…"*

He slid to his knees next to the bed, and gently rubbed her shoulder. "Shhh. Kenzie. Ye're safe now. No one is going to hurt ye'."

She jerked her shoulder away from his touch. *"Please. I've told you the truth."*

"Ye're safe, lass. Open yer wee eyes." He was tempted to use Gaelic to calm her as he often calmed James Cullen and Lincoln. But in her delirium, she might be as afraid of a Scotsman as she was of her captors.

Her eyes popped open and darted suspicious glances from side to side. "Where am I?"

Answer her questions, but keep it simple.

"At the Ritz in London. It's June 5, 1944. Military Intelligence had ye' prisoner for over thirty hours."

Her face when pasty white. "1944?"

"Aye, remember ye' were at Bletchley Park?"

"With Turing?"

"Aye. Ye' were going to work for him, but MI thought ye' might be a spy."

She shook her head. "Not a spy."

"I know ye're not." It would be so easy to say, *Ye're from the future.* But he couldn't bring himself to confess. Not yet.

She stared at him, blinking as if she wasn't sure she believed she had been rescued. "How did I get here?"

Was she asking how she got to the Ritz or to 1944? He was sure she meant the Ritz.

"Zoey, Molly's roommate, saw yer abduction. From her descriptions of the men and the vehicle, I assumed Military Intelligence had arrested ye'. As soon as I found out, I went straight to London, hired a detective, and with some random luck we located ye' and extracted ye' early this morning."

"Why did you go to all that trouble for someone you don't know?"

He should tell her the truth. If she had a temper like the colonel's, she'd come after him with an automatic, start with a bullet to each knee, and work her way up until he resembled a silhouette target full of holes.

Charlotte had been furious when she discovered he had implanted a tracking device in her hip. Even though it saved her life, she still didn't appreciate having her privacy violated. And Meredith had been ticked off when he locked the cave.

From his experience, if he was going to protect a lass, he needed to be subtle about it. There was nothing subtle about the way he had handled Kenzie. He thought back to the moment at Claridge's when he had her to himself. He should have told her then who he was and why he was there, but he hadn't. He'd wanted her for himself then, and he wanted her now.

He got up and crossed the room to a table holding a dinner tray that he had ordered. "I do know ye', lass, and ye' were in trouble and needed my help." He removed the lid from the soup bowl. "The chicken soup is cold. I'll have the kitchen warm it for ye'."

"I'm so hungry I'll eat it cold." She made a move to sit up and groaned.

"Let me help ye'. Yer ribs are bruised and ye'll be sore for a few days."

She pulled the sheet almost to her chin. "I can do it, thanks."

To give her privacy, he turned his back and fiddled with the food tray. Her attempt at modesty reminded him that he had packed clothes for her, but giving them to her now required full disclosure. And besides, not having clothes kept her safer. She couldn't go out or answer the door, and she couldn't bolt.

The first chance he had, he would call Teasdel and ask him to buy a few items on the black market. David knew he couldn't get her to stay in bed naked for more than twenty-four hours. An active woman like Kenzie wouldn't tolerate being cooped up. Even battered and bruised, she would find a way to exercise, even if all she did was stretch.

When the bed quit squeaking, he assumed she was settled, so he turned with the tray in his hands. At the sight of her, his hands jerked, rattling the dishes and almost slopping the soup. If he had thought she looked beautiful before, she was exquisite now, in spite of—or perhaps partly because of—the damage done to her. A ray of morning light picked up the gold in her red hair, and the mass of tangled waves tumbled around her shoulders, creating an angel's halo. Her large, round hazel eyes glinted green and gold, and he was enchanted beyond words, lost in a magical moment in time.

She held up her hands. "Are the bandages your handiwork?"

He cleared his throat, but his voice was husky with desire when he said, "Dr. Sterling attended to ye'. Ye' got some nasty bruises, but nothing's broken, and ye'll heal up fine." He set the tray on her lap, then turned away to pull himself together—again. "Do ye' want to talk about what happened?"

Aye, let's talk about what happened so I won't think about how much I want ye'.

He sat in the chair and casually stroked his jaw in an attempt to appear calm, studying her while trying to ignore his body's urgent demands.

She looked at him, her eyes dilated. She quickly broke eye contact and jabbed at the noodles in her soup bowl.

Dial it back, McBain. Ye're sending signals ye' shouldn't send, and she's receiving them.

After a moment she said, "I didn't know what they wanted from me. I'm sure they're not happy I escaped. I need to get out of London fast. I can't go back to Bletchley. I'm sure Molly's worried."

"We'll figure that out tomorrow. Today ye' need to rest."

Tell her the truth so she won't worry. Odd. Was that the same voice he heard during the rescue?

As much as he knew he should, David couldn't stand the thought of breaking the intimate bond building between them. "There are safe places in the country. We'll find a place, but today is for rest."

When she finished the soup, he took the tray, and she nestled back into the covers. "Do I need to get up anytime soon? I'd like to sleep for another couple of hours, maybe days."

"Take as long as you need. I'm not going anywhere." He yawned. "Resting is the best thing ye' can do right now."

She patted the empty side of the bed. "I don't mind sharing the bed. That chair looks uncomfortable."

He stretched out his long legs, crossing his stocking feet at the ankles. "I'm fine. I've slept in worse places. Go back to sleep."

"If you change your mind later, you won't wake me."

Lass, if I lie next to ye', it won't be sleep I'd be wantin'.

She closed her eyes, and within minutes had drifted off again. He watched her for a while until his eyelids became too heavy to hold open. He jerked several times to wake himself but finally fell under sleep's spell.

"Stop. Please stop."

Kenzie's screams woke him. He jumped and moved quickly to her side. The covers had fallen and she was uncovered to the waist. The bruising on her breasts was darker, and so was his anger. He sat on the bed, leaned against the headboard, and pulled her gently to his chest. "Shhh, lass. I'm with ye' now. Ye're safe." He pulled the quilt to her shoulders while she shivered against him.

"I don't know where I am." She buried her face in her hands and sobbed. "I'm so lost."

"Ye're at the Ritz in London. It's June 5, 1944. Ye' were rescued. Ye're not in danger."

"It was happening all over again," she said, sobbing harder. "The board, the water, the jeers, the taunts, the threats. They didn't rape me, but I can still feel their filthy hands on me. That was worse than the water torture. I couldn't stand their mouths on me. When I screamed, they laughed."

A shot of whiskey poured directly on his ulcer wouldn't burn his stomach as badly as the anguish in her voice.

"They tried to drown me. And then it became a game for them. They poured water into my mouth and nose until I almost blacked out, and then they would stop and fondle me again. I finally didn't care anymore. They must have known, because they untied me and took me to another room."

He wrapped his arms around her. "They won't hurt ye' again."

"They would have killed me."

From the documents he had read describing the atrocities that had taken place at the Cage, if the testimony of German officers was to be believed, he didn't think the British soldiers would have killed her intentionally, but she could easily have died as a result of their overzealousness. He hated them for what they had done under the guise of war. But the bulk of his anger was directed at himself. Ultimately, he was to blame. Instead of taking her home when he found her, he bought her champagne, ruined her jokes, and let her fall into the hands of Military Intelligence.

He combed his fingers through her hair, gently working out the tangles, crooning *a chuisle mo chroí* in her ear.

"What does that mean?" she asked.

He couldn't tell her the true meaning was "pulse of my heart," so he said, "Sleep, my little one."

"Oh, that's nice." She relaxed against him, and her breathing returned to its normal rhythm—a rhythm that had become dear and familiar to him. After a moment she said groggily, "I like you combing my hair. It reminds me of my mother. She was Scottish, too."

"Is that the Wallis in yer name?"

"Yes, but she's dead now."

"I'm sorry."

She looked up at him. "She and her family didn't see eye-to-eye on her marriage to my father. He's not Scottish, and...well, I think they had other plans for her."

His lips were only inches from hers now. And with willpower more powerful than any he had ever exercised before, he kept his distance.

She reached up, cupped his neck, and pulled him closer until their lips touched.

"I...I don't think..."

"Don't think, McBain. Just make love to me." She turned in his arms, groaning slightly from the effort, and kissed him. "I don't want to think about the past week and all I've been through. I want to erase the memory of those men and what they did to me. I want to forget about the waterboard and the deprivation. I want to forget about the bombs and the danger. I want—no, I need you. Don't say no."

She eased down on the bed, her arms reaching for him. "You want me. I know you do. Take me and make me forget."

God, yes, he wanted her, and right now it didn't matter whether she belonged to someone else or not. Once he told her the truth, she would never speak to him again anyway. He might as well have the memory of being a part of her.

He held himself above her. "I don't want to hurt ye'."

"You won't, but you can erase what's happened to me." She grabbed the tail of his undershirt and pulled it over his head. "You *are* gorgeous. Just as I suspected." She ran her fingertips through the light dusting of chest hair, then up to his neck and down his arms, slowing at the rise and fall of his muscles. Then her hands ventured down his chest to his waist and the buttons of his kilt. Instead of unbuttoning it, she opened the flap and reached for him.

He sucked air through his teeth and firmly reminded himself that he wasn't a teenager. He could last longer than ten seconds. "Are ye' sure, lassie?"

Gazing into his eyes she said, "I've never been so sure."

He had lost count of the number of times he imagined himself above her like this, poised to enter her, possess her, claim her, and once he did, he would never let her go. Never.

A knock on the door pulled him from the brink of his heart's desire. "Major McBain."

"Christ," David said.

"Don't answer it," Kenzie said, lifting her hips up to him.

"Major, I have a telegram for you."

David threw his head back, gritting his teeth. This hadn't happened to him since he was a teenager. "Slide it under the door," he croaked. The telegram whisked across the hardwood.

He glanced down at Kenzie to see her mouth set in a hard line. "I have to get it. Don't move." He shoved off the bed and scooped up the telegram. "It's from the commander at Bassingbourn Air Base." He ripped opened the envelope and pulled out the missive. "God *damn.*"

Kenzie sat up, her flushed face now faded to white. "What happened?"

He crushed the letter into a ball and threw it on the table, where it bounced and rolled to the floor. If Jack wasn't dead, he would kill him for going on a mission, and then time travel back to before the crash and kill him again for interrupting this moment with Kenzie.

"Cavanaugh's plane crash landed in the Channel, and Jack was with him."

"Oh, my God." She sat and wrapped the sheet around her toga-style. "Is that it? No other news about the crew, or what happened to Jack?"

"Nothing more."

"What was he doing on a B-17?"

David's temper snapped. "Chasing a goddamn story." David sat on the bed next to her and pulled her into his arms. "I know ye' care for Cavanaugh. Air-Sea Rescue recovers most of the crews that crash into the channel. They'll be all right."

"But you're so worried. I can see it in your eyes."

"Jack has a habit of taking risks without considering consequences. He promised me he wouldn't do anything stupid." David tipped up her face with his finger so she would look at him. "I have to go. I don't want to leave ye', but I have to find Jack and check on Cavanaugh and the rest of the crew. Promise me ye' won't leave this room or let anyone in."

"How long will you be gone?"

He traced a finger along the line of her jaw, to her ear, and then tucked her hair behind her earlobe, all the while holding her gaze with calm reassurance. "The 65th Fighter Wing has a rescue command center at Saffron Walden."

"That's almost to Cambridge."

"I'll wait there for news. The rescue craft will take the crew to the closest port. From there they'll evac the injured to the hospital, and the rest will return to Bassingbourn."

"You could be gone several hours."

"Ye're safe here, lass. There are only three people who know ye're at the Ritz, and I trust all three to keep that a secret. If ye' get hungry again before I return, call the front desk and ask for Neil."

"Is he one of the three?"

David nodded. "Whatever ye' need, he can get it. While I'm gone, ye' can have several hours of interrupted sleep, room service, and a bath. But don't leave the room or let anyone else in."

She tugged at the sheet. "I'm not exactly dressed to receive company."

"Ye're dressed perfectly for me." He pinned her with his eyes and tried to hide his worry in a gentle smile, but even he could hear it in his voice. He kissed her lightly. "I need to change."

He took a duffle into the bathroom and returned a few minutes later in uniform. "If ye' have any trouble, call this man." David jotted down Teasdel's name and the phone number of the pub. "He's the detective who helped with yer rescue. He'll come immediately."

She followed David with the tail of her toga dragging across the floor.

"Lock the door behind me, and don't open it for anyone. I'll call as soon as I get news."

She linked her hands behind his head and rose up on her toes to reach his mouth. The sheet dropped to the floor. The wanting of her was a constant roar in his blood, and it increased now with the feel of her against him, all soft and warm and wanting.

She studied his face, her breath hitching.

"I'll be back, and we'll pick up where we left off." He kissed her again. A touch at first, molding shape against shape, and then with his tongue deep within her mouth, while he battled fierce need and lust and insatiable hunger.

"Ye're okay, Kenzie."

The brooches could go hang. He could never let her go. He left the room, cursing reckless Jack and the blasted emerald.

49

Air-Sea Rescue Command Center, Saffron Walden, England, June 5, 1944

WHEN DAVID REACHED the crowded hotel lobby, he was still cursing Jack and the brooch. He would give his right arm to return to Kenzie and finish what they started.

He casually scanned the lobby and the entrance to the bar. Most of the men were reporter types, sniffing the air for a big story. If they knew the invasion was less than twenty-four hours away, they would be hounding every officer in the lobby for an interview.

Kenzie's Fedora Man wasn't among the two dozen or so gathered there, at least not wearing his overcoat and hat. There were men wearing hats, but none of them appeared to be paying attention to him, and David's early-warning tickling sensation didn't intensify. He relaxed a bit, confident MI hadn't followed him to the hotel. Kenzie would be safe while he was gone. If she stayed in bed, by the time he returned, she would be well-rested and hopefully eager to...

Stop it. She's not yours.

He could tell himself that, but his heart refused to believe it. And besides, Kenzie didn't act like a woman in love with another man. He decided to hold on to that thought even though he was pretty sure it would earn him a front row seat to someone else's love story.

At the concierge's desk, he telephoned the commander at Bassingbourn Air Base. It took five minutes to get through to the airfield's operator and connected to the commander's aide. It took another five minutes for the commander to quit barking orders, which David could hear clearly in the background, before he turned his attention to the caller.

"Colonel Ballard."

"This is Major McBain. I received yer telegram. Do ye' have any news of Cavanaugh's plane?"

"Not a damn thing," Ballard said brusquely. "We're still waiting for news."

David didn't expect any news, but there was still a tightening in his chest at Ballard's answer. "I'm leaving London now for Saffron Walden to monitor the rescue. If I hear anything, I'll let ye' know."

"Thank you, Major. Cavanaugh is one of my best pilots. If that tin can he's flying will hold together long enough, his crew will be climbing aboard a rescue craft laughing about their adventure. Your friend couldn't be in better hands."

Cavanaugh's hands didn't worry David. He was Kenzie's soul mate. He would survive. It was Jack who had David's stomach twisting into knots.

When David walked out of the Ritz, he noted that there were few soldiers on the streets, nothing like the numbers days earlier. Those soldiers who were still in London were assigned here. The absence of thousands of soldiers freed up the taxis, but still there were none on the street. And he needed reliable transportation. He could commandeer military transport, but using a vehicle and driver for personal reasons didn't sit well with him.

He could take the train or drive the clunker. The old girl had a few rough miles left in her, but he didn't trust her. He kicked a small chunk of concrete to the curb. "Damn."

Based on what he learned from the command center, he might have to go to a hospital or an airfield. Having his own transportation would make it easier and faster to get from one place to the other. Luckily, he had envisioned the possibility of an emergency and asked Teasdel to buy more petrol off the black market.

However, repairing the old rattletrap was out of the question.

The best auto mechanics in London couldn't fix that jalopy. Resolved to drive and trust the Powers That Be to get him where he needed to go—and back—promptly and without incident, he aimed his footsteps toward the storage building where Neil parked the car. As he walked, he further relieved his tension by blistering Jack's hide *in absentia*, using words that would make Auld Fraser blush.

The jalopy sputtered and stopped. David hit the steering wheel with the heels of his hands. He wanted to kick the tires to ribbons out of sheer frustration. He didn't want to leave Kenzie, and he didn't want to go to the command center. Not knowing what happened to Jack and the crew might be better than learning the truth. It was one of those damned if ye' did and damned it ye' didn't moments.

He restarted the engine. And it sputtered and stopped again. "Come on, auld girl. It's time to strut yer stuff. Ye' can do this."

The third time was the charm, or so he thought until a loud bang accompanied the sputtering. The muffler probably had more holes than a small sieve, and the car jerked with every gear change. But it kept moving and finally picked up speed, if forty miles per hour could be called speed.

Not far from London, he saw a convoy of United States Army vehicles, no doubt carrying troops to their embarkation points. David stopped the car and got out. While the trucks whizzed by, he saluted, wondering how many of these lads would lose their lives on Omaha or Utah Beach. He turned slowly, still at attention, his salute still in place, until the last of the vehicles disappeared around the bend in the road. Then he snapped his salute down, turned smartly, and returned to his jalopy, once again praying the old Crossley would get him to his destination.

Finally, he was alone on the road again, his only company the clunking engine, his only thoughts were of Kenzie. Making love to her would be almost as dangerous and irresponsible as Jack's most recent stunt. If Cavanaugh ever learned David had almost seduced her, he would deserve whatever punishment Cavanaugh decided to mete out. He had more self-control than that. Thank God they were interrupted. The telegram had saved them from making a serious mistake.

When he returned to the hotel room, he would tell Kenzie the truth immediately. That should make mincemeat of any inclination Kenzie might have to pick up where they left off.

It took an hour and a half to reach the Air-Sea Rescue Command Center. The bright red doors of the two-story brick Saffron Walden Grammar School were guarded, but when he flashed his ID, he was allowed in.

He followed the signs to the airfield's commander's office, where he introduced himself to the aide and explained why he was there. After a ten minute wait, the aide said, "Colonel Hicks will see you now."

David rushed into the office.

"I understand you're from Supreme Headquarters to observe operations," Hicks said.

"I *am* from headquarters, and I'm here to observe, but I'm only interested in a B-17 out of Bassingbourn that ditched in the Channel a few hours ago. What can ye' tell me?

"The pilot had time to send a Mayday, and we tracked the plane until it ditched. A long range craft has been dispatched. The good news is we know where the plane is."

Alarm bells sounded in David's brain. "What's the bad news?"

Hicks lit a cigar and puffed. "The closest rescue craft was more than two hours away."

"Was?" David asked. "Where is it now?"

"Best guess, not much closer. You're welcome to spend time in the Command Center to observe our operation. We're proud of what we do here, and are pleased to be able to demonstrate it for a representative from SHAEF."

"I'm only a liaison."

The commander gave David a look that spelled out his expectations. "Liaisons write reports too."

"Indeed, and I'll do what I can." David wasn't sure how he'd manage, but if agreeing gave him carte blanche access to the

Command Center, he would figure out a way to reciprocate.

50

The Ritz, London, England, June 5, 1944

AFTER DAVID LEFT, Kenzie snuggled back under the covers. How in the world she could have been so ready for sex while feeling like crap she'd never know. Hormones. That's all she could think of.

She prayed Cav and his entire crew were okay.

From what little research she had read about the Mighty Eighth, she knew thousands of men were killed during bombing runs over Germany, but the crews who ditched in the Channel had a very high recovery rate. Air-Sea Rescue was a priority. Planes could be replaced easily enough, but crews could not, and every crew would be needed for the invasion. David's friend Jack was the weak link, though. He wasn't a trained member of the crew. He wouldn't know what to do, and wouldn't have practiced an evacuation.

Cav would get him out, though, or he'd go down with the ship trying. He was that kind of man. She smiled, thinking of her John Kennedy-esque pilot. He was an intelligent and intriguing man, just like McBain, but McBain had something Cav didn't. He reminded her of the Navy SEALs she had met—deadly and daring. Sex with him would be memorable—the feel of his skin under her hands, the sturdy shoulders, the play of muscles...

And that was the last thought she had until she awoke two hours later in the throes of the most erotic dream she had ever had. When she realized she was entangled in the bedsheet and not in McBain's plaid, she sighed heavily.

While she untangled herself she did a quick assessment. The soreness had diminished considerably. It never took her long to recover from endurance races, and while she wasn't typically punched in the ribs, she was used to taxing her system with hundred-mile bike rides followed by twenty-six-mile runs. What Military Intelligence had put her through was more emotional trauma than physical torture—no rack and thumbscrews. Yes, she would have nightmares for a while, but there would be no lasting pain. If she had a couple of ibuprofen, she would hit the gym right now, but neither ibuprofen nor a gym were available.

She had no clothes to wear, no TV to watch, and—she glanced around the room just in case—no books to read. Bathing, eating, and sleeping were the only forms of entertainment available.

After unwrapping her bandages and checking the sizes and purple hues of her bruises in the mirror, she climbed into a tub filled with soap bubbles and hot, steaming water. It might be wartime, but the Ritz had a reputation to maintain, and she would certainly take advantage of the luxury.

She dozed again and woke up in a bathtub full of cool water.

51

Debden Airfield, England, June 5, 1944

DAVID STOOD AT the back of a glassed-in corner of the control room watching aides rip off sheets of paper from the teletype machine, hand them over to another soldier, who would then determine coordinates and stick a red pin on a large map of the English Channel and North Sea.

After two hours and three cups of watered-down tea, the message he'd been waiting for arrived.

"Major, the crew of the *Shamrock* has been picked up. One was killed when the aircraft ditched, two others were injured and will be transported to a hospital in London, and the remaining crew will be flown to Debden Airfield for transport back to Bassingbourn."

"Do ye' have names, or even the name of the hospital where the injured will be taken?" Since Jack didn't know ditching procedure and had never practiced an evacuation, he was likely among the injured; he was also just as likely to be among the dead. David squeezed the bridge of his nose. He and Jack had prepared so well for this mission, and yet it had been a colossal fuck-up from the beginning.

The soldier shook his head. "No names. Only numbers. We'll get a full report when they land at the air base."

"I'll go there now." David hurried out of the room and headed toward the main entrance. He stopped at the front desk for directions. "Which way to Debden Airfield?"

"I'll draw you a map," the aide said.

Colonel Hicks came up behind David. "I heard the *Shamrock's* crew is on the way to Debden."

"I'm going there now."

"I look forward to reading your report," Hicks said.

"I'll be sure ye' get a copy." David took the map from the aide, reviewed it to be sure he understood the directions, then slipped the sheet of paper into his pocket. Two minutes later he chugged along Ashdon Road for the three-mile hop to the airfield. He could almost run faster than the damn car. He floored the accelerator and picked up speed—two whole miles per hour faster.

David was sweating profusely. How in the hell was he going to explain Jack's injuries or his death to anyone? He knew he would soon be facing one or the other, and imagined the tearful conversations with Elliott and Charlotte, especially with Charlotte, who was so close to delivering her second child.

The control tower came into view only seconds before he spotted a B-17 approaching the runway. He had to pull to the side of the road to get a grip on his emotions. He'd been through war, but preparing to hear of his best friend's death or serious injury was far worse than anything he had experienced in Afghanistan. What could he have done differently to have kept this from happening? The answer was simple. He should have ignored Jack's pleas to be included.

No passing the buck on this one. The responsibility was his and his alone.

He pulled back on the road and drove to a guarded entrance to the Eighth Air Force Base, where he showed his credentials. "I'm here to meet the crew of the *Shamrock*."

"Check in at the control tower," the guard said.

David parked the car in a designated spot and walked over to the tower as the B-17 he spotted from the road taxied toward the tarmac.

A member of the ground crew was standing near the door smoking a cigarette. He dropped the smoke on the ground, smashed it with his foot, and saluted.

"At ease," David said. "Do ye' know if this plane is carrying the crew of the *Shamrock?*"

"I don't know, sir, but I can find out."

David squinted into the sun with his hands on his hips, and tapped his fingers impatiently. "Do it."

The crewman opened the door to the tower steps and disappeared.

David checked the time. He'd been gone from the Ritz for three and a half hours. He needed to call Kenzie, but until he knew more, he didn't want to interrupt her sleep.

The plane parked and shut down the engines. The hatch near the waist gunners' windows opened and a man jumped out, followed by another one. David didn't know any of crew except Cavanaugh and Rainer. He kept his posture at ease even though World War III was going on inside his belly. One man jumped out, laughing, and then Rainer appeared at the hatch. He glanced in David's direction and waved.

David walked cautiously toward the plane. Rainer hit the ground and Cavanaugh followed. The relief at seeing Cavanaugh was so small as to be almost negligible. Then at the entrance he spotted Jack. David's legs wobbled. He steadied himself, took a deep breath, and then jogged the twenty-plus steps to the door, arriving just as Jack swung to the ground.

"What are you doing here?" Jack asked, grinning.

"I thought I was here to collect your personal property."

"Sorry to disappoint you."

"I am, too." David slugged Jack, hitting his jaw hard enough to knock him to the ground. Jack stayed where he landed, rubbing his jaw. "What the hell was that for?"

"If you have to ask, ye' learned nothing in Washington."

Rainer reached out to help Jack up. "If it wasn't for Jack, we might all be dead,"

"None of us paid attention during the evacuation drills," a man carrying a Norden bombsight said. "We figured if anything ever happened to the plane, we'd bail out over land, not in the middle of the Channel."

Rainer gave Jack a friendly, man-to-man whack on the back. "Mallory, here, got the life raft into the water, pulled Deke out of the bombardier's station, went back for his Norden bombsite, and pushed Lieutenant Cavanaugh out the window," Rainer said.

David glared at Jack and said through gritted teeth, "I don't give a damn how many lives ye' saved. You're at least half responsible for the most godawful, gut-wrenching four hours of my life, and I include Afghanistan in that. Gather yer gear, wrap up yer assignment, and get yer arse home. Now."

David turned on his heel and headed back to his car.

"Wait," Jack said, running after him. "What happened to Kenzie?"

"When I left her at the Ritz four hours ago, she was sleeping. I won't get back for another two and a half hours. I just hope to God Military Intelligence hasn't found her again while I've been chasing after ye'. Do us both a favor and get Cavanaugh out before he's sent off on a D-Day mission. Got it?"

Jack squared his shoulders. "Look, I know you're hopping mad, but you've got to listen to me. I think we've got this wrong. Cav's not Kenzie's soul mate."

David threw up his hands. "I never should have brought you along. But since ye're here, do yer job. I'm going back to the hotel to get Kenzie, and then we're getting the hell out. If ye' stay behind, ye're on yer own."

David marched away, and then remembered Colonel Hicks' request. He whirled back toward Jack, fisting his hands. If he'd been a boiling pot, the water would be hissing over the sides. "In your debriefing, mention that Colonel Hicks at Saffron Walden was extremely helpful in expediting the recovery of the *Shamrock's* crew."

He didn't wait for a response, but climbed into his car, slammed it into gear, and drove off, spitting out another round of curses about Jack and the damned emerald brooch.

52

London, England, June 5, 1944

AFTER DRYING OFF, she dug through the duffle bag McBain had left in the corner of the bathroom, looking for a T-shirt to wear. She pulled one out and sniffed it. It smelled clean and Downy fresh. She sniffed again. Call her crazy, but the shirt *did* smell like Downy fabric softener. She looked at the label. Jockey. XL. An expert on men's underwear she wasn't, but she would bet her portfolio the T-shirt in her hand hadn't been made in the twentieth century.

A very icky feeling settled in her stomach.

She carried the bag into the bedroom and dumped out the contents. Piled on the bed were David's clothes, a thick wad of pound notes, a women's WAC uniform, shoes, underwear, military credentials, a thick file folder labeled KENZIE WALLIS-MANNING, and a Dell laptop.

"I fucking don't believe this. Who the hell is this guy?"

The punch to her gut was ten times worse than the ones she'd received from the guards. This one was hard enough to break her ribs, and definitely hard enough to break her heart.

She grabbed the shoes and threw them against the wall as tears streamed down her face. She was quivering with the intensity of her raw, searing anger at him and at herself. She had almost made love with him. What a lying jerk.

A corner of one of the pages in the folder had slipped partially out, and she spotted her father's name. "What does *he* have to do with this?"

The manila folder was an inch thick. The first document she found when she opened the file was a memorandum from McBain to a man named Elliott Fraser dated a few days after her disappearance. According to the memo, a man named Jim Manning had called McBain asking for help in locating her. Who was Jim Manning? And why would he care where she was?

The first line of the ten-page document was a knife to her already broken heart. Every succeeding page twisted the knife deeper. The memorandum was a litany of betrayal and lies spelled out in black ink on crisp, laser-printer paper. Her instinct was to crush each page into an individual ball and swat the whole lot across the room with the same brute force McBain had used with the telegram.

For God's sake, she had a half-brother who had never wanted to meet her. If she had known about him, she would have crawled through fire to see him. She had always wanted family. And her father had kept his son from her.

Lies and betrayal.

Anger like she had never known knocked her to the floor. She pulled herself into a fetal position and wept, but even when her tears finally dried up, the anger at her father and McBain remained. Both men had lied to her, telling unforgiveable lies, and she hated them for it. If McBain had only told her who he was when they met Saturday night, they could have gone home, and the last few days would never have happened.

When she started shivering from the drafty floor, she returned to the bed and crawled under the quilt. The pillows were saturated with McBain's musky scent. She tossed them aside, not wanting to be reminded of how easily she had fallen under his spell. He was a lying son of a bitch and she couldn't trust him. If she couldn't trust McBain, what about Mallory?

She backtracked through the memo to Fraser and reread a paragraph about the contents of her bookcase. *Although Miss Wallis-Manning had a copy of Jack's recent release on her bookshelf, we don't believe she will recognize him out of context.*

"I did recognize him. I did. And damn if McBain wasn't right. I didn't believe he was the author Jack Mallory from the twenty-first century."

They had all tricked her. Played her for a fool. If she had a gun, she would use them all for target practice. Her father would be first. McBain would be next.

Don't forget Military Intelligence.

Oh, she wouldn't forget them...or what she had almost done with McBain.

Out of frustration, she picked up the memorandum and continued reading. The document referenced the redacted copy of a memorandum to Churchill she had discovered in the archives. The only way McBain could have found the copy was by reading her emails.

"He *read* my emails?" She bared her teeth, ready to bite a chunk out of his ass. When she saw him again, she would...What? Kill him? She couldn't do that. He was her ticket home. After they returned to the future, then she would extract her pound of revenge.

She read on and found a list of the items in her medicine cabinet. Seriously? He listed the brand of toothpaste, condoms, and....

Heat flushed through her body and her muscles quivered. This invasion of her privacy was not inconsequential. The violation was as serious as what the guards had done to her. The guards could almost justify their behavior. They were trying to extract information to win a war, but what was McBain trying to do? Complete a mission. Bring the little girl home.

Her head was splitting. She could bang it repeatedly against a concrete wall and it wouldn't hurt more than it did now. She turned to the last page of the memorandum and found an unredacted copy of the Churchill memorandum. When she got to the last page and read that MI had thrown Lieutenant Manning under the bus to protect their top secret operation, she had learned more than enough about the perfidy of men. She tossed the file aside.

According to the clock on the table, it was five o'clock. At nine o'clock, Lieutenant Manning would rendezvous with his MI handler. The handler would then escort him to the pub for a meeting with the IRA agent. At that meeting, Manning would be killed.

After all the treachery, she couldn't allow that to happen. She had a uniform, identification, money, and a destination. The Second Ranger Battalion was marshalled near Weymouth. She studied her credentials again. She was assigned to Supreme Headquarters. That should get her inside the marshalling area. Once inside, all she had to do was find Lieutenant Manning. If she didn't find him there, she would go to The New Inn at West Knighton.

After she stopped her grandfather from walking into a trap, she would come back and deal with McBain. If changing the past changed the future, so be it.

She opened the duffle to repack it and found a small package stuck on a grommet on the bottom of the bag. She pried it lose and opened it.

"I'll be damned." Inside were her Rubik's cube and class ring, but no brooch.

Anger sizzled along her nerve endings. If MacBain walked in the room at that moment, with the adrenaline rush she had going on, she'd be strong enough to truss him up and pitch him out the window.

"He stole my emerald. Ha. Won't he be surprised when he tries to use it and it doesn't work? Serves him right. I hope he's stuck here for the rest of his fucking life."

Then it occurred to her that he must have one of his own, and his brooch probably worked, or how else could he have come after her? At least now she knew for sure she could return home.

She repacked the duffle and returned it to the bathroom. Then she calmly composed a letter for McBain that read, "Teasdel found me a dress and shoes. I've gone for a walk. I'll be careful. Can't wait to see you."

Can't wait to see you…you egotistical son of a bitch.

She left the note on the pillow. He would look there first, expecting her to be waiting for him. Adding Teasdel's name was a touch of brilliance. McBain would check with the detective before he went searching for her. If he believed she was dressed in civilian clothes, then he wouldn't realize yet that she had gone through his bag and discovered he was from the twenty-first century, too.

It occurred to her that she could use his help to rescue her grandfather, but dismissed the notion, because McBain might simply toss her over his shoulder and return to the future before she had a chance to right a wrong.

Now she knew the players, she had an advantage, and she wouldn't be taken by surprise again. If all went as planned, she would be back in the room before McBain learned she was gone. She couldn't wait to see his face when she confronted him with the truth. He would be profoundly sorry, but that wouldn't cut it with her. He lied, put her life at risk, and then almost made love to her, knowing how angry she would be when she learned the truth.

In her book, that was the definition of dishonorable.

53

The Ritz, London, England, June 5, 1944

DAVID REENTERED HIS room at the Ritz and was met with the complex fragrances of luxury bath products he had requested for Kenzie. He warmed at the thought of her, sweetly scented, waiting for him. But when he saw the bed made and the room empty his blood pressure went off the charts.

The door hadn't been forced open. He would have noticed immediately. The furniture was upright and in place. There weren't any dirty dishes. If Kenzie ordered food, the trays had already been removed.

Then he saw the note on the pillow. He snatched it up, read it, reread it, and crushed it into a tight little ball.

"*Fuck!* What the hell was she thinking?" He paced the room, then stopped at the window, planted his feet, grabbed the sides of the window frame, and stared out at the late spring sky. Did she go for a walk? Did she run away? Was she abducted again and forced to write a note?

He put a call into the pub for Teasdel and then waited thirty minutes for a callback. "How long ago were ye' here? And how could ye' let Kenzie go off by herself?"

"Whoa," Teasdel said. "I don't know what you're talking about."

"I had to go out. When I came back, I found a note from Kenzie saying you brought her some clothes. I want to know how long ago that was. She's not back yet."

"I haven't seen or heard from Miss Wallis-Manning since I dropped you off this morning."

David's life flashed before his eyes. Whatever fears he had before now paled in comparison. "Forget it. I know where she's gone."

"Do you need my help?" Teasdel asked.

"I'll call ye' back if I do." David hung up, grabbed his duffle from the bathroom, and dumped the contents onto the bed. The WAV uniform, Kenzie's credentials, and her class ring were gone.

He opened the file folder and found the documents out of order. He sat on the bed and dropped his head into his hands. This was worse than his worst nightmare. He now had to assume Kenzie knew her father asked for help to find her, that she had a brother no one bothered to tell her about, that her grandfather was falsely accused of being a spy, and that David lied to her about his identity.

At least there was nothing in the notes about the purpose of the brooch. He had her emerald in his pocket and Jack had the ruby. She would need him to go home. But as mad as she had to be, and rightfully so, would she even want to go? She had to be feeling betrayed on all fronts.

Her credentials would get her into the marshalling area if she decided to find her grandfather. If she could make sure Lieutenant Manning didn't leave the restricted area, he wouldn't be shot. David checked the time. It was too late to go to the marshalling area near Weymouth, but he could make it to the pub in case she failed to stop her grandfather. She was a soldier and wouldn't give up.

With a plan in place, he packed what he needed into a smaller bag and left the clothes. While they looked authentic, the fabric was a higher quality than what was available in the United Kingdom during the war. On close inspection, someone would notice. He would tell Neil to fetch the bag, hide it, and never speak of it to anyone.

He conducted one more search of the room for anything he might have missed, then closed the door. He stopped in the lobby and pulled Neil aside.

"I left a bag in my room. Keep it for me and don't tell anyone you have it. If anyone asks for me, tell them I've gone home. Got it?"

Neil nodded. "Yes, sir."

David gave Neil a handful of pound notes and slapped his shoulder. "Ye're a good man."

He left the hotel for what was probably his last twentieth century visit. As soon as he found Kenzie, they would be going home.

54

Bletchley Park, England, June 5, 1944

KEVIN STOOD IN a wooded area outside Bletchley Park in the midafternoon sun, scanning the area. There were a few tourists around, but no one seemed especially interested in him. He stepped back into the trees and opened the sapphire brooch.

Kit, Braham, Charlotte, Jack, and David had all been through the fog, and now it was his turn. Elliott had given him a specific, limited assignment: find David, give him the message about Cavanaugh, and come straight back.

He knew, though, that best plans often went awry.

Stay alert. Be careful. Follow the plan.

Elliott's last words were embedded in his brain. If Kevin ever wanted to go on another adventure, and he was convinced there would be more, he had to prove he could be trusted. This trip was not the time to yield to his curiosity.

"Chan ann le tìm no àite a bhios sinn a' tomhais a' gaol ach 's ann le neart anama."

Kevin watched a peat-scented fog creep up his legs to his knees, to his waist, and then cover him completely, sending him into a crazy, spinning, flipping ride that made him dizzy and sick to his stomach. The ride had no sooner started than it stopped. He opened his eyes, blinked, and immediately threw up. Why hadn't anyone told him traveling in the fog was like riding the scariest amusement park ride in the world? If he'd known, he wouldn't have overindulged the night before on a sendoff dinner of French cooking and a bottle of wine.

He rinsed his mouth with the bottled water he had poured into a canteen and packed into his small duffel bag along with a change of clothes, credentials, and money.

He had spent the morning touring Bletchley Park to familiarize himself with the layout and security, and knew the mansion on the other side of the barbed wire fence was the main building used by the codebreakers. So he was in the right place, hopefully at the right time.

Before leaving home, he outlined his steps so he would stay on task. He was easily sidetracked, and couldn't afford to go wandering off on a side exploration right now. To find David, he had written on his notecard, start at the Inn.

He shouldered his pack and followed the path to town. After asking for directions from a kid on the street, he found the Inn.

"I'm looking for Major McBain," he told the man at the front desk.

The Innkeeper put aside the mail he was opening and scratched his chest. "McBain, hey? He left two days ago."

"Do you know where?"

The Innkeeper inclined his head. "Didn't say. Took the old car he bought off of me and left."

"Was he alone?"

"Don't know. But his room is available if you need accommodations."

"Gone two days. Hmm." David hadn't returned to the future, Kevin knew that. So where did he go? Kevin didn't waste time wondering. Next on his list was to call Jack. "I'll take the room, and I need to use your telephone." Kevin signed the register and paid for one night's stay.

He dialed the number David had written in the note. When he was connected to the Bassingbourn Airbase operator, he asked for Jack. A few minutes later, a man answered, identifying himself as the commander.

"Sir, I'm Kevin Allen. I'm Jack Mallory's colleague. I asked for him, but the operator passed me on to you instead. I hate to trouble you, but could you send me back to the operator?"

"The operator sent you to me because Mr. Mallory is in a debriefing."

"When can I talk to him? It's important."

"An hour, more or less. Mr. Mallory has become the star of the story he's writing. Quite the hero. Saved several members of the *Shamrock's* crew when it ditched in the Channel."

A hero? Kevin wondered what David thought about that. "Is David McBain there?"

The commander laughed. "He slugged Mallory with a right hook that knocked him to the ground and then drove off in an old clunker. Don't know where he went. Probably back to SHAEF."

Supreme Headquarters?

Wherever David went, it wasn't to SHAEF. Kevin covered the mouthpiece and asked the Innkeeper, "Is Kenzie Wallis-Manning here?"

He shook his head. "I haven't seen her in at least two days. Her room's paid for, though, through Saturday."

Kenzie and David both left the Inn two days ago. David had punched Jack out earlier that afternoon, and Jack was a hero. Kevin checked the time. "Would you be willing to give Jack a message and ask him to meet me at The Eagle Pub in Cambridge as soon as possible?"

"Tell me your name again."

"Kevin Allen. And thanks for your help." He hung up and said to the Innkeeper. "Guess I won't be needing the room after all."

Kevin left the Inn, pocketing his refund minus outrageous charges for a phone call, and caught the next train to Cambridge, considering his assignment carefully. If David was already pissed at Jack, Kevin didn't want to make any mistakes that might make David angry with him, too.

From the train station he took a taxi to The Eagle Pub. Jack would probably be another hour or so. Kevin would nurse a beer while he waited, but he didn't have to.

Jack was sitting at a corner table with a half-empty beer glass, wearing his usual three-day growth of facial scruff, looking rather downtrodden. He waved. Surprise barely registered on Jack's face. "I couldn't get here fast enough. I know you're here because of Meredith. Her cancer's back, isn't it?"

Kevin dropped his duffel behind the chair next to Jack's bag and ordered a beer. "She's scheduled for surgery. But that's not why I'm here."

Jack's back straightened and there was a new quiver in his voice, something alert and fearful. "*Oh, God,* it's Charlotte. Something's happened to her or the baby."

Kevin made a calming gesture with his hands, palms down, moving them slowly up and down. "Both women are fine. I'm not here about them. It's about Cavanaugh. Where is he?"

Jack nervously twisted the Mallory family crest ring he always wore on his left ring finger. "He and his crew flew out right after our debriefing. He couldn't tell me where he was going, only that it was a special assignment. I should have taken him into the fog right then, but I couldn't." Jack stopped twisting his ring and upended the glass of beer. "He's not Kenzie's soul mate. I tried to tell David, but he wouldn't listen. I'll have to find a way to deal with David over this, but I know my gut's right."

Kevin sank into his chair. "You did the right thing. He's not for Kenzie."

Jack held up his glass to let the waitress know he wanted another round. "You agree with me? That's a surprise."

The waitress delivered their drinks and Kevin sipped. "Crap. Hot beer is godawful. Don't they have refrigeration? How can you stand to drink it?" He pushed the glass aside.

"It grows on you," Jack said. "So what makes you think he's not for Kenzie?"

Kevin rested his forearms on the table and leaned forward. Speaking quietly, he said, "After the war, Cavanaugh will marry his high school sweetheart and have five children. His only daughter will marry a man from Chicago named Kelly. They'll have a son named Trey."

Jack stared, open-mouthed. "Jesus Christ. Trey Kelly? Kenzie's friend?"

"The one who saved her life," Kevin said.

Color drained from his face. "If I'd taken Cav to the future—"

"He wouldn't have had a grandson to save Kenzie's life."

Jack sat in stunned silence for a minute. "How did we get this so wrong? If Cav isn't Kenzie's soul mate, then who is?" He took a deep, shivery breath and then another one.

"We don't know. Kenzie may have met someone you don't know about." Kevin shrugged. "Elliott wants everyone home for now. Later Kenzie can decide what she wants to do once she has all the facts."

"That makes sense." Jack finished his beer and dropped money on the table. "Our job's done. Let's get out of here."

"Do you know where David and Kenzie are?"

Jack stood and picked up his duffel bag. "David said he was going back to the hotel to get her. I assume he meant back to the Ritz. Anyway, he told me to get Cav and go home. I figured he was going to do the same. At any rate, my job's done."

Kevin picked up his bag and glanced up at the ceiling. "Look at all those signatures."

"British and American flight crews sign their names with lipstick and candle smoke."

Kevin grabbed the candle off the table. "Cool. Let's write ours."

Jack grabbed him by the collar. "How about we get out of here without leaving any more evidence of our passing than I already have?"

Kevin returned the candle to the table. "After what you did, saving Cav and his men, you'll be all over the history books. You might as well leave your name."

"I'll be a postscript at the bottom of a report, that's all."

As they walked out into the lobby, Jack said, "I think I'll call the Ritz to check on David and let him know I'm leaving."

"Are you going to tell him I'm here?" Kevin asked.

"I'll have to. He'll ask me about Cav."

They stopped at the front desk and Jack asked to use the phone. He placed a call to the Ritz and asked for Neil. "This is Jack Mallory. David McBain's friend. Is he in his room? He's not…What time did he check out?…Did he say anything?…Huh…Okay…Thanks."

"Well," Kevin said.

Jack nodded to Kevin to follow him outside. "Neil, the front desk clerk, said David checked out about six o'clock and told him if anyone asked for him to say he'd gone home."

"Do you believe him?" Kevin asked.

"I have no reason not to. David said he was going to the hotel to get Kenzie—"

"And go home, right? You said that before."

"You've known David longer than I have. What do you think?"

"David has yelled at me for years for doing something that didn't suit him. If David told you to go home, I'd go, especially since you know he's checked out of the hotel."

"I'd feel a lot better if we were all going together."

"If he doesn't come home, we can always come back, right?" Kevin asked.

"Maybe. Probably. Honestly? I don't know."

"I think maybe you're taking this a trifle too seriously. Your job was to manage Cav. You did that. Your job is over. Elliott told me to come right back. I'm going to follow orders. You do whatever you have to do." Kevin sniffed the air. "I can smell the ozone. It's going to storm."

"It's the storm that postpones D-Day. The largest amphibious military assault in history is only hours away. I want to stay and be a part of that."

"Tagging along for a D-Day story is a good way to get yourself killed."

There was a small and nearly imperceptible wince in Jack's eyes, but that was about it. Kevin would have missed it completely if he hadn't been looking directly at Jack when the clouds scuttled by and the full moon surfaced. "I'm not looking to die today. Let's go home."

"You sure?" Kevin asked.

"I'm sure."

Kevin held up the ruby brooch. "Your brooch or mine?"

55

MacKlenna Farm, Lexington, Kentucky, Present Day

ELLIOTT SAT AT the mahogany desk in his office at MacKlenna Mansion, hunched over his laptop reviewing Stormy's book of a hundred and twenty mares. Not bad for a time-traveling horse who had never run a race. His best-selling progeny were responsible for bumping his stud fees up into the high five figures. Elliott doubted Kit would be surprised by her horse's success.

He thought of his goddaughter often, especially when he was dealing with Stormy or recalcitrant time travelers.

"Does Stormy have a date today?" Meredith asked.

Elliott glanced up from his laptop, smiling at his beautiful wife. His heart melted with love for her. She sat in the leather wingback chair near the dwindling fire, her leg tucked up under her hip, her brown hair draped over one shoulder. If Meredith had to have chemo, she would lose her hair again, but he didn't care about her hair. It would grow back. He only cared about her health.

"At eleven o'clock. Do ye' want to walk over to the breeding shed with me?"

"Calling that place a shed is a misnomer. It's a multi-million dollar complex." Meredith removed the glasses perched on her nose and set them aside, along with her laptop. "I'd like to go for a long run afterwards. If I have extensive surgery tomorrow, it will be a few weeks before I'm released to run again."

"How far are ye' going? I might run with ye'."

"Ten, I think, depending on how I feel."

"Never mind."

"Aww, come on. I'll do an out and back so you can run whatever distance you want."

Elliott's cell phone rang. He glanced at the display. "I'll be damned. It's Jack."

Meredith came to her feet instantly, stepped over to the desk, and rested her hip against the edge. After the fourth ring she said, "Stop looking at it with that puzzled expression. Answer it, for heaven's sake."

Elliott shook his head as if coming out of a fog. He hadn't been expecting a call from Jack, and that worried him. "Fraser," he said before switching the call to the speakerphone.

"It's Jack. Kevin and I are in Cambridge."

"Welcome back. Ye' didn't bring Cavanaugh with ye', did ye'?"

"No, I'd figured out before I saw Kevin that he wasn't for Kenzie."

Elliott glanced at Meredith and she gave him a thumbs up.

"That should make for an interesting story. Where is the lass? And David?"

"You haven't heard from him?"

Elliott was suddenly chilled by the note of disbelief in Jack's voice. "When'd ye' see them last?"

At this question, Jack stopped speaking for a moment, and only the sound of his rapid breathing came through the phone. "I saw David a few hours ago. We met at an airfield in Debden. He told me to rendezvous with Cavanaugh and go home, and that he was going back to the hotel to get Kenzie and do the same."

"How long ago?" Meredith asked.

"Maybe two...two and half hours. I called the hotel, and the clerk said David checked out and left a message that if anyone came looking for him to say he'd gone home."

Elliott's heart was beating fast, but he remained outwardly calm. "I wouldn't worry about it, then. I'll hear from him soon."

"I'm only worried because of what happened to Kenzie."

Elliott glanced at Meredith. Her erect posture told him she was alert but not overly concerned. "What happened?" he asked.

"She was abducted by Military Intelligence following a cabaret at Bletchley. Hey, did you know David played the saxophone?"

"*No,*" Elliott said sharply, irritated by the right turn in the conversation.

Meredith smiled slightly.

"Looks like Meredith knew, though."

"He's quite good. He played at the cabaret to a standing room only audience."

Meredith's smile turned to a twinkle, and she wiggled her eyebrows. "I bet most of the audience was female."

"It was, and they were eating it up. Kenzie, too."

Meredith's smile now reached her eyes, and that irritated Elliott, too. His wife was reading something into Jack's statement, and Elliott had no idea what she'd noticed that he hadn't.

"Then what happened to Kenzie?" he asked.

"David found her. When I saw him, he said he was going back to the hotel for her. He wasn't in a mood to talk."

"Why not?" Elliott asked.

"It's a long story. What I need to know now is, where should we go? To Fraser House? To London? To the farm?"

"Go to London and wait for David and Kenzie. The plane's at Heathrow. As soon as they arrive, come to Lexington. Meredith's surgery is scheduled for tomorrow afternoon."

A muffled conversation took place on Jack's side of the phone. "Kevin wants to know how Meredith is feeling, and if James Cullen's cold has gotten any worse, and I want to know about Charlotte and the baby."

"They're all fine. Call when you check into a hotel. Are ye' staying at the Ritz?"

"Yes, and call me if you hear from David. I'll be the last person on his call list, and I'd rather not wait twenty-four hours to hear that he's okay."

Elliott disconnected the call and stood, pulling Meredith into his arms, stroking her back, tenderly. "Jack and Kevin are home, thank God. I'd give him time to call Charlotte, then ye' might want to check with her to see what time their flight gets in."

They stood in front of the floor-to-ceiling window overlooking a paddock full of mares and yearlings prancing around. It had always been Elliott's favorite view from the mansion. He'd seen Sean and Mary MacKlenna stand in the very same spot, but mostly he remembered their daughter, Kit, standing there alone, grieving for her family.

He squeezed Meredith closer. He would never stand in that spot and grieve for her, because if he lost her, he would surely die, too.

"I'm glad Charlotte and Braham will be here tomorrow," Meredith said. "Charlotte can talk surgeon talk and get better answers. You'll be too distressed to remember details."

Elliott stepped back, cupped Meredith's face, and kissed her. "I know ye're worried, lass. I am too. But we have each other, and we'll get through this just like we did last time."

She kissed him back, then rested her head on his shoulder. "Do you think it's odd that David and Kenzie are unaccounted for?"

Elliott cleared his throat of the knot lodged there. "If Jack and Kevin were unaccounted for, I'd be worried, but I'm not worried about two soldiers. They can handle anything thrown at them."

"Even love?"

He thought he detected amusement in her voice and kissed her forehead. "Love? Kenzie and David?"

Meredith looked at him curiously, her head held to one side. "If Cav isn't Kenzie's soul mate, then who is?"

"She might not have met him yet."

Meredith stepped back, folded her arms, and tapped her cheek with her fingertip. "Let's think about this. If Jim hadn't asked David to find his half-sister, David never would have met her."

"Just because they met under unusual circumstances doesn't make them soul mates."

She arched her brow. "Maybe. Maybe not."

Elliott tossed his head back and laughed. "They may not be soul mates yet, but I have a sneaky feeling if they aren't lovers by the time they return, ye' and Charlotte will be donning yer professional matchmaking hats."

"I don't know if Dr. Mallory-McCabe will have time to be a matchmaker with a new baby on her lap, but even if I'm undergoing chemo, *I'll* have time."

Elliott checked his wristwatch. "Speaking of matchmaking. Stormy has a date with a mare in five minutes."

"Hmm," Meredith said, slipping back into Elliott's embrace. "I think I'd rather have some personal time with my own stallion."

"I thought ye' wanted to run."

She took his hand and tugged him toward the door. "I'll run later. All this talk of love and hooking up has my mind racing with possibilities."

They passed the doorway into the kitchen, where Mrs. Collins, the cook, was busy preparing dinner. "If anyone's looking for us, tell them we're in a conference." Elliott winked at his cook before following his wife toward their master suite.

"Does that include Sandy, who's coming up the back walk?" Mrs. Collins asked.

"Especially Sandy. Ye' know the drill, emergencies only." The farm's marketing manager had been trying to tie Elliott down for the past three days to commit to a marketing plan, and Elliott had no interest in even considering new projects until after the surgery.

Meredith closed the door and locked it. "Turn off your phone, Dr. Fraser. I won't be interrupted today." She pulled her T-shirt over her head and fell onto the bed with her arms open to him.

"God, ye're beautiful." He yanked off his MacKlenna Farm polo shirt and hopped on one foot to pull off his khakis.

Thirty minutes later, they lay nestled in each other's arms. "Can I turn my phone on now?" he asked, grinning.

She swatted him with the sheet. "I hope you didn't think of your phone the entire time."

"With ye' under me, I canna' think straight, I want ye' so bad."

"Then turn it on. Maybe you have a message from David."

Elliott checked for messages and missed calls. "Nothing."

She checked her messages, too. "David didn't reach out to me, either. Call him."

Elliott punched David's number, and after four rings, the call went to voicemail. He looked at her, mouth downturned, and Meredith's brow creased with worry.

"Leave a message," she mouthed.

"Jack and Kevin have returned…" Elliott swallowed and tried to hold his voice steady. "They're on their way to London to wait for ye'. The plane is there to bring ye' to Lexington. Call me." He dropped his phone on the bedside table and kissed the top of Meredith's head. "I don't know Kenzie, but I know David, and if Cavanaugh's not her soul mate, David will sense it. Chances are, they're in bed together somewhere."

"You're that sure of it, are you?"

Elliott pulled her over on top of him, and this time he intended to go slow and easy. "Bet on it, Mer."

56

Broadmayne, County of Dorset, UK, June 5, 1944

KENZIE CAUGHT A train for Dorset at London's Waterloo Station for a three-and-a-half-hour trip to the D5 Marshalling Area used by the Second Ranger Battalion.

Most of the battalion had been consigned on board English ships for a few days, but her grandfather remained in the marshalling area overseeing the transportation of the battalion's supplies. Not his job normally, but one he volunteered for. From reading the memorandum in David's file, she knew her grandfather volunteered so he could meet with the IRA agent and fulfill his obligation to Military Intelligence.

If only he had embarked from Weymouth with the rest of his unit, Military Intelligence wouldn't have had a chance to screw him.

Before the night was over, she intended to rectify the situation.

Would it change her history? She didn't know, and at this point she didn't care. Most of the time change ripple, she assumed, would be felt by her father. But she was no expert on time travel. McBain was, but he could go hang himself. The lion's share of her anger was directed at her father, but a remaining cub-sized share was aimed at McBain, and she looked forward to having it out with him.

If he had only told her the night they met who he was, she would have asked him to take her home, and she would have avoided the water torture. But she would have missed being in London during the war, discussing Churchill with Uncle Clifford, kissing Cav, and interviewing with Turing.

And she wouldn't have learned about her grandfather, and found a way to help him.

You can't have it both ways.

She stared out the window into the darkness, drumming her fingers on her knees and watching the rain and high winds lash out at the countryside while she mentally lashed out at three men. Her grandfather for being stupid, her father for being insensitive and hateful, and McBain for being a jerk. He might be a jerk…but worse than that, he was sexy as hell, and she was crazy about him.

Whoa. Where'd that come from?

She wasn't crazy about him. It had only been stress sex. Right?

No. So admit it. Okay. I have feelings for McBain, a handsome, sexy, caring, lying jerk with potential.

And while she was admitting her feelings, she had to acknowledge that they had been there since the moment they sneaked away to the alcove for fresh air. Then when she heard him play the sax…

She yawned, relaxed her head against the seat, and closed her eyes, picturing clearly the documents she had read. A plan began to materialize.

The credentials David had made for her were impeccable, and it pleased her that he had made her a captain. Tonight, of all nights, no one would take the time to telephone SHAEF for verification. All she had to do was flash her creds and ask to visit her brother before he shipped out.

What could be easier?

When she stepped off the train at the Dorchester West Station, two captains disembarked with her and headed for a jeep parked next to the platform. "Excuse me," she said. "I need to go to the Marshalling Area Camp D5 Headquarters at Chalmont House. Can you tell me how to get there?"

"We'll do better than that," the driver said. "Jump in."

She got a look at his insignia and said, "Thanks, sergeant." Then she squeezed into the backseat of the jeep with one of the captains and all the luggage.

"What are you doing out on a night like this?" her seatmate asked.

"My brother is a Ranger—"

The driver swerved to miss a giant pothole. "They shipped out."

"I know, but he's still here. I just want to see him for a few minutes then I'll get back on the train to London."

"Is your brother one of Lieutenant Colonel Rudder's Rangers?" her seatmate asked.

"Yes, they'll be landing at Pointe du Hoc."

The driver drove past a row of terrace houses and pulled to a stop in front of a large home at the end of Main Street. "How do you know?"

"Because I'm assigned to SHAEF and made it a point to find out. He's with Dog Company."

The driver opened the Jeep's front door. "That's a fine outfit."

"He thinks so, too." She climbed out of the backseat. "They've trained hard, and they'll succeed in their objective."

The quiet captain sitting in the front seat said, "Thousands of men will depend on their success,"

"A lot of men will die, but this time next year, the war in Europe will be over." The men's eyebrows furrowed. "Well, that's my prediction anyway."

"Good luck, ma'am. I hope you find your brother." The driver said.

She thanked them for the ride, entered the house, and was quickly met by a harried corporal. "I'm looking for Lieutenant Robert Manning. His unit is billeted in Camp C."

"They shipped out of Weymouth this morning."

"I know. But he's still here, I just don't know where."

The corporal reviewed the log on the desk next to him. "Lieutenant Colonel Rudder left him to see to the final shipment of supplies, ladders, ropes. Those sorts of things. I'll take you over to Camp C. That's where the truck is."

Kenzie looked at the clock behind the desk. It was eight-thirty.

She had thirty minutes to find her grandfather and convince him not to leave with the MI agent. "Anything you can do, I'd appreciate it. I have to catch a train back to London within the hour. I barely got permission to come, so I can't be late in returning."

"It's a short walk, but a wet one."

"Doesn't matter," she said. "Lead the way."

He gathered his rain gear and offered Kenzie a poncho for the walk to the camp. "There are a couple of jeeps, along with the supply truck in a Nissen Hut. Everything's being shipped out within the hour. You got here just in time." The corporal left her at the door. "Come back to HQ, and I'll find you a ride back to the train station."

"Thanks." She entered the hut, surprised by how easy it all had been, probably because the three thousand soldiers who had camped at Broadmayne were gone. After a quick conversation with her grandfather, she'd be back on the train to London, and then home to her time to complete her coursework and graduate. She was pumped now and could almost smell the finish line.

Inside the barely lit building, she wound around the vehicles and worked her way toward the rear of the hut, listening, but hearing nothing, she called out, "Lieutenant Manning. Are you here?" She kept walking until she reached the opposite end, and there he was, clipboard in hand, sitting on the rear of the truck, smoking a cigarette.

"Lieutenant Manning?"

He turned toward her. "Yes."

"We met a few days ago at Bletchley Park."

His gaze roved over her. Then he tossed the clipboard into the back of the truck and the cigarette onto the floor. "Miss Wallis-Manning...I mean...Captain," and then he saluted.

She returned his salute. "At ease."

"I didn't know any WACs were stationed here."

She took a deep breath. *Easy. Take your time. Be convincing.* "I'm not. I came to see you."

He averted his eyes. "I'm married, ma'am. I'm sorry if I gave—"

"No. No, that's not it at all. I know you're married. Your wife is from Ireland, and she's been trying to immigrate, but the American Embassy won't help you."

He lit another cigarette, and blew out the smoke.

"I know you contacted Military Intelligence," she continued, "to see if you could trade your connections in Ireland for help with your wife's application."

He took another draw and his hand holding the smoke had a slight tremor.

"I've come to stop you from leaving the restricted area. You're walking into a trap, and what you do tonight will impact your family for generations."

"Bravo."

Kenzie spun on her heel in the direction of the voice, and there was Fedora Man pointing a gun at her. Again.

He gave a sinister chuckle. "I knew you were dangerous, Miss Wallis-Manning, I just didn't know *how* dangerous. Wherever you turn up, trouble follows." He gestured with the gun. "Lieutenant, are you related to this woman?"

Her grandfather stepped away from her to put distance between them. "I had never seen or heard of her before a few days ago. We met at Bletchley Park."

"Well, well," Fedora Man said. "What are we going to do with you? I don't know whose side you're on, but I can't have you meddling in tonight's activities. Tie her up," he said to Manning. "And be careful. She has a few clever moves that might put you on the ground."

Her grandfather grabbed a length of rope from the back of the truck. "Turn around." Then he whispered, "I won't tie this tight. You'll be able to get free as soon as we leave."

"Don't go with him," she said, not caring whether Fedora Man heard her or not.

Manning tied her hands behind her back and spun her around. Fedora Man tossed him a handkerchief. "Put this in her mouth."

Manning followed orders.

She tried pushing it out with her tongue, but it was wedged too tight.

"We can lock the door on the way out. No one will find her."

Fedora Man aimed the weapon. "I can't take that chance."

"There's no reason to hurt her. She's done nothing wrong." She heard the panic in her grandfather's voice. "I didn't sign up for this," he added.

Fedora Man shoved her grandfather. "She's a loose end. Stay out of the way."

Grandfather rushed the agent. "You can't shoot her." This was her chance, she had to make a move. She pitched to the side, ducked, and ran.

"Now, look what you've done."

Kenzie kicked off her shoes and darted between the vehicles.

"If you want my help, leave her alone."

The voice of the Devil himself said, "Don't threaten me, Manning."

The click of the agent's boot heels warned her he was closing in. If she could reach the door, she could disappear into the darkness. They didn't have time to chase her. She would be safe.

It had all been too simple. And it had gone to hell so quickly.

Ten more steps and she'd be free of the hut. Nine. Eight…The clock was ticking…Seven more steps…Six…Five…The door was within reach…She would hit it with her shoulder…Four…She could taste the finish…Two…One…

Duck, Kenzie!

She did, just as a gun exploded.

Searing pain ripped across her scalp. Her knees buckled, and she collapsed on the wood floor. The dimly lit room went totally black.

57

London, England, June 5, 1944

DAVID TOSSED HIS bag into the backseat of the car he had nursed and cajoled through two insane dashes across England. Did the old girl have one more miracle left in her engine? She started like a sweet song, but after three blocks of grinding, she stopped abruptly.

"*No. Don't stop now.* Come on lass. Ye' can do this." He kissed the air. "Ye' can do it." He turned the key to restart the engine. "Come on sweetling. I know ye' got something left."

Click. Click. Click.

He tried again, pumping the gas.

Click. Click. Click.

He dropped his head on the steering wheel. The torrential downpour pelted the car, and the dying vehicle shook, battered by high winds. "I'll get there, Kenzie. I promise."

He didn't know how he would manage it, though. He hadn't had time to double-check train schedules, and he had little faith in a train getting him there in the next few hours. Never before had he been out of options, with no fallback plan.

Kenzie was walking into a highly dangerous situation, and he had to be there to protect her. If ever he needed a miracle, it was now.

The car stopped at an intersection two, maybe three blocks from Waterloo Station. Since there were absolutely no vehicles on the street, walking was his only option. He grabbed his duffle and abandoned the vehicle, unreasonably grateful when there was a sudden break in the weather and the downpour turned into a sprinkle.

He walked into the train station, dreading what he would discover about the schedules and possible delays, when he remembered exactly where he was—across the street from the Union Jack Club. All British servicemen, regardless of the century, knew to go there for assistance. The odds of catching a ride to Dorset, while not guaranteed, had just moved into the high probability category.

When he entered the large Edwardian Building, he wasn't skipping, but he wasn't dragging his feet either. He was cautiously optimistic he would find a travel solution. The offices were closed, but the bar and restaurant were open. As much as he didn't want to take the time, he needed a bite of a biscuit and a cup of tea. He hadn't had anything to eat since early morning, and if he expected to be at the top of his game, food and a power nap were essential.

He entered a long, narrow room. As was his habit, he took in all the details, and then set most of them aside, including the handful of men and women sitting at tables covered with white tablecloths. He decided to plant himself on a stool at the bar. As much as he wanted a shot of whiskey, he couldn't afford to irritate his stomach tonight. The barman took his order and returned a couple of minutes later, placing the steaming tea, scones, and jam in front of him.

"Quiet night," David said.

"Something's about to happen. It's been like this for the last two days."

"Is anybody around? I need a ride to Dorset."

"I doubt you'll find one tonight. Check at the office in the morning. I'm sure they can arrange a lift."

David glanced at the floor convinced he would find his heart there. "That'll be too late. Do ye' have a train schedule?"

"A soldier left a few minutes ago saying only a few trains are available now and they're backed up. They'll leave when they can."

Had Kenzie boarded a train before the backup? She wasn't inside the station, or he would have seen her.

"I have to find a car."

"I don't think there are any in the motor pool. Everyone was heading to the ports yesterday and today." He handed David a napkin and eating utensils and then said to someone else, "Are you leaving, Lieutenant Roberts?"

David cocked his head to see the two women he had noticed earlier. They were walking toward the bar.

"Been a long day, Fred." The woman glanced at David. "You look like you just lost your best friend." She held out her hand. "I'm Faith Roberts."

"If I don't get to Dorset, I probably will."

"Sounds serious," Faith said.

David picked up the cup of tea. "It is."

Faith pointed to the other woman who had kept walking and had almost reached the door. "My friend is headed that way." Faith called out, "Lily, wait. I found you some company."

"Sorry. But I have to go to work."

Faith put her hands on her hips and rolled her eyes. "Not that kind of company, silly. The major needs a ride to Dorset."

Lily beckoned to him. "Come on, then. I'll take you."

Had he heard correctly? She could be flying a broomstick or driving a clunker like the one he'd abandoned. He didn't care. He swallowed the last gulp of hot tea, grabbed the scones, dropped money on the bar, and picked up his duffle.

The sweet-looking woman with blond hair and big blue eyes held out her hand. "I'm Lily Ellis."

He returned her strong, warm handshake. "David McBain. And ye're about to save my life."

"That sounds ominous."

"Let's just say a lot is riding on my arrival in Dorset in the next two hours. And unless you can drive ninety miles an hour, I'm not sure we'll make it."

"I'll see what I can do." They walked out into the drizzle. "My jeep's right around the corner."

Even from the distance he could tell it was reliable transportation. It had four good tires and no rust or dents. He dumped his gear in the backseat next to hers and settled into the front. He doubted she would drive very fast in this weather, so he prepared to take over the driving, even if he had to be forceful about it. He didn't have time to creep along England's country roads.

"Why are you in such a big hurry to get to Dorset?" she asked.

"I have a meeting in Broadmayne. If I'm late, someone could die."

"We should be able to make it."

David checked the time. It would be close. "What kind of job do you have that sends ye' out on a night like this?"

"I'm a ferry pilot. Tonight I'm flying a Piper L4 'Grasshopper' artillery observation aircraft from White Waltham Airfield to Station 454."

A pilot?

"It's a replacement aircraft required by a US artillery unit based at Piddlehinton Camp in Dorset. The airfield is only a short walk to Broadmayne."

David felt as if he'd been lifted out of his body. This was no coincidence. He didn't know what it was, but it wasn't a coincidence.

Because he had to know, he asked, "Ye'll fly in this weather?" He'd flown in worse storms, but not in a lightweight Piper. And not all pilots would take the risk.

"What's a little rain when our boys are dying on the battlefield?"

He studied her features. She was a strong woman, not particularly pretty, but her spirit made her beautiful. The Allies were lucky to have her on their side. "How long have ye' been flying?"

"When the war started they were looking for ferry pilots, and were accepting women. I joined the Air Transport Auxiliary in 1940, learned to fly, and have been ferrying planes for four years now. I've flown all over the UK and even made a trip to the United States."

"What other types of planes do you fly?"

"When I started, I could only fly Tiger Moths, but now I fly everything."

The heavy weight of worry lifted off his chest. "I'm impressed."

"I'm making a contribution, and I'd much rather do this than work in a factory."

"What about after the war? Will you continue flying?"

She took a curve without slowing down. David hugged the door. "I haven't really thought about it. I guess I'll get married and start a family."

"If you enjoy it, don't quit. There'll be a huge expansion after the war. A lot of the pilots will continue to fly, but many will have seen too much war and will gladly give up their wings."

"I'll keep that in mind."

Thirty minutes later, she pulled into White Waltham Airfield and stopped at the gate. David handed her his credentials to show the guard, who saluted smartly.

"SHAEF? I didn't know I had such an important passenger. I'll get you out of here as soon as possible." She pointed ahead. "There's your ride."

A Piper L4 Grasshopper sat on the tarmac. The little single-engine, fabric-covered airplane flew low and slow, and was the perfect aircraft to spot German tanks and artillery. Any other time, he would have taken the opportunity to study the plane, but this time all he wanted to do was get in and go.

"Stow your gear. We'll leave in ten minutes."

Faith entered the terminal and David jogged over to the plane. The fuselage in front of the tail and the upper and lower surfaces of the wings had been painted with alternating black and white bands.

"New paint job?" David asked.

A member of the ground crew said, "Don't want the plane to be hit by friendly fire. We're painting the stripes on all our planes."

He checked the time. It had been over an hour since his car died, and he was about to board a Piper for a thirty-minute flight. Unless they had a weather delay, he would make it to the pub with time to spare.

He climbed into the backseat and waited, mentally laying out his plan for what he would do as soon as he landed in Dorset. Kenzie had anywhere from an hour to a four-hour head start. She had taken plenty of money from his duffle to hire a car, take a train, or even buy a barely serviceable vehicle like the one he had been driving. She was a skilled military officer. What would she do?

She would take the most reliable option. The train. Depending on when she departed, she would have had time to go to Broadmayne and search for her grandfather. David didn't have time to go there first. As soon as he arrived he would go to the pub, stake it out, and make a move as soon as he spotted Manning.

Faith climbed into the pilot's seat. "Ever flown in one of these?"

"I've flown in a lot of planes, but never a Piper."

"The Piper is used every day to spot artillery, flying at five to six hundred feet regardless of the weather."

"How does it handle in this wind?"

"In thirty mile winds I almost have enough lift just by pulling back on the stick. It'll be bumpy, but this girl can take it. You ready?"

They were in the air within minutes. Bumpy was an understatement, but Faith handled the controls with the same professionalism and competence he had seen in female pilots in his war.

"I'll be ferrying another aircraft back if you need to return tonight."

"What time?"

"How much time do you need?"

"Two hours."

"I'll be waiting."

"If I'm not back by then, go on without me." He didn't know what he would find at the pub, or what would happen with Kenzie's grandfather, but as soon as he found Kenzie, he was taking her straight home.

Lily radioed the tower for landing instructions. "Got a major on board from SHAEF. He needs transport to a meeting location."

"Car and driver will be waiting. Over and out."

If the rest of the evening went half as well, he'd be back home in time to watch the late night news. He pressed his hand against his pants pocket and fingered the outline of the brooch beneath the thick wool trousers, and then closed his eyes for a few minutes. He didn't need much rest to be primed and ready for whatever happened next.

Faith landed the Piper in some of the worst weather England could throw at a pilot. She taxied to the parking spot indicated by flares. "Looks like your ride's waiting."

"What can I do to thank you?" he asked.

"Thanks aren't necessary. I'm just doing my job."

"Keep doing it. Ye're a hero tonight."

She smiled. "Glad to have you onboard, Major McBain."

David jogged across the tarmac and hopped into the waiting jeep.

"Where to, sir?"

"The New Inn at West Knighton. Do ye' know it?"

"Yes, sir. I'll have you there in ten minutes."

It took eight. David barely had time to run through his plan again. The driver stopped the car near the front door of the Inn. "Should I wait, sir?"

"No, but thanks for the lift."

The car drove off and David looked for a place to leave his duffle without it getting soaked. He dropped it behind a rock wall and covered it with wood from the wood pile. Then he checked the rounds in his Colt. Satisfied, he entered the Inn.

There was an elderly gentleman at the bar, another man at a table, and the barman. David ordered a beer and took a seat at a table at the back of the room with a clear view of the door and waited, sipping occasionally at the warm beer.

At 9:15 a man entered, ordered a beer, and paced the room before sitting at a table near the window. He didn't drink the beer, only tapped his fingers against the sides of the glass.

Ten minutes later, another man entered. When he removed his hat, David stilled himself. The man was a masculine version of Kenzie, a little taller and thicker around the chest, but his wavy red hair matched hers, along with the high cheekbones and deep set eyes. He nodded to the barman and then took a seat with the man sitting near the window. David gave them a couple of minutes to talk and then he approached the table.

"Rob? Rob Manning? Is it ye', man? Haven't seen ye' since before the war." David pulled up a chair, sat next to Manning, and slapped him on the back.

Manning's eyes darted back and forth from David to the other man at the table.

"Ye' don't remember me, aye? We met at a pub in Belfast through yer wife, Della O'Brien. The lass wanted to go to America. Did she get out before the war?"

Manning stammered, "Ah…I don't…I don't remember meeting you."

"Ye' don't. I've got a picture of the three of us in my duffle, but I left the bag in my car. Come out wi' me, and I'll give it to ye.' I'm sure ye'd like a photograph of yer wife."

"I've never met his wife," the other man said in a heavy Irish brogue. "Is she bonny?"

"Bonny she is," David said.

"Go get the picture," the man said. "I want to see what she looks like."

Manning stood. "Sure. Let's go."

If this worked, David was going to Sunday mass with Alice when he returned home.

He and Manning walked toward the rock wall where David had hidden his duffle. The hairs on the back of his neck itched like crazy. "If ye' want to see Della again, do everything I say. Ye're being set up. Don't do anything stupid, and we'll get out of this mess."

"I don't know what ye're talking about."

"Don't play dumb. Have ye' seen Kenzie tonight?"

He gasped. "Yes, and she's hurt."

David wanted to wrap his hands around Manning's neck and squeeze, but that could get them both killed. After they got away from the Inn, he would drag the details out of him, and might still wring his neck. "When we reach that wall, jump over, and take cover." They were within a foot of the wall when a voice said, "Stop right there."

"Now," David said. They jumped the wall and rolled to the ground. Shots rang out. *Ping. Ping. Ping.* Bullets dug into the stone wall, barely missing them. Pieces of stone pelted them like shot from a shotgun. David returned fire, emptying his weapon, and then reloaded. "Where is Kenzie?"

"The man shooting at us is with Military Intelligence. He shot Kenzie and dumped her body into the supply truck."

David closed his eyes and asked, "Is she dead?"

"I don't know," Manning said sadly. "She was trying to escape."

David knew she wasn't dead. She couldn't be dead. His heart would know. She might be injured, but not dead. He had to get to her quickly, though. She would need medical attention. "We've got to get out of here. Do you know yer' way back to Broadmayne?"

The intermittent downpour started up again.

The agent yelled, "Come out, Manning. We've got a deal. If you want Della out of Ireland, come out now. Let's finish this."

"If ye' go out there, he'll shoot ye.' If ye' want Della out of Ireland, ye've got to show up with yer men at Pointe du Hoc." David secured his bag on his back. "Let's get out of here."

"Manning, if you love your wife, come out." The agent fired several rounds and the bullets pinged off the stone.

David returned fire. "Yer' cover is blown. Yer' wife's only chance now is based on what ye' do next."

"Okay, let's go."

David got off a couple more rounds before they belly-crawled through the mud toward the hedge surrounding the Inn.

"When we get on the other side of the hedge, run up the side of the lane through West Knighton village and make a left at the bend," Manning said. "Stay on the track until you see a sign for Higher Lewell Farm."

"Thanks for the directions, but ye're going with me."

"I just wanted you to know where to go in case…in case something happened to me."

David grabbed his jacket collar. "Nothing's going to happen, soldier. Move yer arse."

When they reached the farm, both men were breathing hard, Manning whispered, "We're right behind Camp C now. We have to cross the field. Be quiet. If we alert the cows or the guards, there'll be too much explaining to do and we don't have time."

The animals probably wouldn't hear them through the roar of the wind and rain, but David kept silent. They crossed the field without alerting the cows and reached a gate that led to Watergates Lane, which they followed until they reached a ford.

"When we reach Fryer Mayne Farm, we'll have to ask for help. The guards will be out even in this weather."

"Do ye' think anyone will help two mud-caked soldiers."

"It's one of the Rangers' best kept secrets," Manning said.

When a farmhouse came into view, Manning said, "Let me do the talking."

They dashed to the house and Manning knocked. A little girl about James Cullen's age opened the door. "Betty, we need help distracting the guards."

She looked both David and Manning up and down several times, as if trying to decide what to do. Then after a moment she said, "Let me get my slicker."

"Betty's seven. She's helped me and a lot of other soldiers sneak back into camp. Her father was killed during the Battle of Britain. It's just her mum and her. Sometimes we'd sneak out just so we could ask for help to sneak back in. She wouldn't take our money unless she could do something for us. So we made it into a game. She has an imaginary dog she searches for."

David gave her several pound notes. "Thanks for yer help, lass."

She pocketed the money. "Thank you, sir. I'll go distract the guards now while you sneak down the path." She ran off calling for her dog. "Pebbles. Come heeere, Pebbles."

David followed Manning down a path that led to a clearing. "This is where we were camped. The hut with the truck is over there."

David sprinted, hit the door, ripped it open, and came to an immediate halt. The room was empty. "Where'd the truck go?" he demanded.

Manning shook his head. "The vehicles and equipment were being loaded on an LCT in Portland Harbor. I thought we had time."

"That's miles away."

Manning leaned against the door jamb and pulled out a pack of Lucky Strikes. He offered one to David.

David shook his head. "We've got to find a way there. Now."

Manning lit the cigarette and took several draws, then threw it down and smashed it in the mud. "Come on. I know where we can get a ride."

David followed him into Broadmayne and down a long street to a large house. "This is D5 Headquarters. I suggest we steal a vehicle, since we don't have time to ask."

They circled around to the back of the house. Manning lightly punched David's arm and pointed ahead. Parked near the rear door was a jeep.

"Hope the keys are in the ignition."

"I can start it without keys," Manning said. He didn't have to try, though. The keys were in the ignition. They drove out onto the street and within minutes were on the road to the harbor.

"Tell me about Kenzie," David said. "Where was she shot?"

Manning's jaw was working as if he was in pain. "If she hadn't ducked when she did, she would have been shot in the back. The bullet grazed the side of her head. She was breathing when we dumped her in the back of the truck."

David was filled with rage. He grabbed Manning and shook him. The car swerved, and David released him. "*How could you not help her?*"

Manning made a sharp right turn. "The only way I could help her was to get back to her as soon as possible, or he might have shot me, too."

David pressed his lips tightly together to stop the trembling. His hands remained fisted. If anyone stopped them, he was prepared to beat the crap out of them.

Fifteen agonizing minutes later they reached the port. David grabbed his duffle and ran to the dock with Manning right behind him. Two men in rain gear were walking toward a small stone building.

"Have you seen a truck loaded on an LCT in the last hour and a half?" Manning asked.

"A truck was the last thing loaded on the bow of an LCT that departed about fifteen minutes ago."

"We need to catch up with it. Any other ships going out?" David asked.

"The men shook their heads. "Not tonight."

"We need to borrow something. What's available?" David flashed his credentials. "It's imperative I reach that landing craft in the next few minutes."

"There's a MGB tied up over there. It was deemed unserviceable for the invasion but the repairs were done, and it's waiting for engine trials, you could borrow it. I'll take you out. But you'll need to sign a requisition form in the office."

The motor gun boat worked for David. "Let's do it."

He signed the requisition, and within ten minutes they were out on the rough seas. The sailor estimated they were thirty-plus minutes behind the LCT. The rain let up shortly after they boarded, and approximately twenty minutes later the sailor radioed the LCT for permission to come aboard.

A rope ladder was tossed down. "Would ye' take Lieutenant Manning out to the HMS Ben My Chree to meet the Rangers bound for Omaha Beach?"

"Sure," the sailor said. "We'll catch up with that packet steamer in no time."

Manning shook David's hand. "I hope Kenzie's okay."

"Good luck to ye'," David said. He climbed aboard the landing craft and, after explaining the situation to the captain, went to the bow where the truck was lashed to the deck. His heart was pounding as he climbed into the back of the truck.

"Is she there?" the captain asked.

David lifted the tarp and found her bound and gagged. "Aye, she's here." He pressed his finger against her carotid artery. She had a steady pulse, thank God. He removed the gag and cut away her restraints to find her head was soaked with blood. "Jesus Christ." He picked her up and sat on the back edge of the truck with her in his lap.

"We don't have any medical supplies aboard, and we can't turn around and go back to port," the captain said.

"If ye' see the HMS Ben My Chree, we'll transfer her."

The captain left him alone, and David sat there with Kenzie in his arms, checking her wound carefully. There was a laceration in her blood-soaked hair, but she was alive, the wound wasn't deep, and it would heal…but he wasn't so sure about the scars seared into her psyche from the trauma of the past several days.

"It's time to go home, now, lass."

He carried her onto the deck of the landing craft, opened the emerald brooch, and spoke the words, *"Chan ann le tìm no àite a bhios sinn a' tomhais a' gaol ach 's ann le neart anama."*

The fog engulfed his feet, and he held her closer still. When the penetrating mist reached his chest, totally engulfing Kenzie, David jumped into the sea.

58

Normandy, France, Present Day

WHEN THE FOG lifted, David was sitting on a sunny beach with Kenzie in his lap. Neither of them was wet. David glanced up and down the beach. There were several people in small groups. Based on what they were wearing—jeans and T-shirts—he assumed he and Kenzie were back in the future. He kissed her forehead.

"We made it back, lass." He checked her pulse. Still strong. Blood had soaked her hair, streaked her face, and stained her jacket, but the wound wasn't life-threatening. He'd seen plenty of those, and thankfully, this wasn't one of them. He ripped the bottom of his shirt into strips and wrapped her head.

She'd been...what? Lucky? Is that what he was going to call what happened in the past twelve hours? Luck? No, it had nothing to do with luck, and everything to do with the emerald. He closed the gem and pocketed the brooch.

He shook off his duffle and dug through the pack for his satellite phone. He turned it on and clicked the Google Maps icon to check his location.

Normandy?

That surprised him. He didn't know why the brooch had transported them there. He had thought they would come out of the fog on the British coast somewhere. That would have made it easier to get home. Now Elliott would have to send the plane to pick them up in France.

He glanced down at Kenzie and caressed her shoulder reassuringly. She was beginning to stir, and he wanted her to know as she regained consciousness that she was okay. Even with blood-matted hair, she was beautiful. He pulled her closer, protectively, and punched Elliott's number.

"Ye're back," Elliott said with a heavy sigh of relief. "Where are ye'?"

"According to my GPS, we're on Omaha Beach. Where're Jack and Cavanaugh?"

Elliott didn't say anything for a minute then said, "Jack's in London with Kevin. They arrived a couple of hours ago. I'll explain later about the pilot. Are ye' and Kenzie okay?"

"Kenzie was shot. Fortunately, the bullet only grazed her head. She's not in danger, but she needs medical attention. Will ye' send the plane and Kevin? If I take her to the hospital, they'll want to know what happened, but the wound needs to be stitched."

"I'll send a car to pick ye' up from the beach."

"And make us a reservation at the Hotel Villa Lara in Bayeux. I've stayed there before. It's a great boutique hotel. Tell them…I don't know…tell them we've been filming a D-Day scene for a movie and decided to stay over, but we don't have any luggage. We'll need clothes and toiletries."

"On it," Elliott said. "And ask Kenzie to call her father. He's worried sick."

The thought of Kenzie calling her father tugged on David's heart. He didn't want her to be subjected to the man's temper until she'd had a few days to recover. "That's not going to happen right now. She's rather pissed at the colonel."

"General." Elliott said. "And why is she angry with him? He's got a few hard edges, but I've enjoyed his company. He's here at the farm now. Meredith adores him."

David's neck started tingling. Something was off. Way off. "Are we talking about the same person? Kenzie's father is a retired colonel and he's an arse. Kenzie's anger is legit. He lied to her.

Never told her about her brother. The guy's a jerk."

"What do ye' mean? Jim loves his sister."

David held his arm over Kenzie protectively, as if she was in the front seat of a car and he had stopped suddenly. "They don't even *know* each other."

"David," Elliott said in the soft voice he used when he spoke to his son, James Cullen. "Are ye' sitting down?"

"Yes, sir," David answered automatically.

"What happened while ye' were in the past? Did ye' change anything, because we've got conflicting realities."

David scrubbed his face with his hand. "We changed Kenzie's grandfather's war history. Give me an hour to get her settled, then we'll talk. In the meantime, I need a complete history on the general, his father, Kenzie, her mother, and Jim Manning. I need to find out what's different so I can prepare her for the changes in her life. Answer me this…is she still reading law at Cambridge?"

"Yes, and Jim's references went a long way in getting her into the program."

"Ye' need to stall her father, and I'm not talking to Jim until we've reviewed notes. Ye'll have to stall them both."

"Consider it done. I'll call Jack and Kevin, and will text ye' with their ETA."

David clicked off just as Kenzie opened her eyes. They widened when she recognized him. Her hand went to the side of her head. "Where are we, and what happened to my head? It feels like it's been in the jaws of a nutcracker."

"We're in Normandy."

"Seriously. How'd we get here?"

"Ye' can thank the emerald."

"The only thing I'm going to thank that gem for is the money I make when I sell it."

"Glad to see yer sense of humor is intact. And in answer to yer question, ye' were shot in the head."

"It was Fedora Man. That son of a bitch. What happened to my grandfather? Do you know?"

"Last time I saw him he was on his way to meet up with his Ranger battalion."

She looked at him coolly, assessing him in one long take that seemed to last for minutes—although it really didn't—and he couldn't read what she concluded.

She only said, "We've got a lot to talk about."

He swallowed hard, knowing she would hold him accountable for putting her life in danger. And she'd be right. "I know. Do ye' think ye' can walk?"

She made a move to crawl out of his lap. "Let me try."

He stood and reached for her. She stumbled and grabbed his arm.

"Take it slow. We're in no hurry." He slung the strap of his duffle around his shoulder. "Ye' ready?" She nodded. He put his arm around her, and they walked up the beach toward the parking lot. "Let's sit on the bench and wait for the car."

Gingerly, she sat, her teeth set in her lower lip. A minute and a few deep breaths later, she said, "Won't people wonder what happened to me?"

"Our story is that we've been filming a D-Day movie and the blood isn't real."

"Tell that to my head."

"I'm sure it hurts, but as long as ye' don't pass out, we'll be okay. We can't afford to have the police investigating a shooting."

She closed her eyes and turned her face up to the sun. "How did we get here?"

"To Normandy? Or back to our time?"

"Both, I guess."

"After ye' were shot, ye' were dumped in the back of a supply truck. The truck was driven to the Portland Port, loaded onto an LCT, and shipped out. Yer grandfather and I got a ride on an MCB and chased after ye'. When I found ye', I said the old Gaelic words, and here we are."

"Did you use my brooch or yours?"

David leaned forward and braced his forearms on his legs. He was tied up tighter than a triple knot and could feel it all the way across his back. "The emerald. I gave the sapphire to Jack."

"I tried to use the brooch to go home shortly after I arrived, but it didn't work."

He cocked his head and gazed at her. "Once the brooch takes ye' through the fog, it'll hold on to ye' until it's finished."

"Finished with what?"

He wasn't ready to get into a discussion of the brooch's purpose, and was relieved to see a Mercedes pull into the parking lot. Since there were no passengers, he assumed their car service had arrived. When the driver got out carrying a sign that said McBAIN, David waved.

"Our ride is here."

"How'd you arrange a chauffeured Mercedes?"

He held up his mobile. "I made a call."

Kenzie fell asleep, snuggled next to him, during the drive to the Hotel Villa Lara. Her lips moved briefly, as though she was dreaming, or worse, having a nightmare. He would have them, and he imagined hers would be much worse.

When the car pulled up next to the hotel, he nudged her gently. "We're here."

She rubbed her eyes. "Did you throw sand in my face while we were on the beach? My eyes are so grainy."

"Get a few hours of sleep and they'll feel better." He opened the car door and helped her out. "Lean on me, lass. Ye're still a bit wobbly." He preferred to pick her up and carry her, but the hotel staff might not believe their ruse if she couldn't walk. "Remember, we're actors and the blood isn't real," he whispered as they neared the front of the hotel.

They were met by a man identifying himself as the hotel manager. "We have your room ready, Mr. McBain."

"Excellent," David said, ushering Kenzie into the hotel. "I'm sure Dr. Fraser explained we were shooting a D-Day film and have to stay over unexpectedly."

"Yes, sir, and Dr. Fraser's assistant sent an email with your sizes and preferences. Our personal shopper has gone to purchase clothes for you and Miss Wallis-Manning. The room is stocked with toiletries, and the cook is preparing a tray of fresh pastries, cheese, and fruits. If you need anything else, please call the desk." He handed David a key card. "Your suite is on the second floor."

"You have an excellent makeup artist. That blood looks real," the desk clerk said.

"The best in the business," Kenzie said.

While the staff frowned, they didn't seem nervous, but David needed to squelch any possibility they might doubt the story once they talked among themselves. "If ye' think the lass looks bad, ye' should the German she killed. Made a bloody mess of him." The manager and the clerk both laughed, and a bit of relief seeped into David's concern.

"Plus, I have a monster of a headache from filming dozens of retakes," Kenzie said. "Will you send up some ibuprofen?"

"The pain reliever was on Dr. Fraser's list. A bottle is in the bathroom."

"Good." David pushed the elevator button and the door opened. As it closed, Kenzie said, "How is all of this possible? We just arrived and a personal shopper is purchasing clothes for me."

"Elliott makes things happen."

The elevator door opened and Kenzie stumbled. David caught her. "Easy now. You've had a hell of a week."

"Which reminds me, I'm pissed at you for lying to me."

David swiped the card in front of the electric sensor and opened the door. "Let's hold that conversation until after we've cleaned up, eaten, and rested. I know I have a lot of explaining to do, and I will, but not right now."

"I'll agree to postpone the discussion as long as you promise to answer all my questions. No lies, no cover-ups. Just the truth."

"I promise, but first I need to clean yer wound."

She shook her head, then grimaced, and gently touched the bandage. "I can do it. Why don't you go shower first. I'd like to soak for a while."

He could argue with her or he could jump in and take a quick shower. "Ye' need ibuprofen and an icepack." He went into the bathroom and grabbed the bottle of ibuprofen and a glass of water. "Take two of these." The ice bucket had already been filled. He tied the plastic liner holding the ice and wrapped the pack in a washcloth. "Keep this on yer head. The ice and ibuprofen should kick in soon and make cleaning the wound easier on ye'."

She sat on the sofa, put her feet up, and the icepack on her head. "Take your time. I want to sit here and enjoy the view and the peace and quiet. It feels like I just fell off of a high speed rollercoaster. I need to catch my breath."

"Catch yer breath. I'll be back in less than five minutes." He took a hurried shower, then wrapped a towel around his waist, and returned to the sitting room.

She stared at him with frank expression, her eyes dilating. And that pleased him. Maybe she wasn't as angry as she claimed to be.

"You're a damn sexy man, McBain, but you lied to me, and I don't know if I'll ever get over that."

He cleared his throat of the disappointment lodged there. "We'll deal with everything later. Right now, I need to wash your hair and clean the wound."

"*I can do it.*"

"I know you can, but you can't see it as well as I can."

She eased to her feet. "Okay, but don't try to kiss me."

He crossed his heart and held up his fingers in a pledge. "Ye' have my word." Giving his solemn word was the only way that would guarantee he'd keep his hands off her. They walked into the bathroom. "Shower or tub?"

"Shower. I don't want to sit in all this filth. I'll soak when I'm clean."

Kenzie stripped and started removing the bandages around her ribs that weren't as neatly wrapped as the doctor had done. "I'll do that," he said. It took every ounce of control he could muster, but he kept the towel wrapped around his waist, hoping she didn't notice his obvious erection. His first ever shower wearing a towel.

He unwrapped the bandage around her head. The wound had stopped bleeding but would probably start up again. He poured shampoo into his hands and massaged her scalp, taking special care of the wound.

"Ouch." She pulled away from him. "If you're going to be rough, I'd rather do it myself."

"I'll go easier." He normally had a very easy touch, but right now it eluded him. He shook out his fingers and tried again.

"Ah, much better. You've done this before."

"A few times—but not lately," he added quickly, like that would make him sound like less of a rake. He kept getting harder until his erection couldn't be ignored. "I apologize if my reacting physically to ye' is offensive."

"Women react, too. We're just not as obvious."

He tried not to read between her words, but couldn't help it. Did she want him as badly as he wanted her? He rinsed the blood from her hair. "I'm going to clean the laceration now." He cupped water and poured it over the wound. "It cut open your scalp about an inch and just missed shaving off the top of your ear. The blood makes it look much worse than it is."

"How deep is it?"

"Not very deep, but it needs a few stitches."

"You're not going to do it, are you?"

"I could, but I won't. Kevin's coming. He'll do it." He soaped the area around the cut and then very gently moved closer and closer until he was funneling soapy water into the laceration.

She hissed.

He backed off. "I'm sorry."

"Keep going. It has to be done, but talk to me so I won't think about what you're doing. Who's Kevin?"

"Elliott's aide." David went back to cleaning the laceration. "He's also a paramedic. He can stitch ye'. He does an even better job than Elliott."

"So Elliott's a doctor?"

"He's a veterinarian. If ye'd rather go to the hospital, I'll take ye'."

"It would be less complicated if Kevin can do it. So where is he now?"

David washed the remaining soap from her hair. "He and Jack are in London. They're bringing the plane to pick us up."

"Whose plane? Yours?"

"No. Elliott's."

"Are you kidding me?"

"It's a lot to take in."

"Really? Ya think? I need a scorecard to keep up with all the players." She turned, faced him, and gazed into his eyes. "Look, I'm angry, tired, hungry, and my head and ribs hurt. That's a lousy state to be in, but I want to finish what we started."

David's body reacted immediately. "I promised not to kiss ye'."

"I don't remember asking you to." She untucked his towel, and it dropped to the shower floor. She narrowly eyed his erection. "I...I changed my mind." She raised her eyes. "Kiss me."

He didn't stop to analyze what they were doing or the need that surged through him—the hunger to take her, to experience the fire that roared within her. He had to touch her, kiss every curve, taste her skin, and plunge himself into her now-trembling body. And he had do it without hurting her.

His hands roved over the sleek, graceful lines of her neck and shoulders, and he pulled her closer, careful not to hurt her breasts. Desire darkened her eyes.

There was a knock on the door. "Room service."

"Damn it, McBain." There was only a hair's breadth between their mouths. "If you answer the door again, I'll be really, really pissed."

If this was the way she expressed her anger, he'd take it any day.

As if under a spell, his gaze was drawn to her lips, parted and full, and he imagined them wrapped around his cock. Her shallow breathing filled him with a fierce longing. He wanted her more than he had ever wanted a woman. Answer the door? Hell, no. Not now. Not ever. He would find a way to bolt it from the outside so she could never leave him. He'd lock her up in a tower like Rapunzel so he would never have to share her.

"I don't want to hurt ye'."

"I'll tell you if you do."

Her hips undulated against him, demanding what he had longed to give her. Something primitive tightened in his gut and lust coiled around him.

Her amber eyes smoldered and darkened. She wrapped her arms around his neck and gripped his hair, then combed through it as she clung to him. "Don't make me wait, McBain." A smile curved her lips and she kissed him, lifting her leg to hug his hip. His desire matched hers, hard and powerful and dangerous.

He picked her up and she wrapped her legs around him. He groaned when he entered her and she melded to him with an answering groan. Her mouth met his with equal demand.

She would never know the anxiety, the fear that had gripped him when he thought he wouldn't reach her in time, when he found her bound and gagged and covered in blood, and the raw relief when he knew she was alive.

Where had she been all his life? He turned and pressed her back against the wall of the shower, and his legs wobbled, not from her weight but from the fullness of his heart.

He loved her.

He groaned as he palmed her buttocks and sank into her. A sensation unlike anything he had known before arched up his spine and bowed his back. He wasn't even all the way in and he was ready to come. His hips jerked again and he was in, surrounded by her liquid heat, and he was never coming out. He dropped his forehead against hers, trying to cool his raging hunger. He wanted her to remember this, not as a quick coupling, a release of days of stress, but as a passionate and erotic adventure with the promise of a lifetime commitment.

She rocked against him until she screamed, "Don't stop," and bucked into his thrusts. Her desperate pleas broke him, and the need for her burned in his veins. He didn't stop, he couldn't stop, and with each thrust he wanted her more. And more.

"Ye're mine, Kenz. Ye'll always be mine." He had spoken the words out loud. He hadn't intended to, but they burst out, and he didn't care. He wanted her to know this wasn't just a moment of unbridled passion.

He kissed her deeply, and his hips hammered harder with every stroke. He swallowed her cries and held her tightly while she shuddered. Then his orgasm hit, swamping him, and a fierce roar ripped from him as their releases merged into one long, satisfying surrender.

His heart was pounding and his loins were drained and weak and empty.

And it had lasted only two minutes.

59

Bayeux, France, Present Day

AFTER KENZIE'S BATH, she snacked on cheese, fruit, and fresh pastries, and then curled up for a nap. David stretched out beside her and watched her sleep, afraid to leave her side, a primitive part of him worrying that she might stop breathing at any moment. He had done the same with James Cullen and Lincoln, putting his hand lightly on their chests to feel the slight rise and fall as they breathed, but he'd never been inclined to do it with a woman. Until now.

Until now, he'd never been so quick either. He cringed every time he thought about it. He was known for his stamina in the bedroom, but with Kenzie he barely lasted two whole minutes.

Then there was a matter of protection, or lack thereof. Another first for him. Kenzie hadn't been worried about pregnancy during their first attempt. So maybe she thought she was safe.

Safe or not—it didn't matter. Protection was his responsibility, and he failed.

He'd been doing a lot of that lately.

The lines of stress around her eyes had disappeared in her sleep, and she looked goddess-like. He casually stroked her arm while he typed a memo one-handed on his laptop. There was a completeness in the way he felt when he was with her. He didn't know how this was going to play out, but he would do whatever he had to do to win her heart.

In the memo to Elliott, David laid out the facts, even the parts Kenzie wouldn't want him to share, but David wanted Elliott to know everything.

The summary he requested from Elliott came through. David read it quickly to get the gist, then more slowly the second time. The third time, he took it all in. Their fiddling with history had made significant changes in Kenzie's life.

Elliott suggested having Jack talk to her since he was the only one who could really understand the adjustments she would have to make. From David's perspective, they were all positive.

The news of Lieutenant Robert Julian Manning was more startling, and now David understood why the brooch brought them to Normandy. But the most startling news of all was that Cavanaugh was Kenzie's best friend's grandfather.

His phone rang. "We just landed in Caen," Jack said. "We'll be there in thirty to forty minutes."

"Be sure Kevin brings his medical kit. He needs to stitch Kenzie's head. I don't want her going out until she's sewn up and bandaged."

"He's on it. See ya' in a few."

Kenzie rolled over and gazed up at him. "Was that Jack?"

"He and Kevin will be here in thirty to forty minutes. Kevin will stitch up your head, and we'll get out of here."

"I love this hotel. I've never been to Bayeux before, and the view of the Cathedral is breathtaking. I wish I had the energy to go see it." She snuggled up next to him and put her bandaged head on his bare chest. "I've got to get back to London right away. I've got classes and a paper to finish."

He kissed the top of her head. "We're going to Lexington first. Elliott's wife is having surgery. Yer father will be there, and so will Jim Manning. Ye'll need to make an appearance."

"I'm not ready to see him yet, but I might as well get it over with now. Just be prepared for him to go off on me. He's not an easy man to deal with."

"I've met him, and I agree. If it's needed, I'll run interference."

David found it difficult to believe Kenzie's father had changed that much.

"What kind of surgery is she having?"

"She's had breast cancer twice, and the doctors just found spots on her lungs."

Alarm darkened Kenzie's face. "That's not good."

David took a deep breath and blew it out slowly. None of them would function well without Meredith. Elliott might be the clan leader, but Meredith was its heart.

"I know, and that's why we'll all be there tomorrow. Jack's sister, Charlotte, and her husband, Braham, will be there, too. Ye'll like them. Charlotte met Braham in October 1864. He was a major in the Union Army and a spy for Lincoln."

Kenzie sat, holding the sheet to her breasts. "Wait a minute. Are you saying he's from the nineteenth century and personally knew Abraham Lincoln?"

"He was bent on stopping the assassination, too."

"Oh, my God. That would have been a huge disaster."

"Yeah, that's what Charlotte thought."

"Obviously he didn't, or the Lincoln Memorial wouldn't be sitting on the National Mall. If Lincoln had remained President after the war, he might have been impeached by his party for the actions he took. I doubt they would have built a memorial to him."

"I only mentioned it so ye' can see how actions we take while in the past can easily change the future in dramatic ways."

"When we get on the plane, you'll need to tell me everything."

He leaned over and caught her in a tender, lingering kiss, caressing her lips lightly with his tongue. Then he raised his head and stroked his thumbs across her chin and along her jawline. "I'll tell ye' everything I know, lass. Everything." He intended to confess his feelings, and come clean about invading her privacy *and* falling in love with her.

"So we're flying to the states for Meredith's surgery, to say hello to my dad, and then I can leave and return to London."

"We'll fly back on the jet. I need to go back to Scotland and finish a project I was working on." His phone beeped. He checked the face to see the caller ID. "They're almost here. We need to dress."

She yawned. "Ask them to come back tomorrow."

"I know ye're tired, but the advantage of flying on a private plane is that there are no airport hassles, you eat great food, and have a comfortable bed. Ye' can get nine uninterrupted hours of sleep on the plane."

She rolled into a ball and snuggled into the comforter, covering most of her head. "I'll have to do some quick shopping here or in Lexington. I might need more than running clothes."

"Ye' can do all the shopping ye' want, but I asked Jack to stop by yer flat and pack a suitcase."

Her head popped out of the covers. "Without asking? How did he get in?"

David patted her bottom as he stood, wearing only a pair of boxer briefs courtesy of the hotel's personal shopper. "Kevin is very resourceful."

"He isn't the only one." She threw back the comforter, revealing her hip and long leg, and he couldn't keep his eyes off of them, or his mind clear of the memory of her wrapped around him. "How did you get from London to Broadmayne? I was on the last train."

He turned his back to her before she noticed his erection and shoved his legs into a pair of khakis with a heavily starched crease, just as he had requested. When he got himself tucked in, zipped up, and covered with the tail of a polo shirt, he turned back. "I...flew. And that rather remarkable part of the story can wait until later. I still haven't gotten it straight in my mind."

She swung her legs over to the side of the bed. "I'm getting up now, and I think you should go into the other room. I'm naked, and I noticed you're still aroused. So unless you want to promise not to kiss me again..."

"I'm leaving, but only because Jack and Kevin will be here any minute," and then David laughed. "I'm sorry I didn't last longer. If ye' give me another chance, I promise to do better."

"I don't think you could have done any better, McBain. It was exactly what I needed."

Now he smiled. "Then I better leave before I try to convince ye' that ye' need me again."

She tossed a pillow at him. "Go."

He took his phone and laptop and closed the door to the sitting room. He stood in front of the wall of windows and looked out onto the city of Bayeux and the Cathedral. He could easily stay in these rooms for a week, live off room service, and make love to Kenzie until he convinced her he was the love of her life.

A car pulled up to the front door and delivered Jack and Kevin. Kevin entered the hotel and Jack stood on the sidewalk talking to the driver. David had sent Jack instructions to pass along to the driver, out of Kevin's earshot, that David wanted to make a stop before returning to Caen. Kevin had a big mouth, and David was never sure what would come out it. Most of the time Kevin said things just to annoy David, and today he wanted to make sure it wouldn't happen.

The phone in the room rang, and he answered, "McBain."

"You have a visitor—Kevin Allen. Should I send him up?"

"Yes, and prepare the bill. We're leaving within the hour." David hung up and opened the sitting room door. "Are ye' dressed? Kevin is coming up now."

Kenzie walked into the sitting room, looking fresh in black running tights, a pale green, long-sleeve tee, black vest, and Asics running shoes.

"Ye' look gorgeous."

"Thank you. I have this same outfit in my closet."

"It's easy to shop for a lass when her sizes and preferences are on a store's computer."

She wandered over to the window looking out over the front of the hotel, and David joined her there. "What's Jack doing?"

"Probably trying to sell books to the driver."

"I've never met a New York Times bestselling author before, especially one I enjoy reading."

"Please don't tell him. He can get obnoxious when he talks to fans."

"You haven't told me what happened when they ditched in the Channel. They all survived, right?"

There wasn't any point in telling her about the men who were lost, so he said, "Jack was a hero, so don't mention that right now, either."

"There's so much I don't know, and with all that has happened, I don't even feel like the same person."

"Ye've been through a horrific experience. Now ye're back, it might, for a while, seem like ye've been living a dream."

"Not a dream, a nightmare. At least some of it…most of it. A few parts were nice." She smiled. "I enjoyed dancing, meeting Turing, the cabaret…until I got kidnapped…seeing how London looked during the war, hearing firsthand reports of Churchill. We packed a lot into a week."

"It shouldn't have lasted a week, and that's my fault. We'll talk about that part later, okay?"

"Let's not put it off longer than a day or two. I need to talk about what happened. Not only about what happened in the past, but what happened in here, in this room."

David closed his eyes for a moment, took a deep breath, and then opened them again. "When ye're ready, I'll tell ye' everything I know."

Kevin knocked and David answered the door. "Come in." They fist bumped.

"Welcome home," Kevin said.

"I could say the same, but I didn't know ye' were going anywhere."

Kevin extended his hand to Kenzie. "I'm Kevin Allen, and I'm under the threat of serious bodily harm if I don't get you stitched up and out of here as quickly as possible…plus I have to do it without spilling any MacKlenna family secrets. So let's get to it."

Kenzie laughed. "I don't know anything about you, but based on that rehearsed speech, I have a feeling you're not normally as uptight as you appear to be. So relax. I won't ask you any questions." She glanced at David again. "McBain has promised to tell me everything."

Kevin's brow arched. "*McBain?*"

Kenzie frowned and shot a glance from David to Kevin and back to David. "That's his name, isn't it?"

"Yeah, but…"

David cuffed him affectionately on the jaw. "Do yer job, lad, and mind yer manners. I'll be downstairs."

He barely made it out of the room without grabbing Kevin by the shirt collar and yanking him off his feet. He had no doubt Kevin heard the intimacy in the way Kenzie said *McBain*.

She probably wasn't even aware of the way she said his name. He was, though, and he resented the fact that Kevin noticed. It was only a matter of time before Elliott's entire inner circle knew he had slept with her. Using that phrasing was a joke. He hadn't slept with her. He'd had quickie shower sex. A sixteen-year-old would have lasted longer than he had.

David jogged down the steps instead of taking the elevator. He needed to regain his composure before he talked to Jack in person. He not only needed to control his anger at his friend for going on the ride-along with Cavanaugh, but he also needed to put a damper on his out-of-control attraction for Kenzie.

Jack was sitting at a small table in the Hotel's courtyard and studied David closely when he pulled up a chair and joined him. "How's Kenzie?"

"She got a bath and a nap and…"

"Had sex?"

"It's none of your business."

Jack threw his head back in a fit of laughter.

David wondered if he had blown it, thrown away his one chance with her as easily as Manning carelessly tossed away his cigarette butts. He should have waited until she had time to recover. In a few weeks, he could have called her in London and asked to take her to dinner. Court her like she deserved to be courted, and make love to her like she deserved to be loved.

"Your single days are over, my friend. I can hear hearts breaking all over the UK. David McBain is off the eligible bachelor list. Did you use a condom?"

Denying it would serve no purpose. "No."

Jack slapped him on the back and laughed again. "I *am* going to be your best man, right?"

"There's not going to be a wedding."

"Go ahead. Keep thinking that. The fog got you, man, just like it got Kenzie. You can try to step out of it, but you know that's impossible. Hell, you even jumped into the sea, which I might add, was a pretty risky move, but the fog didn't let you go."

"How do ye' know...?" David stopped and remembered the detailed report he had written. "Elliott told ye' about jumping off the boat."

"That was the only thing he told me. He said I would appreciate knowing you had made such a dumbass move."

David chuckled. "It probably was, but I couldn't show up in the future with a ship full of men and D-Day supplies. And before ye' get carried away with all this wedding talk, I'm not the man for Kenzie."

"Oh no? Then who is? It's not Cav."

"Maybe this story ends differently. Maybe the reason she went back in time was to rescue her grandfather, and it had nothing to do with finding a soul mate. When I talked to Auld Fraser, he hinted there might be different purposes for the brooches. That could be the case here."

"I doubt it, but it will make for an interesting discussion later. Here she comes. My God, she's a beautiful woman."

David turned in his seat. The sun glinted off the few golden strands in her red hair. Kevin had combed it so the waves covered the incision. She walked toward David with an ease that sent his heart pounding and his mind flashed back to the shower, to her moans of pleasure, to being inside her.

Jack interrupted David's thoughts saying, "Elliott told me about her altered history. Do you want me to talk to her?"

"Let's wait until we get to Lexington."

"Sure," Jack said.

"Are ye' ready?"

Kenzie turned in a slow circle, taking in the view. "I don't know when, but I'm coming back here. This place is not only beautiful, but peaceful. There's a presence here, a...I can't explain it any better than that."

"Ye' don't need to try. I understand." He opened the car door and followed her into the backseat.

The driver headed southeast on Place de Quebec toward Allée des Augustines, and less than half an hour later pulled into the parking lot at the American Cemetery.

"Where are we?" Kenzie asked.

David opened the door and took her hand. "The American Cemetery. There's something I want you to see. Will ye' come with me?" Before he closed the door he told Jack and Kevin, "We might be an hour."

"Take your time," Jack said.

David and Kenzie left the parking lot and took the path toward the entrance.

"I've never been here, but have heard so much about it. It's laid out like a Latin cross."

They walked past the Wall of the Missing, and the colonnade with the narratives of the military operations, and the bronze statue, *Spirit of American Youth Rising from the Waves*.

"This is amazing, and it's so quiet."

"The reflecting pool reminds me of Washington, D.C.," David said.

"Which way do you want to go?"

David pointed with his chin. "Let's go down the central mall." They walked down the path that extended west from the reflecting pool and divided the graves. When they reached a narrower north-south mall that intersected with the central mall, David turned left. He turned up a row of graves and counted them until he reached the one he was looking for. He took Kenzie's hand and knelt.

"I left yer grandfather on the MGB. He was going to catch up with his battalion on the HMS Ben My Chree. I wished him good luck, but, Kenzie, I was so worried about ye' that I didn't give a second thought to sending the lieutenant on his way."

She knelt beside David and ran her hand across the name on the marker. "This is his," she said in a whisper. "Oh my God," she started crying. "He died here? At Normandy?

"He was one of two hundred and twenty-five Rangers who landed on the beach to scale the cliffs at Pointe du Hoc under heavy fire. Their objective was to seize a piece of real estate the Allied leaders claimed was the most important on the whole Normandy coast, and silence the six 155 mm howitzers aimed at Omaha and Utah."

Kenzie's soft sobs filled the air.

"They were young men—kids really—facing an entrenched enemy. The Germans stood on the edge of the cliffs tossing down grenades and firing machine guns. The Rangers shot rope ladders over the edge of the cliffs and began to climb. When one Ranger fell, another took his place. When a rope was cut, a Ranger would grab another rope and begin to climb. They didn't quit. And when they reached the top, they discovered the guns they had come to destroy had been moved.

Kenzie wiped her face with the back of her hand.

"Your grandfather led a few men to search for them, and they found the guns down the road and spiked them so they couldn't be used again.

"There was a counter assault, but the Rangers held their position, waiting for reinforcements that didn't come for two days. By then the force was reduced to ninety men. Colonel Rudder called for air support and ordered an American flag be used to mark their position. Yer grandfather crawled out with the flag. He was shot multiple times, but he didn't give up until the flag was spread out enough to be seen from the air. He died with a corner of the flag gripped in his hand.

"What the Rangers did at Pointe du Hoc will never be forgotten."

Kenzie's hand traced the words etched down the cross. "He was awarded the Medal of Honor."

"He died a hero, Kenzie."

She leaned into David, weeping. "Why couldn't he have survived?"

"I don't know the answer, but I once heard a story told by Somerset Maugham about a servant who went to the market in Bagdad to buy provisions. While he was there he saw Death. The servant was so afraid he rode away to Samarra. His master was told of this. He went to the market and asked Death why she made a threatening gesture to his servant. Death said it wasn't a threatening gesture. She said she was surprised to see him in Bagdad, because she had an appointment with the servant later in Samarra."

"You can't cheat death. Is that what you're saying?"

"When yer time comes, ye' can't run away. Yer grandfather died, but because of what ye' did, he died a hero."

"It was what you did that saved him. Not me."

"It was yer decision. I was prepared to take us home until I discovered ye' had gone."

Kenzie and David sat huddled on the ground for over an hour, crying, holding each other, shivering in their grief.

"I'm ready to go, I think."

David stood, helped her up, and kissed her tear-streaked face. On the way back, they stopped at the overlook, a small jut of land north of the memorial with a view of Omaha Beach below and the English Channel.

"I think we did the right thing." he said.

She swiped at her tears. "I hope so, but right now I feel responsible for his death." They walked back to the car, arms entwined. "Thank you for bringing me here."

"I didn't," he said. "The emerald did."

60

MacKlenna Jet, Somewhere over the Atlantic

KENZIE SLEPT THROUGH most of the transatlantic flight. She woke to the sound of raised voices, one with a Scottish brogue, but rolled over on the bed and fell back to sleep immediately.

"Kenzie, wake up," David said. 'We're landing in an hour. If ye' want to shower, ye' should do it now."

She sat and stretched. "I've never taken a shower while flying. Is it safe? I mean the plane could dip and I could fall. Experience, you know, is a hard teacher. First the test—"

"—Then the lesson. Ye'll be fine."

"One of these days, I'll tell you a joke you haven't heard."

"I can't wait to hear it. In the meantime, ye' need to shower and eat. Kevin left a cap out for ye' to protect the incision. He said he would change the dressing after ye' clean up. There's a laundry bag in the bathroom. Put yer dirty clothes in there, and they'll be returned to ye' cleaned and pressed." He kissed her forehead. "If ye' need anything else, push the buzzer on the wall inside the door." He turned to walk away.

"McBain, wait." She reached her hand out for him, and he squeezed it affectionately. "I heard raised voices. Were you arguing with Jack?"

He kissed the back of her hand. "No more than usual, but mostly we were clearing the air. We had a difference of opinion."

"About me?"

He pulled her to her feet and wrapped his arms around her, hugging her gently to him. "Indirectly, but mostly I was pissed that he went on the bombing run and almost got killed."

It was so natural to slip into his arms. She stood up on her toes and kissed him. The kiss moved like a warm light from the center of her heart. His beard stubble rasped her chin, and his tongue stroked against hers in an irresistible and erotic rhythm. Tingling desire flashed through her, burning hot and wet, and she wanted him. Now. She moved her hips against him in a slow grind.

"Take a shower with me." She cocked her head to gaze into his eyes, and the sunlight coming through the slats of the blinds hit her face, momentarily blinding her. She shaded her eyes, remembering where she was, and while the idea of becoming a member of the Mile High Club sounded enticing, it wasn't very responsible with Jack and Kevin in the next room. "I guess that isn't such a good idea."

"It's a perfect idea, but the next time I make love to ye', I don't want any time constraints." He squeezed her butt, pressing her harder against him. He was fully aroused, and she smiled, pleased she had that effect on him. "Go, before I change my mind and set another personal record for a quick release."

She laughed. "I see a challenge. I bet I can make you come in less than two minutes."

"As hot as I am for ye', lass, I don't doubt it a bit. What do ye' want if ye' win?"

He tugged her closer with powerful arms, consuming her mouth with a kiss surely driven by the desire to prove her right. She returned his kiss with more force, sliding her tongue between his lips. When he cupped her between her legs, she slipped out of the embrace and darted toward the shower.

"Hmm. Can I get back to you on that?"

He laughed. "Sure, but don't take too long."

The hot steamy water splashed on her face and neck as erotic images from their two minutes in the shower at the Hotel Villa Lara played vividly in her mind.

"Are ye' okay? Do ye' need anything?"

Her eyes popped open. David stood at the shower door with his hands pressed against the Plexiglas. "Are you stalking me?"

"Aye."

She held the soap in her hands and worked up a lather and then ran her hands down her neck, over her breasts, down her abdomen."

"Ye're trying to torture me, aren't ye'? Well, it's working."

"Serves you right. You shouldn't barge into a woman's bath time uninvited."

"Is it too late to accept yer earlier invitation?"

"Go away, McBain. We're not having sex again until we have a long talk."

"So…that means we *will* have sex again? Real sex. Slow sex. The kind that takes all night long?"

"Depends on what happens when we talk."

"I don't want to say anything that might ruin my chances, so are there some topics I need to approach with caution?"

"I don't know what all the topics are yet, but I'll go as easy on you as I can." Her hand drifted down between her legs.

"I'll be glad to help ye' wash the parts harder for ye' to reach."

"I've been washing myself for almost thirty years, I can handle it."

He snapped his fingers. "Damn. Maybe next time, huh."

"Maybe. Will you hand me a towel?"

He grabbed a fluffy white towel and held it open for her. She stepped out of the shower, and he wrapped her up in its warmth. "Kevin wants to know if ye'd like breakfast, lunch, or dinner."

"Breakfast, I think."

"How about an omelet and coffee?"

"Sounds wonderful. Tell him to put everything he has in with the eggs."

"Kiss me, and I'll convey yer message."

She cupped the back of his head with one hand while holding the towel with the other and flicked her tongue along the seam of his lips. "Considered yourself kissed."

He slapped his chest. "Ah, yer breakin' my heart." He opened the door and whistled his way out.

She could get used to this, to him, but they had a lot of talking to do first. She dried off and went through her cosmetic case. Jack had even packed her never-before-used diaphragm. Her doctor had suggested the contraceptive device since she wasn't in a relationship, which reminded her…McBain hadn't used a condom. But it was the end of her cycle, so she should be safe for now. She just couldn't afford to be stupid again.

She dressed quickly and found her breakfast ready to serve when she returned and took a seat opposite McBain. "How long until we land?"

He removed the lids to a plate with a delicious-looking omelet and another with toast. "About thirty minutes. We still have time for ye' to win yer bet."

She kicked him under the table.

"Ouch, what was that for?"

Kevin poured her a cup of coffee. "If he's giving you trouble, I'll make him move. The only time he has to listen to me is when we fly."

She glowered at McBain. "Hmm. Maybe I'll let you stay for now."

Kevin winked at her. "Do you want juice or a bloody Mary?"

"Bloody Mary sounds wonderful, but I'll wait until I face the colonel before I start drinking."

David cleared his throat. "He's…yer father is a general now."

General? She must have heard wrong. "What did you say?"

"I can give ye' a list of all the things ye're going to find have changed in yer life, but until ye' see the difference, ye' won't believe me."

"A general? Really? That will take some getting used to. Will you whisper in my ear and give me a heads up so I won't get blindsighted?"

He reached over and traced her ear with his fingertip, tickling her, and she didn't want him to stop. "I'll be glad to whisper in yer ear."

She went back to her breakfast, trying not to think about how uncomfortable the meeting with her father would be. If he was a general now, he might be twice as difficult.

After she finished her omelet, Kevin brought her a fruit bowl from which she chose a plump strawberry and bit into it. The sweet fruit exploded in her mouth. "Yum."

David lowered his mouth to hers and licked the juice from her lips. "Come with me to the bedroom and I'll let ye' win yer bet."

She glanced out the window to see miles of pastures enclosed in white plank fences. "The ground is coming up fast." She winked. "Maybe faster than you."

He crossed his hands over his heart. "Yer breaking my—"

"—Don't say it."

"What?"

"That I'm breaking your heart."

"Oh, but ye' are."

She plucked a strawberry from the bowl, bit into it, then put the other half to his lips. "I bet you wish you were a kid again."

He ate the fruit, smiling. "Why?"

"Because skinned knees are easier to fix than broken hearts."

Kevin came through the cabin and picked up the dishes. "We're on our final approach. Turn off all electronics, buckle your seat belts, and be sure your seatbacks are in an upright position. We'll be on the ground in a few minutes."

David buckled his belt, turned off his laptop, and placed his water bottle in the cup holder. Then he smiled at her. "It pleases Kevin that I have to listen to him in this one instance. I try to make a big deal out of it."

Just when she thought she had McBain figured out, he did something to surprise her. He was a multifaceted man, and she was enjoying peeling back his layers.

A limo was waiting on the tarmac. Private cars and private planes. Returning to her life as a student might end up being a bigger adjustment than coping with wartime London. She didn't know where McBain would go following Meredith's surgery, but she knew where she was going—back to school. Acclimating would be difficult, but not if she signed up for a race. Maybe she'd register for an Ironman. She'd be so busy with school and training she wouldn't have time to miss him.

Go ahead. Try to believe that one.

He would be on her mind through every swim, bike ride, and run. He was in her blood now. And it would take more than an exchange transfusion to get him out of her system.

They exited the plane and walked toward the waiting vehicle.

"Looks like Jake's driving today. Wonder what's up?" Kevin said.

David held the car door open for her. "Jake's head of security at MacKlenna Farm. He usually sends someone on his staff."

"Thanks for picking us up," Kevin said.

"I have one car out with the McCabes and the boys, and another one with Louise, Evelyn, and the general. It's a busy afternoon. Everyone at the farm is praying for Mrs. Fraser."

"Prayers don't go unanswered. We might not like the answers, but God doesn't ignore us," Jack said.

David gave Jack a puzzled look. "That was profound."

Jack settled in the seat on the other side of Kenzie and buckled his seat belt. "It was on my mind when the plane crashed in the Channel. I thought I'd send God an easy request and just ask him to keep the plane afloat. B-17s only float about thirty minutes. I tied a few floatation devices under the wings, more for something to do while we waited than any hope they would work. She was still floating when the rescue boat arrived. They called in a salvage tug. I don't know what happened to her after that."

Kenzie squeezed Jack's hand. "I'm glad you, Cav, and Rainer got out. I'm sure you've got a great story cooking in that creative mind of yours."

"Along with a notebook full of notes written in chicken scratch, which I was barely able to keep high and dry. I hope I can decipher them, though. That's where the real story is. Not in my brain," Jack said.

"When you're scared you don't remember much. You're too focused on staying alive, or in your case, writing it all down so you wouldn't forget. I look forward to reading the book you'll write about this experience."

"I'll drop you off at the hospital's side entrance, then park, and wait," Jake said. "There're no MacKlenna vehicles here and I'm sure you don't want to be stranded."

They entered the University of Kentucky Medical Center, and Kevin led the way up the back stairs to the second floor surgery waiting room. He and Jack went in, but before Kenzie could enter, David blocked her way.

"Before ye' go in, consider this a whisper in yer ear. There'll be a room full of people all jabbering at the same time. Smile. Hug everyone. Tell them ye're glad to be back, that ye' had an incredible adventure, and as soon as ye've processed it all, ye'll be glad to talk about it. But today is all about Meredith."

Kenzie kissed him, very softly. "Thank you. I needed that." She took a deep, slightly shaky breath, and stepped into the waiting room and into her altered universe.

A ruggedly handsome, tall, athletic man with silvery hair and deep, chocolate eyes held court in the center of the room. Her eyes roamed over his supple leather boots, up his knifed-creased kakis, past a washboard-flat belly, to the green MacKlenna Farm polo shirt, identical to the ones David and Kevin wore.

"My, my, my," she murmured under her breath.

David whispered in her ear. "Elliott has that effect on all women."

Her face heated. Elliott was old enough to be her father, and one father was more than enough for her. "Are you jealous, McBain?"

"A few years ago, I would have been, but not now. He only has eyes for Meredith."

Elliott sauntered toward her, and when he reached her he gave her a warm, reassuring hug. "Welcome home. Ye've come back to a larger family than ye' had when ye' left. How was the flight?"

"Fine, I guess. I slept through it."

"Meredith usually does too." Elliott's face darkened for a moment, but he recovered quickly and said, "I want to introduce ye' to some people. Yer' father ye' know, but he's a retired general now."

She hugged her father. "Congratulations on your promotion."

"I've been so worried about you."

"Please, let's not get into it now," she said tersely.

He flinched. "We'll talk when you're ready."

She had expected him to overreact and criticize, and when he didn't, she wasn't sure how to respond, nor was she sure what to think of the absence of alcohol on his breath. "Maybe tonight."

"It's your timetable, sweetheart. I'll be nearby."

David shook her father's hand. "General Manning, nice to see you again."

"You, too, Major McBain. Thank you for bringing her home. I look forward to your briefing."

Kenzie eyed them both before turning her attention to the man Elliott was introducing to her.

"This handsome devil," Elliott said, "was a star forward on the University of Kentucky basketball team under Coach Joe B. Hall. He's a lawyer, and a damn good one."

"I'm Jim, your brother, or half-brother, and this is my wife, Judy." He stood awkwardly, his hands clasped, as if trying to keep them from pulling her into a hug, too.

"Jim might be unsure of what to do, but I'm giving you a hug," Judy said. "Welcome home, Kenzie."

David whispered. "Jim and Judy love ye'. They haven't seen ye' since ye' went to London last summer."

Elliott put his arm around a very pregnant woman. "This is Dr. Charlotte Mallory McCabe, surgeon extraordinaire, and Jack's sister."

Charlotte patted her stomach, "And Kitherina McCabe."

"Soon, it looks like," Kenzie said.

"Any day now, and I was going to be very upset if Jack and

David didn't make it back in time." Charlotte smiled at Jack, but there was a noticeable undercurrent of tension.

"Charlotte's pissed about Jack's adventure onboard the *Shamrock*." David said.

"She should be. He could have gotten killed."

"Thank you, Kenzie," Charlotte said.

David said, low-voiced, "We'll talk later about how yer running off almost got ye' killed."

Elliott held out his hands to separate Jack and Charlotte and Kenzie and David. "Okay, children. Ye'll all get a chance to verbally beat up on each other later."

A tall, blond, green-eyed man standing next to Charlotte nodded to Kenzie and said, "I'm Braham McCabe.

Another handsome Scotsman. "You're Lincoln's spy. I'm honored to meet you."

Charlotte smiled at her husband. "Please don't gush over him, Kenzie. It will go to his head."

A boy of ten came up and stood next to Elliott. "Is this the Kenzie Mom told me about who would be an aunt like Charlotte?"

Elliott patted the boy's head. "Yes, son, this is Kenzie Wallis-Manning."

"Hi," he said, reaching out to shake Kenzie's hand. "I'm James Cullen MacKlenna Fraser, but my names aren't hyphenated like yours."

"I'm sure you're glad of that. Some people get confused and don't know how to list you alphabetically," Kenzie said.

"Kitherina McCabe MacKlenna Montgomery, my great-great-great-great grandmother, didn't hyphenate her names either. She's Uncle Braham's first cousin."

Kenzie looked over her shoulder at Braham, trying to figure out the connection. "It's too complicated for me. I need a family tree." Kenzie fell immediately in love with the precocious child with big brown eyes and dark brown hair. "I like your boots. Do you ride horses?"

"Yes, ma'am. I have two. One I jump and one I race. I'm going to be a winning jockey when I grow up. But I don't have to grow up much. Jockeys are all short."

"And who is your friend?" Kenzie asked, noticing the little blond boy standing behind him.

"I'm Lincoln Mallory-McCabe. And my names are hyphenated. My mom told me you went back in time like she did, but your boyfriend didn't live in the past like my daddy. Are you and Uncle David going to get married?"

Kenzie hadn't been around very many children in her life, but she didn't think these boys were typical. She had no idea whether Lincoln had come up with the idea of marriage by himself or if he had heard his parents discussing it. "I'm rather mad at your Uncle David right now. We'll have to wait and see."

"My mom gets mad at him, too, like when he locked her out of the cave, but she says she loves him too much to stay mad," James Cullen said. "Uncle David did the right thing locking the door. The bats scared me." He reached into his pocket and pulled out a small chunk of what looked like an amethyst with a piece of silver tracery attached. "I found this in the cave. Isn't it pretty?"

"Let me see that, son." Elliott turned it over in his hand as color bleached from his face.

Kenzie froze. The tracery was identical to that used in the design of her brooch.

Elliott rubbed his son's head. "I'm going to let Uncle David borrow this so he can find out what it's made of. He'll give it back to you."

"Did ye' see any other pieces?" David asked.

"Maybe, but Mom said we had to go, and then you locked the door. Will you look when you go back to Fraser House?"

"I sure will," David said.

Elliott did something with his fingers similar to signals used by baseball catchers, and David responded with more signals.

James Cullen took Lincoln's hand. "Lincoln is my cousin, but we're not really cousins, we just say we are because it's too complicated to say that my great-great-great-great grandmother is his father's first cousin."

"You're right," Kenzie said. "That's very complicated. Will you draw me a picture so I can see how everyone is connected?"

"Aunt Charlotte has lots of greats in her tree, too. I can't keep them straight. I hope they're not as many in yours, but we're related, too. Mom and Dad just haven't figured it out, yet. As soon as Mom gets out of the hospital…"

"Elliott." Everyone turned toward the voice, toward a man in surgical scrubs standing in the doorway.

Elliott hugged his son and motioned for everyone to move closer. Two women Kenzie hadn't met yet stood and joined the circle.

"I've got good news. We biopsied three lesions, and they all came back as histoplasmosis. Meredith is cancer free."

"*Yes*," Elliott said before pulling the doctor into a hug. "*Thank you*."

"Dr. Lyles was right. It was a good call on his part."

"He didn't say anything to me about the possibility."

"He called me right after you spoke to him and suggested we consider it."

"She doesn't have cancer?" James Cullen asked.

"No son, she's doesn't. She's going to be fine."

The little boy jumped up and down, clapping, then he grabbed Lincoln's hands. "Your Aunt Meredith's going to be fine. We can go home now and ride our horses. Daddy, can Jake take us home?"

"After ye' see yer mother. And if ye' want to ride, Kevin will have to take ye."

Lincoln cupped his hand at James Cullen's ear but didn't lower his voice. "Kevin will let us jump the big obstacles, won't he?"

James Cullen put his finger over his lips. "Shhh. If our moms find out, we're in trouble."

Kenzie turned her back so the boys wouldn't see her laughing.

"What's so funny?" David asked.

She pointed over her shoulder with her thumb. "Those two are hysterical. I think I'm in love with a ten-year-old."

David roughed both boys' heads. "Don't get in trouble today, or ye'll have to answer to me."

James Cullen cupped Lincoln's ear and whispered loudly. "He'll take us to the barn and put a strap to our arses, like his da did to him."

Lincoln's eyes widened, and he rubbed his butt. He took James Cullen's arm and pulled him over to the corner where they sat on the floor, turned on their iPads, and quickly became absorbed in a game.

"When can we take Meredith home?" Elliott asked.

"As soon as the anesthetic wears off," the doctor said.

"I'll call Mrs. Collins and tell her to get the celebration dinner ready," Kevin said.

The two women Kenzie had noticed earlier walked up to her. "Elliott didn't introduce us, but considering the circumstances, he's forgiven. I'm Louise and this is my partner Evelyn."

"And you're from Scotland, too," Kenzie said.

"We have a B&B in Edinburgh. I hope ye'll come for a visit."

"That sounds lovely," Kenzie said.

Jack approached Elliott, "I was able to work out that meeting. I thought we'd go now. We'll be back to celebrate this evening."

Elliott waved his hand. "Go. Go. It will be more good news to tell Mer."

Jack waved at Kenzie and David. "Come on. We're making a short trip to Chicago. Everything is arranged. We'll be back in time for dinner."

Charlotte grabbed Jack's arm to stop him. "Where're you going? You just got here."

He kissed her cheek. "I'll tell you all about it tonight."

She rolled her eyes. "You're up to something. Wake me up. I want to hear all about it."

Kenzie's father asked, "Do you mind if I go, too?"

"Glad to have you, sir," Jack said.

"What's this about?" David asked. "Kenzie needs time to relax, have a good meal, and reconnect."

"It's a surprise, and we have to go *now*."

Kenzie's father put his arm around her shoulder. "I know you've got to be exhausted after the week you've had. I saw the race results. You not only PR'd, but you came in third overall. That's impressive. Of all your races to miss, I picked that one."

"Huh?"

David whispered, "This is part of your new reality. Go with it."

"I…ah….I'm sorry you weren't there. It seems like years ago now."

"Tell me about London. What was it like?"

For the next thirty minutes, as they rode back to the airport, Kenzie described the war-torn city. Her father didn't interrupt or criticize. He listened with rapt attention, leaning forward in his seat and hanging on her every word. Who was this man?

If this was her new reality, it wasn't so bad.

61

Chicago, Illinois, Present Day

TEN MINUTES AFTER boarding the plane they were wheels up. David threatened to beat the crap out of Jack if he didn't come clean and tell him what harebrained idea he had cooked up. Jack shrugged it off. David cajoled and threatened some more, but Jack wouldn't budge.

Kenzie spent the trip catching up with her father. "I guess Elliott explained how things are different for me now."

"He did, and I spent a long time with Charlotte. I think I understand, but then I don't really. I'm embarrassed that your memory of me is not very flattering."

She put her head on his shoulder. Something she hadn't done since she was a little girl. "I don't think it will take long to get used to you. You're the way I always hoped you would be."

"Don't get me wrong, I can still be a jerk."

She laughed. "Good, then I won't feel like Alice in Wonderland around you."

"Will you tell me about my father?"

She pepped up. "We looked like brother and sister, and he had such a wonderful sense of humor. We told jokes when we met at Bletchley. I'd tell one and he'd tell one. He was a good man, Dad. I'm sorry you never knew him."

"What you and David did made it possible for him to win the Medal of Honor."

"I know. David took me to the American Cemetery. I saw his grave. He was so young."

"I've been there before. I'd like to go back with you someday."

Until they landed in Chicago, he talked about his mountain retreat and the casserole ladies he enjoyed playing golf and bridge with, and Kenzie laughed at his stories.

"I brought all of your mail with me. You're monthly brokerage statement arrived. If we have time, I'd like you to tell me about your recent investments. The last tips you gave me have turned a huge profit."

Who is this man?

She kissed his cheek. "I love you, Dad, and I'll be glad to share. Matter of fact, just open the statement. If you see anything you like, jump in."

"You wouldn't mind? You're very private about your portfolio. I don't want to intrude."

"Not at all." She reached across the aisle and squeezed David's hand. "Thank you, McBain."

He smiled. "I like the sound of that. It means when I come clean, ye' won't be so mad at me. Maybe ye' can help me out, General."

"Sorry, Major, but I'm not about to get between the two of you."

"Okay, guys, this officer crap has got to stop. Dad, this is McBain. McBain this is Manning."

David made a move to stand. "Sir…"

"Keep your seat, McBain."

"Folks, we have begun our descent into Chicago Executive Airport, where the current temperature is a balmy seventy-nine degrees. We'll be on the ground in about ten minutes. Please prepare the cabin for arrival."

The landing went smoothly, and their transition from airplane to limo was uneventful. The driver skillfully navigated Chicago traffic, turned onto Lakeshore Drive, and pulled into the driveway of a French Chateau-inspired stone house with uninterrupted views of

Lake Michigan.

"I've seen pictures of this house before." She turned to Jack. "The Kellys live here. Don't they? I haven't seen them since Trey and I graduated from West Point. I still had tubes running in and out of me at the time of the funeral."

"You should have prepared her, Jack," David said.

"No, no, this is fine. I want to see them." Kenzie used a dropdown mirror to finger comb her hair and rub away smudges from under her eyes. "Do I look okay?"

David patted her leg that brushed up against his. "Ye' look beautiful. But are ye' sure ye' want to see them?"

"Yes, especially now. Come on. You'll like them."

While they were walking up the stone walk, a woman opened the door. "You're here! It's so good to see you again, Kenzie dear." She gave Kenzie a hug.

Kenzie sniffled. "It's wonderful to see you. I'm sorry I—"

"Shh. We knew you were in the hospital. I'm just sorry we didn't come see you." Mrs. Kelly smiled and patted Kenzie's cheek affectionately. She then turned to greet everyone else. "Come in, General. And you have to be Jack. Thanks for calling and arranging this visit." She shook his hand. "We love your books." Then she extended her hand to David. "And it's wonderful to meet you, David. We've read your books, too."

Kenzie stared at David, "How did I miss that you're a writer, too?"

He shrugged. "I don't have Jack's book jacket smile."

"If Jack had waited another day, we would have been in Italy and missed your visit." She laced her arm with Kenzie's. "Come on back. Trey's dad is in the sitting room." She led them down a hall to a cozy room at the back of the house with a wall of windows overlooking the lake. "We have company," she said as they entered.

"What a gorgeous view," Kenzie said.

"It's our favorite room in the house," Mrs. Kelly said.

Trey's dad was spreading a blanket over the lap of a man sitting in a recliner. He stepped back and smiled. "Kenzie, it's so nice to see you again."

"Nice to see…"

Kenzie's legs nearly gave out, and David was instantly there to support her with an arm around her waist.

"Easy, lass."

She gazed into the dim eyes of the handsome pilot who had, days earlier, twirled her around the dance floor in London. Tears filled her eyes. She sat on a stool next to his chair and took his wrinkled hand in hers. "Hi Cav. It's Kenzie. Have you been doing any dancing lately?"

He laughed in a raspy voice of a man in his nineties. "I gave up my dancing shoes when my sweet Susan died. You never did meet her, did you?"

Kenzie shook her head. "I never did, but I heard Trey talk about his grandmother often. He loved her so much."

"And she loved him. I hear them talking sometimes." He picked up an unlit cigar and rolled it between his fingers then put it to his nose and sniffed. "Can't smoke these any more. My son's afraid I'll burn the house down. So I hold on to it, smell it, remember the flavor." He paused and furrowed his brow as if thinking hard of something he wanted to say, and then his face brightened. "Susan and Trey have been talking about you lately. They were worried, but here you are. You're fine now, aren't you?"

She smiled. "Yes, I am."

"This is Jack Mallory," Trey's mother said.

Cav nodded toward a stack of books next to his chair. "I know that." Then he pointed to David, with the unlit cigar dangling between two shaky fingers. "And he's David McBain. I've read his books, too."

Kenzie glanced at the stack of books. Some written by David and the others by Jack. All of the books were heavily dog-eared. She imagined Cav reading and re-reading every line, looking for answers in their writing that would explain how they could possibly have been part of his past and part of his present, too.

Kenzie's head was spinning. There was so much she wanted to

know since she last saw him at Bletchley. "Cav, what happened to Molly and Rainer? Did they survive the war?"

"Did I hear my name?" a woman asked.

Kenzie jerked her head toward the door and there stood Molly Bradford. While she looked years older, the young woman she had been was still visible in her face. Kenzie hugged her. "I didn't think I would ever see you again."

Molly dabbed at her teary eyes with a lace hanky. "I tried to find out what happened to you, but I was told never to mention your name again. I packed your suitcase and kept it hidden in case you ever came back. I still have it. I know that's silly. But I couldn't bear to throw away your clothes."

"Did you get to travel and see the world?"

She laughed in the same girlish voice. "I married Rainer, we had four children, and I've seen almost all of the world several times.

"You married Rainer?" In Kenzie's mind, Molly was still a young woman and they were sitting on the bed in Uncle Clifford's guest room talking about kissing.

"When he proposed, he said if I would marry him he would take me around the world. And he never broke a promise. We flew everywhere."

"So he kept flying after the war." Kenzie said.

"He flew up to the day he died fifteen years ago. He and Cav and a woman named Lily Ellis started an aviation company and—"

"*Lily* Ellis," David said. "Where did ye' meet her?"

"That's a great story," Molly said. "The *Shamrock* didn't sink when Cav landed in the Channel because a clever crewman, who we now know was Jack, kept her afloat long enough to be towed to port."

Jack laughed. "I prayed she would stay afloat."

"She did," Cav said. "And as soon as she was airworthy again, a ferry pilot flew her back to Bassingbourn. Rainer and I were there to meet the plane and the pilot. We got to talking and decided to get together after the war."

"I met her at the Union Jack Club. I needed a ride to

Broadmayne and she offered to fly me."

"So that's how you got there," Kenzie said. "You were lucky."

"I'm not sure it was luck," David said.

"She was like that. She would go out of her way to help someone." Molly's lip quivered. "We lost Lily—"

"Ten years ago," Cav said. "Seems like yesterday."

"But she was a firecracker, wasn't she Cav?" Molly said. "If you asked her why she wanted to start an aviation company, she'd say a Scotsman she met during the war told her there would be a huge expansion in aviation, and if she enjoyed flying she shouldn't give it up." Molly smiled at David. "That was you, wasn't it?"

"Yes, it was." David scratched the back of his head. "I don't get it. How did you put this together? When Trey and Kenzie were at West Point?"

"When Jack's first book came out, we were shocked," Cav said. "Your picture looked exactly like the Jack Mallory we met during the war. We thought we must have met your grandfather. But when David's book came out, and we saw his picture, we knew it wasn't a coincidence. The kicker was when we met Kenzie at West Point."

"When you went to London to read law at Cambridge, we figured it was close to the time you went back to the war. We've been expecting you," Molly said. "Every morning Cav would say, 'Do you think it will be today, Molly?'"

"Susan's been gone eight years now, and Rainer, fifteen," Cav said. "We miss them a lot, don't we, Molly?"

Molly took his hand. "Yes, we do, but we have each other, and lots of wonderful memories, and now we have Kenzie, Jack, and David to share our memories with."

Kenzie wiped her eyes and turned to Trey's mother. "And you knew all this?"

"We didn't believe it at first, but when four people are so adamant, no matter how crazy it sounds, you have to fall in line eventually," Trey's mother said.

"Trey saved me in Afghanistan, and twice while I was in the past."

"He saved ye' again during the rescue from the London Cage. I'd slung ye' over my shoulder and was running down an alley. We were being fired at, and I heard the word *duck*. I did, and the bullet zoomed over our heads. If I hadn't ducked..." He took a deep breath and looked away. His chin quivered.

Kenzie stroked David's arm, letting him know she understood how overwhelming it was to know you had a guardian angel. "He was with me constantly while I was held by MI, telling me never to give up hope. He knew you were coming for me."

David pulled her into his arms. "This is a lot to process."

"Well, I hate to break up the party, but we have to get back to Lexington, and these folks have a trip to get ready for."

"Are you going, too?" Kenzie asked Molly.

"No. Cav and I will stay here. We're both ninety-two years old, so we don't travel anymore. We read and go for walks and tell stories instead."

"May I come back to visit?"

"Please do," Molly said. "We have so much catching up to do."

Kenzie hugged the woman who had appeared when she had nothing, and had filled her life with an abundance of help, hope, and possibilities in just a few days.

"Oh," Molly said. "I almost forgot." She reached in her pocket and then opened Kenzie's hand and placed a pair of diamond stud earrings there.

"My earrings, but how...?"

"I knew you wouldn't take the money from me, so I asked Uncle Clifford to pretend to sell them. I never had the chance to return them before you disappeared, but for some reason I was sure I should keep them. That I'd be able to return them to you someday."

The general picked up an earring and looked at it closely. "If I'm not mistaken, you talked me into buying those at that jewelry store near West Point."

Kenzie looked at her father and then at Molly. "You two knew each other?"

"We had never met," Molly said. "But we all knew he was your father. We went to your graduation, and I spotted him going into the store and decided to get a look at what he was going to get you for graduation. When he couldn't make up his mind, I suggested the earrings."

"You told me to tell her never to take them off," the general said.

Kenzie put them back in her ears. "And I never did, until I had to sell them."

They said tearful good-byes and made plans for a longer visit, and by the time Kenzie left the Kelly's house her head was splitting. She had cried and laughed until her sides hurt and she had no more tears to shed. She sat in the backseat between her father and David, and across from Jack.

"I don't know about you guys, but that was too much to take in all at once. I'd like a glass of wine, a hot bath, and some quiet time."

Jack scrolled through his iPhone and read messages. "You won't get much quiet time at MacKlenna Mansion."

David pulled out his iPhone and sent a text message. "But ye' will at the cottage. I just sent Jake a message to send the cleaning crew over to freshen it up."

"There's no food there," Jack said.

"There will be," David said, sending another message.

"Are you going to squirrel my daughter away, McBain?" the general asked. "I've hardly had time to visit with her."

"I thought I would, sir. If ye' don't mind. I have some explaining to do."

The general arched his brow. "You're asking the wrong person."

"Yeah, you're asking the wrong person. Where's the cottage?" Kenzie asked.

"Behind MacKlenna Mansion, but it's not really a cottage, it's just a smaller mansion. Elliott lived there when the MacKlennas were alive."

"But Elliott is expecting us," she said.

David put his mobile in his pocket and rested his arm across the back of the seat. "He likes having his family and friends around. But he'll understand. Meredith is home. She'll soon be well, and all's right with his world."

Kenzie snuggled up close to David and closed her eyes, wishing all was right with her world, too. Maybe after they talked it would be, but until then, her world was a bit off-center.

62

MacKlenna Farm, Lexington, Kentucky, Present Day

JAKE STOPPED THE car in front of a two-story, white brick, neoclassical residence surrounded by pastures filled with horses—probably Thoroughbreds, Kenzie thought, since MacKlenna Farm was a Thoroughbred breeding operation.

"This is the mansion, right?" she asked.

"This is the cottage."

"Yeah, right," she said. "This is gorgeous and if it's a cottage, somebody needs to look up the definition."

David laughed. "That's exactly what Meredith said when I dropped her off here over ten years ago."

He held the car door for her. "Thanks, Jake," he called to the driver as he closed the door and escorted her up the steps. "The original frame house was a cottage, but it was demolished in the 1930s. When this was built some time later, it kept the name. It was used as a guesthouse until Elliott moved in. He lived here nearly thirty years, until the MacKlennas died. Then he bought the farm and moved into the residence."

"They didn't have any children to leave it to?"

"Their adopted daughter Kit traveled back in time to 1852, fell in love, and decided to stay. She started a winery in Napa, and that's where Meredith grew up."

"That's the person James Cullen was telling me about."

"She was Elliott's goddaughter. When she left, it tore him up.

He met Meredith a few months later."

They stepped inside the house and David removed his aviators and his mobile and left them on the table at the door. "There's a tradition that when ye' come inside, ye' leave yer mobile devices here. This is a place to relax, and ye' can't do that if ye're tied to yer phone."

She held out her hands. "As you can see, I don't have either one."

"The master bedroom is this way. Yer suitcase should be in there. If ye' want to take a bath, I'll start the grill. I thought I'd grill steaks or salmon, whichever ye'd prefer."

"I'd love a steak."

"Then steak it is."

They passed a grand staircase that hugged the wall and continued down a hall lined with paintings of Scottish castles. "These are beautiful. Are they real places, or just an artist's imagination?"

"They're all castles in the Highlands."

The master suite had cream-colored walls that brought out the colors of the Highland landscapes that dotted the room. The focal point of the suite was an enormous four-poster bed. "You could get lost in that bed."

"I doubt it. There's a Maine Coon cat who comes over here and plops down in the middle of this bed. Her name is Tabor, and she's The Queen. There's also a golden retriever who is always close by. His name is Tate, and they both have the run of the mansion and the cottage, which means—"

"They sleep there. Glad to know." She crossed to the windows and opened the blinds. "Wow, what a view."

"I think it's the prettiest on the farm."

"Are those Thoroughbreds?"

"Aye. Those are the mares, and the wee horses are yearlings."

She nodded.

"Let me show ye' where things are. The bathroom is to the right, and the door to the screened-in porch is to the left. I'll leave you to clean up, and I'll go start dinner."

"Hey, McBain. Why haven't you tried to kiss me?"

He stopped at the door to the room and held onto the doorknob. "We need to talk before anything else happens between us."

"You sound so serious."

"I am serious, Kenzie. I've done some things in the last few days I'm not proud of, and after ye' hear them, ye' might never want to see me again. I'll be in the kitchen."

"Wait, if that's a possible outcome, I'm not sure I want to hear it."

"I couldna make love to ye' again unless ye' knew everything that happened from the moment I heard ye' had disappeared."

"Okay, but if I ask you to stop and not tell me anything else, will you?"

"It doesn't work that way. Go on and get your shower. I'm hungry, and I know ye're hungry too."

Kenzie turned on the top- and side-mounted jets and stood in the sprays for half an hour. Fearing she might shrivel up if she stayed any longer, she stepped out and dried off with another one of the MacKlennas fluffy white towels. She would definitely splurge when she returned to London. Her sheet-thin towels had to go.

Dressing quickly, she followed the tempting aromas wafting down the hall, pulling her into the kitchen. "Something smells delicious."

"Ye'll have to thank Mrs. Collins for the potatoes, vegetables, and salad. I'm only grilling steaks."

"Anything I can do?"

"Take this glass of wine and follow me to the porch."

She sniffed the red wine. "Yum."

"I knew ye' liked red wines. This is one of Montgomery Winery's Cabernet Sauvignons—bold, elegant, and balanced. A great pairing with a bone-in ribeye."

She swirled her glass, sniffed, and then tasted. "If the steak is half as delicious, I'm in for a treat. You're not having any?"

David put down his bottle of seasoning and said, "Here's the first of several confessions. I have an ulcer, and whiskey and coffee are my downfalls. Like Elliott, I'm a Scotsman. We don't drink wine. We drink whiskey."

"How'd you get an ulcer?"

"Confession number two. Stress mostly. I fell into writing after my deployments. I enjoy it, but Jack and I are writing for many of the same readers. Since he's so well known, it puts more pressure on me. In a few weeks, it will all pick up again when we start the first drafts of this adventure."

"You're going to write a book about what happened in London? About me? About the torture?" David was silent. She sipped her wine then shrugged. "I don't guess it matters. No one will believe the story is real. Write whatever you want."

"I was hoping you would say that, but don't tell Jack."

She laughed, put the glass and wine bottle on a tray with the steaks, and followed him to the porch. "What's confession number three?"

"I never told Jack I played the sax, because I never told anyone. My da was drunk one night and tripped over the instrument. Beat the crap out of me. Told me to get it out of the house. By then the music was in my soul, and I couldn't quit playing, so I kept it a secret."

"You have incredible talent."

He tossed the steaks on the grill while she gazed out over the pastures.

"It's so beautiful here. Can you swim in the lake?"

He joined her at the edge of the deck. "Aye. It's man-made, fed by an underground spring, and kept clean to swim in. There's a small dock over there," he pointed. "And you can see the boys' rowboats tied at the end of the dock."

"They take them out by themselves?"

"Kevin takes them."

"It sounds like Kevin is very involved in their lives."

"That's because he's a kid himself."

"I suspect you're the only one who sees him that way."

"Maybe." David went back to the steaks while she explored the heavily scented garden, walking a brick, S-shaped, lighted path. The stars lit up the night sky while fireflies with brightly lit tails flitted about. "They try to imitate the stars," her mother had said. "But they can't sustain the brilliance of the sky even if you collect them and put them in a jar." And as a child, Kenzie had tried, but then her mother died, and she never tried again.

For the first time in twenty years, she wished she had a jar.

She sat on a bench and closed her eyes, listening to the rustle of the plants in the breeze and the buzz of insects. She didn't want to think. For a moment, she just needed to be.

"Kenzie, the steaks are done. Will ye' get the rest of the food? We'll eat in the screened-in porch."

She shook her head, letting loose of the memories, and returned to the house.

The table had been set with china and candles. She glanced at the steaks. "Wow, those look scrumptious, and cooked just right."

"Confession number four. I read all yer Facebook postings, and there was one about going out for a steak dinner with friends from West Point. Ye' said yers was cooked to rare perfection."

"How'd you read my postings? They're set to private."

He cleared his throat. "That's why I prefaced it by saying it was a confession."

"You hacked my Facebook account."

"I didn't see it as hacking. I was investigating a disappearance. Besides, it resulted in you having a steak tonight that's cooked exactly the way you like it."

"But, that's an invasion of my privacy. It's bad enough that my father opened my mail and used it as an excuse to start a fight—"

He made a T with his hands. "Let's call a time out so we can enjoy our dinner. Afterward I'll make a full confession, and ye' can go off on me all at once instead of in minor eruptions."

"If my Facebook account is any indication of what you've been up to, I'd better have another glass of wine."

He refilled her glass. "I have several bottles on standby." He lifted her chin and kissed her, then he brushed his lips across her face, not so much a kiss, as a thorough, slow, tactile exploration of the lines of her face, the contours of her cheeks, and the skin below her ear, memorizing her in a way no one had ever done before.

When he released her she licked her lips. "Hmm. I might have to switch to whiskey. Love the taste."

"I have plenty of that, too."

They devoured their dinner and sat quietly, sipping their drinks, enjoying the cooler temperatures, the insects' songs, and idle conversation while letting their food settle.

After a while Kenzie started fidgeting, and finally shifted to face David. "What's confession number five?"

"Ye're keeping close tabs on the numbers." He took a healthy swig of his whiskey, sighed, and turned toward her. "Number five is that I read all your incoming and outgoing emails from the past six months."

"You didn't."

"Number six. I went through all of your investment statements for the past year."

She got up and strode across the room, poured another glass, and sat on a chair at the table, swinging her leg to match her rising heart rate. "Go on."

"Number seven. I went through all yer drawers, cabinets, bookshelves, dirty clothes pile, and computer bag. I know yer bra size and panty size. I know yer preferences for toothpaste, deodorant, and soap. I know the last time ye' visited yer gynecologist, and I know what ye' put on yer application to West Point. I know how many lovers ye've had, or how many ye've confessed to. I know ye' once colored yer hair because ye' hated it being red. I know all yer college grades and the titles of papers ye' wrote."

She jumped to her feet. "I was joking when I asked if you were stalking me, but this borders on some kind of sick obsession."

"I know what they did to ye' at the hospital in Germany to put ye' back together again. I know ye' hate to have your picture taken, and that ye' love pedicures. I know ye' love dogs, aren't crazy about cats, and would own a closet full of shoes if ye' had a place to put them."

She downed the rest of her glass of her wine.

"I know ye' love to dance, love music, and ye' tell jokes to keep people at a distance and get them to like ye' at the same time."

"You're sick, McBain. You know more about me than most married couples know about their spouses."

"I know you like hot, fast sex, and that you orgasm quickly—"

"I could be faking it."

"But you never would. If a man doesn't please ye' he'll never get a second chance."

She swatted at a fly buzzing the room and considered pretending it had landed on McBain's chest. "Why did you do all of this?"

"If I was going to find ye', I had to know everything about ye'."

"And you found me, but how?"

"When we found the packaging from Solicitor Digby in yer flat, we knew ye'd gotten a brooch and gone back in time. We just didn't know where. It took a while to narrow it down."

"And then you came after me."

He got up and walked toward her, but she stopped him with a rigid, mute, palm-out gesture.

"We found ye' within a few hours of arriving in London."

"Instead of introducing yourself with a bottle of champagne, why didn't you tell me who you really were?"

"I should have."

A coldness seeped into her bones and it wasn't from the cool breeze or the ceiling fan. "If you had, we would have left right then." She snapped her fingers. "Poof."

"Are ye' sure?" He looked at her oddly and seemed about to say something more, but changed his mind.

"Did you really think I wanted to be there? Well, I didn't. I wanted to go home. I didn't want to be in a war zone."

"I didn't know why ye' were still there. The brooch has always let travelers come and go. So I figured ye' were staying for a reason, and the only reason that made sense to me was to help yer' grandfather. I thought ye' might run away if ye' knew I was there to take ye' home."

"You could have helped me."

"I was against altering history. Jack nearly got himself killed, and made drastic and unwelcome changes to his family history when he went back in time. We didn't want that to happen again."

She stared at him with her hands on her hips, elbows jutting out. "*We?* Who's we?"

"Elliott didn't want us to do anything other than find you and your soul mate and return immediately."

"Wait a minute. Who said anything about a soul mate?"

"That's the purpose of the brooch. It takes ye' to the love of yer life."

"Seriously? You were going to kidnap...well, it could only have been Cav. And, even worse, this is the first I've heard of it?" She threw up her hands and began to pace. "Now I've heard everything."

"Jack wanted to take both of you back to the present that night. But I wanted to be sure Cav was the right man for ye'."

"You...?" She swallowed, hard. "*You* wanted to be sure he was the right man for me? Have you *listened* to yourself?" She sat in the middle of the swing so he couldn't sit beside her, and pushed with her feet. The chain creaked where it held against the metal ceiling bolts.

"Not only were you invading my privacy but you and your...your *co-conspirators* decided to make a major life decision for me."

She couldn't bear to look at him, refused to acknowledge the anguish in his expression. "I went through hell when I was captured, and it could have been avoided, so easily. Do you know what they did to me?" She pierced him a look as ferocious as her anger. "*Do* you?"

"I saw the bites and the semen," he said, very quietly. "I was afraid ye'd been raped until the doctor examined ye' and said ye' weren't."

"And I bet you stood right there and watched the entire examination. You *are* sick. Since you were so interested in what happened to me, I'm going to tell you everything—"

He stood rigid, blank-faced. "Ye' don't have to."

"But I'm going to, and I hope you have nightmares about it for the rest of your life. I was strapped to a table naked. They covered my face with a towel and poured water in my nose until I thought I was going to drown. They did it over and over again, demanding to know who I was. Then they fondled me and sucked and bit my breasts and nipples. *They bit me.* And I threw up on myself.

"One of the guards masturbated in front of me and came all over my pubic hair. And when they finished, they tossed me in a room without clothes or a blanket, and I shivered until I wanted to die.

"And you could have prevented all of it. I'm going down to the lake now, and when I come back, I'd like you to be gone."

She took one last swallow of wine.

"No, before you leave, I want to know one more thing. How did making love to me fit into your sick plan?"

David jerked, paled, and said hoarsely, "Ye've misunderstood the whole—"

She turned her back, ran out the screen door, down the steps, and across the backyard toward the lake. Her surroundings had turned dark and ugly, like a Grimm's fairy tale. She dropped down at the side of the lake and wept.

63

MacKlenna Farm, Lexington, Kentucky, Present Day

IT WAS CLOSE to midnight before the tears finally stopped. She had never worn a watch because she had a reliable internal clock and was never off by more than fifteen minutes. Her clock was telling her now that she had been sitting on the grass with her head resting on her arms on top of bent knees for at least three hours. No wonder her neck and back were stiff and achy.

Flashes of the worst argument of her life came rushing back. It had been so similar to the hundreds she'd had with her father. Intellectually, she understood McBain did what he did to rescue her. Emotionally, she struggled to accept his behavior. It was like her father opening her financial statements and telling her she acted irresponsibly.

McBain was not her father. He read her emails and financial statements, not to criticize her, but to understand her. She had been in the Military Intelligence Corps and understood it was imperative to know everything about your target. That's what McBain had done. Not to hurt her but to protect her.

A slobbery tongue licked her face. She jerked up and found herself eye to eye with an elderly golden retriever. "You must be Tate," she said between hiccups. He nosed her arm and she scratched behind his ears. "If I write a message to my dad, will you carry it to him? I don't feel like seeing anyone right now, and I want to go home."

Which home did she have in mind? London or her father's mountain retreat?

The mountains would be nice, and with her father as pleasant to be around as he was now, she would enjoy being with him...

If McBain had told her immediately who he was, she wouldn't have been tortured, but neither would she have tried to rescue her grandfather and ended up with a new version of her father.

Tate sat next to her and laid his head on his paws while she continued to scratch his head.

"I bet you've known McBain all your life. You probably like him. I did, too, but he made bad choices." He sure had, but she had too. She had run off and put others in danger. If she had stayed and had it out with him, they could have gone together to rescue her grandfather.

Tate nudged her hand to remind her to keep scratching him.

"Except for not telling me who he was when we met, everything he did while in the past was for what he believed were good and honorable reasons, and he did risk his life to save me."

Tate looked up at her and made a friendly noise in his throat, encouraging her to go on. "If I'm honest, he's been nothing but solicitous and protective. And I know it's not just about sex. I can tell when a guy's in to me. And he is. What do you think, Tate?"

She rubbed both of his ears and scratched his long back.

"Sex isn't what's driving him right now. He didn't have to make all those confessions. That cost him. It made him vulnerable to serious rejection, but he took the chance because he wanted me to know what he did. You know what else he did?"

Tate whined as if asking what.

"He played the sax in public for me."

Tate looked at her with his dark brown eyes.

"Oh, you didn't know, either? That took a lot of guts, don't you think?"

Tate shook his head, jingling his collar, then climbed to his feet, licked Kenzie's face, and trotted off toward the house.

"If you see him, tell him I'm still thinking my way out of the box he put me in." He probably already moved his gear into the Mansion. The Big One. Just as well.

She lay back on the grass and gazed up into a night sky. Electricity danced in the air, reminding her of when she and David danced that night in London. His hands had been so powerful and warm to the touch, and when she gazed into his eyes she nearly passed out from the raw need she saw there.

That's what made this so confusing now. She had been drawn to him from the moment they met, and now her feelings were tied up in knots, especially now that she knew his main purpose had been to pair her with Cav.

Getting those feelings untied and sorted out wasn't going to be easy.

So where did that leave her? She didn't want him to suffer, and denying herself his company would make her miserable. He was everything she had ever wanted in a man—an intelligent leader, honest, faithful, an unusual sense of humor, loved children and animals, and despite his brief performance, he was one hell of a lover.

The raw pain she'd seen in his face was heartbreaking.

They had both been hurt enough.

The soulful sounds of a sax floated on the June breeze, and even the horses stopped and perked their ears. She rolled over on her stomach and looked toward the cottage. David was sitting on the deck playing "Somewhere Over the Rainbow."

"Keep playing," she muttered, "and I'll have this all figured out in a jiffy." And then he blew her away with "My Heart Will Go On."

She smiled through her tears. "I love you like crazy, too."

She stood and walked toward the dock, stripping off her clothes. When she reached the end, she turned and yelled. "This isn't an invitation to quickie sex. It's an invitation to a lifetime of it, long and slow and beautiful."

She eased into the water, and when she surfaced, he was standing there.

"I love ye' Kenzie Wallis-Manning. Will ye' marry me?"

"Don't ever lie to me again, or avoid telling me the truth because you think you're protecting me. I want to be treated like your partner, and you have to respect my space. Can you do that?"

"Aye, if ye'll forgive me when I mess up, because as sure as I'm standing here, I will."

She held out her arms. "Come here, and I'll give you my answer."

He undressed and dove in, and when he surfaced she wrapped her arms and legs around him and gave him a sweet, urgent kiss. It wasn't a hungry, devouring kiss, but while it was slow, it was driven by a need to be with him, completely with him.

The kiss had begun as a spring bud in war torn London, and now fully blossomed under a Kentucky sky. He entered her with a powerful thrust. "I want ye' so bad, I won't last a minute. I surrender the bet to ye' now, but don't plan to get any sleep tonight in that big bed. There are too many parts of ye' I haven't tasted yet to leave time for sleep.

Moments later, he came inside of her. "That's twice I've come in ye' without protection."

"I think we're safe, but if we're not, James Cullen and Lincoln will have another cousin to travel through time with sooner than they might have if we'd planned ahead."

"Ye' think?"

"Bet on it, David. Now kiss me."

64

Fraser House, the Highlands, One Year Later

ELLIOTT ENTERED THE first floor master suite of Fraser House and found his wife sitting up in bed reading. He kissed her soundly on the mouth. "How are the wee ghosts tonight? Have ye' heard any bloody screams?"

Their bedroom had been used as a meeting place by brave Highland lads fighting in the uprising, and Auld Fraser had delighted in telling tales of ghost sightings. Elliott didn't believe the stories for a long time, but since he met Meredith, he had become more open-minded.

She put her folder aside, turned out her bedside light, and snuggled under the comforter. "They usually come out on stormy nights, but so far they're as quiet as the *wee* mice you can't get rid of."

He sat down beside her and stroked her head, weaving his fingers through her hair. It was grayer now, but it was still long and silky, and he loved the feel of it draped across his body. "Tabor doesn't have any interest in them now. I'm afraid the old girl might not live much longer."

She swatted his hand. "Don't you dare say that, and don't let James Cullen hear you, either. We all know Tate and Tabor are old, but they're family, and losing them will devastate all of us. Even Annabella."

"Annabella tried to get Tate to run through the house tonight, but he wouldn't leave his pillow by the fire. I'm afraid he might not make it back to the farm."

"Don't be ridiculous. Of course he will. He'd haunt you for sure if you didn't bury him on the farm."

"He's twelve and Tabor's fifteen. One of us has to talk to James Cullen about the inevitable," he said.

"You do it, and then you can explain why you're a veterinarian and can't save the family pets."

He picked up her folder and thumbed through the pages. "Ye're not making this any easier on me." He scanned the first page of a memorandum from her genealogy research team. "When did ye' get this?"

"Last week. I put a copy on your desk. Didn't you see it?"

He put the folder back on top of a stack of spreadsheets. "I think so, but I had to put it aside, and then forgot about it. Did you send a copy to David and Kenzie?"

"I did, but neither of them were surprised. They'd already figured out that Kenzie was related to the MacKlennas somehow, but didn't know how far back the researchers had to go to find the connection."

"How far did they go?"

"You would have known if you had read the report. Kenzie's grandmother was a MacKlenna, and a direct descendant of James Thomas MacKlenna. It will make more sense after the family tree is completed."

"If we keep adding branches, it might never be completed."

Elliott pushed the covers back, and her creamy skin quivered under his gaze. He ran his fingers teasingly down her neck, her shoulder, her arm. "Did I thank ye' for all the work ye' did getting the internment arranged? The service was beautiful. Ye' negotiated difficult waters with aplomb, and the Wallises were glad to finally have Laurie buried in the family plot, and Kenzie knows the true story about her mother's relationship with her parents."

The sweetest smile curved her lips. "Uh…no. You didn't, but I forgive you. That is unless you stop doing what you're doing." Her eyes gleamed up at him, liquid and sleepy with desire. "Did you know there's a rumor that you were the father of the baby Laurie miscarried?"

"I heard that, but it's not true. We dated but never had sex."

"You were a teenager, Elliott. Now you're sixty-one, and your libido hasn't slowed down since the day I met you. You expect me to believe that?"

He teased her with his fingertips, brushing them lightly across her brow, her eyes, her nose, her nipples. "Okay, once or twice, but she wasn't pregnant when she ran off with Kenzie's father. We'd had a fight and hadn't been together for three or four months."

"Fine," she said on a breathless sigh. "Tell me about the cave. You were down there today. Did you wear your mask?"

He kissed her, and they didn't break the kiss until he pulled away and pressed his lips against her neck just beneath her ear. "What do ye' think?"

"About what?"

"Whether I wore my mask."

She moved her hips, rolling to the rhythm of the rain pattering against the windows. "I don't care. Why are you torturing me?"

"Because I love ye'." His finger trailed a path up her leg and hip and arm, and across her upper lip to her other ear and back again. "The mining crew should have the final load of boulders removed within a few days. Once the door is exposed, I know Jack will want to explore."

"I don't care about the cave." Her cheeks were the color of a soft pink rose. "I don't care about anything. Don't stop." She grabbed his T-shirt and hauled him down to kiss her again. Her tongue was soft against his as he slipped into her mouth. Every time she tried to finish the kiss he pressed harder. Until finally he let her go.

"The brooch indentations above the archway are enough to tempt even me."

"Are we still talking about the cave?"

"Did ye' lose the conversation thread during all those gyrations?"

"I wasn't gyrating."

"I beg to differ. You were somewhere between a four and five on the Richter scale."

"Don't go near that door."

"What door?"

"You've lost the thread, too."

"Unlike ye', I can keep up with the conversation."

"We'll see about that. Take off your clothes. Come to bed."

Elliott nibbled at her bottom lip just to hear her low, throaty moans. "Without the brooches in place, the door won't open. And we don't have enough brooches for the six slots."

"There may be more slots on the door, too. You've only seen the top of the arch. What about the piece of amethyst James Cullen found?"

"Its shape and workmanship are consistent with the other brooches, but so far no other pieces have been found. The other brooches may never come into our possession."

"Since the brooches are finding their way to you, I think you're meant to be the new Keeper. They'll show up." She tugged at his T-shirt again. "You've had a long day with the internment service and the christenings. You're tired."

He got up and emptied his pockets at his dresser. "Alice went above and beyond with the reception this afternoon and dinner tonight. With the entire inner circle here, it gets crowded."

"And noisy. Did you tell Alice thank you?"

"Several times. Did ye'?"

"Yes. I saw you and David in a huddle. What did David say?" She rose up on her elbow, and the sheet slipped, revealing the tops of her breasts.

"About what?"

"You're thinking about making love to me instead of the conversation."

"I think of that a hundred times a day." He put his phone on vibrate and plugged it in using the charger on the table by his side of the bed. "In answer to yer question, David said Jack would have to go by himself next time."

"I don't' believe that, do you?"

Elliott dimmed the lamp on the table. "I'm staying out of it."

"Until James Cullen decides to go back. What will you do then?"

"I promised him we'd go see Kit. I'd like to do that."

"If you do, I'm going, too."

He stripped down to his boxer briefs and slipped on his robe. "I'm going to check on the kids."

She sacked her hands behind her head. "I thought you did that already."

"You distracted me. When I come back we'll…"

"Finish this?"

"No, we'll continue this."

She smiled lazily. "I'll be waiting."

Elliott walked down the hall and opened the door to the nursery. The sweet baby smell hit him, and his heart expanded. James Cullen's sleeping bag was spread beneath the crib where Kenzie and David's three-month-old twins, Henry and Robert, were sleeping; and Lincoln's sleeping bag was beneath the crib where Charlotte and Braham's nine-month-old Kitherina slept.

The boys had toy swords and helmets at their sides with their loose-fitting, calico Jacobite shirts and kilts neatly folded.

He stepped gingerly to avoid the iPads and iPhones and kissed the tops of the babies' heads. Their fine baby hair tickled his lips and made him smile. Then he laid his hand gently on their chests to feel the rise and fall of their breath.

Satisfied they were warm and dry, he knelt and kissed the boys before moving their plastic swords within easy reach. "Ye' never know when the lads and lassies will need yer protection. Keep them safe from harm."

His knees popped when he stood. He was getting old, he couldn't deny it. His final resting place in the family cemetery was near his da's and Auld Fraser's, but it would lie empty for a couple more decades. At least until James Cullen was old enough to lead the clan.

Tabor rubbed against his leg and he leaned down to pet her. "Watch over them now and always," he whispered.

He paused at the door, Tate trotted down the hall and joined him, and he stood there with Tate and Tabor, silently marveling at all the blessings he had received since the day his goddaughter walked out of his life and left her beloved animals in his care.

"Wherever you are, Kit, may God hold you and these precious children in the palm of his hand."

I hope you enjoyed THE EMERALD BROOCH and will consider leaving an honest review on Amazon. Reviews make a difference and are greatly appreciated.

About the Author

Katherine graduated from Rowan University in New Jersey, where she earned a BA in Psychology with a minor in Criminal Justice. Following college, she attended the Philadelphia Institute for Paralegal Training before returning to Central Kentucky, where she worked as a real estate and tax paralegal for over twenty years.

Katherine is a marathoner and lives in Lexington, Kentucky. When she's not running or writing romance, she's enjoying her five grandchildren: Charlotte, Lincoln Thomas, James Cullen, Henry Patrick, and Meredith Lyle.

Please stop by and visit Katherine on her social media sites or drop her an email. She loves to hear from readers.

website: www.katherinellogan.com
blog: www.katherinelowrylogan.com
Facebook: www.facebook.com/katherine.l.logan
Twitter: @KathyLLogan
LinkedIn: www.linkedin.com/in/katherinellogan
Pinterest: pinterest.com/kllogan50
Shelfari: www.shelfari.com/o1518085100
Goodreads: goodreads.com/author/show/5806657.Katherine_Lowry_Logan
Google+: plus.google.com/+KatherineLowryLogan/posts
Email: KatherineLLogan@gmail.com

Want to read Kit and Cullen's love story? It's told in
THE RUBY BROOCH.
(Celtic Brooch Series Book 1)

* * *

Meredith and Elliott's love story is told in
THE LAST MACKLENNA.
This story is not a time travel (Celtic Brooch Series Book 2)

* * *

And for Charlotte and Braham's love story, read
THE SAPPHIRE BROOCH.
(Celtic Brooch Series Book 3)

* * *

If you would like to receive notification of future releases

Sign up today at KatherineLowryLogan.com or

Send an email to KatherineLLogan@gmail.com
and put "Sequel" in the subject line

Look for THE DIAMOND BROOCH in late 2016

Author's Notes

A note about Kenzie and Molly. The real Kenzie—actually McKenzie—and Molly are identical twins. McKenzie was diagnosed in February 2011 with Stage III Hodgkins Lymphoma. On November 8, 2013 Molly donated her bone marrow, and as of June 26, 2014, McKenzie has been cancer free. Throughout most of her treatment McKenzie continued to attend classes at Morehead State University in Kentucky. She is now a registered nurse in the NICU at Cincinnati Children's Hospital. McKenzie is a young woman filled with grace and an indomitable spirit, and she is an inspiration to so many. I was thrilled to be given permission to use her as the model for my character Kenzie Wallis-Manning.

~*~

From flying on a B-17 in Richmond, Virginia, to running on Omaha Beach, the research and writing of this book have presented the most exciting challenges and opportunities of my writing career, along with the most memorable experiences. It far exceeded my expectations.

With a few exceptions, I have always enjoyed World War II movies and books. When I first considered writing my own war story, I wanted to focus on a very small window of time—the week leading up to D-Day. The challenge was fitting a suspenseful romantic adventure into that time frame. Ideas for the stories popped up in the mostly unlikely places.

Irishman Collin Taylor, our Normandy guide, came up with the idea of using an IRA spy. Steve Ellis-George from Broadmayne, UK, made dozens of fantastic suggestions about David's race to find Kenzie and save her grandfather. The pilot, Lily Ellis, is a combination of his daughter's name and a family name. While Lily wasn't a real pilot, she is a representative of the ferry pilots' invaluable contribution to the war effort.

Professor Thomas Appleton and I shared several lengthy discussions about London, the war, and research at the archives. It was from one of those discussions that the idea for the redacted memo arose.

My author friend, Mark Wilson from Edinburgh, gladly answered dozens of questions about Scotland. He has been a wonderful resource for all of my books.

I connected with Sana Mason and her husband Kevin early in the writing process. Sana graduated from West Point in 1987. She provided great insight about the curriculum and training and helped to shape Kenzie's character, and Kevin was always available to answer military questions.

This book could not have been written without the input, support, editing, and encouragement from Faith Freewoman, Demon for Details Manuscript Editing. From character traits and weaknesses, to plot issues and resolutions, to themes and settings and funny jokes, Faith was an email away with an answer or suggestion. She's a wonderful collaborator with creative solutions.

A note about Bletchley Park: There are very few pictures and diaries about what happened at Bletchley during the war because of the secrecy involved. I doubt anyone could have gotten through the gates without identification. In order for the story to work, I had to take a few liberties.

The scene at Claridge's when Kenzie insults the general is solely my creative mind at work. However, it is based on fact. Major General Henry J. F. Miller leaked details of the invasion date at a dinner party in April 1944. He was reduced to his permanent rank of colonel and sent home.

Turing and the Rubik's Cube: Thanks to Dan Garcia, Ph.D. and Christos Papadimitriou, Ph.D., author of *Turing (A Novel about Computing)*, professors at the University of California, Berkeley, for their insights and suggestions.

The London Cage did exist. Colonel Scotland wrote a book about the Cage a few years after the war, but it was heavily censored. I doubt they would have taken Kenzie there since she wasn't a German officer, but the torture complex provided an interesting backdrop for Kenzie's story.

My early readers are awesome, and I am deeply indebted to them for their interest in my work and their thoughtful suggestions: Joan Childs, Theresa Snyder, Nancy Qualls, Lynn Wilson, and Shirl Deems.

My special thanks and deep appreciation to Dr. Ken Muse (my medical advisor, tour guide, and sweetheart) who escorted me to:

- **In the United States:** The National WW II Museum, New Orleans, LA, National Museum of the Mighty Eighth Air Force, Savannah, GA, The National Museum of USAF, Dayton, OH
- **In Europe:** Imperial War Museums, Churchill's War Room, Tour of Mayfair and St. James, Museum of London, Chartwell, Home of Winston Churchill, Imperial War Museums at Duxford, Oxford University, Bletchley Park, Normandy, Hotel Villa Lara

Consultants and Experts

- Special Military and West Point Consultants: MAJ Kevin G. Mason, USA (Retired), MAJ Sana M. Mason, USA (AUS) USMA 1987
- Commemorative Air Force Gulf Coast Wing (Texas Raiders B-17)

- Pat Elliott, pilot of *Texas Raiders* (B-17)
- Mark Wilson, Author (Scotland)
- Thomas Appleton, Ph.D., Professor of History, Eastern Kentucky University
- David Teasdel, aka/Author David Rashleigh (London)
- Neil Bright (London – Blitz Walkers)
- Colin Taylor (Normandy: Overlord Tours)
- Steve Ellis-George (Broadmayne)*

*Reenactments – next year Broadmayne D5 will be bigger than before, with a second event called Armor & Embarkation. Armor & Embarkation is the UK's largest coming together of mobile WW2 armor and support vehicles. The goal of combining the two events is to create the largest, most accurate D-Day embarkation experience ever.

Steve is also working on a project to create a permanent local D-Day memorial/education center. Currently there is no memorial in the UK that recognizes the sacrifices made by the brave American servicemen and women who lived, loved, and died there.

Bibliography

Secret Postings: Bletchley Park to the Pentagon, Charlotte Web, BookTower Publishing; 2 edition (October 11, 2014)

London's War: A Traveler's Guide to World War II, Sayre Van Young, Ulysses Press (December 9, 2003)

Half a Wing, Three Engines and a Prayer: B-17s over Germany, Brian O'Neill, McGraw-Hill Education; 1st edition (May 21, 1999)

The Lost World of Bletchley Park: An illustrated History of the Wartime Codebreaking Centre,

Sinclair McKay, Aurum Press Ltd; 1St Edition edition (November 1, 2013)

8th Air Force: American Heavy Bomber Groups in England 1942-1945, Gregory Pons, Histoire & Collections (July 1, 2006)

Dog Company: The Boys of Pointe du Hoc—the Rangers Who Accomplished D-Day's Toughest Mission and Led the Way across Europe, Patrick K. O'Donnell, Da Capo Press; First Trade Paper Edition edition (November 6, 2012)

The Boys of Pointe du Hoc: Ronald Reagan, D-Day, and the U.S. Army 2nd Ranger Battalion by Douglas Brinkley, Publisher: William Morrow; 1 edition (2005)

B-17 Flying Fortress Units of the Eighth Air Force (Part 1) (Osprey Combat Aircraft S.): Pt.1 by Bowman, Martin W. (2000), Publisher: Osprey Publishing

A WANDER THROUGH WARTIME LONDON: Five Walks Revisiting the Blitz by Clive Harris, Neil Bright, Publisher: Pen and Sword (February 2011)

Intact: a First-hand Account of the D-day Invasion from a Fifth Rangers Company Commander

by John C. Raaen Jr., Publisher: Reedy Pr (April 30, 2012)

Style Me Vintage: 1940s by Liz Tregenza, Publisher: Pavilion (November 1, 2015)

The London Cage by Lt. Col A. P. Scotland, OBE, William Clowes and Sons, London.

The Savoy of London by Compton MacKenzie, George G. Harrap and Co, Ltd., London, England, first edition, 1953,

Walking the London Blitz by Clive Harris, Publisher: Pen & Sword Books (January 1, 2004)

The Ultimate Guide to U.S. Army Combat: Skills, Tactics, and Techniques Paperback – July 7, 2010 by Jay McCullough, Publisher: Skyhorse Publishing; 1st edition (July 7, 2010)

The Soldier's Friend: A Life of Ernie Pyle by Ray E. Boomhower, Publisher: Indiana Historical Society Press; 1st edition (August 15, 2006)

Betty's Wartime Diary 1939-1945 by Nicholas Webley, Publisher: Thorogood (April 1, 2003)

West End Front: The Wartime Secrets of London's Grand Hotels, by Matthew Sweet, Publisher: Faber & Faber; 1St Edition edition (November 1, 2011)

London 1945: Life in the Debris of War by Maureen Waller, Publisher: St. Martin's Griffin; Reprint edition (June 13, 2006)

The Secret Lives of Codebreakers: The Men and Women Who Cracked the Enigma Code at Bletchley Park by Sinclair McKay, Publisher: Plume; Reprint edition (September 25, 2012)

Assignment to Hell: The War Against Nazi Germany with Correspondents Walter Cronkite, Andy Rooney, A.J. Liebling, Homer Bigart, and Hal Boyle by Timothy M. Gay, Penguin books, NYC, 2012

Cronkite by Douglas Brinkley, Publisher: Harper Perennial; Reprint edition (May 21, 2013)

Citizens of London: The Americans Who Stood with Britain in Its Darkest, Finest Hour by Lynne Olson, Publisher: Random House Trade Paperbacks; Reprint edition (May 3, 2011)

By Rick Atkinson D-Day: The Invasion of Normandy, 1944, Publisher: Henry Holt and Co. BYR) (May 21, 2014) NYC

B-17G Flying Fortress – Walk Around No. 67 by David Doyle, Publisher: Squadron/Signal Publications; First Edition edition (August 23, 2011)

Belly Gunner by Carol Edgemon Hipperson, Publisher: 21st Century (September 1, 2001)

Blue Guide London: 18th edition (Eighteenth Edition) by Emily Barber, Paperback: 600 pages, Publisher: Blue Guides Limited of London; Eighteenth Edition edition (August 13, 2014)

Big Bombers of WWII: B-17 Flying Fortress by Frederick A. Johnsen, Chester Marshall William N. Hess, Hardcover: 431 pages, Publisher: Lowe & B. Hould; First Edition edition (1998)

The Mighty Eighth: The Colour Record by Roger A. Freeman, Hardcover: 224 pages, Publisher: Cassell (June 30, 2001)

New York Times Complete World War 2: All the Coverage from the Battlefields and the Home Front by The New York Times (Author), Richard Overy, Hardcover: 612 pages, Publisher: Black Dog & Leventhal; Har/Dvdr edition (November 5, 2013)

Overlord D-Day, June 6, 1944 by Max Hastings (Author), 65 Photos/12 Maps/12 Drawing, Hardcover: 368 pages, Publisher: Simon and Schuster; Book Club Edition edition (1984)

Operation Overlord by Jack Patterson, Paperback: 80 pages, Publisher: Xlibris (January 12, 2010)

War Stories of D-Day: Operation Overlord: June 6, 1944 by James D. Brown (Author), Michael Green, Hardcover: 320 pages, Publisher: Zenith Press; First edition (October 8, 2009)

Walking D-Day (Battleground Europe) by Paul Reed by Paul Reed, Publisher: Pen & Sword Battleground (17 May 2012) (1600)

Art of the Flight Jacket: Classic Leather Jackets of World War II (Schiffer Military Aviation History) by John P. Conway (Author), Jon A. Maguire, Hardcover: 176 pages, Publisher: Schiffer Publishing, Ltd. (September 1, 1995)

The Normandy Battlefields: D-Day and the Bridgehead, by Leo Marriott (Author), Simon Forty, Hardcover: 192 pages, Publisher: Casemate (March 19, 2014)

B 17: Flying Fortress, by Roger Freeman (Author), Rikyu Watanabe, Hardcover: 56 pages, Publisher: Crown Publishers; 1st edition (September 24, 1984)

The Longest Day: The Classic Epic of D-Day by Cornelius Ryan, Paperback: 352 pages, Publisher: Simon & Schuster (May 1, 1994)

The Bletchley Girls: War, Secrecy, Love and Loss: The Women of Bletchley Park Tell Their Story)] by Tessa Dunlop, Publisher: Hodder & Stoughton Ltd (June 1, 2015), London

Codebreakers: The Inside Story of Bletchley Park by F. H. Hinsley (Editor), Alan Stripp, Paperback: 360 pages, Publisher: Oxford Paperbacks; Reissue edition (August 9, 2001)

Our Longest Days: A People's History of the Second World War by Sandra Koa Wing, Paperback: 320 pages, Publisher: Profile Books (January 1, 2009)

Ernie Pyle's War; America's Eyewitness to World War II by James Tobin, Hardcover: 312 pages. Publisher: The Free Press; 1st edition (June 10, 1997)

An Emotional Gauntlet: From Life in Peacetime America to the War in European Skies by Stuart J. Wright, Paperback: 358 pages, Publisher: University of Wisconsin Press; 1 edition (March 21, 2008)

The Guns at Last Light: The War in Western Europe, 1944 by Rick Atkinson, Paperback: 928 pages, Publisher: Picador; Reprint edition (May 13, 2014)

Ernie's War: The Best of Ernie Pyle's World War II Dispatches by David Nichols, Hardcover: 432 pages, Publisher: Random House; 1st edition (July 12, 1986)

The Press of Battle: The GI Reporter and the American People, Jack Edward Pulwers, Hardcover: 850 pages, Publisher: Pentland Press (NC) (November 24, 2003)

Bomber Command (Zenith Military Classics) by Max Hastings, Paperback: 400 pages, Publisher: Zenith Press; Reprint edition (September 23, 2013)

Jimmy Stewart: Bomber Pilot by Starr Smith (2005), by Starr Smith, Publisher: Zenith Press (1700)

D-Day Illustrated Edition: June 6, 1944: The Climactic Battle of World War II by Stephen E. Ambrose, Hardcover: 768 pages, Publisher: Simon & Schuster; Ill edition (May 6, 2014)

CPSIA information can be obtained
at www.ICGtesting.com
Printed in the USA
LVOW05s1604120117
520749LV00014B/2449/P

9 781519 359773